A book in the series

RADICAL PERSPECTIVES

A Radical History Review book series

SERIES EDITORS:

Daniel J. Walkowitz, New York University

Barbara Weinstein, University of Maryland, College Park

History, as radical historians have long observed, cannot be severed from authorial subjectivity, indeed from politics. Political concerns animate the questions we ask, the subjects on which we write. For over thirty years the *Radical History Review* has led in nurturing and advancing politically engaged historical research. Radical Perspectives seeks to further the journal's mission: any author wishing to be in the series makes a self-conscious decision to associate her or his work with a radical perspective. To be sure, many of us are currently struggling with the issue of what it means to be a radical historian in the early twenty-first century, and this series is intended to provide some signposts for what we would judge to be radical history. It will offer innovative ways of telling stories from multiple perspectives; comparative, transnational, and global histories that transcend conventional boundaries of region and nation; works that elaborate on the implications of the postcolonial move to "provincialize Europe"; studies of the public in and of the past, including those that consider the commodification of the past; histories that explore the intersection of identities such as gender, race, class, and sexuality with an eye to their political implications and complications. Above all, this book series seeks to create an important intellectual space and discursive community to explore the very issue of what constitutes radical history. Within this context, some of the books published in the series may privilege alternative and oppositional political cultures, but all will be concerned with the way power is constituted, contested, used, and abused.

"Fly Me? Go Fly Yourself!," Kathleen Barry's title for the final chapter of her sparkling history of airline attendants in the United States, reminds us of one of the most memorable and disturbing hypersexualized images of advertising and popular culture in the 1970s. But the title also signals the lively and contested story of stewardesses' resistance. Airlines hired women to "service" their passengers, hoping that their glamour, allure, and charm would spur sales. They did not expect that stewardesses would use femininity to claim public space in which to air their grievances about sexual harassment, age discrimination, and appearance and marital requirements. Stewardesses countered with what Barry calls the "wages" of femininity. To keep their jobs, stewardesses had to perform "femininity," to work at maintaining the perfect body, to express "caring" sentiments, and then to attend to passengers with seeming effortlessness—all despite long shifts serving cramped and at times demanding flyers. Thus the history of flight attendants—located between femininity and feminism, professionalism and unionization—allows Barry to tell a paradigmatic story of the new workplace in which the growing majority of working women in twentieth-century United States were required, again in her words, to "perform gender *as* the job."

FEMININITY IN FLIGHT

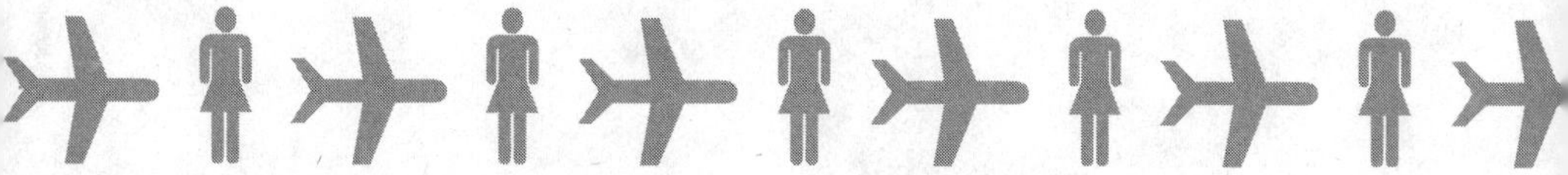

Kathleen M. Barry

FEMININITY IN FLIGHT

A History of Flight Attendants

Duke University Press   Durham and London   2007

© 2007 Duke University Press
All rights reserved.
Printed in the United States of America on acid-free paper ∞
Designed by C. H. Westmoreland
Typeset in Adobe Minion by Keystone Typesetting, Inc.
Library of Congress Cataloging-in-Publication Data appear
on the last printed page of this book.

FOR CHARLES

CONTENTS

LIST OF ILLUSTRATIONS

ACKNOWLEDGMENTS

It is impossible to acknowledge all the support I have received from advisors, colleagues, students, librarians, archivists, friends and family, and flight attendants throughout the long process of turning what started as a graduate seminar paper on the group Stewardesses For Women's Rights into this book. But I am grateful for the chance to offer at least some thanks.

I have enjoyed an extended sojourn at the University of Cambridge in recent years among an illustrious community of scholars in the Faculty of History and at Jesus College. At Cambridge, a Mellon Research Fellowship in American History, a generous multiyear postdoctoral fellowship, has enabled me to finish this book, among other things. I want to thank especially Tony Badger and Michael O'Brien and gratefully acknowledge the Mellon Fund of the History Faculty. Others who deserve mention include Ann Holton, Josh Zietz, and Dan Rodgers, who graciously provided comments on the project while a visiting Pitt Professor. Thanks also to the students I have taught at Cambridge for many interesting discussions of America past and present.

The History Department at New York University offered a nurturing community during my graduate studies. I was lucky enough to have as my advisor Lizabeth Cohen, who always offered incisive criticism and counsel, as well as crucial mentoring. Daniel J. Walkowitz was unstintingly generous with his time and provided invaluable advice at every turn in dissertation research and writing. I hope he sees in this book how much all that red ink helped. Though absurdly busy, Robin D. G. Kelley provided brilliant comments and suggestions at key junctures. David

Reimers and Susan Ware offered yet more insight and encouragement. Fellow students made life at NYU even more intellectually enriching and quite often fun, particularly Micki McElya, Rebeccah Welch, Kevin Murphy, Lori Finkelstein, Molly Mitchell, Ellen Noonan, John Spencer, Karl Miller, Bill Mihalopoulos, Andrew Darien, Joong-Jae Lee, Erin Clune, and Rachel Mattson. My dissertation group provided astute critiques and encouragement: Cindy Derrow, Karen Krahulik, Michael Lerner, Louise Maxwell, and Joan Saab, who helped at early stages; and Kirsten Fermaglich, Neil Maher, and Debra Michals, whose later help was vital. A special nod is due to Joan, who presciently suggested "Femininity in Flight" for a title many years ago, when this project was a rough draft of a dissertation prospectus. I have never come up with one I like better. The Graduate School of Arts and Sciences at New York University provided crucial financial support with a Henry Mitchell MacCracken fellowship from 1994 to 1999. I am grateful also to the American Association of University Women Educational Foundation for an American Dissertation Fellowship for 1999–2000, and to the NYU History Department for a Margaret Brown fellowship for 2000–2001.

It is a pleasure to note additional intellectual debts that I have accumulated in the course of this work. Eileen Boris gave me my first chance to publish something on flight attendants in 1999. Her ongoing interest and support, and careful review of the entire manuscript, have been invaluable. Dorothy Sue Cobble, whose own scholarship has been a singular influence on how I think about service work and women's activism, provided a detailed critique of the manuscript that could not have been more helpful. Their insights have improved this book in many ways. Nan Enstad's comments on the manuscript and encouragement were a most welcome contribution too. For much-appreciated readings of portions of this work stretching from 2006 back to the late 1990s, thanks to Julie Greene, Lynn Abrams, Ava Baron, Maggie Walsh, Heidi Gottfried, Nancy Gabin, and Pat Cooper; seminar participants at the University of Wales, Swansea, the University of London, Oxford, and Cambridge in 2004 and 2005; and audience members at the "Labouring Feminism" conference (2005), the conference of the British Association for American Studies (2005), the annual meeting of the American Historical Association (2002), the North American Labor History Conference (1999), and the Berkshire Conference (1999). It was a treat and a learning experience to share the podium with two fellow scholars of flight attendants, Drew

Whitelegg and Bobbie Sullivan, at the BAAS conference in 2005; thanks to Drew for organizing our panel and more generally for his collegiality and fascinating scholarship. While working at the Gilder Lehrman Institute of American History from 2002 to 2003, I did not learn much about flight attendants, but I did learn a good deal about the practice of public history; thanks to my colleagues there, especially the institute president, Jim Basker. And cheers to Valerie Millholland and her colleagues at Duke University Press, and the co-editors of the Radical Perspectives series, Danny Walkowitz and Barbara Weinstein, for their commitment to this book.

At the Archives of Labor and Urban Affairs at Wayne State University, the knowledgeable and efficient staff, especially the archivist Bill Gulley, enabled me to navigate large, unprocessed collections during all-too-brief visits. Library staff at NYU and Cambridge University provided access to a wealth of far-flung sources. I am particularly indebted to the staff of the Robert F. Wagner Archives and Tamiment Library, especially Andrew Lee and Gail Malmgreen, where I completed a major portion of my research (and was employed part-time during graduate school).

Special acknowledgment is due to the former and current flight attendants who have shared their insights over the years that I have been researching and writing on their occupation. Many go unnamed in the following pages, but their help—from interviews, to e-mails, to informal chats about their experiences, to the gift of a t-shirt inscribed, "A Flight Attendant is here to save your ass not to kiss it"—has provided invaluable source material, not to mention great conversation. I want particularly to thank Jeanne Notaro, Gloria Whitman, Diana Bristow, and Janet Corcoran. I hope all find the book worthy.

Finally, I want to acknowledge the loved ones who have contributed to this work in more ways than they probably realize: my parents, Ann and Frank Barry; my sister Allison Barry; and my brother Kevin Barry, his wife Patti Jeanne, and their four wonderful kids. My family helped me with this project from day one in various tangible ways. But I am even more grateful for the intangible gift of their love and unstinting support since long before this project began, and throughout it. I am grateful too for the support of the Kassoufs, Spratts, and Prems in recent years. For Charles Kassouf, to whom this book is dedicated, I hope just a few words will go a long way. In countless ways he has made this book possible and life so often a true joy. I am thankful above all else for him.

FEMININITY IN FLIGHT

Trans World Airlines flight attendants, newly graduated from training, Paris, August 1965. © Bettmann/CORBIS.

INTRODUCTION

"Stewardesses are America's vestal virgins," remarked a male passenger traveling on United Airlines in 1966. The comment captured how firmly lodged female flight attendants—"stewardesses" until the 1970s—were in the popular imagination of the mid-twentieth-century United States. These young, single, white women's good looks and unusual occupation prompted reverence, envy, and desire. Since 1930, when the first stewardesses took flight, airline marketing and employment policies succeeded brilliantly in creating a select corps of airborne "Glamor Girls," as *Life* Magazine called them in 1958, to help sell seats. What airlines had not counted on, however, was that lurking among the glamour girls were some militant union organizers and feminists. By the 1970s, when skimpy uniforms, airline slogans like "I'm Cheryl—Fly Me," and pulp novels like *The Fly Girls* lent stewardesses a more provocative aura, flight attendants emerged as among the most outspoken and successful workplace feminists.[1]

Stewardesses' historic mystique hardly suggests a penchant for union activism or feminism. But on closer inspection, the history of flight attendants in the United States is a story in which glamorization and organization, and femininity and feminism, uniquely shaped the efforts of a cultural elite among working women to claim greater respect in an archetypal "women's job." Stewardesses working in the two decades after the Second World War relished their celebrated popular identity, but also unionized. They were joined by the small number of men who worked alongside them as stewards and pursers, but whose presence rarely registered in popular ideals or airline marketing until the 1970s. Postwar flight attendants picketed and threatened strikes against airlines (and indeed struck on more than one occasion) and lobbied the federal government for safety certification. Union activists also demanded an equal place at labor's table at a time when labor leaders found it hard to take pink-collar workers seriously, especially such a young, glamorized group. Postwar flight attendants fell short of obtaining many of their goals. But their efforts—and occasional outpourings of militancy—made plain that the rewards of belonging to a glamorous coterie did not substitute for being respected as workers with distinct skills. Gracious and charming steward-esses were, docile they were not.

By the mid-1960s, with two decades of organized activism behind them, stewardesses were quick to take advantage of an increasingly rights-oriented era to wage war on gender-biased work rules and patronizing attitudes. Fed up with airline policies that dictated retirement at marriage or at the age of thirty-two, female flight attendants seized on new legal tools banning sex discrimination in employment to force change. In less than a decade stewardesses' lawsuits and union activism ended age and marriage restrictions, and then won them the right to fly as mothers. Flight attendants also remade their unions, transforming what had been adjuncts of male-dominated parent unions into independent associations run by, and for, cabin crew alone and committed to women's rights and concerns. Finally, as stewardesses' reputation changed from the long-glamorized one of ideal brides to that of sexy swingers, flight attendants used their public relations acumen to debunk their hypersexualized im-age and demand respect as safety professionals. Though the cultural baggage of glamour lingered, flight attendants would meet the challenges of recent decades with the fruits of their feminist activism in the late 1960s and 1970s: a more diverse and stable workforce, independent and feisty unions, and growing recognition of their role in passenger safety.

Perhaps it should not shock us that female flight attendants of the late 1960s and 1970s, co-opted as commercial symbols of the sexual revolu-tion and subjected to some of the most rigid sex discrimination then faced by female wage-earners, fought back during the heyday of the women's movement. But how do we account for the union activism and professionalizing efforts of stewardesses in the postwar era, when, as one later recalled, "next to being a Hollywood movie star, nothing was more glamorous"? Stewardesses generally considered themselves lucky mem-bers of a handpicked elite, but few stayed in the job long in any case before the 1970s. Thanks to the no-marriage rule, annual turnover held steady at 30 to 40 percent, with average tenure at about two to three years, from the 1930s through the 1960s. Why would short-term, glamorized workers bother to muster the energy and commitment needed to union-ize, to struggle for professional recognition, and to demand that labor leaders take them seriously?[2]

I argue that the activist history of flight attendants from the late 1940s onward is not just the little-known labor history obscured by the cultural history of the iconic "stewardess." Rather, the labor history cannot be separated from the cultural history: glamorization was a double-edged sword that motivated and shaped flight attendants' activism, and in turn their contributions to working women's struggles for more respectful treatment. As five female flight attendants committed to feminist and union activism complained in 1977, "The airlines would have us believe that we are too glamorous to be considered workers. And the public considers us too frivolous to be taken seriously." Flight attendants en-gaged in activism to be taken seriously as workers with real skills, rather than celebrated exclusively as embodiments of femininity.[3]

The stereotype of female wage-earners as less than serious about work and political action—not "real" workers like male breadwinners—is a durable one in the United States. Women who worked for wages—that is, doing the kind of "work" recognized as deserving pay and conferring economic citizenship—found themselves marginalized as mere seekers of "pin money." As the growing scholarship on women's work and activism has shown, the desire for respect as real workers, with economic needs and skills as real as men's, has long motivated women to demand better treatment from employers, unions, and the state. For female flight atten-dants, however, the problem was not so much that they were dismissed as less important, less serious than male workers; rather, it was that their mystique of glamorous femininity made them unrecognizable as workers of any kind. Airline marketing and cultural representations cast pas-senger service aloft as an essentially feminine exercise in exuding charm, looking fabulous, and providing comfort. Stewardesses seemed merely to be masterly performers of womanhood. Flattering as it may have been, glamorization left no room for recognition of the distinct skills and arduous labor required by flight attendants' multifaceted work.[4]

Ironically, stewardesses had to work quite hard to seem not to be working at all. The job required a range of service and safety tasks, from serving food and beverages, caring for ill or infirm travelers, and simply chatting with passengers to enforcing safety rules and remaining ever watchful for possible emergencies. To this already complicated mix of mental and manual labor airlines added exacting appearance and deportment standards. From the first job interview onward, stewardesses were expected to remain perfectly groomed, maintain a willowy figure, and conjure an unending supply of cheer and concern for passengers. Female flight attendants worked mightily at what feminist social scientists call the labor of femininity, that is, they worked at having the kind of body and expressing the emotions demanded of women by white, middle-class, heterosexual standards. But such work, as scholars have pointed out, is neither measured nor compensated as "real" labor, even when required by an employer. Female flight attendants were thus doomed to have the discipline, effort, and skill that they devoted to meeting airlines' appearance and behavior standards dismissed as doing simply what women naturally know how and want to do: to look and act like proper women. Yet the ultimate challenge for stewardesses was to perform *every* aspect of their multifaceted work with such unwavering charm and attractiveness that *none* of their labor was evident: they were supposed to provide service and safety as well as smiles with an appearance of effortlessness. The more effectively stewardesses did their job, by airline standards, the more complicit they became in concealing their own skills and hard work.[5]

Being glamorized exemplars of femininity certainly had its benefits. Not least, stewardesses enjoyed regular travel, a rare privilege until recently, and the independent lifestyle that their job afforded. They also claimed the pride of a high-profile chosen few, who had "as sure a path as any to the altar," as an admiring female reporter noted in 1955. But what we might call the "wages of glamour" still came at a cost. Along with demanding hard work that seemed effortless, feminine charm required youth and availability by the airlines' account. Airlines considered stewardesses obsolete upon marriage or reaching their mid-thirties and offered them scant long-term benefits or promotional opportunities if they managed to stay for more than a few years. Stewardesses' celebrated image also affected their interactions with passengers and co-workers in troubling ways. Airline marketing that promised perfect hostesses left air travelers ignorant of flight attendants' mandate to enforce safety rules and prevent disruptive behavior in the cabin. Stewardesses' reputed desirability also invited sexual harassment from male co-workers and passengers alike.[6]

Stewardess activists occasionally drew explicit links between the burdens of their glamorized image and their goals and demands. More often they did not, at least until the feminist ferment of the 1970s. Still we can—and I think should—see the entire history of flight attendants' organized activism as inseparable from the labor, rewards, and burdens of representing glamorized femininity. Postwar stewardess activists strove to supplement the wages of glamour with recognition as professionals and capable trade unionists. In doing so, they drew on the strong occupational bonds that flight attendants shared, even as stewardesses' elite identity made many uneasy with labor organizing. But as the sexual revolution and the women's movement unfolded, a later generation of flight attendants increasingly found glamorization itself to be problematic. For a time in the mid-1960s, when public policy began broadly to demand non-discrimination in workplaces, stewardess activists used their mystique to publicize and challenge the gender-biased rules that airlines had long imposed on them. But the more airlines resisted changes in employment policy, while also marketing a more prurient vision of alluring stewardesses, the more flight attendants sought to replace the wages of glamour altogether with respect as professionals.

WORKING WITH GLAMOUR AND CARE

Dictionaries note that Sir Walter Scott, the nineteenth-century novelist, introduced "glamour" to the English language, adapting an older Scottish word for enchantment. But how it went on to become a ubiquitous yet ill-defined buzzword in popular culture has generated little scholarly analysis. As the historian Jill Fields observes, "Though utilized frequently as a descriptive term, glamour's definition has remained as elusive and indeterminable as the aura of power it imparts to particular objects, bodies, and processes." A handful of scholars have glimpsed the birth of glamour in Victorian barmaids, the visual idiom of the Belle Époque painter Giovanni Boldini, and popular actresses and showgirls of the late-nineteenth- and early-twentieth-century stage; a few others have sketched glamour's growing importance in the twentieth century through the evolution of intimate apparel and Hollywood's impact overseas. Glamour, these scholars basically agree, was a byproduct and catalyst of the modern emphasis on appearances and self-display that grew with urban consumer culture and centered on female bodies in particular. In perhaps the most concise formulation to date, the Italian studies scholar Stephen Gundle defines glamour as "the language of allure and desirability in capitalist society" in the twentieth century.[7]

Though widely adaptable, glamour's historical career has been primarily in the "business of female spectacle," in Linda Mizejewski's succinct phrase. In part, this profitable business has been the display of fashionable female bodies on stage and screen and in print. It has also been the related project of convincing female consumers that they need only buy the right products and services to look and live like Hollywood stars, socialites, débutantes, beauty pageant winners, models, and other popular icons of feminine attractiveness and allure. For feminine glamour to be desired and consumed, of course, it had to be produced—not only by those who have made glamorizing goods and services, but also those who have embodied it. For débutantes and beauty queens, representing glamour may have been a career of sorts, but it was not wage work per se; for others, like stewardesses, models, and actresses, evoking glamour was part, if not the sum, of their paid labor. Jill Fields, in her history of intimate apparel, attributes much of glamour's power and importance to how it separated consumption from production: the conceptual divide between the "fashion" and "apparel" industries, she argues, disassociated clothing and its glamorous possibilities from the unalluring world of garment factories and workers. In airline passenger service, we can also see glamour at work in rendering labor invisible. In stewardesses' labor of feminine embodiment, however, where the point of production and the point of consumption were inseparable, glamour meant concealing labor even as it was being performed.[8]

But the cultural luster of being a stewardess also depended on bringing domesticity to the alien space of an airliner. Indeed, stewardesses' elevated cultural status was as much about caregiving as cosmopolitanism and allure. The nurturing required by airline service standards meant constant menial labor and emotional caregiving, qualities in tension with beauty, enchantment, and sex appeal. As one former flight attendant who worked in the 1950s responded when asked whether she considered her job "glamorous," "It's difficult to be 'glamorous' while attempting to serve drinks, meals, and other cabin services to 88 passengers and 3 cockpit crew on a 1 hour 15 minute leg . . . by yourself." Coping with ill-behaved children, violent drunks, and panic-stricken travelers, even without time pressures, could hardly be described as glamorous work either. The overarching ideal of femininity that flight attendants represented was an evolving blend of traditional domestic expectations and more modern ideals of attractiveness and charm on display—in other words, part glamour, part nurture.[9]

Yet if the carework and glamour aspects of flight attendants' work were in tension, both lacked cultural and economic value as labor. Nineteenth-century industrialization, Jeanne Boydston and others argue, engendered a new ideological divide between "home" and "work" that eroded the economic value attributed to housework. Instead, women's domestic duties in the home were idealized by the emerging white middle class as "effortless emanations of their very being, providing for the needs of their families without labor, through their simple presence in the household," in Boydston's words. The twentieth century brought many changes in housework, but not in its fundamental status as a supposedly noneconomic labor of love. The effort and skills that flight attendants put into their jobs were thus doubly obscured by the mystification of both women's domestic and glamorizing labor as something other than work.[10]

THE EXPANDING PINK-COLLAR WORLD OF WORK AND ACTIVISM

Though stewardesses enjoyed an iconic status all their own, they had much in common with other women who toiled in the feminized realms of clerical and service work and received little recognition of their skills and labor. From "office wives" (secretaries) fetching coffee for the boss to waitresses obliging male customers with playful performances as scolds or vamps, female wage-earners in many clerical and service fields have been expected not only to perform gender on the job but to perform gender *as* the job. The appearance requirements, early retirement, sexual harassment, and patronizing attitudes from male labor leaders that flight attendants faced have many parallels in the history of nurses, telephone operators, shop clerks, domestics, teachers, waitresses, and secretaries, among others. Indeed, one waitress's recollection in 1940 that management scrutinized "every gesture" and "every word" uttered to customers, "and every detail of her appearance," suggested just how much service employers had in common in assuming the right to control female workers' bodies and personalities as well as labor. The stewardess mystique was only one example of the managerial packaging of femininity for customers' consumption (and male co-workers' enjoyment) that marked the expanding world of pink-collar work. What made stewardesses' work and popular appeal distinct was that management's demands for flawless femininity from this comparatively small group were more stringently uniform—and better marketed—than in similar pink-collar occupations.[11]

The rise of this pink-collar work was the result of two larger, related historical developments that have reshaped American life over the last century: the movement of women into the labor force and the burgeoning of the service sector. The general growth in female employment, with some exceptions during national crises of war and depression, was steady and dramatic. In 1900 one in five women in the United States worked for wages, a total of five million; by 1990, three in five did, and they numbered more than fifty million. In those same decades wage work became the norm for women across class and racial lines and over the lifecycle, and married women, including those with young children, eventually outnumbered single women. The expansion of the service sector was equally dramatic. By the last decade of the twentieth century, services accounted for two-thirds of national income and service occupations for more than three-quarters of nonagricultural employment in the United States. While scholars find many causes for the rise of the service economy, the service sector's growth and the feminization of the labor force were mutually reinforcing: as more women worked outside the home, demand rose for consumer services formerly provided by unpaid female domestic labor, and growing demand for services created more jobs filled by women.[12]

Where service jobs involved public contact, employers typically sought out white women, or better still, young, native-born white women, for their relatively high levels of education, sociability, ornamental qualities, and modest wage expectations. Women of color generally inherited paid domestic work, the traditional female service field, but also found new opportunities in other service jobs, though on a predictably unequal basis in status, wages, benefits, and job security. Female flight attendants were at the leading edge in particular in the 1930s of commercialized "hostessing," where young white women were hired to bring female nurturing, plus a profitable dose of charm and attractiveness, to the growing travel and hospitality industries. As the term "pink-collar" was coined to suggest, women took up an array of female-dominated clerical and service occupations which were generally cleaner and safer than blue-collar work, but which because of gender segregation and discrimination had lower pay and status than traditionally male white-collar work. The problems that flight attendants confronted, and the ways they chose to organize and protest, reflect these changes in work, even as they tell us a particular story about femininity in the airline industry.[13]

Stewardesses' glamorization helped Americans make cultural sense of women's movement into paid work and the increasingly commonplace experience of purchasing mass-produced services. In celebrating stewardesses as charming, attractive hostesses who made passengers feel "at home," airlines, journalists, popular culture producers, and the public overlaid a fantasy of nurturing and alluring femininity on new commercial relationships and spaces. The fantasy mitigated the potentially unsettling realities that stewardesses might have represented: that they were gracious and attentive because they were paid to be, and worked about as far removed physically from the domestic realm as possible. As the objects of the fantasy, stewardesses carried considerable cultural weight and material burdens. As the gender and technology scholar Cynthia Cockburn has observed, work is a gendering process and workers produce culture along with goods and services; work is a race-making process too, as others have added. But stewardesses more than other workers not only performed gender and race and produced culture at work; they served the entire nation as emblems of white, middle-class femininity.[14]

The stewardess mystique was certainly not the sole creation or property of management. Airline managers' desire to sell tickets with the promise of an attractive, gracious hostess required female bodies, effort, and ingenuity to fulfill. Tellingly, it was a woman wanting to work for the airlines who first suggested hiring female cabin crew in 1930, not an aspiring Ziegfeld in the ranks of airline executives. In the years since, stewardesses have managed, like other women, to put feminine ideals to work for themselves, as a source of pleasure and pride, an economic resource, and even a means to promote social change. When activist stewardesses used their privileged cultural position to draw public attention to the discrimination they suffered, they co-opted an employer-defined vision of femininity for feminist goals. They often found their grievances all but lost amid flattery, chivalry, and irreverence when they made their case to the news media and politicians. But a glamorized popular identity provided stewardesses with a cultural visibility that few other working women enjoyed, and they proved quite adept at making the most of both the power and objectification that it entailed.

This history of flight attendants has benefited from the insights of other scholars who have written on the occupation. Sociologists, including Arlie Russell Hochschild, have drawn broad conclusions from flight attendants about work and gender in postindustrial capitalism. For Hochschild the occupation exemplifies the emotional labor required of service workers and the risks of alienation that the commodification of feeling carries. For others, such as Melissa Tyler, the occupation evidences in the extreme the gendering and the resultant devaluing of women's work. Sociologists and historians have also seen flight attendants as agents and representatives of changes in women's work in the 1970s, and Georgia Nielsen's landmark union study of United flight attendants locates the roots of change in the postwar era. The historical emphasis on the 1970s in most of this work is understandable, as they were dramatic years of change for female flight attendants as for other working women. But the effect, with few exceptions, is to suggest that flight attendants were previously a contented, docile bunch. Flight attendants' union history tells us otherwise. More generally, the literature on flight attendants leaves disconnected their seemingly disparate roles as icons of femininity, both exploited and privileged, and as ambitious activists who alternately ignored and protested the constrictions of feminine ideals. This book is an attempt to connect those two roles over several decades by taking glamorization and activism as inseparable features of flight attendants' collective experiences, and of their relevance to the broader history of femininity, work, and pink-collar activism.[15]

1

"PSYCHOLOGICAL PUNCH"
Nurse-Stewardesses in the 1930s

In 1933 a reporter from the Toledo *Sunday Times* took dramatic note of a new job for women in Depression-era America. The airline stewardess "goes to work 5,000 feet above the earth, rushing through space at a rate of three miles a minute. She has been eulogized, glorified, publicized, and fictionalized during her comparatively short existence. She has become the envy of stenographers in New York and farmers' daughters in Iowa. She seems to be on the way to becoming to American girlhood what policemen, pilots, and cowboys are to American boyhood." With rhetorical flourish, this female journalist heralded the arrival of America's newest icon of femininity, the airline stewardess.[1]

Though small in numbers, no more than a thousand by the end of the 1930s, female flight attendants sparked the imagination of many writers amid America's worst economic disaster. Aviation inspired excitement and romance during hard times, and stewardesses brought an air of reassuring femininity to the rough-and-ready world of flying. As many reporters declared, they met the challenges of rudimentary technologies and unpredictable passengers with unflappable charm, courage, and ingenuity. Amid economic hardship, social dislocation, and tendentious debates over women's right to employment, female flight attendants quickly gained a permanent place in airplane cabins and in popular culture as enviable "sky girls," with good looks, flawless hostess skills, and exciting jobs.[2]

The flight attendant occupation took permanent shape in the 1930s as "women's work," that is, work not only predominantly performed by women but also defined as embodying white, middle-class ideals of femininity. As the nascent commercial aviation industry sought to lure well-heeled travelers into the air, airline managers and stewardesses together defined the new field of in-flight passenger service around the social ideal of the "hostess." A stewardess's foremost duty was to mobilize her nurturing instincts and domestic skills to serve passengers, much as middle-class, white women were expected to treat guests in their own homes. The early airlines' crystallizing ideal of the stewardess also demanded, however, that the hostess be as desirable as she was nurturing. From the start, stewardess work was restricted to white, young, single, slender, and attractive women. Female flight attendants quickly earned an enduring reputation as representing the best of American womanhood.

The hostess ideal and hiring restrictions not only stamped the flight attendant occupation itself as archetypal white "women's work" but also helped to shape racial and gender hierarchies in the culture and economy of the early-twentieth-century United States. African American male railroad porters, who numbered more than twenty thousand in the 1920s, had long embodied service expectations in long-distance domestic travel. Commercial air carriers elected instead to offer passengers a genteel "hostess," rather than a racially subordinate servant. By hiring only white employees for flight crews, airlines linked whiteness to technological prowess in an industry widely hailed as being at the cutting edge of modern commerce and mechanical ingenuity. But in segregating the flight crew by sex—men in the cockpit as pilots and women in the cabin as passenger attendants—airlines confirmed popular equations of masculinity with mechanical mastery and femininity with technology's domestication. Stewardesses entered the popular cultural imagination as the female "pioneers" of the modern frontier of flight—a feminizing influence in a race-coded paradigm of progress, with American aviation advancing capitalism and civilization throughout the nation and world.[3]

With their "sky girls," airlines also contributed to elaborating the division of labor in the service economy as paid domestic labor declined and commercialized services burgeoned outside the home. Women's employment and the service sector would grow together, but higher-status public contact work would be largely reserved for whites, while racially subordinate groups would be segregated in lower-status, behind-the-scenes service jobs. The first generation of female flight attendants quickly became a glamorous aristocracy in the expanding pink-collar service hierarchy. As such, they helped define employers' and customers' expectations of feminized service in a commercial context, and the physical and social profile of the women who could best impress customers. The popular début of young, white women in airline passenger service in the 1930s would resonate for decades to come in commercial aviation, the service economy, and cultural fantasies of femininity in the United States.[4]

CONQUERING THE SKIES FOR COMMERCIAL TRAVEL

The first stewardesses who took flight in 1930 embodied the growing efforts of airlines in the United States to lure passengers from other means of travel by providing transport that was not only faster but safe, reliable, and comfortable as well. For more than two decades after the Wright Brothers' historic flight at Kitty Hawk in 1903, airplane rides represented thrilling entertainment or military derring-do to Americans, rather than a way to travel. Despite America's "airmindedness," in the historian Joseph Corn's phrase, it was western Europe that initially led the way with airline passenger transport in the wake of the First World War.[5]

By the late 1920s, however, the government and public gave American carriers a new incentive to focus on passenger transport. Beginning in 1925 the federal government began more purposefully to nurture a passenger-focused airline industry by enacting legislation to turn over air mail to private contractors, fund the development of aviation technology and infrastructure, and then adjust the mail contract system to encourage the carriage of passengers along with mail. The Post Office in the later 1920s and early 1930s also promoted airline consolidation by generally awarding its most lucrative contracts to the largest, most well-established carriers, rather than the lowest bidders. Government officials used the mail contract system to ensure the growth and stability of the industry and especially to promote passenger service, which they hoped would eventually free airlines from the need for subsidies. Airlines based in the United States received an additional boost in 1927, when Charles Lindbergh enthralled the nation as the first aviator to complete a transatlantic flight. The feat won international acclaim for "Lindy" and served the aviation community as an advertisement for the growing reliability of aircraft and engine designs. Lindbergh's historic solo flight to Paris sparked unprecedented public interest and investor confidence in aviation.[6]

In the late 1920s commercial aviation in the United States grew explosively. More than one hundred carriers were flying passengers, mail, and other cargo on routes connecting the nation's major cities and spanning the continent. Amid the flurry of start-ups, mergers, and acquisitions spurred by the aviation boom, the historic "Big Four" domestic airlines—United, American, Eastern, and TWA—and the international carrier Pan American emerged as industry leaders. By the end of the decade they were flying twelve-seat planes and experimenting with passenger-only routes. Passenger traffic on all of the nation's airlines expanded rapidly, from less than 9,000 in 1927 to more than 400,000 in 1930, despite the national slide into economic depression. Having been slow to start, by the late 1920s the airline industry in the United States outdistanced its European and Canadian competitors in total passenger traffic. By 1933 the Big Four alone carried more than half a million passengers.[7]

During the 1930s aircraft manufacturers increasingly geared their designs to the growing business of passenger transport. In just a few years small planes of wood, wire, and fabric gave way to larger, sleeker metal craft with upholstered, climate-controlled interiors, prompting favorable comparisons with the Pullman rail cars that defined luxury travel on the ground. Douglas's DC-3, introduced in 1936, was the culmination of these trends and a watershed in its own right. It offered spacious, reclining seats for twenty-four for daytime flights, or berths for sixteen and two dressing rooms for overnight flights. With greater speed and hauling capacity than its predecessors, the DC-3 became the workhorse of the airline industry for decades. "It freed the air lines from complete dependency on government mail pay," remembered C. R. Smith, president of American Airlines, because it was "the first airplane that could make money just by hauling passengers." Within just a decade or so, technological advances and federal money enabled airlines to become a major competitor for American travelers' business.[8]

THE "FELLOWSHIP" OF WHITENESS ALOFT

In the later 1920s most travelers were understandably reluctant to choose airlines over railroads or ships, for flying was generally more expensive and widely perceived as more dangerous. As for comfort, as one historian has quipped, early commercial air travel often "verged on torment." Before the DC-3's arrival, cabins were cramped and offered little protection from temperature extremes, fuel odors, or the vibration and deafening roar of engines and propellers. Planes flew through rather than above the weather, making airsickness all too common. With rudimentary technologies on the ground as well, flights were often interrupted or canceled because of weather conditions or mechanical failures.[9]

To woo the affluent traveler who could afford airfare, some carriers began to follow European airlines' practice of employing cabin attendants to offer the personalized attention and at least some of the creature comforts found on the rails or at sea. Carriers in Europe, then the United States, turned first to young, white men to attend to passengers. The first-ever flight attendants were teenagers hired as "cabin boys" by German and English airlines in 1922. By the later 1920s several European airlines were employing "stewards," adult men recruited from first-class hotels, restaurants, and ocean liners. America's first flight attendants took flight in 1926, when Stout Air Services of Detroit hired male "aerial couriers." Soon the overseas carrier Pan American and others followed suit. By the end of the decade several American carriers employed couriers or stewards to serve gourmet fare, chauffeur passengers to the airport, answer their questions in flight, and handle baggage and paperwork.[10]

In looking to and across the Atlantic for their service standard, airlines eschewed what might have been the more logical model to emulate, that of their main competition. With the exception of Pan Am, airlines in the United States battled for market share with the railroads. The railroads since the later nineteenth century had famously relied upon male African American attendants to embody their ideal of passenger service. As black porters played host on luxurious Pullman cars, the role of the racially subordinate servant ultimately defined their relationship to affluent, white passengers. Indeed, popular cultural images collapsed porters into the racist caricature of "George," a docile, slow-witted, buffoonish attendant, and a close cousin to "Sambo," the simple-minded slave of the white antebellum imagination. Passengers, for their part, often invoked the stereotype by summoning porters as "George." Pullman's all-black maids, while far fewer in number, reinforced the racial inequalities of railcar service and made clear how gender and sexuality intertwined with racial stereotyping. Maids were employed to attend especially to women passengers, a means of mitigating the perceived dangers of intimate contact between porters and white women; maids also received lower wages than porters and harsher treatment from management. The black servility marketed by Pullman was belied by the skilled service that porters and maids provided, as well as the militant labor and civil rights activism of the porters' pioneering union, the Brotherhood of Sleeping Car porters. Still, racist custom and the Pullman Company's own advertising, though eager to portray attendants' competence, invited white rail passengers to expect racial dominance as part of the service they purchased.[11]

Yet as railroads enabled the white traveler in effect to play master or mistress to black attendants, the commercial basis of this unequal relationship was explicit: passengers were expected to tip and had to pay for meals, drinks, and the use of pillows. In fact, part of the "George" stereotype was his shameless pursuit of tips—compensation that the Pullman Company used to justify low wages for porters. Tipping was well established in other travel and service industries as well by the twentieth century. On ocean liners passengers tipped their stewards, or less often the small number of stewardesses who, like Pullman maids, waited on lady passengers. In restaurants and hotels too, personal service typically generated gratuities that grew with the level of luxury offered. Travelers and diners may have liked to judge the attention they received in a noncommercial language of "courtesy" versus "rudeness," but tips cast porters' and other workers' service as undeniably for hire. As for the workers themselves, "tips go with servility," remarked a journalist in 1902, who marveled that "any native-born American could consent" to accepting a gratuity.[12]

Early airlines distinguished themselves from the railroads and other sellers of service by offering the "fellowship" of whiteness and banishing tipping. The high cost of air travel skewed its possible customer base toward wealthy and thus largely white travelers, but even so, airlines reportedly discouraged the patronage of African Americans (calls for reservation were racially screened by residential address). To serve their white clientele, airlines employed passenger attendants to act as both host and servant, much like railroad porters, but the airlines also sought out "professional" and "attractive" young, white men and prohibited them from accepting gratuities. As an aviation writer later observed, airlines decided that "they would let George, the Pullman porter, collect the quarters and the half dollars." Customers "feel happier and impartially serviced" when "tipping for special attention is painlessly removed." With no charges or tipping, another writer elaborated, the airline attendant could "meet every passenger . . . with a pleasant smile, and

on a more or less personal basis of genial good fellowship." Gratis service and racial "fellowship" eased the problem of white male subservience
and encouraged a sense of exclusive community in the face of fear and far
less comfort than Pullman cars or ocean liners offered. Airline management further diminished any servile connotations attached to stewards'
work by treating it as a possible stepping-stone to positions as pilots or
executives.[13]

Though servility and white male identity had little shared history to
begin with in the United States, airlines had special incentive to distance
their stewards from any hints of servitude. Unlike the railroads, airlines
needed to provide basic reassurance that the transport being sold was
fundamentally safe. White male attendants did what racial stereotypes
would not allow black male attendants to do: signal to fearful air travelers
that they were safely in the hands of those able to master the new technology of flight. In 1931 an aviation journalist who praised the one American
airline that did briefly employ African American attendants ironically
made clear why stereotypes associating technological prowess with white
masculinity ultimately barred black men from the job. In a leading aviation journal, C. B. Allen explained that the porters of the short-lived New
England and Western Airways, "once they overcame their nervousness
about flying," were proud of their jobs and "of course, had the necessary
training and background to render the right sort of service." For the
novice passenger, Allen added, the experiment was "very reassuring, for it
supplied the familiar atmosphere of the Pullman car and made flying
seem a lot less strange." The "nervousness" that Allen attributed to the
porters, if fleeting, indicated that calmness aloft was not to be expected of
African American men, however well-suited for the "right" type of service and however reassuring in their familiarity. Equanimity on aircraft
circa 1930 was a tall order for anyone, but stereotypes dictated that it
would most likely come from white male attendants. With uniforms that
echoed the naval-style garb of pilots, stewards reassured passengers that
the white men in the cabin as well as the cockpit were competent and in
control.[14]

Whether or not early passengers felt safe with stewards, the airline industry's initial reliance on male cabin attendants proved a halting experiment. Stewards only gained a foothold in the late 1920s on some routes
flown by a limited number of carriers. Most early passengers relied on the
co-pilot for sporadic service or simply fended for themselves. While the

commercial air transport industry managed to grow despite the onset of the Depression, hard times still prompted the elimination of much of the small steward corps in 1930. At least one well-placed observer concluded that white men were simply not cut out for passenger service anyway. In 1931 the same aviation journalist who depicted African American porters as "nervous" but well-suited for "the right sort of service" offered a contrasting picture of white stewards' ineptitude. "Over-zealous" stewards, he contended, too often annoyed passengers. Several had reportedly awakened travelers from naps only to point out uninteresting landmarks, while in other cases, he claimed, stewards had become so airsick themselves that they required care from passengers. But the frustrated pundit did find cause for hope in one airline's solution to the problem of cabin service: Boeing Air Transport's young, white nurse-stewardesses.[15]

THE "PSYCHOLOGICAL PUNCH" OF WHITE FEMININITY

The feminization of cabin service was initially the idea of Ellen Church, a nurse and trained pilot who wanted to work for the airlines. Airlines did not consider hiring women as commercial pilots regardless of qualifications, as Church knew. So on 12 February 1930 she paid a visit to Steven Stimpson, a manager at Boeing Air Transport (BAT, a predecessor of United Air Lines), and proposed that nurses could be an asset in cabin service. According to aviation lore, Stimpson had recently decided that Boeing needed to add cabin attendants to its flights, and was considering young Filipino men for the job. As with Pullman porters, affluent travelers would have already associated Filipino men with personal service in ocean transport, restaurants, hotels, and private households. Airlines, however, had already demonstrated a preference for white cabin staff, though as Stimpson's idea suggests, this racial typing was perhaps still uncertain. For unknown reasons, Stimpson's first proposal never took hold. What we do know is that Church persuaded Stimpson of nurses' potential as cabin crew, and Stimpson wrote a historic memo to his supervisors. Though his packaging of Church's idea reflected the immediate needs of airlines in 1930, when fear of flying was the paramount concern, his memo presciently outlined why airlines would prefer young, white women to serve passengers for decades thereafter.[16]

"It strikes me that there would be great psychological punch," Stimpson wrote, "to have young women stewardesses or couriers, or whatever you want to call them. . . . Imagine the national publicity we could get from it, and the tremendous effect it would have on the traveling public." But that was not all: "Also imagine the value that they would be to us not only in the neater and nicer method of serving food and looking out for the passengers' welfare, but also in an emergency." As Stimpson made clear, though, the possibility of emergencies was something best keep quiet. The airline should hire only trained nurses, he argued, but not advertise the fact, since it would suggest that medical personnel were required for passenger safety. "But," Stimpson noted, "it would be a mighty fine thing to have this available, sub rosa, if necessary either for air sickness or perhaps something worse." Nurses were additionally valuable because "the average graduate nurse is a girl with some horse sense" who "has seen enough of men to not be inclined to chase them around the block at every opportunity." Nurses would be disciplined, intelligent, and able to handle onboard clerical duties "better than the average young fellow."[17]

Stimpson's supervisor initially offered a curt, one-word reply: "No!" Boeing officials were reportedly concerned that "girls" would interfere with discipline on the plane. Pilots, in a typical defense of occupational exclusion, disdained the idea of having "flying nursemaids" encroach on their all-male territory. But Stimpson eventually talked the company president into a three-month trial. Boeing hired Church as the world's first airline stewardess and charged her with selecting seven other young nurses. After interviewing more than one hundred candidates Church made her choices, and on 15 May 1930 stewardess service began on the Oakland–Cheyenne–Chicago route on ten-passenger Boeing 80s. After the trial period the carrier hired twenty more women, and by 1933 it employed more than fifty. Boeing reported receiving hundreds of letters from passengers lavishing praise on the new cabin attendants. Pilots soon relented too, since stewardesses lessened the cockpit crew's concerns for passengers' welfare and brought them meals and coffee. Even better for Boeing, stewardesses garnered the publicity that Stimpson had predicted. Though few in number, the "sky girls" quickly became a popular subject for aviation reporters, novelists, and even Hollywood filmmakers.[18]

Noting Boeing's success and its stewardesses' popularity, other major airlines placed women in the cabin: Eastern in 1931, American in 1933, Western and TWA in 1935. TWA, for one, decided that even though its passengers professed satisfaction in surveys at being served by co-pilots,

"The Original Eight": the world's first airline stewardesses, hired by
Boeing Air Transport in 1930. © Bettmann/CORBIS.

customers were voting with their feet by patronizing other carriers that had stewardesses. Notably, when it hired its own stewardesses, TWA decided to emphasize its commitment to passenger comfort by making the popular label of "hostess" their official job title. Estimates of the size of the growing stewardess corps varied, but by the mid-1930s two to three hundred women worked aloft. By the end of the decade, when passenger traffic on airlines based in the United States topped three million, flight attendants' number had more than tripled, to around one thousand.[19]

The flight attendant occupation was not feminized entirely in the wake of BAT's successful "experiment." Although more and more carriers hired women by the end of the decade (most but not all nurses), some continued to employ stewards as well. In 1937 the *New York Times* noted that 105 male stewards worked alongside 286 stewardesses on American carriers. Pan American relied on male attendants exclusively until the 1940s, because it considered the extra clerical work and physical challenges on its long overseas routes too strenuous for women. Eastern uniquely flip-flopped over the 1930s and into the 1940s on the sex of its cabin attendants. Some carriers simply could not afford cabin staff. National had to let its first and only stewardess go after a year to help pay for a new plane in 1938. But if not all air travelers in the 1930s enjoyed the attention of a stewardess, the growing number of women in the job profoundly shaped passenger service and its central place in airline marketing.[20]

Stimpson's evocation of "psychological punch" succinctly captured the objective of stewardess service. In an era when women routinely earned lower wages than men, airlines were willing to pay stewardesses about as much as stewards. Airlines did get extra value for their hiring dollar with women who held nursing degrees, which were not required of men. But the general parity in pay, working conditions, and benefits indicates that labor costs had little to do with the feminization of passenger service. Instead, airlines quickly came to see female cabin attendants as uniquely valuable in marketing. As many contemporary observers contended, if young, white women were flying, then wary travelers would be encouraged to brave the skies: other women would be reassured, and men would be dared to prove their own fortitude. Airlines worked hard to convince the public that flying had emerged from its barnstorming and wartime roots as a safe, modern means of travel, and relied on women to help them. Female pilots, women such as Amelia Earhart, Ruth Nichols, and Jacqueline Cochran, whose record-breaking exploits made them national celebrities, served as publicity agents. Airlines hoped that Earhart and her colleagues would appeal especially to women, who industry marketers worried not only refused to fly themselves but also kept husbands grounded. Yet it was the stewardess, rather than the "aviatrix," who proved more effective for public relations in the long run. Stewardesses showed that planes were not only safe enough for intrepid women to fly and live to tell of it, but for respectable young women to ride at ease and play hostess in them.[21]

The racial, class, and gender identities of stewardesses were all crucial to the airlines' hope of challenging widespread fears of flying. Like stewards, stewardesses shared a "fellowship" with their passengers: according to the *New York Times* in 1936, "Because of the confined space and intimate atmosphere of the airplain [*sic*], a fellowship exists between passengers and hostess that has no counterpart in any other type of travel. Many friendships are formed." Airplane cabins were indeed confined, and airlines expected cabin staff to treat passengers as personally as possible. Most notably, attendants were required to learn and use each passenger's name. But more important, the stewardess's race and respectability made her an appropriate companion—a "friend" who legitimated the risky business of flying for the middle and upper classes. And a stewardess, instead of a steward, presumably made the plane seem even safer, for she suggested that masculine technological savvy was unnecessary outside the cockpit. As a writer for the *Atlantic Monthly* explained in 1933 of the stewardess's soothing role on a rough-weather flight, "The passengers relax. If a mere girl isn't worried, why should they be?"[22]

As the same writer recognized, however, the "mere girl" reassured passengers so effectively because she distracted them with "cheerful chatter" and refreshments. In other words, the symbolic effects of gender, race, and class had to be backed by an enactment of domesticity. While airlines eschewed the railroads' model of racially subordinate servitude, the infant air transport industry trod the path of public domesticity blazed on the railroads and refined in hotels, department stores, and other commercial venues in the later nineteenth century and the early twentieth. As Amy Richter has argued, the "public domesticity" that railroad owners, customers, and staff together created moved the values and behaviors of private life into the commercial realm of rail travel, transforming both in the process. The resulting shared fantasy of public domesticity did not mean that people actually mistook a railcar for a home. But it did regulate interactions among mixed-sex strangers through an adapted code of Victorian respectability, which offered order, comfort, and familiarity amid rapid cultural and social change. While airlines courted an affluent public for which commercial interactions and long-distance travel were no longer so novel and potentially unsettling, the advent of regular passenger flight represented a cultural and technological innovation of enormous magnitude. Not surprisingly, airlines pursued the well-established goal of attempting to make customers feel "at home" far away from home. An all-inclusive ticket price, with gratuities prohibited, helped banish hints of commercialism from airplane cabins, and furnishings that resembled domestic spaces as far as possible engendered homely familiarity for travelers. But what better way to lend a homelike quality to the modern marvel of flight, airline managers soon realized, than hiring white, female attendants whose very presence and labor invoked domesticity?[23]

HAND-PICKING THE HOSTESSES

Following Ellen Church's original vision of nurses as ideal cabin crew, early airlines required a nursing diploma of their hostesses. The nursing qualification, many airline managers, passengers, journalists, and stewardesses agreed, attested to a unique facility for handling the public that came from years of special training and hard work. By hiring nurses, airlines hoped to guarantee themselves a workforce of unusually intelligent, disciplined young women able to cope with any situation or personality. Nurses had also figured in many hospitals' efforts from the beginning of the twentieth century to lure more middle-class patients by lending their furnishings and service a more obvious appearance of domesticity. Making patients feel "at home" in the foreboding space of a hospital closely resembled the challenge that airlines set for themselves. But in their eagerness to reinforce the idea that flying was above all safe, airlines did what Stimpson had advised: they insisted that nurses were valuable in passenger service as paragons of domesticity, and kept "sub rosa" the value of their intricate knowledge of bodily care. As managers, journalists, and many stewardesses intoned throughout the 1930s, health-care expertise could prove useful, but it was interpersonal and domestic skills that made graduate nurses perfectly suited to serving airline passengers.[24]

Nursing, as one scholar has succinctly put it, "is the quintessential female profession." With roots in the home, as an extension of women's domestic duties, nursing has long been associated with womanhood and vice versa, even with the growing technical knowledge and training that it required by the twentieth century. Airlines' view that the nursing experience was "grand training for any girl," as one manager explained in 1933, was hardly novel or unusual. By denying that nurses' expertise in caring for the injured and ill might also be important, however, airlines immediately swept cabin safety issues under the rug and marketed flight attendants' service role solely instead. This may not be surprising, nor was it unique. The Pullman company was no more forthcoming about porters' safety duties on the rails; it also eagerly sought (though did not require) trained nurses for maid positions, yet presented them to female passengers simply as domestic servants at their disposal. Still, it was disingenuous for the infant airlines to claim that stewardesses' hospital training hardly mattered in an era when airsickness was rampant and crash landings alarmingly frequent. In the long run, early airlines' emphasis on service in defining flight attendants' work would make it exceedingly difficult for later generations of cabin crew to peg professional aspirations to expertise in passenger safety. In the short term, it meant that airlines did not really need nurses in a pinch. When military mobilization for the Second World War caused a national shortage of nurse labor, airlines dropped the nursing requirement. They did so quietly, with no real disruption to their hiring goals and practices or to the ideal of the stewardess. The nursing qualification was useful, but ultimately expendable.[25]

The airlines would prove much more strongly attached to other elements that gave stewardesses their "psychological punch." From the start, airlines required that stewardesses be not only white and female with a nursing degree but also young, single, slender, attractive, and personable. These early managerial decisions about the particular vision of white femininity that airlines wanted in the cabin would define stewardesses' qualifications long after widespread fears of flying had passed and the nursing qualification disappeared. A distillation of how gender, race, and class biases shaped employment opportunities more broadly, these restrictive assumptions of which kind of white, female bodies and personalities made for the best passenger service quickly became cherished tradition for airline managers, and for many stewardesses themselves.[26]

Age, physical dimensions, and marital status offered the airlines relatively unambiguous criteria for defining the ideal stewardess. Stimpson later explained, "I wanted enthusiastic girls, so I set an age limit of 25." Though the particular age ranges varied slightly among carriers, airlines in the 1930s quickly settled on the early twenties as the only years when women were suitably mature yet still vivacious enough for cabin service. To work on the cramped and weight-sensitive planes of 1930, the first stewardesses had to stand about 5' 4" and weigh no more than 115 pounds. As aircraft grew more solid and spacious, airlines raised the height and weight ceilings—but only barely, to around 5' 8" and 130 pounds. Airline managers considered marriage no less a threat than aging or spare pounds to women's suitability for the job. Wedlock, they reasoned, would detract from stewardesses' devotion to serving passengers, and the physical rigors and long, odd hours of flying would interfere with wifely duties at home. Boeing and soon its competitors thus hired only single women for cabin service positions. And single, as career guides warned prospective applicants, did not include being separated, widowed, or divorced—in other words, single meant being respectably innocent of, but available for, marriage. A few major carriers did allow some stewardesses to continue flying after marriage (though supervisors warned that these exceptions would end the moment any married stewardess's performance was seen to slip). But a handful of exceptions at management's whim only proved the singles-only rule.[27]

Discrimination against older and married women seeking wages was widespread at the time. The Bell system of telephone companies, the largest employer of women in the early-twentieth-century United States, similarly restricted the hiring of its all-female operator workforce on the basis of age and marriage. The Depression intensified many employers' resistance to employing married women while male "breadwinners" suffered widespread unemployment. New Deal federal policies discouraged married women's wage-earning. By immediately defining stewardessing as a necessarily temporary interlude of self-support between school and marriage, age restrictions and the no-marriage rule insulated stewardesses and airlines from debates over women's right to work outside the home. But as a small group of workers in a new, expanding industry, stewardesses were more a curiosity than a substantive presence in an especially competitive labor market. Airlines' age and marriage policies served mainly to ensure the youthful appeal of stewardesses and their

dedication to a challenging but clearly short-term career. As a TWA manager reportedly told the carrier's first class of hostesses in 1935, "If you
haven't found a man to keep you by the time you're twenty-eight, then
TWA won't want you either." While airline managers complained about
the costs and inconvenience of high turnover rates caused by "Cupid," the
no-marriage rule also guaranteed that few stewardesses would fly long
enough to expect promotions, significant raises, or other longer-term job
benefits.[28]

The airlines' stipulations regarding marital status, age, weight, and
height all dovetailed with their less precise but crucial ideal of respectable
allure. Stewardesses did not have to be "raving beauties," as journalists
surmised, but they did need the "good looks of the 'well-bred' American,
not the 'show-girl' type." Airlines wanted good teeth, clear skin, glossy
hair, and no evident physical flaws. Visible scars prompted the immediate
rejection of otherwise suitable candidates; corrective eyewear would not
do either, so near perfect vision was required as well. Airlines demanded
virtual perfection literally from head to toe: in 1935 TWA delicately informed candidates for its first hostess class, "With all passengers seated in
the plane, a hostess' feet are especially conspicuous. If you know that your
feet are larger than average for your height and weight, we ask that you
discuss the matter with the local TWA representative and possibly avoid
an unnecessary trip to [the final interview]."[29]

The airlines' vision of female attractiveness was only partly based on
meeting the physical ideal of the well-bred American woman. Stewardesses also had to exemplify charm and grace. From the early 1930s on,
larger carriers regularly reported receiving thousands of applications an-
nually for a handful of openings. By 1935 United had received fifteen
thousand applications in the five years since it began hiring stewardesses,
yet hired only a few hundred. In 1939 alone American Airlines interviewed fewer than one hundred of five thousand hopefuls, and hired a
mere twenty. To choose among the hundreds who met the physical requirements and had the requisite nursing or, less often, business experience, airlines demanded intangible qualities such as "poise," "tact," and
"character." Whatever class background aspiring stewardesses claimed,
they needed to have mastered middle-class manners and deportment to
represent the airlines. Personnel officers scrutinized candidates' family backgrounds, conversational skills, posture, vocabulary, diction, and
even how gracefully they used their hands and how "well" they wore their
clothes.[30]

In "hand-picking" their stewardesses, airlines sought still more than evident refinement and physical perfection. Personnel officials also looked for young women who struck them as intelligent and having common sense, wit, and a sense of adventure, but who understood the job to be hard work and ultimately temporary. Finally, airlines apparently wanted young women refined enough to socialize with wealthy travelers, but not too cosmopolitan or pampered to serve them. The chief stewardess for American Airlines explained in the *New York Times*, "The girl from Peoria or Podunk has just as much chance of becoming an airline stewardess as the young woman from New York or Chicago, and, in fact, usually turns out to be the better hostess." Nursing schools in the early twentieth century similarly favored small-town and rural recruits, who were expected to be more accustomed to hard work and discipline, and less likely to have suffered moral lapses, than their urban counterparts. Airlines continued that preference in seeing Middle America's finest girls-next-door as closer than big-city sophisticates to their hostess ideal.[31]

Airlines devoted such extraordinary care to screening candidates because appealing to all passengers at all times was no small challenge. The stewardess acted as both companion and servant to white, affluent, and mostly male passengers, thus walking a fine line between deference and gregariousness. She had to seem capable of offering to shine one passenger's shoes, soothe the nerves of the next with pleasant conversation, and tactfully decline a date from another. To make matters more complicated, the stewardess, while under the command of the pilot, was also the authority figure in the cabin, enforcing safety regulations and taking charge in an emergency. Whatever duties she performed and in whatever circumstances, the stewardess had to seem as appropriately gracious as possible—friendly but not too familiar, accommodating socially but not sexually, competent but not intimidating. As a chief hostess for TWA summed it up, a stewardess had to be able to "spill a cup of coffee in a man's lap and get away with it."[32]

Like other service providers, airlines sought representatives who met customers' expectations of a pleasant appearance and demeanor. From private-duty nursing to department-store clerking, hairdressing, and waitressing, an attractive face, figure, and personality were considered important if not essential attributes for female service workers engaged in public contact work. But by choosing white women for in-flight passenger service who were not only acceptable but exceptional by normative standards of charm and beauty, airlines assembled an elite corps of "superwomen." An article in *Literary Digest* from 1936 titled "Flying Supermen and Superwomen" noted that airlines put as much extraordinary care into selecting their stewardesses as they did with pilots. Would intermarriage between the two groups, the article breathlessly asked, yield "a race of superior Americans"?[33]

THE UNIQUE CHALLENGES AND
REWARDS OF AIR HOSTESSING IN THE 1930S

The idea that stewardesses were exemplars of femininity would endure for decades, as would the restrictive employment policies that encouraged it. But the actual labor that the first generation of sky girls performed and the respect they earned for it were in many ways unique. The nurse-stewardesses of the 1930s met distinct challenges in attempting to make commercial aircraft feel like home for passengers and were congratulated for bringing "professionalism" to the task.

There were many good reasons why thousands of women clamored for the chance to domesticate the skies. "Women," TWA's first chief hostess Ruth Rhodes proclaimed in 1937, "haven't enough adventure in their lives." Flying, Rhodes believed, was the most romantic thing that a woman could do. As Ellen Church, a licensed pilot, understood when she first suggested the idea of stewardesses, cabin service offered the only practical way for women to win employment aloft in passenger transport, the most prestigious area of the exciting new business of aviation. As many stewardesses explained, airline passenger service represented an appealing alternative to shifts in hospital wards or private-duty nursing, as well as most other earthbound occupations open to women. One stewardess informed a correspondent for the *New York Times* in 1936, "Oh, there's a freedom—a mental stimulation to this work. It hasn't the routine that there is in a hospital, yet there's the same interesting contact with the public." And as a female reporter noted, "A job which puts a premium on chatting easily with a screenland Romeo and calls it duty is apt to keep one smiling."[34]

With the airlines' high standards for stewardesses so well advertised, earning stewardess wings also meant joining the ranks of a nubile elite— among the most "marriageable" women in the country, as many journalists had it. One member of this exclusive group later recalled that she "was never any great shakes with the boys" in her hometown, "but the minute I got that airline job they came out of the woodwork." The reputation for matrimonial success that came with the job was flattering and an important benefit to many stewardesses. While many female workers in gender-segregated clerical, service, and industrial jobs spent most of their working hours with other women, and nurses tended the ill and infirm, stewardesses regularly held the attention of healthy, affluent male travelers and of their esteemed male co-workers in the cockpit.[35]

Perhaps most important of all, the job offered a steady, decent pay-check during the Depression, when many workers, including unprece-dented numbers from white-collar and professional ranks, were hard pressed to earn a living or even find work at all. Stewardesses received on average $100 to $125 a month, more than most nurses earned for hospital or private-duty work. It was also more than what white women typically earned in industrial, service, and clerical jobs and approximated salaries in feminized professions, such as teaching and librarianship. In addition, stewardesses received paid vacations, insurance coverage, and expense allowances for layovers (though some complained that airline outlays fell short of providing for decent lodging and meals). Finally, stewardesses enjoyed the rare treat of low-cost or gratis air travel for themselves and their families.[36]

In the 1930s, moreover, stewardess "pioneers" enjoyed respect for their work and skills that later generations would find elusive. Their ability to cope with a motley assortment of duties while tending their nervous human cargo impressed their passengers, employers, and the press alike. In the early 1930s, when airlines had only rudimentary maintenance crews, stewardesses performed a variety of pre- and post-flight chores, from sweeping and dusting cabins, cleaning lavatories, and making sure that seats were securely bolted to helping to refuel planes and roll them into hangars. The growth of the airlines quickly relieved stewardesses of their screwdrivers and brooms, but brought new work as the industry scrambled to put more comfort into flying. Stewardesses maintained increasingly diverse inventories of items for passengers' use, including typewriters, stationery, checkerboards, and electric shavers. One writer quipped in 1937 that American Airlines' equipment for sleeper flights "makes an imposing array which would do credit to a modern drug store." Before, during, and after flights, stewardesses completed a variety of reports for the airlines on passengers, cargo, and equipment.[37]

At the same time, uncomfortable, unpredictable, and even dangerous conditions demanded extraordinary interpersonal skills and sensitivity to passengers' varying psychological states. Stewardesses supplemented offers of refreshments, pillows, blankets, reading materials, cigarettes, and chewing gum (to relieve ear pressure) with improvisational care giving, socializing, and policing. Panic attacks and airsickness among passengers of course required prompt and sympathetic responses. Stewardesses also plied bored passengers with entertainment, by organizing games or engaging in pleasant conversation. Nearly all air travelers were curious about flying. Stewardesses fielded queries about airline routes, geography, weather patterns, and aerodynamics, among other subjects. "The stewardess," a career guide noted in 1940, "is the reference library of the upper atmosphere." Airlines also looked to stewardesses to minimize as diplomatically as possible the theft of such valuable items as airline-engraved silverware. Early passengers, contemporary sources claimed, demonstrated a startling propensity for claiming souvenirs. Finally, in an age when many air travelers had never before seen an aircraft interior, stewardesses remained vigilant for any who might mistake the exit for the lavatory door.[38]

In addition to earning respect for the sheer diversity of the duties they performed, early stewardesses distinctly enjoyed a reputation for bravery. Airlines hardly advertised the possible dangers of flying, but reporters and commentators in the 1930s repeatedly emphasized courage among the qualifications for the job and among the attributes that stewardesses routinely demonstrated. The closing of one profile of stewardesses from 1936 typically surmised, "The life of the flying hostess . . . takes plenty of courage, but she always seems to have it." Stewardesses proved their mettle to observers by meeting adverse weather conditions and mechanical mishaps with an air of confidence. More simply, stewardesses' willingness just to fly regularly inspired tributes. One male passenger penned a poem for Mildred J. "Sugar" Kane, a flight attendant for United in 1936 and 1937: "Little Lady of the Air / Flitting here and flying there / Over mountain tops and lakes / Courage real is what it takes / To go on from day to day / On your highly dangerous way / Yet you smile and carry on. . . ." Far less often, stewardesses won even higher praise for performing heroic acts. Nellie H. Granger, a hostess for TWA, garnered national press coverage in 1936 for her life-saving efforts in a crash that killed eleven people. Standing 5′ 2″ and weighing 101 pounds, Granger pulled two badly wounded survivors out of the wreckage, walked four miles to summon help, and then returned to the scene on foot to care for the two passengers she had saved. The *New York Times* noted, "Any one of her co-workers, Miss Granger will tell you, would have met the emergency with the same coolness and courage."[39]

Popular novels and films of the 1930s further promoted the image of the courageous stewardess. In a particularly dramatic yarn, Ruthe S. Wheeler's novel *Jane, Stewardess of the Air Lines* (1934), Jane Cameron and her colleagues suffer multiple travails, including a passenger's appendicitis, food poisoning, and airborne crime, as well as several crashes. On flights that repeatedly place passengers' and their own safety in jeopardy, the plucky stewardesses triumph. Jane helps pull an injured pilot from a plane wreck about to ignite, foils an attack by air bandits, and then lands a job as a stunt pilot for a Hollywood film. Steel-nerved Jane was merely one heroine in a broader genre of air crime and aviation dramas popular with American readers in the 1930s. But few authors after Wheeler would create a stewardess character of such crisis-tested bravery or one whose technological mastery of flying rivaled, even exceeded, that of male pilots, the usual subject of aviation hero worship. Popular romanticizing of air travel and its possible dangers in the 1930s enabled stewardess "pioneers" to stand as exemplars of airborne courage, in fiction and real life.[40]

Variously marveling at the bravery, tact, and sensitivity that stewardesses mustered, admirers offered early stewardesses high praise: they labeled their efforts "professional." Newspaper and magazine features often noted the high level of interpersonal skills needed to play hostess aloft. In a profile in 1932 of the United stewardess Olette Hasle, W. B. Courtney of *Collier's* recalled how Hasle had calmed a panic-stricken female passenger: "There was professional suavity in the undertones in which she talked to the woman, and practical skill in the manner in which she patted the frightened creature's trembling hands." "What unsuspected processes, I wondered," mused the military pilot and *Atlantic Monthly* essayist Francis Vivian Drake in 1933, "might not have been going on in the mind of my girl in green as she had handed back my ticket? Behind that friendly smile, for instance, had she been filing me away for future reference: 'Business man—seen better days—give him a match box and some gum'?" This "girl in green," Drake concluded, who among other accomplishments managed to relax her passengers in stormy skies, had "obviously been recruited from professional ranks."[41]

The apparent "professionalism" of early stewardesses that struck admiring observers like Courtney and Drake would prove fleeting. First, appreciation of early stewardesses' "cool professional air" reflected the novelty of their work and its setting. As flying became a more common-place activity for affluent Americans, stewardesses' nonchalance would no longer seem so impressive in and of itself, or even "a gift of Heaven," as Drake reckoned in 1933. Second and more important, making the cabin seem homelike emerged as stewardesses' foremost duty. When meeting that challenge was linked to the estimable skills of nursing in the 1930s, stewardesses' rendition of it seemed a "professional" achievement, particularly when it was juggled with so many other responsibilities and in such a foreboding setting. But the more airlines repeatedly intoned that a stewardess simply did what a gracious hostess would do in her own home, and the more flying lost its alien, novel qualities, the less anyone but flight attendants themselves would view their efforts as worthy of the label "professional."[42]

What is more, to be praised as going about your work professionally, as early stewardesses were, was one thing, but to enjoy the privileges and prestige of working in a recognized profession was another. As many historians have argued, "female" and "professional" have been a problematic pairing. The supposedly objective criteria that defined professions by the late nineteenth century—including esoteric knowledge, altruistic service to the public, state-certified credentials, autonomy in work, and self-monitoring of occupational standards—resulted from the exclusionary strategies and self-justifying ideals of male occupational groups and their elite sponsors. By design, the prerogatives of the professions were reserved de facto, if not also de jure, for men. In male-dominated professions, such as medicine and law, women struggled for the right of entry and, once in, confronted contradictory ideals of femininity and masculine professionalism. In historically female-dominated occupations that have fought for recognition as professions, such as social work and nursing, practitioners have earned the unequal designation of "semiprofessionals" in popular and sociological typologies of work. By the circular logic of gendered understandings of professional status, women could appropriately enter and excel in a field such as social work because it was a "caring" profession, but it was something less than a fully recognized profession because women predominated in it. Even when nursing degrees offered stewardesses a certifiable professional credential, their claim to professional status was limited by the desires of the airlines and the public to sanction their work outside the home, like nursing and women's employment more generally, as properly feminine.[43]

While closely linked to nursing, moreover, airline passenger service belonged to an expanding range of "hostess" jobs in travel and hospitality industries that generally lacked even an equivocal claim on professional status. "It's open season for women hostesses these days," reported *Independent Woman*, the journal of the National Federation of Business and Professional Women's Clubs, in 1938. Airline stewardess jobs took center stage in the magazine's survey of employment opportunities for women, but the article also publicized new hostessing options on ships, and at hotels, restaurants, and tourist attractions. "All a woman has to do when she finds herself out on a limb with a wolf or two howling," it concluded, "is to ask herself: 'Where can I roll out the red carpet where it has never been rolled before—where can I commercialize my "hostess sense"?' " As *Time* Magazine surmised in 1937, "U.S. railroads, long addicted to the Negro porter as a factotum, have seen the signs of the times in the sky," and began to hire young, white female nurses as "stewardesses" too.[44]

Though airlines conflated stewardesses' work with the honing of innately feminine talents and inclinations, stewardesses themselves demystified and dignified their job on their own terms. In 1938 one stewardess, Jeanette Lea, proclaimed in an article in *Popular Aviation* on behalf of her colleagues, "We *don't* fly for love." Just because a third resigned each year to marry, she explained, "does not mean that all of us sit on a perch in the sky waiting for Dan Cupid to soar by and take a pot shot at us." While publicity had attached what Lea aptly called an "aroma of romance" to stewardesses, she believed that they regarded themselves as "regular businesswomen" who worked "sincerely and efficiently" and did their best to promote the interests of their airline. Another stewardess, Marjorie Parker, explained in 1941, "As a general thing, hostess work is routine just like any other job," though she did confess that her job was often more interesting than earthbound employment.[45]

But if passenger service was ultimately just a job, stewardesses also made clear that it was distinctly demanding. In one breath Olette Hasle of United explained passenger service to readers of *Collier's* as "taking our home-making instincts into the cabins of the commercial airlines," but in the next she reported that stewardesses had "to know more than how to smooth a pillow and serve a lunch." Because of the unique psychological and physical strains that passengers experienced, Hasle felt that her work

A hostess for the Pennsylvania Central airline, Washington, 1941.
Library of Congress, Prints & Photographs Division, FSA-OWI Collection,
LC-USF34-045056-D.

was "only remotely analogous" to any kind of earthbound hostessing. Hasle believed that only arduous nursing training enabled stewardesses to handle multiple menial service duties while providing adept passenger care. Ellen Church, the world's first stewardess, believed that airline passenger service required a nurse's "sound knowledge of human psychology," among other attributes. To many early stewardesses, homemaking instincts helped them in their work, but as Florence Nightingale had argued of nursing itself, it also required skills and training beyond those of womanhood.[46]

As airlines in the United States strove to make a lucrative business of the modern technological conquest of the skies, the pioneering "sky girls" of the 1930s impressed the nation by bringing feminine charm aloft. In the midst of the national nightmare of the Depression, they demonstrated how attractive, refined, efficient, and adventurous women could be— even when hurtling through the sky in a vulnerable metal contraption.

And they accomplished this in the reassuringly domesticated role of a hostess. For their efforts, pioneering stewardesses were rewarded with a regular paycheck, the chance to travel, and widespread admiration for their pluck, respectable allure, and "professional" devotion to making passengers enjoy air travel.

The first generation of stewardesses thus participated in constructing enduring boundaries around their occupation by fulfilling the airlines' ideal of the hostess. Their bodies, personalities, and social graces gave shape to the restrictive vision of femininity that airlines would market for decades. The nursing qualification and the need for unusual courage passed with the 1930s. But the "aroma of romance" that Jeanette Lea found attached to her occupation in 1938 grew stronger as the culture and business of passenger transport matured. By the postwar years, airlines promised their elite but expanding customer base a more luxurious, leisurely party among the clouds, along with hostesses whose duties increasingly focused on making the party as entertaining and lavish as possible. For postwar stewardesses, beauty and charm would become even more central in defining their work and glamorizing their popular image. In "exercising the skill of a Nightingale, the charm of a Powers model and the kitchen wisdom of a Fanny Farmer," as a female journalist marveled in 1943, early stewardesses pioneered an occupation so saturated with ideals of femininity that the distinct challenges of hostessing aloft would soon be thoroughly obscured.[47]

"GLAMOR GIRLS OF THE AIR"
The Postwar Stewardess Mystique

In August 1958, when American Airlines opened a new stewardess training facility, *Life* marked the occasion with a frothy tribute to air hostesses. Aptly entitled "Glamor Girls of the Air: For Lucky Ones Being Hostess Is the Mostest," the magazine enticed readers with a cover photo of two brightly smiling stewardesses. Inside it pictured stewardess trainees and proclaimed airline stewardessing "one of the most coveted careers open to young American women today": "The job they want does not pay extraordinarily well, only $255 to $355 a month. The life is irregular and the opportunities for promotion are small. But the chance to fly, to see the world and meet all sorts of interesting people—mostly the kind of men who can afford to travel by plane—gives the job real glamor."[1]

The cover feature in *Life* succinctly captured the intensifying glamorization of female flight attendants and their work in the postwar United States. Flying for a living no longer demanded as much courage and forbearance; postwar stewardesses enjoyed admiration instead for their cosmopolitan life of travel on increasingly luxurious aircraft. No less important, serving prosperous, white, and predominantly male travelers offered stewardesses abundant opportunities for upwardly mobile marriages. By the mid-twentieth century, journalists and airline publicists began to proclaim that the job itself was "bride school," exemplary training for already desirable young women to take on future roles as wives and mothers. Good marital prospects were an estimable advantage for young female wage-seekers in an era when the marriage rate boomed, the average age at marriage dropped, and few Americans thought that a single person could be happy. Postwar airlines had stopped requiring a nursing degree, so competition for stewardess positions broadened to other young, white, slender, single women with a few years of college or business experience. But only those within this already narrow group who impressed airlines as especially attractive and charming got to enjoy a few years of travel and flattery as glamour girls of the air.[2]

The mystique that enveloped airline stewardesses by the postwar years carried complicated and even contradictory implications for the women who predominated in the flight attendant occupation. On the one hand, glamour amounted to distinct rewards that stewardesses enjoyed simply because they embodied the airlines' ideal of femininity. Glamour represented in this sense nonmonetary wages, the status and material benefits —from the interest and admiration of the media, to travel opportunities, to reputed desirability as wives—that stewardesses reaped as members of an elite. The "wages of glamour" were a middle-class, feminine variant of the "wages of whiteness" that scholars like David Roediger have recently explored, taking up W. E. B. Du Bois's insights from decades earlier. In surveying the aftermath of Reconstruction, Du Bois argued that white workers enjoyed a "public and psychological wage" of racial superiority, which could compensate when real wages fell short. Stewardesses similarly, though more distinctly, enjoyed a wage of race, class, and gender supremacy for representing idealized allure and domesticity.[3]

Yet the wages of glamour did not accrue automatically to stewardesses —they worked hard to earn them. On the plane and off, stewardesses labored to craft bodies and personalities that met their employers and customers' expectations of respectable and alluring femininity to the last detail, from the neatness of their hair, to the width of their hips, to the lilt of their voice, to the grace with which they handled difficult passengers. For all these achievements to convey the desired image of femininity, however, they had to appear effortless. Glamour, on the other hand, was an ongoing performance that demanded a lot of work to produce, but succeeded ultimately only when the labor was unrecognizable as such to the audience.

Stewardesses' mystique of glamorous femininity had crystallized into an implicit contract that defined female flight attendants' labor and compensation. Stewardesses earned unique benefits and plaudits for flawlessly enacting feminine nurturing and attractiveness in the cosmopolitan context of postwar aviation. But glamour, as both the goal of and

"A Pair of Smiling Stewardesses" appeared on the cover of
Life, 25 August 1958. Courtesy of Peter Stackpole/Time & Life
Pictures/Getty Images.

compensation for the performance, obscured the reality that airline passenger service was definable work, with distinguishable skills, other than expertise in femininity. The wages of glamour thus came to stewardesses at a cost in the respect and rewards that they could claim as workers. Understanding the historic activism of flight attendants requires first understanding how glamorization shaped flight attendants' work and collective identity by the postwar era.

MARKETING LUXURY IN A NEW ERA OF REGULATION

In the 1930s nurse-stewardesses were a popular frill that not all young airlines could afford. By the late 1940s carefully chosen hostesses became more central to the maturing airline industry's marketing and service objectives because other avenues of competition had narrowed. After the federal government undertook economic regulation of the industry in 1938, airlines staked their reputations more closely on the quality of in-flight services and the charms of the stewardesses who delivered them. The regulated airlines scrambled to win travelers' business with luxurious innovations in air transport and even more emphasis on fulfilling the promise of an attractive, attentive hostess.

Economic regulation was a development that the airline industry encouraged and from which it richly benefited. A national scandal over corruption in the awarding of airmail contracts and several well-publicized crashes in the 1930s prompted leaders of the young industry to lobby for more rationalized federal oversight and support. In 1938 Congress obliged by passing the Civil Aeronautics Act to promote "the development of a commercial air transportation system to meet the needs of the foreign and domestic commerce of the United States, of the postal service and of national defense." The act centralized aviation policy making in the Civil Aeronautics Authority (CAA). The new agency was charged with regulating safety as well as business practices, including routes, fares, loans, and mergers. The act also attempted to reconcile private airlines' need to turn a profit with the national interest in an extensive air transport network. It included a crucial provision to supplement the indirect, haphazard subsidies of mail contracts with direct federal subsidies to underwrite airline operations on unprofitable routes.[4]

The new regulatory structure would serve the airline industry well for many decades. The Civil Aeronautics Board (CAB), the policy-making and rate-setting successor of the CAA as of 1940, pursued its mandate of providing the nation with a stable, efficient system of air transport by fostering "managed competition" in the airline industry. In practice the CAB's managed competition policy nurtured extant airlines with federal money and permanent route awards. The CAB allowed larger, established airlines ("trunk" carriers in industry parlance) to maintain their overlapping but distinct national route maps and steadily grow them over time. After the Second World War the board also allowed several leading domestic carriers to enter international travel markets, which had previously been the exclusive province of Pan American. The CAB helped smaller regional ("feeder") lines as well by allowing them to compete on lucrative routes and generously subsidizing them to provide air transportation to underserved areas. Because the CAB parceled out new routes only to established carriers as a rule, upstarts were exceedingly rare. CAB fare mandates, moreover, eliminated cutthroat price competition. Airline executives were often not pleased with the CAB's specific rulings or its power over their corporate affairs. But the new system of permanent route certificates, pricing constraints, and direct subsidies offered airlines a much more predictable, stable context in which to battle for market share than the previous system of unbridled competition and contingent awards of airmail contracts. With the government overseeing where they provided service and at what price, airlines would focus their competitive energies on how they served passengers—and who did the serving.[5]

The outbreak of war temporarily sidetracked the airlines from their focus on upgrading passenger service, but wartime profits helped to underwrite their postwar emphasis on luxury and with it, the stewardess mystique. Like other industries that the U.S. government deemed vital to national defense, the airlines abandoned business as usual to assist the nation's military and industrial mobilization. Throughout the early 1940s, the government depended on commercial airlines to help move men and matériel around the country and overseas. The industry maintained scheduled passenger service, but with many seats and entire planes requisitioned for military purposes, airline managers had no need to worry about attracting customers. Because aircraft manufacturers were deluged with military orders and half their equipment was taken over by the government, airlines had to make do with reduced, outdated fleets and ask their regular clientele to suffer more spartan treatment. But for doing their part for national defense, many carriers enjoyed lucrative government contracts. All wartime airlines profited from predictably fuller planeloads, a considerable boon for an industry in which every seat unsold is revenue irrevocably lost. Leaps in engine and aircraft design and navigation equipment, funded by the military, benefited commercial carriers for decades to come. The exigencies of war also showed the benefits of commercial air travel to many military personnel and civilians who otherwise could not, or would not, have patronized the airlines. Though many carriers struggled in the immediate postwar years to reconvert to peacetime operations, airlines emerged from the profitable war years poised for a new era of explosive growth in domestic and, increasingly, international operations.[6]

The regulated postwar airlines competed for a growing population of air travelers with promises of convenience, comfort, affordability, and lavish service. Many Americans still found air travel prohibitively expensive, and fear of flying still kept the wary to the ground, traveling by railroads, buses, ships, and private automobiles. By 1962 fewer than a quarter of Americans had been on a commercial airliner; and of those who had, a mere 15 percent of repeat flyers accounted for 64 percent of the trips. Still, the decreasing relative cost of air travel went a long way to building airlines' business. As early as September 1945 airfares were cheaper than the most expensive first-class rail tickets on several heavily traveled routes. Postwar airline credit plans ("Fly Now, Pay Later") and lower-cost "coach" fares on domestic routes and "tourist" fares overseas made air travel even more comparatively affordable. Annual passenger totals on airlines based in the United States increased from 1.4 million in 1938 to 25 million in 1952 and 38 million in 1955. International passenger traffic, while a small percentage of total business, mushroomed from nearly 110,000 in 1938 to more than 3.4 million in 1955. By the end of 1953 airlines had decisively topped railroads in carrying Americans distances of two hundred miles or more, and in 1958 airlines surpassed ocean liners for the first time in overseas travel.[7]

As the relative cost of flying came down, comfort and convenience increased. The long haul, four-engine propeller aircraft introduced in the late 1940s could fly fifty to sixty passengers at around three hundred miles an hour cross-country, with few scheduled stops. The new planes boasted pressurized cabins that enabled them to soar comfortably above the weather. They also featured posh interiors, including "conversation" lounges, "Honeymoon" suites, and dressing rooms. With the introduction of even more powerful craft in the early 1950s, airlines offered non-stop flights across the country and over the Atlantic.[8]

The capstone of airline efforts to win over postwar travelers was the promise of stellar service. Airlines sought to make air travel a norm rather than a luxury, but at the same time make the experience of flying itself as luxurious as possible, particularly for "first-class" travelers. Pan Am's "President's Special" to London and Paris offered seven-course meals and gifts of orchids and perfume for female passengers and cigars for men, while TWA's "Sky Chief" provided overnight sleeper accommodations with breakfast served in bed. With its cross-country "Mercury" service, American promised "door-to-door" baggage pickup and delivery. In 1957 Continental Airlines extended royal treatment to coach class with its "Gold Carpet Service," which literally included a rolling out of a gold carpet for boarding passengers (and a parade and salute from gold-clad maintenance workers as the plane departed!). But whether postwar air travelers paid full fare or saved with a coach ticket, all could expect an "ever-attentive" hostess or host—the embodiment of the regulated airlines' promises of the utmost in passenger service.[9]

THE LABOR OF LUXURY AND OF GLAMOUR

The unparalleled luxury of postwar flying lent an increasingly cosmopolitan air to playing hostess aloft. It also demanded even more work on stewardesses' part, not only to provide the extensive labor required for lavish service but to exude glamorous femininity at the same time. Luxury service included the flattery of being served by a glamorous hostess, and glamour demanded a front of flawless femininity. Stewardesses were expected to work hard serving passengers, yet do it so charmingly that it seemed as if they were not really working at all.

Postwar stewardesses and their less numerous male co-workers devoted an increasing amount of effort to plying passengers with food and drink, a prime symbol of luxury in both coach and first class. By 1941 every domestic carrier boasted some form of food service, most including hot meals; by 1947 the CAB estimated that domestic carriers spent $11 million on catering alone. Despite the high costs and practical challenges of serving gourmet fare aloft, postwar airlines worked mightily to lure passengers with diverse, appetizing, and attractively presented snacks and multi-course gourmet meals. While it may be hard for twenty-first-

Stewardess serving food on a flight from Washington to
Los Angeles, December 1941. Library of Congress, Prints &
Photographs Division, FSA-OWI Collection,
LC-USF34-081914-EE.

century air travelers to believe, airline food in the postwar years was
reportedly quite good.[10]

In the later 1950s airlines added liquor to the gourmet experience aloft.
Prohibition ended in 1932, but airlines were reluctant for many years after
to invite public opprobrium by serving alcohol, though they repeatedly
considered the possibility. Since the birth of scheduled passenger service
in the late 1920s, airlines did not allow travelers to bring their own tipple
along for the ride. One of the flight attendants' responsibilities was to
confiscate as tactfully as possible any flasks or bottles that passengers
secreted aboard. By the 1950s mainstream cultural attitudes toward drinking had liberalized considerably, and cocktails had become an integral part
of leisure. For postwar "organization men" and VIPs, airlines' primary
customer base, drinking carried little of its previous social stigma. During

Stewardess for American Airlines making up bunk on an overnight flight in view of male passenger, December 1941. Library of Congress, Prints & Photographs Division, FSA-OWI Collection, LC-USF34-081807-E DLC.

Stewardess at work on a flight from Los Angeles to San Francisco, December 1941. Library of Congress, Prints & Photographs Division, FSA-OWI Collection, LC-USF34-081895-E DLC.

the 1950s domestic carriers abandoned dry tradition and, following inter-national carriers' lead, added wine and cocktails to their menus.[11]

Airlines' ever-loftier strides toward luxury made for a more physically arduous and contradictory work experience for flight attendants. Before the advent of service carts in the late 1950s, one to three flight attendants had only a cramped galley as a base for preparing, serving, and clearing multi-course meals and drinks for planeloads approaching one hundred passengers. A pedometer worn by one stewardess on a routine flight from Chicago to Miami in 1948 registered an exhausting eight miles. And then there were the distinct challenges of serving alcohol. Drinks not only added another item to service routines but invited unruly behavior by passengers, an annoyance and possible danger to crew and other pas-sengers alike. For stewardesses in particular, cocktails and wine also pro-vided amorous passengers with liquid courage, worsening the burdens of sexual harassment in an industry quite serious about the dictate that the customer is always right.[12]

We may well wonder how a stewardess was supposed to lift, bend, and fetch repeatedly and spend hours on her feet, yet never let a hint of sweat soil her uniform, allow her make-up to smudge or her hair to muss. We may also wonder how challenging it was to fulfill countless requests for help and attention without ever snapping back at drunk or excessively demanding passengers. But that is precisely what a stewardess was sup-posed to do throughout her career with the airlines. A career guide from 1951 highlighted this central contradiction: stewardesses worked too hard to "feel" glamorous, but they had to look and act the part anyway. The author, Mary Murray, told the prospective "sky girl," "You may think you want to be a stewardess just to wear a smart uniform, fly off to wondrous places, and meet the famous people who travel via the airlines. The career is glamorous, exciting, and adventurous—*to the spectator*. The stewardess is likely to be working so hard, however, worrying about her passengers, bad weather, delayed flights, problem children, ticket reports, and food service that she is far too busy to feel very glamorous." "But," crucially, "she is smiling anyway, with a poise that is stressed during her training as a most valuable asset." Airlines carefully trained and expected steward-esses to keep up the appearance of glamour with a "smile" and "poise"—work unto itself, but work that made all of their labor seem effortless.[13]

To be as attractive and gracious as airlines demanded required both considerable self-discipline and submission to further management by airline trainers and supervisors. Ironically, while airlines portrayed stewardesses as "naturally" talented at caring for others and looking lovely, elaborate training, not to mention hefty employee manuals, betrayed in painstaking detail the effort and discipline demanded of the airlines' glamour girls. To win the job in the first place, women had to prepare themselves to meet recruiters' high standards. Career guides like Murray's offered prospective applicants tips on how to dress, walk, and speak to impress. However poised and well-groomed new hires already were, postwar airlines demanded increasingly elaborate schooling for stewardesses in becoming more attractive and charming in a more standardized way. Large carriers like United and American built lavish training facilities ("charm farms" in flight attendant argot), where candidates spent up to six weeks earning their wings. The training included technical schooling in airline operations, safety procedures, and service routines, but it devoted more time to socializing stewardesses in the airlines' strict standards of behavior and appearance. As American promised prospective recruits in 1961, "At the Stewardess College, a staff of professionals is on hand to help you learn proper hair-styling, tricks of good grooming, make-up and figure improvement. You'll learn to walk, talk, and think with new poise." Training at airline facilities also reinforced the importance of respectability. Candidates were housed in dormitories under the watchful eye of a "matron" and subject to rigid curfews and restrictions on male visitors.[14]

Many carriers let enterprising "experts" at commercial stewardess schools prepare young women for the occupation. Airlines saved themselves considerable expense by farming out training, because the prospective stewardesses paid for it themselves with tuition. Candidates in the airlines' own training programs at least received free room and board and perhaps a partial salary or expense allowance. Delta, for one, explained in its recruiting literature, "As in other recognized professions, the cost of training must be borne by the individual." Few other recognized professions, however, demanded expensive formal training in what the carrier considered the vital areas of posture correction and figure control. One former flight attendant recalled paying $325 for an eight-week training course at the McConnell School for stewardesses in Kansas City in 1948; another juggled three jobs in New York City at the age of nineteen to pay for training by Grace Downs, who broke into the stewardess schooling business after establishing a famous chain of modeling schools. Steward-

ess jobs were not necessarily guaranteed upon graduation, despite un-
scrupulous recruiters' promises. The emphasis in commercial courses was
even more squarely on charm and beauty and general ideals of gracious
service than at the airlines' own facilities, since the commercial schools
were preparing women for work on any carrier. At Grace Downs's school,
for example, as *Life* proclaimed in 1947, "girls learn how to take care of
drunks, diapers, and double chins," while at McConnell's, a graduate
recalled that the program included "daily exercise classes, grooming, and
practicing walking up and down stairs in high heels." A few accredited
universities also offered stewardesses training programs developed in
cooperation with airlines, starting with De Paul University in 1942. In the
early 1960s Continental bypassed specialized training altogether and sent
its hostesses to the Powers Modeling School (supplemented with a mere
half-day of specific guidance on emergency procedures).[15]

Whether trained by an airline, commercial school, or university, all
stewardesses-in-the-making could expect the "beauty makeover," the
key visual component of the standardization process that airlines used
to produce perfect hostesses. The makeover typically meant a haircut—
airlines required "neat," collar-length hairstyles—and application of
makeup, followed up by tutoring in how to reproduce the same effects
with approved products and techniques. By many stewardesses' accounts,
it was a traumatic experience. Betty Turner Hines, a former flight attendant for Pennsylvania Central, recalled the shock during their training in
1943: "When we got back from our all-day beauty overhaul, we all burst
into tears. We couldn't believe our eyes: we all looked alike—we were
clones of each other!" The desired look may have changed over the years,
but the process was the same two decades later, when the flight attendant
and writer Liz Rich found herself in a newly minted "regiment of Barbie
dolls." In some cases, airline stylists required physical alteration well
beyond hair and makeup, such as having teeth ground to achieve a "perfectly even" smile.[16]

Being wedged, sometimes painfully, into a feminine mold by training
prepared stewardesses to represent airline-defined charm. Upon graduat-
ing, stewardesses continued to labor on the job and on their own time to
remain flawlessly attractive. Stewardesses had little choice but to do so,
for supervisors routinely checked their weight, uniforms, and grooming.
As a former hostess for Continental Airlines explained, "While on duty,
we were required to wear a girdle, carry extra nylons (pre-panty hose!)

"How Is Your Appearance Today?" Delta stewardesses
preparing for a flight, 1956. © Bettmann/CORBIS.

and carry an extra pair of white gloves . . . Our total appearance was
observed at all times by our supervisors. Any hostess who did not meet
standards could be sent home without pay." A former attendant for
Eastern recalled being "written up" for a tear in her uniform that occurred as she reached up to stow pillows and blankets *after* the passengers
had disembarked. As for weight rules, supervisors suspecting that a stewardess had put on extra pounds could ask her to jump on the scale at any
time and ground her immediately if she weighed in over her maximum.
Even stewardesses who appeared slender enough were subject to regular
weigh-ins on most carriers. Officially "overweight" stewardesses were
expected to shed pounds steadily (two a week, usually) or face termination. Many airlines also imposed weight minimums; though far fewer
flight attendants encountered difficulties at the lower end of the ranges,
airlines did on rare occasions require that stewardesses gain weight.[17]

Meeting the airlines' demands for unstinting charm and attractiveness
was its own reward, or so stewardesses were told. As Murray explained, if
a stewardess had trouble "with the overfriendly fellow, or the blustering

executive" and handled him with sufficient discretion and tact, or managed to transform unhappy or timid passengers into "pleasant, assured travelers," then "there is no reward which can equal the inner feeling of satisfaction that goes with a job well done." But a stewardess's job well done was meant to go unnoticed. The service of the ideal hostess, she explained, "is so complete and so unassuming that the passenger seldom realizes just *what* it was that made him enjoy Flight #3 more than any trip he has ever taken." It was a complicated performance, invoking the traditional ideals of the servant toiling unobtrusively behind the scenes and of a woman's selfless care-giving in the home. But it also carried a more modern commercial flourish of treating customers to a well-crafted display of attractiveness. Tellingly, a supervisor applauded the work of the American stewardess Barbara O'Brien in 1957 by noting that she fulfilled her duties "with such ease and efficiency one is scarcely aware that you are carrying out a procedure." But while the supervisor considered O'Brien's appearance in uniform "neat and regulation," the manager warned her to check her makeup more often during flights "to maintain a well-groomed look."[18]

Fortunately for postwar stewardesses, taking on the airlines' complex service demands brought them more than the "inner feeling of satisfaction" of womanhood well done. While the work of glamour was burdensome, the cachet that stewardesses enjoyed could also be immensely gratifying. At no time were the wages of glamour as palpable and uniquely rewarding for stewardesses as in the postwar years.

THE WAGES OF GLAMOUR

The mid-twentieth century was a good time to be a glamour girl, especially if your mystique was grounded in girl-next-door wholesomeness, as stewardesses' was. During the national crisis of the Second World War, "glamour" was associated with dangerous frivolity, even while it endured as an ideal of allure. Rosie the Riveter was congratulated for bringing femininity to the factory floor, but was warned against taking glamour too far with flowing hair that might get caught in machinery. After war's end, love of glamour fit better with the national pastime of rampant consumption. Wartime ambivalence gave way to widespread "glamorizing," not only by style-conscious teenagers and adults but also by manufacturers hoping to lend eye-catching flare to such sturdy consumer items as refrigerators and pickup trucks. *New York Times* headlines even referred to a railroad barge and a chimpanzee as "glamour girls."[19]

But it was not to chimps or durable goods that the media and public looked to glimpse fashion, beauty, and cosmopolitan lifestyles. Hollywood continued to be a main source of female glamour icons. Films and celebrity culture served up distilled sexual allure in the curvy forms of the blonde "bombshell" Marilyn Monroe, the tempestuous screen siren Ava Gardner, and the serial bride Elizabeth Taylor, but also celebrated more fresh-faced icons of femininity like Doris Day and Debbie Reynolds. On the smaller screen, the "Miss America" pageant blossomed into an annual celebration of girlish glamour. The pageant began in 1921, but it was not until the director Lenora Slaughter transformed it into a contest for scholarships, with ironclad rules assuring the crown-seekers' chastity, that it assumed unqualified respectability during the late 1930s and 1940s. When a Miss America first received her crown on television in 1954, capturing half the viewing audience, the event became an all-in-one lesson for girls in the requirements of femininity. It was also an occasion for adults to take pride in the best of American womanhood in the making. Although less popular than Miss America, Katy Keene, a comic book heroine who worked as a model and actress, was perhaps just as telling of the postwar fascination with girl-next-door glamour. Beginning in 1945, she proved a hit with young, female consumers of comics, especially because of her wide-ranging and stylish wardrobe, which featured designs submitted by readers. Unlike Hollywood's often troubled and divorce-prone stars or wealthy débutantes and their society elders, Miss America, Katy Keene, and Debbie Reynolds all presented a vision of glamour that was seemingly achievable by the lucky and industrious, and could offend no one.[20]

At any given moment in the 1950s there was only one Miss America and several thousand stewardesses, yet they had much in common. They were attractive, poised young women who enjoyed a cosmopolitan life of travel and public exposure, but no one doubted that their future lay in domesticity. Though stewardesses had been glamorized from virtually the first moment they graced a commercial airliner, their image had evolved in subtle but important ways by the postwar years. The skies seemed less otherworldly by then, and commercial air travel had become more accessible and luxurious. The airlines had claimed since the 1930s that stewardesses were merely doing what women did in their own homes, but by mid-century the comparison seemed less of a stretch to journalists, novelists, and filmmakers. The archetypal stewardess found in popular culture shed her original identity as a curiosity who tackled a strange and difficult job with a professional background in nursing, not to mention plenty of courage. In her postwar guise she had become a young woman enjoying the chance to travel briefly while training *for* the ultimate female "profession" of homemaking. What once fascinated because it was so alien and daring had become "bride school." Siginificantly, postwar airlines dropped any remaining pretenses to quasi-military garb for stewardesses. While the shrinking number of male stewards and pursers continued to don what looked like naval uniforms, female flight attendants began after the Second World War to wear stylish designer suits, genteelly accessorized with hats and white gloves.[21]

Perhaps no popular culture product better captured stewardesses' idealization as cosmopolitan brides-to-be than *Three Guys Named Mike*. A feature film released in 1951 by Metro-Goldwyn-Mayer and produced in cooperation with American Airlines, *Three Guys Named Mike* traces the career and romantic adventures of a stewardess, Marcy Lewis, until she decides to trade her beloved job for even greater fulfillment in marriage. Slightly quirky but supremely charming, Marcy, played by Jane Wyman, breezes happily through the ups and downs of passenger service, while easily winning the affections of the three competing suitors of the title. As much as Marcy relishes life as a stewardess, she opts eagerly in the end for settled domesticity. She chooses the "Mike" who is a small-town science professor over the pilot and the advertising executive. Who better to represent a postwar fantasy of femininity than a spunky, beautiful young woman who has ventured far beyond the limits of domesticity, only to cherish the prospect of quiet homemaking above all else?

Sundry other popular cultural products offered the same basic message: that stewardesses were glamorous but reassuringly domesticated young ladies. In the "Vicki Barr Flight Stewardess" series of mystery novels for girls published in the late 1940s and 1950s, Vicki competed with the popular Nancy Drew for young, female readers' admiration. Dust jackets from the series opined of Vicki, "Charming, bright and hard working, her career as an air stewardess brings her glamorous friends, exciting adventures, loyal roommates and dates with a handsome young pilot and an up-and-coming reporter." The stewardess mystique also lent commercial appeal to many print and television advertisements. Stewardesses hawked not only their employers' and other travel products but also unrelated goods such as cigarettes, soft drinks, hair preparations, and nonfat milk. Playtex strove to glamorize girdles with the help of a stewardess, who in a televised advertisement showed her undergarment to be comfortable enough for passenger care, leisure, and romance on two continents.[22]

Not all visions of stewardesses that postwar American consumers encountered in fiction, nonfiction, and advertisements were the same. There was an undercurrent of more explicitly sexualized images as well, foreshadowing the reputation for promiscuity that flight attendants would acquire, through little effort of their own, by the 1970s. A United stewardess, Barbara Cameron, posed for *Playboy* as "Miss December" in 1955. She appeared again exactly three years later as "The Girl Next Door" in the lineup of "most popular playmates" marking the magazine's fifth anniversary. Flight attendants also appeared in the era's lesbian pulp fiction. Paula Christian based two of her novels on the character of the stewardess Val MacGregor and her awakening to same-sex desire. A feature film thriller from 1956, *Julie*, smashed the mold of *Three Guys Named Mike* with a horrific view of marriage gone wrong: the stewardess heroine, Julie Benton, survives the murderous wrath of her psychotically possessive husband (this fictional airline apparently had no rule against married stewardesses, as almost every real airline did at the time). But while Benton suffered a nightmare of aberrant domesticity on screen, it was nonetheless the beloved leading lady Doris Day who played her. Day's own wholesome glamour-girl image fit well with the usually quite respectable stewardess mystique.[23]

It was an enviable mystique indeed, and one that could bring a variety of additional rewards to the women who claimed membership in stewardesses' illustrious ranks. The making of *Three Guys Named Mike* in 1950 brought Hollywood experiences to two real-life stewardesses. In preparing for the film's production, MGM executives invited American Airlines stewardesses to submit accounts of their work experiences. Dona Lee, whose letter was selected for use, won $100 and a daylong tour and tribute at MGM studios, where Spencer Tracy and Cary Grant, among others, toasted her. Even luckier was Lee's colleague Pug Wells, whose idea the film initially was. Wells was a technical advisor to the production, which won her a spot on the set and a bit part in the film, which she later promoted on a tour of twenty cities. Extended stays in Hollywood were by no means typical, but encountering traveling celebrities was quite common for cabin crew. Many occupied the limelight regularly themselves, moreover, in public relations roles. In addition to appearing in national advertisements for air travel, toothpaste, and automobiles, stewardesses were contestants and judges in beauty pageants and gave radio and television interviews. Simply winning a job as a stewardess often brought the notice of hometown newspapers—and not just in Podunk.[24]

The celebrated sky girls of the United States grew in international prestige, representing American womanhood abroad and setting the benchmark for airline hostesses around the world. In 1949 the traffic manager of India's largest carrier, Air India International, told American reporters, "The stewardesses of this country set the standard for the stewardesses on airlines throughout the world. You can't beat the American woman for friendliness and making the passenger feel at home." National airlines in India and Canada, among other countries, hired stewardesses from the United States to train their attendants. Even Great Britain's state-owned airline, which had resisted feminization of cabin crew along American lines, relented. When transatlantic competition after the Second World War from carriers based in the United States and Canada pushed British executives to begin adding women to their celebrated steward corps, they sniffed that their new hires would be "female stewards" and not "glamour hostesses." Yet by the end of the 1950s British flight attendants looked and acted an awful lot like the glamorous stewardesses of American carriers.[25]

GLAMOUR GUYS OF THE AIR?

What popular culture did not register, and airlines did not advertise, in celebrating the "glamour girls of the air" was that there were male flight attendants too. They were few, except on overseas flights, but they were there nonetheless as seeming anomalies in a job that was feminized in every possible sense. After losing their original grip on cabin crew positions in the late 1920s, white men maintained a perpetual foothold in the occupation, accounting for a shifting minority of 5 to 15 percent of flight attendants over the course of the mid-twentieth century. Men remained in part because airlines early on created an elite niche for them in international flying. Managers believed that the uniquely complex record-keeping and informal diplomacy, as well as grueling travel schedules,

This photo of fifty-three global flight attendants appeared as a two-page color insert in *Life*, 25 August 1958. While intended to show the variety of uniforms, it suggested how homogeneous flight attendants were worldwide: all were slender, light-complexioned women whose uniforms, other than the obvious exceptions, were tailored skirt-suits with demure hats. Courtesy of Peter Stackpole/Time & Life Pictures/Getty Images.

made male attendants better suited to international cabin service. The job category of "purser," the lead flight attendant on overseas routes, remained male-only as a rule until anti-discrimination legislation in the mid-1960s allowed women to enter these better-paid, quasi-supervisory positions. Men also stayed in cabin service as stewards, even into the 1960s when almost no airline still hired male flight attendants for domestic routes, because they were exempt from the age ceilings and no-marriage rules. Unlike stewardesses, they could choose to make a long-term career of flying, and some did stay for several decades.[26]

While male flight attendants did not bask in the flattering glow of the public spotlight as their female colleagues did, they could enjoy the cosmopolitan mystique of flying for living too, as well as masculine privilege in some distinct forms. Pursers or stewards may have received the same basic wage as female colleagues, but male flight attendants generally enjoyed better accommodations on layovers and better benefits. The male minority was also spared the beauty makeovers, weight monitoring, and elaborate grooming codes that governed stewardesses' appearance from head to toe. Many male flight attendants also managed more traditionally male jobs or commercial ventures along with cabin service, nurturing second or subsequent careers on the side. One former steward for Eastern explained that sixteen years of flying to San Juan, Puerto Rico, which required only ten days' duty a month, gave him time to run other businesses. As a female colleague explained, entrepreneurial male flight attendants used their job to meet suppliers and customers, attend trade shows, and otherwise promote side businesses at no cost, while drawing their airline salary. "Others were using it as a step to positions in the cockpit crew," though some "just loved to fly and travel." Maleness carried possible benefits as well in daily work experiences. "Most passengers assumed the male [flight attendants] were management of some type," a former stewardess explained, "and preferred to accept service from 'one of the girls.' They didn't want to bother the guys." She remembered that pilots also preferred to be served by female cabin crew.[27]

Working in what was widely perceived as a woman's job posed challenges nonetheless. As men in other feminized fields like nursing have also experienced, a male minority may carve out privileged niches, but their occupational choice can still lead to their being stereotyped as effeminate and homosexual. A former female flight attendant who flew in the late 1950s explained, "The attitude of much of the public" toward pursers and stewards "was that all were 'Gay,' which, as usual, was very far

Three stewards (airline unidentified), 1941. Library of Congress, Prints & Photographs Division, FSA-OWI Collection, LC-USF34-044973-D.

from factual." By male and female flight attendants' account, the majority of men in the job at the time were in fact heterosexual and married. Many pilots, steeped in the aggressively masculine culture of the military, were just as given to stereotyping as the public. Some cockpit crewmembers remained aloof from male flight attendants; others were outwardly hostile. While one former stewardess claimed that she "never saw [male flight attendants] treated with anything but respect by management, flight crews, and passengers," a male veteran of cabin service remembered that pilots, for their part, "hated" male flight attendants, especially in the 1950s. He recalled too that the men were more likely to receive complaint letters from passengers than the women.[28]

But while some passengers and pilots were prejudiced against male cabin crew, working with a preponderance of gregarious, attractive women was no hardship for "straight" stewards and pursers. As for male flight attendants who were gay, "They held their own on the job, and were a pleasure to work with," one former stewardess later recalled. Perhaps most important, the working relationship between male and female flight attendants was generally pleasant and mutually rewarding by most accounts. One of the very rare male cabin crewmembers in mid-century popular culture was perhaps not far from the "typical" male flight attendant in reality: in the mass-market paperback novel *Carol Trent, Air Stewardess*, the veteran steward Ted Barlow grumbles about overdemanding passengers, speaks often of his beloved wife, and dispenses "fatherly" advice to his novice flying partner, Carol. Yet Ted makes only fleeting appearances in the novel, much as male stewards did in real life. The young, single stewardess Carol was presumed to be the real draw for readers in 1956.[29]

Pride in being an airline "glamour girl" was widely shared among stewardesses of the postwar era. Women who otherwise faced limited and generally low-paid occupational choices had good reason to cherish the status rewards of meeting the airlines' exceedingly high standards of femininity. As Suzanne Lee Kolm has emphasized, that stewardesses could expect to marry easily and well if they chose to do so can hardly be overstated as a distinct benefit of the job in years when most women had little reason to expect economic security and societal approval other than through marriage. Indeed, postwar women's work cultures were "steeped in the cult of marriage," as one scholar has noted, as was popular culture more broadly.[30]

These perquisites were not without costs. If becoming a stewardess improved a woman's prospects in heterosexual competition, success also meant that she would have to forfeit her job because of airlines' single-women-only policy. The glamour of being a stewardess was a double-edged sword in many ways, an exaggeration of the constraints and benefits more generally of endeavoring to meet white, middle-class standards of feminine respectability and allure. Even as stewardesses enjoyed the wages of glamour, they were quite well aware of what that glamour cost them in conformity to stringent airline rules, in meager real wages and no job security, and in working hard at appearing not to be working at all. Given the aura of glamour surrounding postwar stewardesses and all the cultural adulation they received, it may seem surprising that they should also have distinguished themselves by joining the heavily male and blue-collar labor movement. But stewardesses' willingness to work hard extended not only to embodying airline-defined femininity: it extended to having their efforts taken seriously as *real* work too.

3

"LABOR'S LOVELIEST"
Postwar Union Struggles

In November 1958 thirty-two stewardesses on Lake Central Airlines, a small Midwestern carrier, walked off the job for eleven days, demanding better wages and work rules. The small group belonged to the Air Line Stewards and Stewardesses Association (ALSSA), a national union organized in 1946 that by 1958 represented more than three-quarters of the nation's airline flight attendants. The Lake Central strikers played up their glamorous image. They donned sashes like those worn in beauty pageants to proclaim their strike, and smiled for the camera in their stylish uniforms. Yet these charming young ladies were willing to maintain picket lines in four inches of snow and risk their celebrated jobs to win better treatment as workers. While flight attendants in ALSSA had threatened walkouts before, and Pan Am's mostly male cabin crew in another union had struck twice, ALSSA's ability to maintain a successful strike—even by just thirty-two workers—dramatically confirmed the labor militancy of the airline's celebrated hostesses.[1]

The same postwar stewardesses who enjoyed iconic status as glamorous brides-in-training also collectively insisted on being respected as workers by their employers and the labor movement. At the same time, flight attendants made clear that they were not just any workers—they sought recognition as "professionals," for their technical skills in ensuring passengers' safety. An independent, powerful union and professionalization through government safety licensing were inseparable goals, as well as the means through which postwar flight attendants hoped to supplement the wages of glamour with recognition and better compensation for their skilled labor. In struggling to advance their interests through glamour, trade unionism, and professionalism, flight attendants made a distinct contribution to the history of pink-collar labor organizing, and to the broader currents of women's activism that feminist historians have highlighted amid the prescriptive domesticity of the postwar era.

As revisionist scholars contend, the years between the Second World War and the dramatic social upheavals of the 1960s were not monolithically an era of suburban- and family-oriented consumerist bliss, and pressures for women to embrace hearth and home were not all-encompassing. Female union activists, civil rights protesters, leftist political organizers, and members of sexual minorities, among others, promoted their own visions of women's worth and rights—apart from and in opposition to the dominant white, middle-class, heterosexual ideal of domesticity. Scholars have also emphasized that although postwar ideals of womanhood venerated homemaking, they were complex and encouraged achievement in other arenas as well.[2]

However fervently postwar white women embraced domesticity, they were as a group spending more time outside their homes at part-time or full-time jobs. After the temporary spike in female employment and occupational breakthroughs of the Second World War, white American women resumed their steady march out to work and into "women's jobs" over the twentieth century. Women grew from 29 percent of the American workforce in 1950 to 35 percent in 1965. Already in 1950, a third of all women earned a paycheck, half of them for full-time work. In the family-oriented 1950s, the growth in the employment rate for married white women was particularly notable, from 21.6 percent in 1950 to 30.5 percent in 1960. Despite wartime gains, postwar women confronted persistent, if evolving, patterns of discrimination that channeled them into low-paying service and clerical fields. Women nevertheless took advantage of and spurred the nation's postwar economic boom as wage-earning producers and consumers. Cold war anxieties, the Baby Boom, unprecedented affluence, and suburbanization, among other developments, certainly encouraged women to embrace domesticity. But as feminist historians have reminded us, postwar Americans felt obliged to reassure themselves of women's devotion to the family in part because of wives' and mothers' growing participation in the labor market.[3]

Stewardesses were especially apt icons of glamorous femininity for the postwar years as working women who dramatically transcended

Striking Lake Central stewardesses, November 1958.
Courtesy of Francis Miller/Time & Life
Pictures/Getty Images.

domesticity, yet reassuringly represented it. Few women journeyed as regularly or as far from home, or came into contact with the rich and famous as often, as a typical stewardess did. Stewardesses nonetheless embodied women's traditional caring roles in attending to the comfort and well-being of others. Because stewardesses were young and single as a rule, no one worried about whether wage-earning detracted from their homemaking, or vice versa. Better still, passenger service itself seemed to be a good rehearsal for the roles of wife and mother.

Postwar stewardesses demanded respect as skilled workers and trade unionists, however, in ways that defied normative ideals. In the late 1940s stewardesses organized for better wages and work rules in a highly coveted occupation and, in the 1950s and early 1960s, attempted to secure an autonomous place in the male-dominated labor movement. Flight attendants declared themselves professionals with expert knowledge of cabin safety too, and asked male employers, co-workers, and federal policymakers to acknowledge that their feminized service job involved more than good grooming and womanly concern for others. Postwar stewardesses relished being gracious hostesses and glamour icons, but they struggled to make these roles accommodate more progressive notions of women's labor and skills than popular ideals allowed.

THE GLAMOUR GIRLS ORGANIZE

The initial sparks for unionizing among flight attendants were complaints from United Airlines stewardesses about stagnant salaries, the lack of limits on duty hours, and the threat of summary dismissal. On United, the carrier that had first hired women for passenger service in 1930, a starting stewardess in 1945 earned the same $125 a month that the very first "sky girls" received. Worse, the monthly salary was premised on 100 hours of flying time when various duties on the ground and in flight could consume as many as 150 hours. Conditions on United were typical of the industry, and better than on some smaller carriers.[4]

In late 1944 United's chief stewardess Ada J. Brown, frustrated by the company's unwillingness to upgrade conditions, left her management position to return to the all-female rank and file and begin organizing a union. She recalled, "As chief stewardess I tried to get improvements for the girls with salary, flight regulations, and protection from unjust firing. We were always promised things, but nothing was ever done—except to throw parties for the stewardesses." Soon her fellow United stewardesses Sally Thometz, Frances Hall, Edith Lauterbach, and Sally Watt joined Brown. They were hardly experienced labor organizers or experts on the legal grounds for collective bargaining in the airline industry. Whereas many industries fell under the jurisdiction of the National Labor Relations Act of 1935 (or Wagner Act) and the National Labor Relations Board, Congress in 1936 placed airlines alongside the railroads under the Railway Labor Act of 1926, administered by the National Mediation Board (NMB). Along with elaborate mechanisms for mediation and government intervention to forestall interruptions in transport services, the Railway Labor Act also imposes distinct representation requirements. Moreover, there were no official precedents for collective bargaining by flight attendants—only intimidating stories of management's earlier opposition to talk of organizing among stewardesses. According to Brown, "Girls that tried to form an association were fired or threatened."[5]

Within a few months inexperienced but committed stewardess activists had established a viable union movement with three-quarters of United's three hundred stewardesses. By August 1945 the Air Line Stewardesses Association (ALSA) had established local councils in four cities, elected national officers, and drafted a constitution and bylaws. In protracted negotiations with United in the spring of 1946, ALSA leaders persevered on a shoestring budget in the face of the company's intransigence on such issues as hour limits and generally patronizing attitudes from male executives. In April 1946 ALSA signed the first collective bargaining agreement for flight attendants, winning voluntary recognition from the company. The contract provided a $30 raise in starting pay to $155, compensation for ground time, a limit of eighty-five hours of flying a month, and reimbursement for half the cost of stewardesses' first uniform. ALSA also won stewardesses the right to see their personnel files and established grievance machinery for them to challenge disciplinary actions and dismissals. The efforts of United stewardesses soon ignited similar movements on other carriers. Within half a decade 3,500 flight attendants on sixteen airlines unionized, more than two-thirds of the total workforce.[6]

In the mid-1940s millions of American workers engaged in labor protests and swelled the ranks of the labor movement. An unprecedented number of strikes in 1945 and 1946 stunned several industries and brought business as usual in several cities nearly to a halt. Workers throughout the nation who had sacrificed for the duration of the Second World War demanded higher pay and better treatment from employers, many of which, like airlines, had enjoyed large wartime profits and anticipated continued prosperity in the dawning postwar consumer boom. Because of the airlines' important contributions to military and industrial mobilization, flight attendants had good reason to believe their services had helped the nation's war effort and that their circa-1930 wage rates were particularly unfair. They were, as a union official later described, "ripe for organization."[7]

Yet flight attendants were in many ways unlike other workers protesting corporate power and greed in the wake of the Second World War. In building a national union, organizers overcame a distinct array of formidable obstacles. First, flight attendants were a geographically dispersed and highly mobile group. The Railway Labor Act required union representation by "craft or class" carrier-wide. A "local" on any but the smallest carriers had to include employees scattered among airline bases in several cities. Flight attendants typically worked alone in the cabin or in pairs, making the face-to-face work of organizing more difficult (though their habit of sharing apartments and congregating in the same buildings promoted social solidarity). They were also perpetual travelers, working on diverse flight schedules and often at odd hours, and subject to frequent relocation, whether at their own request or the airline's. Simply bringing together a substantial number to discuss union matters was a feat in itself. It was a struggle too to keep track of members and collect their dues. Dues income has always been particularly important to flight attendant unions, because a dispersed, mobile workforce is costlier to represent as a rule than groups centralized in factories, offices, or other earthbound workplaces.[8]

With flight attendants' modest paychecks, the dues were not large in any case. While flight attendants faired relatively well among their pink-collar sisters, they were at the bottom of the wage ladder in the generally well-paid airline industry. In 1955, for instance, the average salary for flight attendants in the United States was just under $3,300, while pilots and co-pilots claimed more than three times as much, and all other airline ground workers (maintenance, clerical, etc.) took home average yearly pay of between $4,300 and $5,300. That same year, the average paycheck across industries (for all production or nonsupervisory employees on private, nonagricultural payrolls) would have amounted to just over $3,500 for fifty-two weeks' work, and for manufacturing workers slightly more than $3,900. Flight attendants' high turnover rates hardly made them ideal union material either. In 1955 a union newsletter noted that the average length of service for stewardesses was twenty-seven months, and 99 percent of resignations were due to marriage. For the union, the no-marriage rule guaranteed frequent loss of members and officers alike.[9]

In addition to practical difficulties, organizers also needed to sell participation in a predominantly male and blue-collar labor movement to a predominantly female, white-collar elite. Trade unions invoked a history of working-class militancy and radicalism, with masculine overtones, that many flight attendants found alien if not also distasteful. Amid the Red Scare of the postwar years, the national labor movement's purge of its left wing for supposed communist domination offered a potent reminder of historic links between labor activism and radical politics. Stewardesses, after all, were typically fresh from college and a middle-class upbringing, neither of which encouraged pro-union sentiment. Some flight attendants did come from union households and needed no convincing to embrace labor organizing. Jeanne Notaro, the daughter of a union motion picture operator, became active in the stewardess association as soon as she could and remained a union leader for four decades. But as Edith Lauterbach, a union pioneer at United, later contended, stewardesses more often "came from families where Daddy just didn't want his daughter to belong to a union."[10]

When stewardesses began organizing, women and white-collar workers were distinct minorities within the labor movement. At the end of 1946 about one and a half million white-collar workers belonged to unions, less than 13 percent of their total number, and some 3.5 million women belonged to unions, 20 percent of the 16.7 million female wage-earners in the United States. At the same time, 34.5 percent of all non-agricultural workers belonged to unions. The one in five women workers who were union members were disproportionately concentrated in a handful of industries, namely garment, textiles, food processing and serving, retail, telephone and communications, and electrical manufacturing. Where women accounted for a large share of union membership, they were underrepresented in leadership positions.[11]

Nonetheless, a significant heritage of pink-collar activism did exist by the mid-twentieth century. Telephone operators, who like flight attendants were almost exclusively young, white, and female, stood for a time in the years surrounding the First World War at the leading edge of female worker militancy. Though their organizing efforts withered in the 1920s under an onslaught of company unionism, organizing among telephone operators revived in the late 1940s out of wartime shopfloor grievances. Waitresses too had begun organizing around the turn of the century, forming powerful locals of their own in the Hotel and Restaurant Employees Union. Waitress unionists transformed the male traditions of craft unionism into an effective tool for defending the collective interests of the primary wage-earners who predominated in the waitress workforce. The American Federation of Teachers and social worker unions, also products of Progressive era organizing, blended professional and collective bargaining goals in the postwar years in ways that paralleled flight attendants' ambitions. Unionizing efforts among clerical and retail workers found some success in the organizing heyday of the 1930s, though they faltered in the postwar decades even as employment in stores and offices swelled. In 1946, the same year in which United stewardesses organized, the American Nursing Association agreed to let its state units engage in collective bargaining, a nod to the growing appeal of trade unionism among nurses. But given flight attendants' backgrounds and occupational identity, it is doubtful that many knew much about the history of pink-collar unions.[12]

What mattered more in encouraging flight attendants to unionize was that organizers took great pains to distance their brand of trade unionism from the working classes and political subversion. Organizers made clear their patriotism and their wish to cooperate with management, but more important, they sought to erase the proletarian roots of labor organizing and cast it instead as respectable, even savvy. "A labor representing organization," a pamphlet in 1946 reassured stewardesses, "if correctly established, properly constituted and efficiently managed, is a business established for the purpose of representing working people. There is nothing mysterious or different about it." The pamphlet urged stewardesses "to build up" their "class or craft of employment into something to be proud of and *not submerged with the masses.*" By this logic, unionization was not a degrading admission of working-class status but precisely the opposite — the way for flight attendants to secure their status as distinct from and superior to "the masses." The same types of arguments would later be used in drives to organize office workers in the 1960s; as a union president observed, "there are lots of ways to give a union the sweet smell of status."[13]

Precisely because flight attendants were such an elite white-collar group, organizers contended, airline exploitation demanded their collective protest. An editorial in the first issue of the flight attendant union publication *Service Aloft* in October 1946 tellingly outlined what organizers considered flight attendants' chief grievances: "The airline industry seems to think they are doing a favor when they give a person a job as a steward or stewardess. They are prone to forget that these people have done more to sell airplane traveling to the American people than any other single factor." Flight attendants' "duties are many and exacting and should be compensated accordingly. A file clerk in any business organization today makes more money" than flight attendants, "and file clerks do not have to buy their uniforms and look like cover girls at all times." Labor organizing, according to this editorialist, was "proper" and indeed necessary for loyal, highly skilled workers who deserved more than other white-collar workers, with lower status, were already getting. The conspicuous reference to "cover girls" also spotlighted the particular burdens of glamour that fell on the occupation's vast majority of women. As the union protested, the image demands of the job were exploitive, and the only way for stewardesses to secure "reasonable" compensation in return, by organizers' account, was by unionizing.[14]

As flying "cover girls," stewardesses already had a strong sense of occupational identity, reinforced by their rather extreme demographic homogeneity. What organizers therefore needed to do was convince enough stewardesses that joining a union did not contradict or threaten their gender and class identity, but flowed naturally from their distinct experiences and grievances. The union founder Edith Lauterbach, who remembered her fellow stewardesses as mostly anti-union by upbringing, also believed that at least half "were willing to go along with organizing to help . . . with the working conditions of the whole group." In the end, organizers succeeded in mobilizing stewardesses' investment in their mystique, as well as their discontent with the low pay and working conditions that accompanied it.[15]

THE PILOTS' UNION TO THE RESCUE?

Union appeals to flight attendants' status consciousness benefited from an impressive example of white-collar organization on the airlines, the Air Line Pilots Association (ALPA). Boasting an exceedingly well-paid membership and considerable influence among federal policymakers, ALPA made craft unionism a bulwark for pilots' professional entitlements. Though ALPA was an affiliate of the American Federation of Labor (AFL) since its birth in 1931, its aloofness toward other unions and jealous defense of its power and independence demonstrated that elite workers could be in the labor movement but keep its working-class majority at arm's length. ALPA, as both a successful model of elite unionism and a domineering ally, cast a long shadow over flight attendants' attempts to find their own niche in the labor movement.

In the days of barnstormers and First World War flying "aces," pilots earned admiration as daredevil "supermen." But by the late 1920s the growing technical sophistication of aviation and the airlines' desire to project dependability led pilots to professionalize. Uniforms like those of naval officers, strict qualifications imposed by federal licensing, and monthly earnings of as much as $600 (flight attendants earned $125) were among the signs of their professional status. But as airlines struggled with the Depression, pilots found that they were not immune from pay cuts, longer hours, and the threat of unemployment—so they unionized to defend their elevated status. In July 1931 pilot representatives from all the major airlines formed the Air Line Pilots Association and elected the charismatic United pilot David Behncke as their leader. Behncke quickly began to lobby legislators and arranged an international charter for the fledgling union from the American Federation of Labor. Many pilots looked askance at including their professional group in the AFL, but Behncke persuaded his members of the need for formal ties to organized labor to strengthen ALPA's authority with airline management. Behncke's acumen paid off. During the 1930s and early 1940s ALPA ensured high salaries for its pilots and stamped their interests on aviation legislation. In the process, pilots paid little heed to other workers in and outside the airline industry, earning them an enduring reputation for haughty self-ishness within labor circles.[16]

By the later 1940s, however, ALPA had little choice but to respond to the aspirations of other workers if it wished to maintain pilots' pre-eminent place in airline labor relations. International unions with broad industrial bases among blue-collar workers, including the Transport Workers Union, the International Brotherhood of Teamsters, and the International Association of Machinists, were actively seeking new members on the airlines. AFL leadership had urged ALPA to assist other airline employees in organizing since the 1930s, but pilots ignored the matter until competition appeared. When ALPA did act, it was to ensure that fellow airline workers' unionization proceeded under the pilots' tutelage. In the late 1940s and early 1950s ALPA chartered several subordinate affiliates for other airline crafts. The first was not coincidentally the Air Line Stewards and Stewardesses Association (ALSSA), established in 1946 as a better-funded rival to the independent union at United, ALSA. The pilots' union generously subsidized the organization and administration of these separate and officially independent subsidiary unions. But the affiliation agreements gave pilot leaders unilateral power to intervene in the subordinate unions' affairs and even sever the alliances outright. ALPA had its own international charter from the AFL, the nation's most powerful labor organization, but ALPA's subsidiary unions were linked to the federation only through their affiliation with the pilots. ALPA thereby subsidized the unionization, while containing the competing ambitions, of other groups.[17]

ALPA's first experiment with subordinate affiliates targeted stewardesses because they were not only organizing themselves already but also
drawing the attention of "outsider" unions. In 1946 the Transport Workers Union (TWU), one of the more militant, left-leaning unions within
the Congress of Industrial Organizations, gained the bargaining rights
for Pan American flight attendants. TWU's entry into the Pan Am cabin
was atypical in many ways. Pan Am, as the only carrier in the United
States with exclusively international routes, was a unique entity, and its
largely male cabin staff was anomalous. Their representation through
TWU proved an exception as well. They joined TWU as the Flight Service
Section of the Pan Am Local, an umbrella local dominated by ground
workers. No other group of flight attendants would share a local with
others outside their craft. But while the Pan Am attendants' unionization
may have been aberrant, it did pique ALPA's concern over competition on
the plane. Compounding pilots' worries in the late 1940s was that white-
collar "insiders" in the cockpit were posing an even more intimate threat.
Third-flight-deck crewmembers, flight engineers who served as in-flight
mechanics, had won a permanent place in the airline industry alongside
captains and co-pilots. As of 1948, after years of having ALPA refuse them
membership, the flight engineers formed their own international union
with the AFL's blessing.[18]

Airline employee representation was a high-profile, competitive field
in the labor movement of the later 1940s, and ALPA was the leviathan
with which management and other unions had to reckon. Lacking practical experience and resources, stewardess organizers had little choice
but to accept much-needed help from pilots and their wealthy, powerful union. An alliance with pilots had much to recommend it. Since
the 1930s pilots and stewardesses had forged overlapping work cultures
socializing on the plane and on layovers, with no small amount of romance and intermarriage between the two groups. Flight attendants
working alone or in pairs necessarily looked to the cockpit for guidance
when in the air, so looking to pilots for help in organizing and bargaining was hardly a stretch. The pilots' union, after all, had served its members quite well. Edith Lauterbach remembered that when ALSA negotiators were struggling on a shoestring budget in their first contract talks
with United, donations from individual pilots were crucial in sustaining them.[19]

Yet heartfelt camaraderie and frequent romancing did not make pilots'

Delta stewardess serving coffee to the pilot and first officer,
January 1956. © Bettmann/CORBIS.

and flight attendants' working relationship any less unequal. As with
executives and secretaries or doctors and nurses, pilots' and flight attendants' interactions on the job were structured by rigidly hierarchical
roles. As the ultimate authority on the plane, pilots were flight attendants'
de facto supervisors and, if conflict ensued, could easily have their subor-
dinates disciplined or even fired. While flight attendants served passengers, they also fetched coffee and food upon demand for the cockpit crew.
Work life on the plane included badinage, horseplay, hazing, and pranks
that presumed women's willing subordination to men and shaded into
what is now considered sexual harassment. For instance, a former TWA
hostess who flew in the early 1950s recalled with amusement, "Sometimes
unofficial girdle checks were made by playful crews!" Whether or not
these gestures were enjoyed by stewardesses, they certainly highlighted
the power dynamics at play: pilots felt entitled to touch stewardesses at
work and did so in a way that replicated, though "playfully," ground
supervisors' "touch checks" for regulation undergarments. If a steward-

ess did marry a pilot, she forfeited her job under airline rules while he, of course, did not. For the small minority of male flight attendants, unwanted sexual attention may not have been a regular problem, but hostility from pilots was. Finally, as Lauterbach's recollections about the generosity of pilots highlight, pilots earned multiples of flight attendants' wages.[20]

A trade union provided a forum where flight attendants might attempt to claim more control as workers—and try they would. But an unaffiliated stewardess union with no more than several hundred members had little chance of competing in the long run with a well-funded ALPA subsidiary for flight attendants. Chartered on 1 August 1946 and provided with a full-time organizer on the pilot union's payroll, ALSSA quickly dwarfed ALSA, the union that Ada Brown and others had formed at United. In December 1949 independent ALSA, representing six hundred stewardesses on United and Western, merged with ALSSA, already representing 2,900 flight attendants on fourteen airlines, including TWA, Eastern, and American.[21]

THE SEARCH FOR AUTONOMY BEGINS

A few years into the history of their unionization, flight attendants assented to an unequal union marriage of convenience with pilots. ALSSA leaders strove to reap the benefits of the alliance for members, but also chafed at its constraints. During the 1950s ALSSA activists went about building their organization and winning steady pay increases and improvements in working conditions for stewardesses, stewards, and pursers on virtually every large carrier in the United States and the majority of smaller ones. In 1951 ALSSA represented 3,300 flight attendants on twenty-four airlines; less than ten years later, it represented some 9,000 flight attendants on thirty airlines. Active ALSSA membership grew from 1,800 in 1953 to 7,000 in 1960, an increase from less than one-third to more than two-thirds of all flight attendants in the United States. Thanks to ALSSA, flight attendants with a year of service on leading carriers saw their monthly earnings increase nearly 150 percent from the late 1940s to the late 1950s.[22]

The first ALSSA convention in 1951 made clear the ambitious plans of flight attendant activists for their organization and their occupation. When delegates elected their first national officials to replace ALPA's all-male appointees, the forty-five women and five men placed female flight attendants in three of the union's four national offices, including the presidency. While future elections would hand power disproportionately to male flight attendants, as we will see, Mary Alice Koos's election to the top post was telling. (When President Koos lost her bid for reelection in 1953, it was because many local officials within ALSSA considered her too deferential to the pilots, according to a union insider.) Delegates also made clear that they considered ALSSA's partnership with the pilot union no more than a temporary expedient. The first official convention in 1951 cemented ALSSA's status as a separate but unequal entity: ALPA replaced ALSSA's "conditional" charter of affiliation from 1947 with a "regular" charter restating pilot leaders' unilateral authority over flight attendants' union affairs. But at the very same meeting, flight attendant delegates voted an agenda that amounted to a bold bid for more power and autonomy. ALSSA's avowed goals as of 1951 were to obtain union shop agreements requiring membership of any flight attendant who worked under union contracts; to win federal certification of flight attendants for safety qualifications; and to apply to the AFL for an international charter to become a fully independent union—even as the ink was drying on the permanent charter of affiliation from ALPA. All three goals variously conflicted with ALPA's interests and policies.[23]

On the subject of the union shop, flight attendants and pilots agreed to disagree. ALPA's stance was that a good union should not need or want to negotiate contracts that effectively force workers to join in order to keep their jobs. Such principled opposition to a basic guarantee of organizational stability and financial security was a luxury that most unions could not afford, especially a dues-poor one like ALSSA with a high-turnover membership. Since pilots hoped that stewardesses would eventually pay their own union expenses, ALPA did not interfere with ALSSA's drive for union shops (though of course the more the flight attendants' union became self-sustaining, the less it would need or want ALPA's help). After 1951 ALSSA included union shop agreements among its top priorities in collective bargaining, and by 1958 it had won them on four major carriers where the financial and organizational benefits of the union shop were greatest. Unfortunately for flight attendants, they would find the pilots' leaders neither so open nor accommodating when it came to differences of opinion over certification and an independent charter from the AFL.[24]

"STEWARDESSES WANT LICENSE . . .
BUT NOT OF THE MARRYING KIND"

ALPA was less forthright, but apparently effective, in opposing safety certification for flight attendants by federal aviation authorities. Although previous studies have treated the historic fight for certification as little more than a footnote, flight attendants themselves have made clear since the early 1950s that it was an important symbolic as well as material goal. Early union organizers believed that without certification, cabin crew would find job security elusive and lack significant leverage in negotiations. Union contracts would eventually provide some security and improvements in work rules, but without federal intervention, flight attendants stood little chance of convincing airlines that they should be treated as indispensable safety workers. As a male journalist succinctly put it, flight attendants' arguments for certification were, "More safety for the public. More status and standing for themselves." And more power should they decide to go on strike, he might have added.[25]

Certification was the ultimate litmus test for flight attendants' claim to a uniquely important role in cabin safety. As ALSSA grew in numbers and resources during the 1950s, the union focused on safety activism as one of its primary goals in improving working conditions and staking a greater claim for its members' contributions to commercial aviation. ALSSA negotiated with airlines and lobbied aviation officials for improved standards in galley design, crew seating arrangements, and other matters affecting flight attendants' on-the-job safety. But ALSSA also considered cabin crew's own well-being part of the larger question of passenger safety and how it might be improved with the expert advice of flight attendants. The cockpit crew held sole responsibility for safe operation of the plane, but flight attendants were the authority figures in the cabin upon whom passengers' safety also depended. Flight attendants enforced preventive measures daily, such as making sure that passengers fastened their seat belts for takeoffs and landings. But they also carried the crucial, if rarely exercised, responsibility for handling passengers in the event of an emergency. As crashes had repeatedly shown since the 1930s, cabin crew could be the sole guarantee of passengers' survival in evacuating a burning or sinking plane efficiently and administering first aid. Under headlines such as "High Degree of Professional Skill" and "Heroines All," ALSSA publications seized on every opportunity to dramatize how potentially difficult and essential cabin crew's safety work was in life-threatening situations.[26]

ALSSA took such stories to the press, to federal aviation regulators, and to Congress in lobbying for certification during the 1950s and early 1960s. Who better than flight attendants, ALSSA contended, to serve as experts in improving cabin safety procedures, since they implemented them daily? And what better guarantee than governmental certification of their training to ensure that flight attendants would be prepared to save lives in a crisis? "Doctors, nurses and airline pilots have to have licenses," an ALSSA official told a reporter in 1961, "Even barbers and beauticians. Almost any individual dealing with public health and safety must. It doesn't make sense not to have flight attendants licensed. The lives of many sometimes depend on their coolness, skill and training. How important it is, then, that they be required to meet minimum licensing standards." Flight attendants felt entitled not only to a better wage from their employers than file clerks earned, but to at least the same state recognition accorded to beauticians for their more important contributions to the public's welfare.[27]

Flight attendants had enforced cabin safety measures and prepared for mechanical failures and other emergencies since the late 1920s. But by the postwar era, cabin safety duties were more complex and in turn more central to flight attendants' assertions that they were "professionals." After airlines stopped requiring stewardesses to be registered nurses during the Second World War, the already limited professional status that stewardesses as a group could claim by dint of their nursing degrees was no longer available. Airlines continued to favor registered nurses, but they were a shrinking elite in the growing flight attendant workforce. At the same time, the increasing complexity and variety of aircraft and on-board equipment meant that flight attendants needed more technical knowledge to perform their safety duties. In the pressurized cabins that became standard after the Second World War, for example, flight attendants needed new skills in operating heavy, difficult-to-open doors that maintained the air seal of the cabin. Higher flight altitudes also required flight attendants to know when and how to administer oxygen to all passengers in emergencies, and to individual passengers who had trouble breathing in non-emergencies. Postwar flight attendants seized on the expanding duties of cabin safety as a specialized, vital body of knowledge and skills that made them worthy of a place among recognized professionals.[28]

By 1962 postwar flight attendants' hopes for licensing came closest to fulfillment when the legislation that they had promoted for years finally came up for congressional debate. Congressional action was needed because the Federal Aviation Administration (FAA) was unwilling to institute flight attendant licensing on its own. What flight attendants proposed, and Congress agreed to consider, was an amendment to the Federal Aviation Act of 1958 to include flight attendants within the definition of "airman" and require that they be certified as such by the FAA. "Airman" was an appropriately gendered title for federally licensed airline workers, for it included occupations composed overwhelmingly of men, and entirely so in the cockpit: pilots and co-pilots, flight engineers, navigators, mechanics, radio operators, and dispatchers. They were also all groups who were directly involved in the operation of aircraft. Flight attendants would have been the sole group among them to work with passengers instead of with the planes themselves. That a well-trained cabin crew was the best guarantee of passengers' survival when other certified "airmen" could not prevent a plane from crashing was the primary justification offered by flight attendants for their demand for licenses.[29]

Flight attendants' licensing legislation stalled after hearings in the spring of 1962 before the House Interstate and Foreign Commerce Committee and never made it out of committee. The most obvious reason for the legislation's demise was opposition from the FAA. Flight attendants had made a great push for licensing legislation in 1961 because they sensed more sympathy than ever before among regulators, but at the hearings in 1962 the FAA's representative protested that licensing of flight attendants would be an unnecessary administrative burden for the agency. To certify a group with such rapid turnover, he argued, would take far more effort than the FAA already devoted to certifying other, more stable male groups. While the FAA acknowledged that flight attendants' criticisms of insufficient training were important, it promised to take care of the problem with tighter regulations on cabin crew staffing and training programs.[30]

Several other obstacles beyond the FAA's opposition contributed to flight attendants' failure to secure licensing. While expertise in passenger safety offered a more specialized claim than a degree in nursing for flight attendants' professional ambitions, it was still a limited platform for translating a self-defined professional identity into federally anointed status. As a group, flight attendants acquired their safety expertise in the airlines' training programs and through time in the job itself, which for most was just a few years. Airline safety training, flight attendants repeatedly contended, was grossly inadequate in many cases. Indeed, flight attendants argued that federal licensing was needed to eliminate the broad disparities in safety training across carriers and its subordination to schooling in service and appearance requirements. As ALSSA's president quipped, "In some training programs there is more emphasis on the proper method of serving a martini than the emergency evacuation of aircraft." Flight attendants in effect resorted to circular logic in their struggle to professionalize as safety workers: certification was needed to make them safety professionals through government-mandated tests and standards, but flight attendants also claimed that they already were safety professionals and thus deserved licenses to confirm that they were. Ironically, flight attendants' own leaders sometimes advocated licensing by warning that stewardesses were often too immature, inexperienced, and ill-trained to act effectively in an emergency. To dramatize the point, the president of ALSSA recounted to lawmakers grim instances when flight attendants' "ignorance" had turned potentially survivable crashes into fatal disasters. While indicting insufficient training the testimony nonetheless cast flight attendants in rather poor light and called into question whether flight attendants were the devoted, skilled safety professionals that they professed to be.[31]

The deck was already stacked against flight attendants in their professionalizing efforts, because of the airlines' refusal to acknowledge their safety role. The Air Transport Association (ATA), representing the industry, stated flatly to the Civil Aeronautics Board in 1957, "Historically the use of flight attendants aboard an aircraft has been prompted by service to passengers, thus, their justification has been economic and not for reasons of safety." During the congressional hearings on licensing legislation in 1962, the head of the ATA repeated that stewardesses were hired to provide service and charm, not safety.[32]

That airlines could so undervalue flight attendants' role in passenger safety underlined the broader cultural and historic obstacles facing stewardesses as they sought membership in the ranks of professionals. These ranks, as recognized by the public and state, were already well established as male-dominated and defined by arduous training, mastery of specialized knowledge and methods, and self-imposed standards that supposedly enabled altruistic service to the public (as well as personal economic gain and prestige). These criteria defined doctors and lawyers as prototypical professionals in the eyes of the state and the public, and enabled others, such as social workers and real estate brokers, to achieve more equivocal professional status. Flight attendants used these criteria themselves as a measure of their professionalism and to justify being licensed: their knowledge and skills, they argued, were unique and essential to the traveling public's safety. The problem was that flight attendants' skills and knowledge in passenger safety were not as quantifiable or evidently specialized as the skills and knowledge of other "real" professions.[33]

The president of the flight attendants' union eloquently explained the nature and importance of cabin crew's safety vigilance to a congressional subcommittee in 1960 in a way that unwittingly revealed why professional recognition proved so elusive. "The job of the hostess and purser requires judgment, ingenuity, skill and independence in an area of the most difficult sort—not handling inanimate and usually predictable machinery—but large numbers of human beings of all ages, walks of life, varied national and racial backgrounds, under panic conditions." "Just as the pilot is trained to keep his mind geared to what he would do at each instant should an emergency arise, so the hostess or purser must be trained to mentally assess the passengers from the minute she or he first sets eyes on them," identifying who seemed most likely to be disorderly and create danger, most able to help in an emergency, or most likely to need assistance. The favorable comparison to pilots, whom the government had been licensing for decades, was not coincidental. As the union leader indicated, safety vigilance was invisible but imperative labor for both pilots and flight attendants on every flight; it was immeasurable and unproductive to employers and customers unless an emergency did occur, but it was vital work nonetheless. To the union official, the stewardesses' challenge was ultimately the more difficult one. Yet for the same reason that stewardesses' preventive safety work was especially difficult— they worked with and managed unpredictable passengers, rather than typically compliant machinery—that work was easily trivialized or ignored. In the cabin alone, as the union official explained to Congress, safety assurance required an expert ability to size up any kind of person quickly and ensure that each behaved cooperatively to minimize potential dangers. However difficult and exacting, this work was done only surreptitiously as part of playing hostess unless disaster struck. Because flight attendants' preventive work in passenger safety was the intangible ability to handle people, the skills required were easily seen as merely part of their care work, if noticed at all.[34]

Flight attendants' safety skills were also the tangible capacity to operate emergency equipment, ensure evacuations, and deliver first aid when necessary, which came closer to the kinds of quantifiable skills that historically defined pilots and other groups as professionals. But here too flight attendants faced quite a challenge in casting their expertise as worthy of licensing. While more palpable than the task of sizing up passengers and invisibly deterring them from unsafe behavior, flight attendants' technical proficiency in safety equipment and procedures was similarly unproductive until needed in emergencies. But more important, that technical proficiency measured poorly on the historic yardstick of specialized knowledge and methods, gained through years of schooling or apprenticeship, that other groups used to justify their elite status. Within the context of aviation licensing, flight attendants could not claim the years of technical military or private training required of pilots, nor the intricate craft knowledge required of mechanics. Flight attendants could and did assert their professionalism in being skilled agents of passenger safety, but their claims were apparently too vague and tenuous to justify licensing in the eyes of federal lawmakers and aviation regulators. Nor did flight attendants' professionalization efforts compel the airlines to treat their safety work as anything more than an in-house secret in the postwar era.

Flight attendants' co-workers did not so easily dismiss the cabin crew's safety role. An individual pilot expressed support for flight attendants' certification cause in *Aviation Week* in 1952, adding, "After all, everyone else connected with airplanes must pass requirements in order to maintain minimum safety standards." Pilots' own professional status depended upon providing safe passage for air travelers, and ALPA led the field of safety advocacy among the airline unions. Throughout the later 1950s, ALSSA often joined its parent union ALPA in lobbying for air safety legislation and publicizing shared safety concerns, such as the possible dangers of inebriated passengers. ALPA leaders also supported higher, more uniform safety training standards for flight attendants.[35]

Nevertheless, ALSSA's drive for federal licenses suffered from a lack of support from pilot union leaders. On the matter of certification, an ALSSA official informed her members in 1961, "The average line pilot agrees with us. However, ALPA doesn't." Though pilot leaders had been paying "lip service" to ALSSA's quest for certification, the flight attendant union's legislative representative had discovered that ALPA lobbyists were hard at work on Capitol Hill undermining her efforts. ALPA, the ALSSA official concluded, feared surrendering authority over whether pilots could continue working if flight attendants struck. That is, if licensed flight attendants walked off the job, they would make it difficult if not impossible for pilots to continue flying if they chose to do so. Not all individual pilots were supportive of licensing flight attendants either. One former flight attendant for Eastern quipped, when asked whether she thought pilots took flight attendants' safety work seriously, "They were mostly interested in what they would be having as a crew meal."[36]

Postwar flight attendants' safety activism and bids for licensing were not in vain. In 1952 the Civil Aeronautics Authority issued its first safety rule concerning cabin crew. Civil Air Regulation 40.265 required an attendant on domestic flights with seating capacity for ten or more passengers to ensure efficient emergency evacuations. In the early 1960s the Federal Aviation Administration (successor to the CAA) introduced specific ratios of flight attendants to passengers and minimum training standards, as flight attendants had long sought. Yet flight attendants' leaders complained that the training standards lacked enforcement mechanisms and, worse, the FAA simultaneously dismissed licensing as an undue burden. With airlines' insistence that flight attendants' purpose was solely to please passengers, any government codification of their safety duties was an important victory. Still, it was all too clear to activists that their safety work failed to inspire the respect they felt due from federal officials, and from their co-workers and union allies in ALPA.[37]

"GIRLS AGAINST THE BOYS"

ALPA's failure to support flight attendants in their licensing drive reflected and fed a larger struggle over flight attendants' self-determination in the late 1950s and early 1960s. Back in 1951, when ALSSA held its first convention, elected its own officials, and set up its own treasury, bylaws, and constitution, both the pilots' and flight attendants' unions celebrated the occasion as confirming ALSSA's new status as separate and self-governing. Flight attendants nonetheless began immediately to bid for more independence by seeking an international charter of their own from the AFL. While the pilots' leaders publicly assented, they privately opposed the charter. National labor leaders, for their part, avoided dealing with the charter request for as long as they could. It was awkward, after all, to deny the democratic aspirations of organized workers. But the AFL constitution did not allow a new charter for a subordinate union unless the parent union agreed. National labor leaders were reluctant to burden further their already difficult relationship with the wealthy, powerful pilots' union by supporting the stewardesses' charter drive. ALSSA's repeated charter requests thus met evasive responses, if any at all, preventing the amicable divorce from ALPA that flight attendants wanted.[38]

But by the later 1950s the prospects for any peaceable parting were quickly dwindling. As early as 1947 the stewardesses' union founder Ada Brown warned members that the pilot union would not support their strikes. More than ten years later, the Lake Central walkout proved her right. The question of support from pilots was crucial, for while un-licensed attendants held limited power to threaten an airline's operations with a work stoppage, pilots could easily shut down an airline by observing picket lines. ALPA's official policy on other unions' strikes, however, was for pilots to honor their employment contracts and continue working, as long as they considered it safe to do so (though not to "scab" by substituting for strikers). ALSSA was a subsidiary of ALPA, but it was not exempt from the pilots' ban on sympathy strikes. When flight attendants had come close to striking on three previous occasions, ALPA officials put them on notice that pilots would keep flying. Even worse for the Lake Central stewardesses, their employer was the only employee-owned airline in the United States at the time, and pilots were the major shareholders. The prospects for a sympathy strike were indeed slim, but ALSSA officials nonetheless approached the Lake Central pilots, only to be rebuffed. The dispute was hardly soothed by an open telegram on the eve of the strike from the Lake Central stewardesses' leader Nancy Silverthorn, proclaiming that any pilot who intended to cross the picket line just because that was ALPA policy lacked "the intelligence or courage of the most junior stewardess." The stewardesses struck on 23 November 1958, and for the eleven days of the walkout Lake Central maintained operations with ALPA pilots in the cockpit and supervisory personnel substituting in the cabin (the pilots had at least refused to fly with newly hired strikebreakers).[39]

Other clashes further poisoned the relationship between the flight attendants' and pilots' unions. In 1958, the same year as the divisive Lake Central strike, ALPA wooed the small group of stewardesses on Mohawk Airlines out of ALSSA and into another of its subsidiaries, the Air Line Employees Association, a small union of ground-based clerical workers.

To ALSSA leaders this was a blatant "raid," a breach of fair play among unions in the AFL-CIO. The new jet aircraft that leading airlines introduced in 1958 added to inter-union tensions. For pilots, whose pay structure was based partly on miles flown, jets meant an automatic pay boost for doing the same basic work during the same shifts, which federal hour limits determined. For flight attendants, who earned flat monthly salaries, larger, faster jets meant increased workloads with no automatic pay hike. Worse, flight attendants suspected that the speed and higher altitude of jet flight threatened their health, through swollen limbs, fatigue, and menstrual irregularities. As the flight attendants' negotiators began to work harder to reduce cabin crew hours when jets arrived, they threatened pilots' earning potential: shorter workdays for flight attendants meant that pilots might either have to work shorter shifts themselves or spend more time on the ground and less racking up miles, to allow for turnover of cabin crews. Jets also promised much larger increases in employment for flight attendants than for pilots. While pilots still outnumbered the cabin crew whose union they oversaw in the late 1950s, some pilot officials worried that ALSSA seemed capable of becoming the proverbial tail that would wag the dog of ALPA. At ALSSA's tumultuous fifth biennial convention in April 1959, the increasingly strained relations between pilots' and flight attendants' representatives nearly broke down. ALSSA's president left the convention authorized by delegates to disaffiliate from ALPA at his discretion, after a study committee weighed in on the matter.[40]

The growing imbroglio over ALSSA's future might have been settled simply had flight attendants been able to secure the independent charter they had sought since 1951. The AFL-CIO did finally rule on ALSSA's long-stalled charter request in the wake of the fractious convention of 1959. It was motivated to do so not only by the worsening relations between ALSSA and ALPA but by the Labor-Management Reporting and Disclosure, or Landrum-Griffin, Act, enacted by Congress in 1959 after revelations of corruption in organized labor during the 1950s. The conservatives who had pushed through the bill took corruption as an excuse to quash what radicalism remained in unions after the anti-labor Taft-Hartley Act of 1947 by placing further restrictions on workers' protests and heightening public scrutiny of labor organizations. But the "mini bill of rights" for union members included in Landrum-Griffin also challenged racial segregation and other practices that deprived workers of equal representation and opportunities to run for union offices. Thus the act outlawed the kind of second-class membership that the federation worried was being provided to flight attendants by ALPA.[41]

The House of Labor's official decision in November 1959 on ALSSA's charter requests was that the pilots ought to provide a more democratic, though still paternalistic, form of representation for flight attendants within ALPA. "As a chartered subsidiary union," George Meany, president of the AFL-CIO, wrote to ALPA's president, the federation considered ALSSA "part of" ALPA—in other words, the pilots' union was flouting the intent, if not the letter, of the Landrum-Griffin Act. "Your international union," Meany instructed, "must assume the responsibility for the welfare and conduct of the Air Line Stewards and Stewardesses." Meany recommended that ALPA establish "a department or division of air line stewards and stewardesses as part of ALPA." As for ALSSA, Meany wrote separately to say that the federation recognized ALPA's right to represent the flight attendants within the federation, and that under the AFL-CIO constitution, ALSSA could not be granted a charter without ALPA's consent.[42]

STRUGGLES WITHIN ALSSA

As the conflict between flight attendants' and pilots' leaders became irreconcilable by the start of the 1960s, intra-union struggles were tearing ALSSA apart from within. The more the leaders clashed in the late 1950s, the more some ALSSA members and local officials found reason to doubt their national officers. Serious discontent within the flight attendants' union began to register at the same moment that disfavor toward the pilots reached a new peak: the Lake Central strike. As the strike made clear, disgruntled ALSSA members worried that their association was becoming an undemocratic trade union led by self-interested men—even as those male leaders increasingly bridled at the pilots' oversight.

ALSSA's second elected president, the Eastern steward Rowland K. Quinn Jr., exemplified male flight attendants' amplified presence in the union's affairs. Either the union's president or its vice-president, or both, was a male flight attendant from the first elections in 1951 until the 1970s, and Quinn himself served five consecutive presidential terms from 1953 to 1963. During Quinn's tenure men accounted for no more than 10 to 15 percent of the ALSSA membership and even less of the flight attendant workforce. Male flight attendants were disproportionately active in the union in part because they stayed on the job longer than stewardesses. But they also had a particular cultural incentive to take on union work and run for office. The postwar cultural climate associated manliness with breadwinning and defined labor organizing as a normatively male endeavor. Male flight attendants earned their living in a short-term, feminized occupation, but they could assume masculine roles in union activism and by demanding better compensation as "family men." Union work and leadership provided a ready way to seek respect and pay befitting "mature" breadwinners. Many stewardesses in turn welcomed male leadership as a means to increase their union's authority and legitimacy. Edith Lauterbach later explained, "Although the membership was almost entirely female, many honestly believed," when Quinn was first elected in 1953, "that a man would be more effective than a woman as president." Quinn did have "manly" credentials, as a trained pilot who had served in the Air Force and earned a degree in industrial management at the University of Michigan before becoming an Eastern steward.[43]

But while male leadership served a strategic purpose, it also invited female flight attendants to link their grievances with the union to suspicions that its male leaders were at best insensitive and at worst domineering. The Lake Central strikers, for their part, later complained that they were bullied by union leadership into signing an agreement and returning to work against their wishes. "The girls all felt we had been 'sold down the river' by ALSSA," their leader confided to another local official. Members and local officials at TWA were no happier with ALSSA headquarters when the members were assessed $2 each, in addition to quarterly dues of $7.50, to provide strike funds for the Lake Central women. In a raft of protest letters to Quinn, they demanded to know why one thousand hostesses on TWA should have to support thirty-odd strikers from Lake Central. Angry letter writers wondered if anyone at TWA had been consulted about the strike assessment and insisted on more financial details from headquarters.[44]

But the letters to Quinn also indicated that many TWA hostesses were upset less about the assessment than with the union's pursuit of security though union shop agreements, especially the one ALSSA had recently negotiated on their airline. Some complained that their contract was substandard, accusing negotiators of having sacrificed better wages and work rules for the union shop. Others felt that the mere fact of the union shop was the problem, since it represented coercion. Echoing several letter writers, Joyce Hills complained that she saw no benefits in her forced membership in ALSSA, and added, "For every one loyal TWA union hostess, you probably have eight that have no idea why they are to pay $7.50 a quarter to belong, other than it saves them from being fired." Shirley Johnson informed ALSSA's president, "I do not believe in most unions as I find that the leaders of these organizations have not been a part of this working group and are in it solely for the money. . . . When were you an airline stewardess, Mr. Quinn???" On the one hand, unhappy members and local leaders demanded a more democratic ALSSA, with greater self-determination at the local level, increased accountability at headquarters, and equity of treatment across diverse carriers. On the other hand, complaints of preferential treatment for the Lake Central strikers and of coercion under the union shop pointed up basic discomfort in the rank and file with trade unionism itself.[45]

Disgruntled ALSSA members would only find more cause for concern as their leaders plunged deeper into conflict with the pilots. When Quinn was reelected in 1959 and empowered by delegates to cut ALSSA's ties to ALPA, some rank-and-file members and local leaders detected a strong whiff of "autocracy." Meanwhile, rumors and press reports encouraged them to suspect that ALSSA leaders might end their oversight by pilots only to invite domination by the Teamsters, the union of one and a half million truckers and other transport workers that was the bête noire of the labor movement. The Teamsters had taken center stage in federal investigations during the 1950s of corruption in the labor movement and links to organized crime. They had also amassed a record of aggressively intruding on other unions' jurisdictional claims, which, along with revelations of corruption, prompted their expulsion from the AFL-CIO in 1957. Wealthy and now independent, the Teamsters no longer had any obligation to recognize the federation's prohibitions against raiding. As of 1958 their president, Jimmy Hoffa, was touting ambitious plans to organize workers on the airlines and in other transport industries in a drive for "transportation unity," and his union made sporadic overtures to stewardesses in the late 1950s and early 1960s. ALSSA leaders denied merger discussions, or even connections, with the Teamsters, who would have been a highly controversial ally at best. Many unhappy members of the stewardess union, however, were unconvinced.[46]

With internal distrust mounting, Quinn finally announced on 5 August

1960 that ALSSA was severing all ties to ALPA. The press found the breakup
a typical instance of womanly pique in a classic battle of the sexes, but the
disaffiliation was no laughing matter for those involved. ALPA immediately imposed a trusteeship on ALSSA. Thirty dissident stewardesses
within ALSSA, both local officials and rank-and-file activists, quickly
called a press conference to express their intention to stay with the pilots.
One told the *Chicago Tribune* that eight of every ten local ALSSA officials
favored a continued affiliation with ALPA. Quinn retorted, "A girl who
makes between $300 and $500 a month doesn't relish having pilots who
make $35,000 a year run her affairs both in the air and on the ground." But
to many flight attendants, it was better to remain subject to oversight by
the pilots' union than risk complete independence, with its attendant
financial peril and exposure to raids by other unions, or, worse, being
swallowed up by the Teamsters.[47]

THE "TERROR OF THE SUBWAYS" VERSUS
THE "LADIES AUXILIARY"

Whatever stewardesses thought of the disaffiliation, they would pay a far
heavier price for their union divorce than pilots. The legal struggle that
pitted Quinn and his allies against ALPA for control over ALSSA eventually produced a staggering fifty-two suits and countersuits that dragged
on into the mid-1960s. ALSSA could ill afford to be embroiled in these
court struggles. In 1960 ALPA claimed assets of roughly $4.5 million; that
same year, ALSSA's income totaled $200,000, virtually its only financial
resource. Even worse for ALSSA, the dues check-off agreements that it had
secured with several large carriers in the late 1950s came back to haunt it.
Management at TWA and American, among other carriers, quickly decided to hold the dues deducted from members' paychecks in escrow
accounts until the legal disputes between ALPA and ALSSA were settled.
Some airlines also refused to negotiate new contracts for flight attendants
or to cooperate with ALSSA in processing grievances while its bargaining
rights were legally in question.[48]

In growing desperation, ALSSA leaders tried one last plea for a charter
from AFL-CIO and, when it failed, looked carefully for a new union ally.
They turned to the only international besides ALPA with an existing claim
on the flight attendant craft: the Transport Workers Union, to which Pan
Am cabin attendants had belonged since 1946. While TWU's strongest

historical base was among subway workers in New York City, it had organized a variety of airline occupations in its air transport division. Pan Am pursers, stewards, and stewardesses had enjoyed what many flight attendants considered among the best contracts in the industry for fifteen years. After a preliminary meeting with TWU officials, Quinn made an official request in February 1961 that the transport workers take in ALSSA. TWU agreed in early March (despite warnings from the AFL-CIO leadership that it would be charged with raiding) and offered ALSSA leaders what they considered an appealing arrangement. ALSSA would join TWU as new Local 550 in the Air Transport Division (Pan Am flight attendants would remain in their carrier-specific umbrella local). Like all other TWU locals, ALSSA would pay per-capita dues to the international and abide by its constitution and bylaws. But otherwise ALSSA would move into TWU with its current structure and practices intact, including control over its treasury, administrative personnel, and choice of legal counsel. TWU guaranteed ALSSA, its leaders believed, more autonomy than ALPA had ever allowed. Delegates at ALSSA's sixth biennial convention in April 1961 ratified the new affiliation.[49]

When ALSSA secured its affiliation to TWU, representation elections had just begun in which every flight attendant who had belonged to ALSSA now had to decide whether she favored ALPA's new "Steward & Stewardess Division" (ALPA-SSD) or "ALSSA, Local 550, TWU" (ALSSA-TWU). Over the course of 1961 and into 1962, those elections would determine the bargaining rights for 80 percent of the roughly ten thousand flight attendants then employed in the United States. In neither case could flight attendants escape oversight by a larger, male-dominated union in their union affairs. The question was which overseer—ALPA, an exclusive, white-collar craft union, or TWU, a diverse, blue-collar industrial union—would allow flight attendants more room to pursue professionalization and operate autonomously.

ALSSA partisans hoped to woo stewardesses by emphasizing that they would be treated "as equals, not as problem stepchildren" by TWU. They asserted that ALSSA-TWU was "the organization best able to improve [the] profession through higher salaries, shorter hours, better working conditions, stronger protection, while, at the same time, establishing a new respect and prestige for the Flight Attendants." TWU International, they noted, readily supported safety licensing for flight attendants, unlike ALPA. Equally important, ALSSA-TWU allowed members to vote on whether to accept their contracts. In ALPA-SSD, as in the old ALSSA, national officers, including the pilot president, still held sole authority to ratify flight attendants' contracts. Better that flight attendants should upgrade their profession on their own terms, ALSSA-TWU organizers argued, than try to borrow prestige as a mere "ladies auxiliary" of ALPA.[50]

Partisans of ALPA-SSD countered that it was better to borrow prestige and power from the pilots than risk being identified with the blue-collar masses in TWU and their corrupt or radical leaders. A typical flyer contrasted the "professional" autonomy that ALPA-SSD would provide with the prospect of being submerged among alien, working-class groups in TWU. The choice stewardesses faced, according to the flyer, was "whether you want to have the freest choice of electing all of your own representatives . . . or whether you wish to be represented by an organization composed of a vast number of people, most of whom work in jobs such as bus drivers, mechanics and tug boat dispatchers, and who know nothing of you and your profession." ALPA organizers also liked to imply that TWU was really the ultimate blue-collar menace, the scandal-ridden Teamsters, in disguise. ALPA advocates exploited fears of incursions from the Teamsters by trying to convince stewardesses that TWU was in league with them and represented the same type of corrupt unionism. The president of TWU International, Mike Quill, was an outspoken, militant veteran of the CIO with historic links to the Communist Party who offered a ready target for ALPA partisans. ALPA officials at Northwest assailed him as the "terror of the New York Subway System," with "ambitions to achieve similar 'Go' and 'No Go' control over the nation's airlines."[51]

ALSSA advocates dismissed such class-based appeals as a red herring. One need only compare paychecks and employee manuals, they countered, to see how much more rewarding pilots' white collars were. But partisans of ALSSA-TWU nonetheless showed plenty of class-inflected aloofness themselves toward TWU. ALSSA organizers needed and welcomed the help of TWU International staff and support from other groups in the transport union, but class difference, as well as gender and age, made the alliance an awkward and sometimes difficult one. As a TWU official put it, "The ALSSA girls do not seem to be disposed to seek advice or help from the so-called mechanical group." Indeed, ALSSA organizers encouraged stewardesses to believe that they need not identify with other, less elite transport workers to enter the TWU fold. A central piece of

Cover of an ALSSA-TWU
organizing brochure, 1961.
Records of the Transport Workers
Union, courtesy of Robert F.
Wagner Labor Archives, New
York University.

ALSSA organizing literature, a pamphlet entitled "Progress thru Unity," expressed the point in stark visual terms. The cover made clear in print that ALSSA was now a subunit of TWU, but the illustration portrayed "unity" in terms of extreme uniformity and exclusivity. It depicted a lineup of stewardesses in two uniform designs with slightly varying hairstyles, their slender bodies otherwise identical in the physical ideal of genteel femininity that they represented. By emphasizing stewardesses' appearance as a unifying, exclusionary source of pride and identity, the illustration promised a union of and for stewardesses alone.[52]

Yet partisans of ALPA-SSD, even with pilots' prestige to back them, felt it just as necessary as their rivals did to dispel the class-coded "stigma" and "shame" that labor organizing threatened. Echoing flight attendant organizers in the late 1940s, propagandists for both camps likened their unions to sororities or professional groups like bar associations. Here apparently was a workforce converted to labor organizing in practice, but still not necessarily in principle. As the battle for stewardesses' loyalty in 1961 and 1962 showed, any pretenses to labor solidarity beyond the plane were merely of strategic appeal, if that, to unionists intent on maximizing their autonomy, power, and prospects for professionalizing.[53]

ONE SUBORDINATE UNION
BECOMES TWO STILL-SUBORDINATE UNIONS

When the dust settled from the intra- and inter-union struggles of the late 1950s and early 1960s, flight attendants ended up split between the new stewardess division in the pilots' union and ALSSA, now a self-consciously white-collar, craft-oriented local in the blue-collar, industrial TWU. Of the approximately 8,000 unionized flight attendants whose bargaining rights were in question, more than 6,500, or roughly four in five, eventually voted on their union representation. At a few airlines, barely a majority of eligible voters cast ballots, but at other carriers turnout reached 90 to 100 percent. ALSSA-TWU edged out ALPA-SSD overall, 54 to 43 percent. Each union won over distinct constituencies, with particular timing to their success.[54]

On the one hand, most small carrier groups and a few larger ones led by opponents of ALSSA's leadership, namely Braniff and United, went with ALPA-SSD. And they did so relatively quickly, while ALSSA-TWU was in dire financial straits and its future sketchy. On regional and local carriers, with small aircraft and typically more paternalistic labor relations, ALPA-SSD had a crucial advantage in the close working relationships between individual pilots and stewardesses. As a TWU staff organizer at Ozark Airlines bemoaned, stewardesses on smaller airlines tended to "base their convictions on the pilot as a person and not ALPA the organization."[55]

On the other hand, ALSSA-TWU fared better in the later elections of mid- to late 1961 and 1962, after TWU International began providing loans and staff assistance. It won over all the "Big Four" airlines except United—TWA, Eastern, and American—as well as some medium and small carriers. Along with timing, the demographics of some larger air-

line groups apparently worked in ALSSA-TWU's favor. Larger flight attendant groups had larger corps of veterans; and TWA, Eastern, and Northwest employed most of the male minority of flight attendants. Seasoned
flight attendants had longer personal memories than their co-workers
about what a subordinate relationship to ALPA was like. The pilots' strategy of "wining and dining" stewardesses certainly met with considerable
cynicism among veteran union women. Male flight attendants, for their
part, were not likely to champion close working relationships with pilots
or ALPA. In any event, ALSSA-TWU ended up with nearly all the male
flight attendants involved in the union struggles, which meant that it
inherited the historic pattern of male dominance in union leadership.[56]

It was also only in ALSSA-TWU that flight attendants found themselves
in another power struggle with their parent union to clarify their autonomy, or rather their lack of it. TWU officials were apparently unaware of
how much of a financial and organizational burden they had assumed in
taking in ALSSA in March 1961. But they soon learned that ALSSA was in
financial ruin, and watched it lose thousands of members to ALPA-SSD.
ALSSA's mounting debt, along with the irrevocable loss of future dues
income, troubled TWU officials, who quickly suspected they had "a bear
by the tail." While flight attendant unionists were not eager to accept help
from "mechanics," TWU officials found organizing stewardesses equally
unappealing. Their reports to the international's headquarters were filled
with complaints of poor turnout at union meetings and of what they
considered ALSSA local leaders' ineptitude. "The generating of interest is
the basic job that has to be done with these people," according to the chief
TWU staff organizer for ALSSA, Frederic Simpson, who blamed the apathy
largely on stewardesses' supposed obsession with men and dating. TWU
officials like Simpson soon concluded that they needed to teach their
"way of doing business" to ALSSA.[57]

The international therefore tightened the reins on its struggling local,
and when Quinn and his fellow officers fought back, ALSSA again found
itself subject to a trusteeship. On 27 June 1963, only three months after
Quinn won reelection to a sixth term, TWU International suspended him
from office, charging gross financial mismanagement. In a replay of earlier struggles, Quinn and his fellow deposed officers claimed that the
financial matters of which TWU complained were for ALSSA alone to
decide and went to court. An exasperated Quinn told members, "If we do
not stand up to this latest assault, the last three years will have been a total

waste of time, money, and sacrifice." But while Quinn and his allies won in trial court, the appellate court ruled that the question of ALSSA's autonomy was not a matter of federal judicial concern. Quinn, personally insolvent by then, gave up. TWU withdrew its trusteeship in early 1964, when its administrator reassured fellow officers of TWU International that the new president of ALSSA, the former elected vice-president Colleen Boland, had "been completely trained in the ways of TWU." Whatever autonomy ALSSA might enjoy was apparently only at TWU's whim.[58]

No power struggle was needed to clarify the limits on flight attendants' self-determination in the Steward and Stewardess Division of ALPA. The SSD was subordinate by design to the pilots' division of ALPA. It elected its own leaders, but the top flight attendant official was merely the SSD "vice-president," whereas the pilots' chief served as ALPA president. Flight attendant delegates voted in the election of ALPA president at the two divisions' joint biennial conventions. But the office itself was open only to pilot candidates, and flight attendants were expected to reserve their votes as a bloc (which they did), to be cast only after the pilots' choice was clear. Flight attendants in ALPA did not vote on their contracts, which were ratified by the signature of the pilot president and the top officials of the SSD. The pilot division, finally, could dissolve the flight attendant division at any time by a simple majority vote. The SSD provided stewardesses with exactly the kind of second-class union membership that it was supposed to revise.[59]

Considering the high rate of turnover and widespread discomfort with labor organizing among postwar flight attendants, the wonder in the end is not that they failed to secure true independence in their union affairs, or to persuade federal regulators to license them as safety professionals. It is that they bothered trying. The typical rank-and-filer may not have cared very deeply about union issues or whether the FAA licensed her. When rank-and-file stewardesses did raise their voices, it was often to complain of forced membership under union shop agreements, express distrust of the leadership, or fret over the possibility that they might become Teamsters. Nonetheless, there was enough collective sense of purpose and militancy among postwar flight attendants to build a successful organization and propel ambitious, though divisive, drives for self-determination. Looking back on his decade as ALSSA president many years later, Rowland Quinn concluded that the flight attendant union women with whom he worked were as militant as the organizational context of the labor movement and the cultural climate allowed.[60]

Other groups disadvantaged in the labor movement hierarchy did not necessarily fare better in the House of Labor after all. Flight attendants shared not only occupational parallels with Pullman porters, but some union parallels as well. The AFL dragged its feet for years in granting an international charter to the porters' union; thereafter the Brotherhood of Sleeping Car Porters (BSCP) and its militant leader, A. Philip Randolph, would continue to struggle with labor's racism as the first AFL international of black workers. Yet the BSCP, in its drive to secure "manhood rights" for porters, relegated Pullman maids and porters' wives and female relatives to subordinate status in its women's auxiliary. Black and white women in various unions' auxiliaries were often celebrated as female helpmeets but denied autonomy whenever male leaders felt that their own interests might be threatened. While several leftist and liberal internationals in the CIO boasted distinguished records on gender equity in the mid-twentieth century, many other unions were fully vested in defending male dominance and white supremacy in the name of the "family wage" system. Labor leaders spoke of the need to bring more white-collar workers into the union fold, but they offered most white-collar unions scant attention and resources; some were persecuted in the postwar Red Scare for being too radical. It was not just labor leaders' own limited vision, however, that made democracy and self-rule elusive for many unionists who happened not to be white, male, and blue-collar. The political constraints of the postwar years hardly encouraged progressive breakthroughs in organizing and empowering women and minority unionists, as state and employer pressure grew to channel labor militancy solely into the legalistic collective bargaining system and keep the labor movement from expanding into new industries or traditionally anti-union regions.[61]

In 1947 the ALPA employee who edited ALSSA's new union newsletter, *Service Aloft*, declared, "Glamour is gone from the air line flight attending profession," replaced by "realism." "The stewards and stewardesses," he contended, "will no longer be pushed around but will be given the fair treatment they are entitled to receive." The staff member was premature in proclaiming the demise of glamour and mistook glamour and realism as being mutually exclusive. That glamour continued to be a source of considerable pride and identity among stewardesses was amply evident in

A Braniff hostess, Muffett Webb, announced as the first Miss Skyway, 1956. This beauty pageant, exclusively for American flight attendants, was co-sponsored by the Air Line Stewards and Stewardesses Association (with Skyway Luggage). **Photo by Arthur Sasse.** © Bettmann/CORBIS.

Service Aloft as it evolved into a better-funded publication edited by flight attendants' own elected leaders. In 1957, for instance, a TWA flight attendant who competed in the Miss America pageant graced the newsletter's front page in a bathing suit and tiara; a story on page two recounted her adventures as Miss Hawaii. But in adjacent news items, the newsletter also noted a new union shop agreement on one airline and summarized recent grievance cases that the union had won. As the official union voice for postwar flight attendants, *Service Aloft* seamlessly blended articles and photographs celebrating stewardesses' attractiveness and romantic exploits with satirical cartoons and writings poking fun at how unglamorous passenger service was, prosaic details of union administration, and tributes to stewardesses' heroism in emergencies. Stewardesses did not need to deny glamour's appeal to embrace "realism" about glamour's exploitative aspects and want an able, autonomous union.[62]

"NOTHING BUT
AN AIRBORNE WAITRESS"
The Jet Age

On 18 August 1961 the *Dallas Morning News* reported a lament by an official of the Air Line Stewards and Stewardesses Association that stewardess work had devolved into drudgery. The newspaper explained, "An ex-airline stewardess who has traveled more than 700,000 sky-miles said Thursday that her former job is 'not a fun profession any more—it's a chore!' " "Pretty brunette Phyllis Young, educational director for the ALSSA, charged that with the advent of jets, the hostess has been chased by drunks, overworked by new schedules and under-trained by employers." Young reportedly proclaimed, "Why, the stewardess is no longer a hostess any more—she's nothing but an airborne waitress."[1]

Phyllis Young's views on the fate of airline hostesses captured some of the intensifying grievances that marked the jet age for flight attendants. As Young indicated only three years after jet-powered aircraft entered regular service in the United States, flight attendants would find that their work bore less resemblance to the airlines' traditional ideal of playing gracious hostess to intimate parties of genteel travelers. Larger, faster jets enabled airlines to cultivate a much larger and more heterogeneous passenger population. Nonetheless, the bread-and-butter customer continued to be the white, male business traveler, who received an increasing share of airline marketers' attention. Airlines courted the American public, but especially businessmen, with grander promises of luxury service and, more amorphously, personal attention and fun aloft. Yet promises of good times and superlative service on more crowded jets did not prompt airlines to increase their staffing proportionately. Flight attendants had to serve increased passenger loads on shorter flights, with more varied duties to perform. The jet age stuck flight attendants with a profound speed-up in their work and an ever-more contradictory service mandate. They were supposed to provide efficient, assembly-line service while delivering customized charm and flattery to every customer. As Phyllis Young's lament about "drunks" suggested, airlines' evolving vision of jet-age luxury also encouraged more bad behavior among passengers of all kinds. Young's remark that the airline hostess had become "nothing but a waitress" became a common refrain for flight attendants chagrined to find their celebrated jobs growing in workaday drudgery and frustration —and losing some of the cultural luster that distinguished their work from waitressing and other service jobs.

While the arrival of jets was reshaping the daily work of airline passenger service, the discriminatory boundaries of stewardess employment were changing too. On the one hand, by the 1960s airlines had become one of the most egregious perpetuators of formalized sex discrimination in the United States. All but a few airlines maintained their requirement that stewardesses be single, past the point when no-marriage rules generally fell out of favor with employers of female labor in the postwar United States. Worse for stewardesses, several carriers introduced age ceilings of thirty-two or thirty-five in the 1950s and early 1960s. But on the other hand, airlines were forced to cede ground on racial discrimination when African American women breached the color barrier in airline passenger service in the late 1950s. Token integration did not change the fundamental whiteness of the occupation, but it did mean that at least one key brick in the edifice of airline discrimination was dislodged. The arrival of jet aircraft marked a whole new era in the culture and business of commercial aviation, with far-reaching and even contradictory consequences for the flight attendant occupation.

"A TIRED BUSINESSMAN OUGHT TO BE ALLOWED TO LOOK AT A PRETTY GIRL"

On the evening of 26 October 1958 the first commercially successful jet-powered aircraft made its début flight, as Boeing's 707 went into regular service on Pan American Airways' transatlantic route. With much publicity, a plane filled with celebrities and VIPs departed from New York and arrived in Paris eight hours and fifteen minutes later, carrying a record load of 111 passengers over 3,300 miles at an average speed of 475 miles an hour. It was a historic moment to rival Charles Lindbergh's epic solo flight from New York to Paris thirty-one years earlier. The Boeing 707 was not the first jet airliner to fly scheduled passenger flights, but it was the first to do it safely and efficiently enough to achieve a permanent place in airline fleets. The commercially viable jet was perhaps the single most important technological advance in commercial aviation. It revolutionized the business of air travel, transformed international commerce and patterns of migration, and shrank political and cultural perceptions of temporal and spatial distance. Jets enabled the global movement of passengers and cargo in a matter of hours rather than days, weeks, or months.[2]

Within a few years of the 707's début, American carriers bought and put into service a range of jets that dramatically increased hauling capacity and reduced flight times in many travel markets. Airlines large and small committed themselves to unprecedented debt financing to secure the increased speed, range, and capacity of jets. Larger and more expensive jets meant that airlines could—and needed to—markedly expand their operations and customer base. The expansion of the airlines succeeded thanks both to the increase in many Americans' discretionary income and to aggressive promotions, economy fares, and vacation packages offered by airlines and related travel industries. By 1970 airlines based in the United States were collectively carrying 150 million passengers, three times as many as a decade earlier. That same year, the number of Americans who traveled abroad reached five million, and only 3 percent chose to go by sea rather than air. While only about 10 percent of the adult population in the United States had flown in an airplane in the late 1940s, almost two-thirds had done so by 1977. In 1973 the Gallup organization determined that no fewer than one in four Americans over the age of eighteen had taken a commercial flight that year.[3]

Still, coaxing more of America's less affluent travelers to fly was not enough for airlines to fill their jet fleets at a healthy profit. In the jet age, American carriers also competed as never before to win the loyalty of the well-to-do regular traveler who continued to provide the bulk of airline income. In 1964 the Port Authority of New York and New Jersey reported that a mere 5 percent of passengers accounted for 40 percent of the airline seats occupied that year. According to airline industry sources, over three-quarters of air travelers in the United States in the early 1970s were "in a professional or business occupation" and earned over $15,000, then a sizable amount. A consultant for TWA bluntly explained in 1972, "The emphasis has shifted from getting the Great Unwashed to fly to getting more of the Great Washed who do." While the jet age gave rise to the so-called jet set—men and women of transcontinental leisure—airlines' most sought-after customer among the Great Washed was the businessman traveling on an expense account.[4]

In the jet age, airline marketing strategies turned more to mass advertising and distinct corporate images. Airlines that had once depended on employees above all to convey a carrier's desired image of courteous, efficient service came to rely instead on expensive advertising campaigns for image-making. By the later 1960s large airlines like United and American spent upwards of $20 million annually on advertising, and mid-sized airlines, like Continental and National, budgeted from $5 to $10 million. In spending more on ads, airlines were less concerned with enlarging the market for air travel than with building their own market shares. To impress the Great Washed, airlines spent more time and money staking competitive claims not only with the concrete details of schedules, fares, and amenities but also with fantasies of sincere friendliness, fun, and special treatment.[5]

Heftier advertising budgets and more imprecise promises to make passengers feel good reflected developments both within and outside the airline industry. In the late 1950s and 1960s a "creative revolution" in advertising encouraged many sellers of consumer goods and services to trade formal, impersonal presentations of specific wares for more generic messages of corporate caring and personality. But airlines in particular also perceived a new and distinct need to personalize their images and raise the emotional expectations of passengers. Airlines feared that for their best customers, flying had become boring and monotonous. No longer was the challenge to convince the public that flying was a safe, uniquely efficient, and increasingly affordable way to travel; in the jet age, airlines worried instead about staving off the well-traveled businessman's ennui.[6]

In seeking to excite and flatter the bored repeat flyer, airline advertisers drew inspiration from not only the creative revolution in the advertising industry but from the broader sexual revolution under way in the United States. By the 1960s postwar mores governing heterosexual relations and especially women's sexual respectability had strained to the breaking point. The approval of oral contraceptives by the U.S. government in 1960 perhaps more than anything brought about sweeping changes in sexual activity and weakened the social stigmas attached to sex outside the confines of marriage and reproduction. As the pill offered American women a more accessible and affordable way to assert control over sexual activity and its repercussions, cultural producers turned more often and openly to sex for popular appeal. The Playboy Clubs that the magazine publisher Hugh Hefner opened in several American cities in the 1960s gained immediate attention and perhaps best signified the increasingly close cultural relationship between sexual provocation and respectable entertainment. At the new nightclubs celebrities and wealthy urbanities bought expensive memberships to enjoy comedy and jazz performances as well as cocktail service by the fabled "Bunnies," young, buxom women in skimpy costumes. With a strict look-but-don't-touch policy governing Bunnies' scripted interactions with customers, the Playboy Clubs melded a stylized display of overtly sexualized female bodies with decorum of a sort. The popular début in 1953 of Hefner's magazine *Playboy*, a self-styled arbiter of bachelor consumerism and sexual gratification, had challenged postwar ideals of propriety for white, middle-class male breadwinners. But the Playboy Clubs' success brought sexually tinged entertainment more firmly into the mainstream.[7]

For advertisers in the 1960s, including airlines, sexual suggestiveness offered an increasingly unrisky way to tout the happiness and gratification that customers could expect from a product or service. "Personal" messages increasingly blurred with sexual messages on Madison Avenue. The airlines in particular had a ready-made corps of young, single, attractive female bodies with which to eroticize their corporate personalities. Mary Wells, the most influential advertising executive to handle an airline account in the 1960s, explained her efforts to spice up Braniff's image in simple yet revealing terms in 1967. Wells told *Business Week*, "When a tired businessman gets on an airplane, we think he ought to be allowed to look at a pretty girl." Of course, restrictive airline employment policies since the 1930s had meant that nearly every American air traveler saw and was served by a "pretty girl." But what Wells suggested was different. A visual display of young, white, feminine allure had become an entitlement of the tired businessman, who could attach to it whatever erotic fantasies he liked. By the early 1970s, as we will see, obvious sexual teases like "Fly Me" and "We Really Move Our Tails for You" had taken firm hold as a predominant theme in airline marketing. The process started earlier and more subtly, with jet-age airlines' ever-loftier promises to please passengers.[8]

Predictably, stewardesses were featured centrally in suggestions that genuine corporate concern, flattering attention, and wholesome or erotic fun were all included in the price of a jet ticket. Since the 1930s stewardesses had been ubiquitous in airline advertising. But by the 1960s they carried even more figurative weight as the embodiments of airlines' mass-marketed personalities. Gone were generic references to friendly staff alongside offers of specific services and amenities; in came promises of a hand-picked servant for every passenger. An advertisement for Eastern from 1967, for instance, titled "Presenting the Losers," pictured a group of nineteen applicants whom the carrier had rejected for stewardess positions. The attractive, slender, and well-groomed "losers" were distinguishable from "winners" only by their frowns and lack of airline uniforms. The text explained that they "were probably good enough to get a job practically anywhere they want," but that because of its high standards of appearance, intelligence, and personality, Eastern turned down nineteen desirable candidates for every exemplary one hired. With mock defensiveness, the ad read, "Sure, we want her to be pretty . . . don't you? That's why we look at her face, her make-up, her complexion, her figure, her weight, her legs, her grooming, her nails and her hair." In addition, Eastern boasted, it screened each applicant for "her personality, her maturity, her intelligence, her intentions, her enthusiasm, her resiliency and her stamina." With such an exhaustive list of qualifications, readers may have marveled (or doubted) that women so wondrous existed, let alone would serve them on Eastern.[9]

Even when jet-age airlines continued the older advertising tradition of specifying the amenities on offer, the emphasis was still on stewardesses' boundless capacity to please anyone. On "the friendly skies" of United, passengers were encouraged to expect signature "extra care." A print advertisement in 1967 opined, "Every United stewardess knows a Friday night face when she sees one. It's the tired face of a businessman who's put in a hard week and just wants to go home." The carrier promised hors d'oeuvres, steak, lobster, a favorite drink, a pillow, and films or music—depending of course on what the passenger felt like having. "Some people want to be fussed over. Some don't. Extra care is different for every passenger. But they all get it." Notably, the accompanying photograph suggested that superlative service included sexual arousal: the man with the "Friday night face" leered at his personal provider of extra care.[10]

In 1969 Delta Airlines ran a full-page advertisement titled "No Floor Show, Just a Working Girl Working" that captured what was new in the jet age, and what had not changed, in airlines' glamorization of steward-esses. The color photo in Delta's ad showed a brightly smiling, blonde stewardess striding confidently down a cabin aisle to deliver a meal. Based in the Bible Belt, Delta shied away from the growing trend in the 1960s toward bolder sexual innuendo and the objectification of stewardesses. Indeed, the ad's title proclaimed that Delta stewardess service was "no floor show," and the photograph reinforced its wholesomeness by show-ing the stewardess to have impressed a smiling female passenger in par-ticular. But while avoiding sexual connotations, Delta's ad put exemplary jet-age emphasis on corporate personality and caring as conveyed by the stewardess. The small print explained, "This is for real. No model. No put-on smiles. Her name is Carol Koberlein." Prospective passengers thus had an authentic name to attach to the smiling, trim figure in the photo. Yet to reinforce the homogeneous appeal of Delta cabin attendants, the text hastened to add that the one pictured could be any one of the 1,724 on its staff. "In her new chic outfit," the fine print continued, "she looks like anything but a stewardess working. But work she does. Hard, too. *And you hardly know it.*" The phrase, "and [rather than 'but'] you hardly know it," told readers that an appearance of effortlessness while doing hard work was not a surprising, laudable achievement but rather a re-quired part of how stewardesses did their job. But since Carol's smile was sincere, "not put-on," serving passengers was not really work to her at all. Carol, of course, was hardly "just a working girl working."[11]

With air travel becoming more commonplace in an increasingly service-oriented economy, airline marketers worked harder to deny that stewardesses were merely one contingent in the expanding army of cus-tomer service workers in transport and other industries. In the jet age, airline marketing continued to obscure stewardesses' labor and skills as airline-promoted glamorization long had done. Indeed, jet-age airlines' commercial messages only reinforced stewardesses' image of feminine nurture and allure with new vigor—and with a new ironic twist of letting passengers in on the industry secret of mass-producing personalized enchantment. In concluding, the Delta "No Floor Show" advertisement declared that Carol's utmost triumph as "just a working girl working" was to put the spotlight on the passenger: "It's no floor show," the Delta ad repeated in its final lines, "But it's funny how you get to feel like a leading man." If passenger service was not a "put-on," jet-age airlines nonetheless invited the tired businessman to imagine himself as an airborne star of a romantic epic, high-tech adventure, or idyllic domestic scene. All the leading man had to do was buy a jet ticket, and then watch and enjoy as a pretty girl served him with apparent effortlessness.

"EXTRA CARE" AT BREAKNECK SPEED

Jet-age airline advertisements that promised "extra care" and the like made flight attendants' job more challenging by raising passengers' expectations of customized service, genuine smiles, and perhaps flirtation as well. Flight attendants' work was made far more difficult by the central and unadvertised reality of the jet age: extra care had to be delivered to more passengers in less time. The arrival of jets confronted flight attendants with a large-scale and permanent "speed-up" in their work. As flight times fell steadily on successive generations of jets from the late 1950s to the late 1960s, flight attendants needed to complete in considerably less time essentially the same service duties as in earlier years, or even more. Flight attendants also faced "stretch-outs," because each cabin crewmember served more passengers on each flight on the larger, more crowded jets. While resistance from flight attendants placed limits on the stretch-outs, the advent of jets brought permanent, dramatic increases in workloads and time constraints.

While flight attendants had experienced increases in service duties and decreases in flight times over preceding decades, the speed-ups and stretch-outs that arrived with jets were unprecedented in their abruptness and intensity. Against union protests, airlines transferred "crew complement" policies (the number of flight attendants assigned to work flights) from smaller, slower planes to new jets. Virtually overnight, flight attendants found themselves serving upwards of twice as many passengers in as little as half the time. In 1963 an official for the flight attendants' union explained typical recent developments at Eastern Airlines. In the days of the piston aircraft, one attendant typically served twenty to thirty passengers, with "no liquor or champagne service or choice of meals offered" on most flights. On jets, cabin crew had to cope with added liquor and meal services and a crew-passenger ratio of one attendant to as many as fifty-one passengers. While older aircraft "lumbered along" at about 250 miles an hour, "jets are zipping along at 600 M.P.H. cutting cabin service time—in some cases—nearly in half." Management, he contended, had "hardly recognized" the problems of understaffing on jets and was "unwilling to formulate an equitable solution." Flight attendants perpetually lobbied federal regulators for higher minimum crew requirements. But aside from a basic standard by the early 1960s of three attendants for any flight carrying ninety-nine or more passengers, incremental changes to government rules generally did little to prevent what flight attendants considered the unsafe as well as unduly stressful understaffing of jet cabins.[12]

Jet-age workloads quickly became a central issue in union demands and protests. As early as 1959 TWA cabin crew threatened to strike over their suspicions that working on jets caused health problems, including swollen limbs, excessive fatigue, and menstrual irregularities. They demanded a reduction in hours until further research determined the medical consequences of jet duty. When Eastern flight attendants picketed during a contract dispute in March 1965, one nine-year veteran on the picket line told a reporter for the *Washington Post*, "The traveling public doesn't realize how much work it is. As far as they're concerned, we're just someone to smile at them and give them something to eat." In the 1960s the unions enjoyed limited success in reducing the maximum hours demanded of flight attendants, winning better pay with special incentives for jet duty, and negotiating marginally lower flight-attendant-to-passenger ratios. Yet they were never able to ease the time pressures that came with shorter jet trips, nor reverse the basic increases in workload—serving more passengers on each flight and working more flights each month.[13]

For flight attendants, time pressures and understaffing on jets were made worse by airlines' heightened sense of competition in providing "luxury" service. In 1968 United's manager of dining service planning explained to the *New York Times* why airlines remained committed to elaborate service despite falling flight times (and flight attendants' complaints). "Today, we're in a most competitive position. We're putting more and more on flights, to be served in less time. More of everything—liquor, food, meals and sandwiches. . . . Airplanes are much the same and so are the flight times. You get down to a few basic service factors, such as food, that can determine whether you get the business." Eastern's dining service manager allowed that trying to squeeze too many services into a short time could backfire. On the briefest flights, she confessed, "The girls run so fast all you see is a blur. It doesn't add to our image of 'substance and quality.'" Not surprisingly, the stewardesses interviewed for the same article in the *Times* painted an even grimmer picture: "You feel like you're throwing food at people . . . They ought to give us roller skates."[14]

Rather than brook flight attendants' demands for staffing increases or scale back services, jet-age airlines focused instead on improving efficiency in the mass production of passenger care. The result for flight attendants was a changed labor process that contradictorily entailed more routinized manual labor as well as more demanding mental and emotional labor that resisted routinizing. In pursuit of efficiency, jet-age airlines developed more technologically advanced, carefully orchestrated methods of packaging and delivering meals, drinks, and entertainment. More than ever before, flight attendants were the final links in airline service assembly lines. Following rigid management-defined schedules and procedures, and with the aid of increasingly elaborate equipment, flight attendants distributed the meals, drinks, movies, and other material trappings of airborne luxury that were supposed to keep passengers contented. As the sociologist Roberta Lessor has described, the "object-work" of passenger service (as opposed to "people-work") became more rationalized and simplified: management took a firmer hand in plotting the means and methods of service delivery, and flight attendants carried out their assigned tasks more quickly and repetitiously.[15]

Flight attendants thus experienced a belated service-work version of what the Marxist critic Harry Braverman broadly defined in 1974 as "the degradation of work in the twentieth century." As Braverman and many labor historians have argued, the principles of "scientific" management pioneered by Frederick Winslow Taylor at the turn of the century inspired a large-scale reorganization of work in factories and offices over successive decades. Signature innovations were increasingly elaborate divisions of labor, more centralized planning and control, and widespread mechanization—all of which eroded workers' skills and non-manual input. Jet-age airlines "Taylorized" flight attendants' work to the extent that they could, with more centralized organization of service routines and more mechanical aids for service delivery. So the "deskilling" and "degradation" of work that Braverman and others have lamented affected flight attendants to some degree. Flight attendants themselves recognized the change by referring to the "mindless" or "robot-like" aspects of their work.[16]

The "people-work" that flight attendants did resisted rationalization, however. Creating a pleasant and safe atmosphere in an airliner cabin, responding to impromptu requests, and exuding attractiveness made for labor not easily broken into simplified tasks or carefully supervised from a central office, let alone automated. Airlines employed "check riders," disguised as passengers, who monitored flight attendants' performance but had very limited ability to manage cabin crew labor in-flight. Supervision, after all, had to be backstage, or it might undermine the ideal of gracious service. At least some of the customers, moreover, inevitably intruded on the best-laid plans for efficient service delivery. As a stewardess complained to the *New York Times* in 1968, "The airlines have spoiled their passengers—taught them to be demanding." Managers could plot service routines and safety procedures, and even suggest in advance scripts for interactions with passengers. Once a flight began, it was flight attendants, individually and as a team, who had to figure out how best to tackle the particular service and safety demands of a given trip.[17]

Thus for flight attendants any "deskilling" in the jet age was far less troubling than the way speed-up and routinization clashed with ideals of gracious, personalized service. Passenger care could be only partly routinized under new time pressures, and routinization itself was bound to annoy some of the passengers. Annoyed passengers, in turn, made the non-routine aspects of service all the more difficult. As a stewardess for United told *Newsweek* at the start of 1968, "To get the work done, you absolutely have to be short with the passengers." Her contention was borne out by a time-motion study, a favored method of the Taylorist search for efficiency. As *Newsweek* noted, the study had found that stewardesses had exactly twenty-three seconds on average to interact with each passenger, based on 122 passengers and an eighty-five minute flight. But when a harried jet-age stewardess managed to achieve time-motion efficiency, she risked alienating passengers. A Pan Am stewardess explained, "The ads promise [passengers] they'll be coddled every minute of the flight. I just can't coddle 130 people at one time. But they all expect it and they get downright rude when they don't get it." The job had come to mean, in another stewardess's words, "food under your fingernails, sore feet, complaints and insults."[18]

THE CHANGING CUSTOMERS

An expanding and more unruly passenger population further complicated flight attendants' labor and threatened its rewards. As we have seen, when flight attendants complained about the jet-age speed-up, they blamed the problem in part on how "demanding" and potentially "rude" customers had become. Customers' unhappiness with sped-up service indeed worsened jet-age workloads for flight attendants—but the growing problems of cabin service went beyond just the speed-up. Exactly two decades into the jet age, two veteran stewardesses painted a stark portrait of what they considered the troubling changes in the passenger population over preceding years. They told a reporter for the *Chicago Tribune* in 1978, "The cheap fares and the charter flights allow all kinds of people to fly who never used to fly before . . . The barroom brawlers, the drunks, the types who get violent, the kind with no class at all." While some elitism was surely at play in these stewardesses' complaint, to a harried jet-age flight attendant the "class" desired in passengers had less to do with wealth or breeding than with courtesy and sobriety.[19]

Flight attendants did not have to be snobbish to find the benefits of association with passengers more elusive in the jet age. In his landmark analysis of the rise of the white-collar class in twentieth-century America, C. Wright Mills observed in 1951 that sales clerks drew satisfaction from their work by "borrowing prestige" from their affluent clientele and the merchandise and décor of fashionable stores. Yet Mills noted that the effort fared better in the more intimate environment of a small-town boutique, where customers were known by name, than in a large and impersonal urban department store. The advent of the jet age affected flight attendants' prospects for borrowing prestige in similar ways. At mid-century, when well-heeled air travelers enjoyed leisurely flights on roomy, well-appointed planes, flight attendants could borrow plenty of prestige from both customer and setting. In 1952 a stewardess described the job as more fun than work, because "you have a chance to sit down and visit with people who are just coming back from a world tour or fascinating holiday," or "maybe you meet a combat veteran, excited over his homecoming." By the jet age, the customers were no longer so exclusive a group, but more important, flight attendants' encounters with them were increasingly abbreviated. Flight attendants could no longer expect as much gratification from personal contacts. Moreover, as *Newsweek* quipped in 1968, the jet-age stewardess had "hardly enough time to recognize Mr. Right, much less dazzle him."[20]

Worse to flight attendants than any sacrifices in passenger-afforded prestige was that the behavior of airline customers, whatever their socioeconomic status, was becoming more erratic. The sociologist Roberta Lessor reported of her interviews with flight attendants in the late 1970s, "I have often heard nostalgia expressed on the part of the older flight attendants for the by-gone years when a 'better class of passengers flew.' Even those too young to actually be nostalgic are wont to say, 'Now we're just the bus in the sky; we get everything.'" But as Lessor cautioned, what her informants were "expressing is not nostalgia for a rich and important passenger, but rather nostalgia for a *predictable* passenger." As memoirs by flight attendants make clear, the privileged and powerful are as capable as anyone of stunningly bad in-flight behavior. Under the conditions of the speed-up, as Lessor argued, the non-routine work of handling difficult passengers, which might have been a welcome challenge to flight attendants' intellect and creativity, instead became a resented distraction from completing service routines. When a union representative solicited "gripes" from stewardesses at Southern Airlines in 1972, two wits listed their chief complaint as "The _____ Passengers! Get rid of them."[21]

The swelling number and growing diversity of passengers alone meant serving and maintaining order among a more complicated mix of humanity. But airline marketing and service policies in the jet age made matters worse by encouraging heavy drinking and chaos aloft. Cocktail and wine service had taken firm hold in the airline industry before the jet age, but now the flow of liquor was ever freer. The result for flight attendants was not only more repetitive manual labor in serving drinks but an amplification of liquor's effects on passengers' behavior. In principle, flight attendants were authorized by airline policies (and eventually government safety rules) to bar drunk travelers from ordering more alcohol or even from boarding in the first place. In practice, their ability to control liquor consumption was severely limited by their employers' and customers' expectations of unfailing courtesy. As a former flight attendant for Pan Am recalled of her shock at finding how difficult her new job was in the mid-1960s, "Try to force a drunk passenger in the back of the cabin to sit down and stop throwing cigarette butts on the floor with gentleness." As early as 1955 the flight attendants' union received word of a drunk passenger who had threatened his seatmate with a switchblade. By 1972, when union safety officials asked members for reports of inebriated passengers' misbehavior, the responses within a month suggested how widespread and dangerous the problem was. The union's newsletter reprinted excerpts from just a few of the more horrific encounters, which included instances of passengers wielding knives, choking and punching flight attendants, and assaulting fellow passengers, not to mention vomiting repeatedly.[22]

The laxity of airline regulations governing carry-on baggage as planes grew more crowded constituted an additional annoyance for cabin crew and potential danger. In 1967 a national newsletter for the flight attendants' union reported that in the two years since liberalized baggage allowances were introduced, "passenger compartments were stuffed with all sorts of strange items," including "portable TV sets, patio umbrellas, a tuba, aqualungs, tricycles, huge hunting trophies and . . . a kitchen sink! . . . We'll never find out just how that kitchen sink was safely and securely stowed." As flight attendants complained, the impossibility of stowing oversize items and excess luggage made the cabin an obstacle course in normal circumstances, but more important, threatened the prospect for speedy evacuation in an emergency. Airlines vacillated on what specific restrictions there should be to meet federal safety guidelines, but were loath to anger passengers by advertising and enforcing them in any case. An inquiry by the Federal Aviation Administration in 1972 uncovered numerous lapses in enforcing federal rules on baggage stowage as well as widespread reports from flight attendants that they had been "severely criticized and threatened by company supervisors for trying to limit the size and amount of baggage being carried on board by passengers."[23]

As chaotic as regular flying became, charter flights were a particular breeding ground for bizarre episodes. Commercial charters grew in popularity in the jet age as a means for travelers to get group discounts and for airlines to maximize use of their costly fleets. Because charters were irregular, airline policies and procedures were looser. In 1971 a stewardess who worked for the Alaska-based carrier Wein Airlines lodged a remarkable complaint during a union discussion of safety about the "cargo" she had confronted on a recent charter flight to a dog show. Over one hundred passengers brought nearly as many dogs along in the cabin. "Can they legally do that?," she wondered. "They said because it was a charter, they could do it." In 1968 a stewardess with Southern Airlines reported a more predictable kind of mayhem. When a men's group from Atlanta chartered a flight to a professional football game, the fraternity-like exploits culminated in such an intense "pursuit" of the stewardesses that the women had to hide in the cockpit until the captain grounded the flight.[24]

As if speed-ups, drunks, kitchen sinks, and canine "passengers" were not enough to bedevil flight attendants, there were still other provocations. The list of new and growing grievances for flight attendants in the jet age could go on and on—from airline attempts to employ foreign nationals as cheaper, non-union labor on desirable international routes, to supervisors' demands that flight attendants take on additional work in cleaning planes (a duty that belonged contractually to other workers). Suffice it to say that flight attendants had more reasons than ever before to find glamour lacking—and exploitation by their employers intensifying—in the daily grind of "extra care" on packed flights.

All these grievances took a toll on individual flight attendants in exhaustion and workplace dissatisfaction. And the growing problems of passenger service produced a jarring dissonance between reality for cabin crew and the image that the airlines worked so hard to cultivate. A female reporter for the *Des Moines Register* wittily suggested how durable stewardesses' image of allure was, even under supposed threat from jet-age realities. Under the headline "Meet the Girl Who Wears Those Silver Wings and a Big Smile," the profile began, "The airline stewardess, 1965, has one of the most frustrating jobs in the world. Male passengers expect her to look like a Las Vegas showgirl, and are angry when she doesn't. Female passengers are angry when she does, and are fond of calling her a 'flying waitress.' Bachelors say she's not as glamorous as she used to be, yet would trade their collection of James Bond paperbacks for a date with her."[25]

Nevertheless, that enviable image was wearing thin for flight attendants themselves as a reward for increasingly difficult work. When two veteran stewardesses described what it was like to be a "hostess" in 1967, their answer was marked by avowed ambivalence: the typical stewardess both "loved" and "hated" flying for a living. "On her good days," they explained, "she is a hostess, the official greeter, the gracious lady of the house entertaining in her 'home.' On bad days she merely puts in time as a drudge, a bored but 'glorified waitress.' " The women hastened to add, "It is the good days that are important to her when she officiates at her gala party in the air." But it was the bad days that were the increasing reality of the jet age.[26]

GROWING WORKFORCE, MORE BLATANT SEX DISCRIMINATION

Even as jet-age stewardessing had come to seem more like "glorified" waitressing, the job grew more exceptional in its discriminatory employment restrictions. While airlines did not meet new labor demands on jets with as many new hires as overburdened flight attendants would have liked, they nonetheless recruited and hired cabin staff in spiraling numbers. The nation's flight attendant workforce doubled in just seven years, from less than ten thousand in 1960 to more than twenty thousand by 1967. Perpetually high turnover rates among the women who made up nearly the entire workforce intensified airlines' recruitment needs, already growing because of expanded jet operations. Airlines might have eased the hiring crunch by waiving marital restrictions for stewardesses, or by hiring more men along with women. A few waived the no-marriage rule, but most did not, and nearly all stopped hiring men altogether. Instead airlines took even greater pains to ensure that stewardesses remained a youthful, nubile group by enforcing more rigid and anomalously discriminatory employment policies.[27]

When the occupation took shape in the 1930s, the airline industry's ban on marriage for stewardesses was but one example of broader and widely accepted prohibitions on married white women's employment, prohibitions which predated, but increased during, the Depression. By the mid-twentieth century, however, official bars to married women's employment had all but disappeared amid labor shortages in the booming economy. The postwar cultural climate prized homemaking as the sine qua non of women's social value and personal fulfillment, but economic and political imperatives also dictated the permanent mobilization of womanpower, including married white women, in the workforce. As postwar policymakers argued, women's paid labor was needed to expand production and stimulate consumption. And during the cold war against communism, the flourishing of American capitalism was also a crucial matter of national security. While postwar opinion-makers worried over the supposed dangers to family life of working wives and mothers, public policy and debate accorded unprecedented legitimacy to white married women's employment. Thus the airlines' decades-old ban on marriage for stewardesses became increasingly atypical and retrogressive. The economist Claudia Goldin concludes of general trends in married women's employment in the United States, "Discrimination never disappeared . . . But after 1950, the marriage bar vanished almost entirely (*except for flight attendants*)."[28]

A growing number of airlines added a new discriminatory policy to their stewardess employment rules in the 1950s and early 1960s, grounding female flight attendants at the age of thirty-two or thirty-five. As with no-marriage rules, airlines since the 1930s had imposed age limits in their initial employment of stewardesses, refusing to hire women past their late twenties. Airlines that employed male flight attendants required them to be no older than thirty-two or thirty-five at the time of hire. But during the 1950s and into the 1960s, several carriers instituted age limits in continued employment for stewardesses only. On most carriers that adopted such age rules, the flight attendants were exclusively female. But on Northwest and TWA, stewardesses faced age ceilings of thirty-two as of 1956 and thirty-five as of 1957, while male flight attendants could fly until they reached their sixties.[29]

As the flight attendant workforce had steadily expanded since the 1930s, so had the number of women who stayed in the job for several years, even while average tenure remained at two or three years. Some veterans took the few routes of career mobility available to female flight attendants, becoming stewardess supervisors or trainers, but most continued to serve passengers. Airlines minimized veteran male and female flight attendants' claims to economic rewards for time served by capping salary increases at eight to ten years and by not offering pension plans or other long-term benefits. But veteran stewardesses, even if relatively economical as long-term workers, still left airlines with the "problem" of employing maturing women in what was supposed to be a temporary sojourn between school and marriage.[30]

American Airlines pioneered the "solution" by declaring that as of 1 December 1953, it would ground stewardesses upon their thirty-second birthday. American's official rationale for the new policy was "based on the established qualifications for Stewardesses, which are attractive appearance, pleasant disposition, even temperament, neatness, unmarried status, and the ability and desire to meet and serve passengers. Basic among the qualifications is an attractive appearance. Such an appearance ordinarily is found to a higher degree in young women. Therefore, the establishment of an age limit will best effectuate and preserve the concept of Stewardess service as it is understood in this Company." The flight attendants' union newsletter retorted, "Since American has taken this position, they are required to support their inference that when a woman reaches the age of 32, she becomes unattractive, querulous, anti-social, and commutes to her job on a broom." "American must be a very courageous outfit," remarked a female reporter in the *Washington Post.* "After all, you don't tell a woman she's no longer charming at 32." Most of the American stewardesses interviewed by the reporter objected to the new rule; they doubted that women suddenly looked old at thirty-two and commented that "the senior gals are among the best." ALSSA objected strenuously to the new policy, but managed only to limit its implementation to new hires.[31]

Some carriers were quicker than others to follow American's lead, but by the mid-1960s fifteen of the thirty-eight federally certified airlines had adopted early mandatory retirement policies for stewardesses. Those carriers together employed nearly 9,000 stewardesses, more than 60 percent of around 14,500 then working in the industry. For the 2,200 female flight attendants then at TWA and the 160 at TransTexas and Southern, grounding came at the not-so-advanced age of thirty-five. Stewardesses employed by the other carriers with age ceilings saw their wings clipped even earlier, at thirty-two. A small minority of stewardesses held union-won "grandmother" exemptions from age ceilings because they were hired before the policies went into effect on various carriers (about 10 percent on TWA, for example). But the rare job security that "grandmothered" stewardesses enjoyed came at the cost of being the unwelcome exception to airlines' increasingly stringent demands for youthfulness.[32]

Several carriers promised to provide alternative employment for stewardesses deemed too old to fly, for example jobs in reservations or as passenger agents, in which they were apparently still acceptable to serve the flying public on the ground. Yet flight attendants charged that such promised ground jobs typically meant an inconvenient relocation and lower pay, or were simply not made available; in any case they were not the jobs to which supposedly "aged" stewardesses had devoted several years. As a writer for the *New York Post* explained in 1965, "Sitting in a back office answering phone calls is just not the same as flying to California twice a week." Little wonder that promises of alternative ground jobs did little to mollify stewardesses who had been told they were no longer glamorous or gracious at thirty-two.[33]

Individual airline rules varied, but most carriers considered it necessary to impose either an age limit or a no-marriage rule, if not both, to maintain the youthful feminine appeal of an expanding stewardess corps. In a significant departure, TWA decided in 1957 to let married hostesses keep their jobs. TWA reportedly dropped its no-marriage rule to relieve annual labor shortages; its hostesses tended to leave to get married in June and August, peak travel months. But not coincidentally, TWA imposed an age ceiling of thirty-five the very same year. Throughout the airline industry, the trend of the 1950s and early 1960s was toward more restrictive employment rules for female flight attendants—a trend increasingly out of step with the broader loosening of official employment strictures on women in the flourishing national economy. Flight attendants thus had to work harder in the jet age at a job with more blatant sex discrimination and even less job security.[34]

"OPEN SKIES FOR NEGRO GIRLS"?

As airlines introduced age ceilings and otherwise constricted further the career prospects of stewardesses, a handful of African American women successfully pressed for their right to join the transient, but glamorized, ranks of airline hostesses. To force any change in airlines' traditionally racist employment standards for stewardesses took enormous concerted efforts by applicants who were overqualified except by their racial identity, and by civil rights groups and sympathetic government officials. But with the help of the Urban League, the National Association for the Advancement of Colored People (NAACP), and New York State anti-discrimination authorities, a few black women managed to breach the color barrier in airline passenger service in the late 1950s and early 1960s.

The airline industry had never bothered to specify "whites only" in stewardess employment, but it did not have to: hiring standards had implicit racial as well as ethnic, religious, and class biases. In demanding exemplary social graces, an unusually attractive appearance, and a respectable background, airlines placed additional obstacles before all but white, middle- or upper-class, native-born, Christian women who met the already formidable age, marital status, educational, and physical requirements. In 1961 Mary O'Connor, a veteran flight attendant for United Airlines who worked as a stewardess supervisor and recruiter, revealed in print what she considered industry-wide assumptions concerning race and class. In her memoir cum career guide, a list of typical questions for prospective job applicants included, "Are your hands soft and white?" Hands that were not only white but also free from any evidence of arduous labor marked the desired stewardess candidate. A researcher in the mid-1960s found, moreover, that virtually all the stewardesses whom she profiled reported Protestant or Catholic backgrounds. The president of one of the two national flight attendant unions commented in 1965 that she knew of "only one girl of the Jewish faith" working as a stewardess.[35]

The few exceptions only proved the rule of racial and ethnic exclusivity. Carriers that operated in Hawaii and the Caribbean selectively employed Latina and Hawaiian attendants to lend exoticized "authenticity" to the travel experience for the growing number of postwar tourists bound for these romanticized destinations. When the giant carrier United won its first permanent overseas route connecting San Francisco and Honolulu in the late 1940s, it added a small corps of Hawaiian stewards to its otherwise entirely white and female flight attendant workforce. The stewards worked exclusively on the Hawaiian run to provide, in United's words, "local color." Aloha Airlines, a small carrier with routes among the Hawaiian Islands, offered an even more vibrant display of "local color" in the late 1950s: Aloha's "Island-born" stewardesses were the first flight attendants to provide regular, live "in-flight entertainment" in the form of singing, hula dancing, and ukulele playing.[36]

In the continental United States, however, airlines had no such exotic niches for hostesses or hosts of color. Only under persistent pressure from aspiring African American stewardesses, national civil rights groups, government officials, and a few high-profile politicians did airlines even begin to consider hiring black women. By the mid-1950s both the NAACP and the Urban League were fighting to integrate the airlines, with a particular eye on flight attendant and pilot jobs. New York State, which had a model anti-discrimination law, was the scene of the most important battles. By late 1957 rejected applicants had filed no fewer than seventeen charges of racial discrimination against airlines with the New York State Commission against Discrimination. Not surprisingly, major carriers drew the most attention: TWA was charged with racial bias in nine cases, American in four, and United in two. The smaller carrier Mohawk

Airlines was not among those formally charged, but it was the first to be persuaded by New York authorities to employ an African American woman for passenger service, in December 1957: Ruth Carol Taylor, who became the first African American flight attendant to work for an airline in the United States. Soon after, TWA relented in the face of a state investigation in the spring of 1958 and hired Margaret Grant, the first African American stewardess on a leading carrier. In October 1959 the New York City branch of the Congress of Racial Equality (CORE) seized on these breakthroughs by leading a protest march through Manhattan and encouraging African Americans to patronize TWA and explicitly congratulate the carrier on hiring a black stewardess.[37]

The two hard-fought victories on Mohawk and TWA were followed by more arduous struggle. Though airlines had been promising to change their ways, no more African Americans had been hired as flight attendants by mid-size or large airlines by 1960. Some airlines turned away black applicants for such alleged flaws as overwide hips and "unshapely" legs, while others did not bother with explanations. The next breakthrough came at the nation's fifth-largest carrier at the time, Capital Airlines, only by order of the New York State Commission against Discrimination (NYSCAD). Patricia Banks solicited an NYSCAD investigation of racial bias at Capital after the carrier had inexplicably refused to hire her. Banks, a graduate of Grace Downs's Air Careers School, had faired sufficiently well in Capital's initial screening process in 1956 to win employment as a stewardess. She had earned a "B+" rating from the chief hostess, which in the carrier's personnel parlance meant "accepted for future employment." But the chief hostess, at the urging of Capital's director of passenger service, changed the status of Banks's file to "see again." When Capital failed to follow up with Banks, and then to make clear why it would not hire her, she took Congressman Adam Clayton Powell's advice and filed a complaint. NYSCAD, after a public hearing, ruled in February 1960 that Capital had illegally discriminated against Banks because of her race, and must hire her. In May 1960, four years after first applying to Capital, Banks finally began work as a stewardess.[38]

Even after being hired African American stewardesses continued to face harassment, as Marlene White found on Northwest Airlines in the early 1960s. Northwest employed White as its second black stewardess in 1962 (she had held a back-office job with the carrier since 1959) only under order of the Michigan Fair Employment Practices Commission. The airline singled her out for degrading treatment, according to White, and then fired her with no just cause. Though White had graduated in the upper third of her stewardess training class, as she later explained to a union official, Northwest had threatened to fire her if she did not consent in writing to the continuation of her probationary status beyond the standard six months. She complied in order not to be fired, but after an additional eight months Northwest terminated her anyway. Her discharge was based on the claim that she had failed to demonstrate sufficient knowledge and proficiency in emergency procedures. "I was given many more tests, both oral and written, on emergency procedures than the other stewardesses," White recalled, all of which she believed she passed. "I have done graduate work in economics at the University of Chicago and have educational qualifications of the sort that makes it impossible for me to believe my grades and discharge were other than discriminatory." National officials of the Air Line Stewards and Stewardesses Association, White's union, filed another complaint on her behalf with the Michigan Fair Employment Practices Commission, and also complained of her dismissal to the President's Commission on Equal Employment Opportunity, citing Northwest's federal contracts as imposing an obligation not to discriminate. Northwest relented, and White resumed her stewardess career eight months later, in December 1963.[39]

By the mid-1960s the perseverance of White and like-minded African American women, and their increasingly powerful allies, forced the entire airline industry at least to begin integrating cabin crews. In 1963, no less a personage than Vice President Lyndon B. Johnson, as head of the President's Commission on Equal Employment Opportunity, made the hiring of black stewardesses a personal cause (and one that he liked to spotlight for the press). His phone calls to airline heads certainly helped move the nearly decade-long fight along. By 1965 seven of the largest eleven airlines in the United States employed black women as stewardesses, and there were approximately fifty African American stewardesses all told in the United States, an exceedingly small but symbolically significant number in a flight attendant workforce of about fifteen thousand. (In 1966 black workers accounted for 3 to 5 percent of the entire airline workforce.) After racial discrimination in employment became illegal throughout the United States under the Civil Rights Act of 1964, airlines began aggressively recruiting African American women. United, American, and others began advertising in black publications, recruiting at historically black colleges, and soliciting referrals from federal job program administrators and the Urban League. As a result, the number of

African American stewardesses on the nation's largest carrier, United, grew from ten in July 1965 to thirty by late 1966, and at American from eleven in mid-1965 to twenty-two by the end of 1966. In May 1967 Joan Dorsey, the first African American stewardess employed by American Airlines in 1963, achieved another landmark as the first black stewardess supervisor in the United States. Just a few months before, American had been singled out for praise by the historic black newspaper the *Chicago Defender* for its "quiet revolution" in implementing equal employment policies. As the number of black passengers grew in the jet age, airlines had even more incentive to employ black stewardesses.[40]

The "quiet revolution" was still to come on other carriers. In 1965 Braniff claimed that it could not find any qualified black candidates for in-flight positions, and in 1970 one of the nation's most prominent civil rights organizations, the Southern Christian Leadership Conference, launched a boycott against Delta Airlines. The group protested that Delta, based in Atlanta, had failed as of 1970 to hire more than a token few African American workers above the level of maintenance personnel. When an aspiring flight attendant of Cuban descent applied for a job with National in 1973, she was told by her interviewer to apply to Pan Am instead, because they "have a more international image."[41]

Even where hiring bars had fallen, moreover, a warm welcome did not always await. Shocked stares and verbal abuse from passengers as well as hostility from some co-workers continued to mark African American stewardesses as unwelcome exceptions. Darker-skinned women faced distinct barriers. As a New York State investigator of airline racial bias explained in 1966, a "white esthetic" worked to exclude "a large proportion of well-qualified applicants with such physical features as dark skin complexions and certain hair textures." Joanne Fletcher, who described herself to the historian Helen McLaughlin as "*black* black," applied to several airlines in 1967. She recalled that her written applications were well received but that she was repeatedly rejected in interviews. "I got the idea," she remembered, "that I was too noticeably black." Fletcher's persistence eventually impressed a personnel officer at Eastern, who hired her in July 1967. When Fletcher arrived for her first flight, she encountered "stony stares" from her fellow crewmembers, who refused to acknowledge her. Soon after, a white female passenger "shrieked" when Fletcher brought her dinner tray, and she later refused to allow Fletcher to handle her coat at the end of the flight.[42]

Hostility was merely one form of the racism that continued to plague

African American stewardesses. Sheila McNutt, who worked on Pan Am's Caribbean routes in the early 1970s and spoke Spanish as needed, recalled a troubling exchange with a white American female passenger. The woman told her, "Oh, you're so pretty! My goodness, your English is so nice! My husband thinks you're from Jamaica, but I bet you're from Trinidad." McNutt recalled the response when she said, "I'm from Philadelphia": "their faces dropped, and you could tell I was only attractive as long as I was exotic. As an American, I was no longer of interest." Some black flight attendants felt themselves especially vulnerable to sexual harassment, particularly from pilots. One recalled in 1972 that she had met many white men on the job "looking for their 'black experience.'" Airlines, by contrast, avoided any "exotic" connotations in employing African American women by imposing implicitly white appearance standards on them. Afro hairstyles, for example, were among those forbidden in the late 1960s and early 1970s. One former flight attendant, Kathleen Heenan, remembered that her airline, TWA, required African American stewardesses in the late 1960s to straighten their hair as part of an overall process through which they "were made to sort of look white."[43]

In the spring of 1963 *Ebony* welcomed the desegregation of stewardess work with the headline "Open Skies for Negro Girls." A columnist in the *Chicago Defender* celebrated too, if more hesitantly, later that year, when American Airlines sent its first black stewardess aloft. "These jet airlines are moving at a snail's pace on hiring Negroes—but we're really thankful for these small blessings. Honest." While any integration was of symbolic significance and cause for the black press to cheer, the token hiring of black stewardesses did little to challenge the normative whiteness of passenger service work. And unfortunately for African American women, their entry to the flight attendant occupation coincided with the growing challenges and burdens of the jet age. But although pioneering black stewardesses' victory was imperfect, it was still impressive. They had forced racial integration on a high-profile industry and demanded that the wages of glamour no longer be available only to white women. As one black flight attendant told a reporter in 1972, "After all, next to being a movie star or beauty queen, no position or job so tenaciously heralds a woman's beauty and femininity."[44]

Eventually token integration gave way to more substantial diversity. By the start of the 1970s there were almost a thousand black stewardesses at work on American carriers, about 3 percent of the workforce. Overall, a study in 1971 found that about 6 percent of flight attendants were of nonwhite racial heritage, including not only African Americans (45 percent) but also Latinas (33 percent), Asian Americans (21 percent), and Native Americans (1 percent). By then airlines were also no longer as biased toward light-skinned women and had stopped encouraging African American stewardesses to bid only for "safe" assignments, that is, to avoid areas like the American South, where they might provoke more hostility from passengers.[45]

By the accounts of the first African American stewardesses, a good number of white flight attendants did not want to share their workplace and image of glamour with women of color. The *New York Times* contended in late 1957 that the airlines' reluctance to hire black women was at least partly based on fear that white women would flee "if the 'glamor' of the job were 'down-graded' by employment of Negro girls." After all, flight attendants collectively enjoyed the racial privilege conveyed by whiteness generally and more particularly by glamour. As attacks on racism in airline hiring grew, flight attendant unionists remained on the sidelines. While professing support for racial equality in principle and backing Marlene White in her dispute with Northwest, the unions otherwise declined to address airline racism in any palpable way in the late 1950s and 1960s. Union contracts included racial nondiscrimination clauses by the mid-1960s, but that was hardly a radical development after years of civil rights pressure on airlines and the passage of a federal nondiscrimination act in 1964.[46]

Yet white stewardesses did not flee en masse when their celebrated occupation was desegregated, nor did their union actively oppose integration. Whether individual stewardesses and their union representatives championed, resented, or were indifferent about the end of their occupation's lily-white status, few could have failed to notice that the civil rights struggle was gaining momentum and had extended into their own workplace. Some might even have reflected on how racial discrimination mirrored the increasingly blatant gender discrimination that they themselves suffered, as age ceilings spread in the late 1950s and early 1960s and the no-marriage rule endured nearly alone on airlines.

There was only so much that stewardesses could do to mitigate the speedups, preposterous promises of "extra care," misbehaving passengers, and other challenges of the jet age. But when liberal egalitarian ideals took firmer hold in the culture and politics of the United States in the 1960s, white stewardesses were quick to recognize that at least one of their grievances, forced early retirement, was suddenly ripe for airing. And air it they did, in a more militant and successful stream of protests than flight attendants had ever before attempted. But like the African American women who made the first successful assaults on airline discrimination in the late 1950s, they would find that airline employment habits would take a fearsome amount of struggle to change.

"DO I LOOK LIKE AN OLD BAG?"

Glamour and Women's Rights
in the Mid-1960s

On 17 April 1963 a small group of activists from the Air Line Stewards and Stewardesses Association struck a shrewd public relations
blow against age discrimination by the airlines. The contract for
American Airlines stewardesses had expired in 1962; one of the sticking
points in protracted negotiations was the union's demand that American
end retirement at thirty-two. After the union called for federal mediation, several activists decided to take their case to the court of public
opinion. "Over-age" stewardesses invited reporters and the public to
decide for themselves if the women no longer embodied the airlines'
famously high standards of attractiveness. At a press conference in New
York City, eight stewardesses turned out who were clear-complexioned,
perfectly groomed, slender, and stylishly uniformed to a one, but who
ranged in age from the twenty-three to thirty-six. The women dared
reporters to find what was wrong with the supposedly unattractive
among them, that is, the four who were past age thirty-two but continued
to fly with union-won "grandmother" exemptions from early retirement.
Barbara "Dusty" Roads, a thirty-five-year-old union lobbyist, even asked,
"Do I look like an old bag?" The response in the local and national news
media was a resounding no. A photographer snapped the women in a
lineup, and when the photo ran in several newspapers, readers were
invited to guess which four of the attractive, smiling stewardesses were
over thirty-two.[1]

While airlines had instituted "early retirement" policies as much as a decade earlier, the policies only began to threaten the jobs of a significant number of stewardesses in the mid-1960s. Because union protests had won waivers for stewardesses already employed when airlines adopted age rules, the most veteran stewardesses, like Roads, were exempt. The vast majority of stewardesses who did not enjoy "grandmother rights" tended to leave the job quickly because of airlines' no-marriage rules. American carriers would not hire women older than twenty-six to twenty-eight years of age for stewardess positions, and most were in their early twenties when hired, so few stayed long enough to reach thirty-two. Thus it was not until the mid-1960s that more than a handful of steward-esses suffered the affront of an exceedingly early retirement.[2]

More important, the delayed impact of the airlines' age ceilings came at a time when sex-biased employment rules in general were coming under new legal attack and public scrutiny in the United States. Flight atten-dants eagerly embraced new opportunities to challenge airline age lim-its and marriage prohibitions under the growing number of legal con-straints on discrimination in private employment. As airlines would find to their chagrin too, when stewardesses pleaded their case before the public, most policymakers and media commentators roundly rejected the proposition that feminine allure evaporated at thirty-two. In the mid-1960s, amid the resurgence of feminism, female flight attendants found more fertile legal and cultural ground than ever before to protest how their employers treated them.

Stewardesses began courting the national spotlight in 1963 with all the charm and attractiveness for which they were renowned and offered a pointed critique of airline discrimination. They did not question airlines' demand for alluring hostesses, but rather how restrictively female attrac-tiveness was defined and how little their skilled labor was valued. Were women really too old to be attractive at thirty-two? Was marriage really detrimental to stewardesses' ability to provide gracious service? Should a dangerous situation arise in flight, wouldn't an experienced, skilled stew-ardess be best qualified to assist passengers and possibly save their lives? Stewardesses made the most of the increasingly progressive times and their own cultural visibility to provoke public disfavor toward the air-lines' gender discrimination.

Stewardesses' strategy of harnessing the power of glamour to promote gender equality did carry the risk of having their protests all but buried in flattery and irreverence. Asking "Do I look like an old bag?" only invited

the kind of objectification with which stewardesses were all too familiar. More important, stewardesses' publicity and lobbying efforts in the
mid-1960s did not alone force material changes in airline policies. The
more the stewardesses attempted to mobilize new public policies and
public opinion against airline discrimination, the more the airlines called
upon their own political and financial resources to forestall change. African American activists had forced the industry to accept token racial
integration by the 1960s—but managers were not about to let the young,
white women who still defined and dominated cabin service force additional change in marketing ideals and employment policies without a
full-scale battle.

WAITING FOR TITLE VII

Flight attendants' assaults on airline sex discrimination in the 1960s grew
from seeds sown in earlier, less hospitable years, as with second-wave
feminism writ large. Postwar stewardesses joined many other women in
unions and other liberal and left institutions in protesting gender inequality at a time when "feminism" was among many "isms" suppressed by a
cold war intolerance of dissent. While organized flight attendants fought
an uphill battle for equal standing in the labor movement in the 1950s and
early 1960s, they also sought ways to undermine age ceilings and prohibitions against marriage. Though many postwar efforts to improve working
women's status found moderate success, especially in more progressive
industrial unions, flight attendants' challenges to gender discrimination
in their workplace were largely futile before the mid-1960s.[3]

Flight attendants began protesting sex discrimination soon after they
first organized in the late 1940s with the tools that unionization afforded,
namely collective bargaining and grievance machinery. The results in
collective bargaining were limited at best. When American Airlines introduced the first age ceiling of thirty-two for stewardesses at the end of
1953, protests by ALSSA forced two significant compromises, which set
the pattern for the spread of age ceilings. First, ALSSA managed to restrict the age limit to new hires. The union immediately saved the jobs
of sixty-four American Airlines stewardesses then already thirty-two or
older and set a precedent of so-called grandmother rights. Grandmother
rights not only protected veteran stewardesses' jobs at American and
other carriers. They also ensured that a few more mature stewardesses

would remain in the job as living evidence of how arbitrary the age ceilings were—a point well made by Dusty Roads and her colleagues at their press conference in 1963.[4]

Second, and less helpful ultimately, ALSSA refused to allow American to write the new age rule into the collective bargaining agreement between company and union. American imposed the age ceiling anyway, as a precondition of employment. New stewardesses then signed a pledge to resign "voluntarily" at thirty-two, a contract provision technically outside the parameters of collective bargaining. But while the union could not prevent the airline from adopting the age ceiling, keeping it out of the collective bargaining agreement indicated the union's noncompliance, or so union leaders hoped. On most airlines that adopted age rules, ALSSA forced management to impose the policy through individual pre-employment, not union, contracts.

Once age ceilings spread, ALSSA officials tried to bargain them away, along with the marriage prohibition. Airline negotiators balked at discussing union proposals, however, or offered unpalatable alternatives. Rowland Quinn, former president of ALSSA, recalled the response of negotiators for Aloha Airlines to the union's request to drop the ban on marriage in the 1950s: "We will negotiate for [stewardesses] to be pregnant but not married." Quinn remembered quipping to the Aloha officials, "Aren't you getting the cart before the horse?" In late 1961 representatives of Pacific Airlines management tentatively agreed to allow married stewardesses to continue working, but as the ALSSA newsletter explained, "insisted that they designate which married stewardesses they would retain and which they would release." ALSSA negotiators rejected the idea. When faced with airlines' intransigence, union officials devoted their energies instead to wages and other working conditions of immediate importance to all members. After all, union leaders could not necessarily count on strong backing from their parent unions (ALPA and, as of 1961, TWU.) or even most of their members in what was obviously an uphill battle.[5]

Grievance proceedings provided another means to protest age and marriage restrictions. By forcing grievances to the final, binding stage of arbitration, an individual stewardess and her union could hope for help from an outside authority. As it happened, referees upheld the airlines' right to impose age and marriage restrictions for nearly two decades. The first grievance against the no-marriage rule at Pan American in 1948 failed, as did subsequent challenges to age and marriage policies until late 1965. The union's position was that the conditions of unionized steward-esses' continuing employment could be determined only through collec-tive bargaining agreements, regardless of what stewardesses individually pledged when hired. Terminations for age or marriage were unjust ex-ercises of unilateral company authority in an area that required union assent—assent that the union had purposely withheld. But referees deter-mined that since union contracts were mute on the issue, and union negotiators were well aware of the age and marriage policies, the union had effectively given tacit consent by failing to negotiate them away. Arbitrators generally understood their official role as only to interpret whether company actions accorded with extant collective bargaining agreements and labor laws, and saw no conflict in the age and marriage rules until the mid-1960s.[6]

But while airlines could easily ignore union demands to loosen gender-biased employment restrictions in the days before Title VII, stewardesses and their union representatives registered repeated protests nonetheless. It is little wonder that they did, since gender discrimination by the air-lines had grounded as many as one in three stewardesses every year since the 1930s. The effects of discrimination were also unsettling for the unions. Turnover among stewardesses perpetually undermined stability in the membership and hindered the cultivation of committed union workers and leaders from among the rank and file. By continuing to contest age and marriage policies at the bargaining table and with griev-ances in the 1950s and into the 1960s, flight attendants at least gave in-house notice to airlines of their commitment to forcing change even-tually. Fortunately for stewardesses, the social and political ferment of the mid-1960s opened new routes to pressing for more equitable treatment. Stewardess activists began to take their complaints about age and mar-riage rules to the media and policymakers, whom they found intensely interested amid the resurgence of feminism.

RESURGENT FEMINISM

In the early 1960s a variety of developments set the stage for the modern women's movement. As with other social and political movements of the 1960s, an example and catalyst was provided by African Americans' in-creasingly vocal demands for civil rights in the later 1950s and early 1960s.

More than ever before, with the cold war and the global spread of anti-colonial movements, elected officials and politicians were anxious to bolster the nation's image as an egalitarian democracy. The civil rights movement effectively highlighted the domestic failings and hypocrisies of America's democratic ideals through legal action and peaceful mass protests against racial segregation. The civil rights movement also provided inspiration and models for action for other disempowered groups. To feminists who participated in or even just observed the rising tide of protests for racial justice, African American women in the civil rights movement powerfully demonstrated women's centrality to grassroots mobilization and their potential for leadership roles. Female civil rights activists' experiences with and challenges to male domination in the growing movement served too to catalyze calls for gender as well as racial equality.[7]

Additionally, by the early 1960s decades of women's activism in labor, left, and liberal circles culminated in public policy breakthroughs favoring enlarged opportunities for women. In late 1961 President John F. Kennedy established the Presidential Committee on the Status of Women (PCSW) to investigate women's progress and make recommendations in several areas: employment by the federal government and federal contractors; social insurance and tax laws; labor laws; political, civil, and property rights; and services for women as wives, mothers, and workers. Many of the PCSW's specific recommendations for federal action on working women's behalf bore little fruit. But more important, the PCSW, the first official body of its kind, and its much-discussed report of 1963, *The American Woman*, conferred new legitimacy on the goal of women's equality. At the committee's urging Kennedy established two permanent federal commissions to monitor women's issues. Several states quickly followed suit, and by 1967 all fifty had established commissions on women's status. Together the state and federal commissions provided venues for activist women's networks to grow and solidify, and when government action fell short of activists' hopes, for new feminist organizations to emerge and press more vigorously for women's rights.[8]

A few months before the PCSW's report, Kennedy's administration had pushed through Congress the Equal Pay Act, the first federal legislation prohibiting sex discrimination in private employment. The act barred employers from paying different wages to workers simply because of their sex. Pervasive occupational segregation kept most women workers from directly benefiting. Far more earned lower wages than men because they worked in devalued "women's jobs," not because male co-workers got higher pay in the same position. The Equal Pay Act also excluded domestic and agricultural work, occupations in which women of color were disproportionately concentrated. But although the act ultimately did little to address the wage gap between men and women—in 1970 women still earned less than seventy cents to male workers' dollar on average—it was an unprecedented federal move to address gender inequity in the private workplace.[9]

Title VII of the Civil Rights Act of 1964 constituted an even greater federal intervention to ensure women's right to equal economic opportunity. Unlike the Equal Pay Act, however, Title VII broadly challenged sex discrimination only because of a rather late addition to a bill that would have otherwise been mute on women's rights. The Kennedy administration's omnibus civil rights bill, introduced in the House of Representatives in June 1963, was intended to bolster African Americans' voting rights and access to public education and to prohibit racial discrimination in federal programs, public accommodations, and employment. Equal employment opportunity bills banning job discrimination by race had been introduced in every session of Congress since 1942, and there had been several proposals to extend the ban to sex, religion, and national origin. As initially drafted, Title VII of the civil rights bill sponsored by Kennedy forbade private employers to discriminate on the basis of "race, color, religion, or national origin," but not sex. As the civil rights movement and Kennedy's assassination in November 1963 gave the Civil Rights Act broader support than any of its predecessors, a "sex" amendment was successfully added to the bill as well.

In an oft-noted historic move, on 8 February 1964 Representative Howard Smith of Virginia, a conservative Democrat, introduced the amendment adding "sex" to the nondiscriminatory provisions of Title VII. Smith opposed the civil rights bill in its entirety, and his irreverent speech proposing the "sex" amendment led observers at the time and historians subsequently to conclude that he acted simply to hobble the legislation with a controversial gesture toward gender equity. Other scholars have seen Smith's action as a more complicated compound of racism and feminism: an attempt either to torpedo the entire bill or, if it passed, to make sure that it provided no protection to black workers that white women would not also enjoy. Smith achieved the latter and less recognized goal. Eight of the nine congresswomen in office at the time rallied around the "sex" amendment and, with little debate, it stayed in the bill.[10]

On 2 July 1964 President Johnson signed the Civil Rights Act into law, with Title VII's prohibition of sex discrimination included. Title VII prohibited discrimination in hiring, employment, and training or apprenticeship programs on the basis of sex, race, national origin, or religion. It applied to private employers of twenty-five or more workers, employment agencies, and labor organizations. The bill created the Equal Employment Opportunity Commission (EEOC) to interpret Title VII and investigate employers' compliance with the new law as soon as it took effect on 2 July 1965. For stewardesses and other working women who did not benefit from the Equal Pay Act, Title VII suddenly outlawed gender discrimination wholesale in American workplaces. In practice, though, as we will see, it would take years of cajoling and agitation by activist women to push federal authorities into actively combating gender bias.[11]

As unprecedented women's rights initiatives made their way through political channels in the early 1960s, feminist stirrings emerged in popular culture as well. In 1962 Helen Gurley Brown's lighthearted best-seller *Sex and the Single Girl* celebrated the "swinging singles" culture of large cities. Brown urged young women to think twice about sacrificing careers and social and sexual independence for the confines of housewifery. In 1963 Betty Friedan's *The Feminine Mystique* attacked the postwar ideal of female domesticity itself. Friedan inspired widespread reflection on what she defined as "the problem that has no name," the stultification and drudgery that she believed plagued white, middle-class homemakers. From women's magazines and interviews with fellow graduates of Smith College, Friedan painted a grim portrait of suburban domesticity as a gilded cage that trapped women in an endless tedium of chores and vapid consumption. Friedan, herself a veteran journalist and leftist activist as well as wife and mother, pleaded for more opportunities for paid work as the best way for women to escape what she provocatively derided as "the comfortable concentration camp" of the suburban home. As critics have charged, *The Feminine Mystique* was a limited analysis of women's oppression. Working-class women and women of color often could not afford to be full-time homemakers, whether they wanted to or not. Some women who were full-time homemakers angrily retorted that they found fulfillment and took pride in their unpaid domestic labors. Friedan's celebration of paid employment ignored the reality that most jobs available to women, however well-educated, offered few intellectual or creative challenges. But by naming "the problem that has no name" and protesting against it, Friedan energized national debate on gender roles and encouraged women to look at their own lives as a subject for social and political analysis.[12]

Thus by the mid-1960s the time was riper for feminist agitation than it had been for many years. The federal government declared that equal work required equal pay regardless of sex and, more broadly, outlawed sex discrimination in private employment. The civil rights movement inspired a growing number of white Americans, especially among the young, to question the status quo. Yet as female activists found, the proliferation of protest movements—demanding racial justice, free speech at universities, and an end to American involvement in Vietnam, among other goals—typically replicated established patterns of women's subordination while otherwise seeking a more just society. Moreover, the mere existence of laws against sex discrimination did not lead to their enforcement. It would take the broad-based mobilization of feminists to make the new laws meaningful and challenge the male domination that pervaded American life in the 1960s.[13]

Stewardesses were among the many women from various walks of life who launched the modern movement for women's rights. They were not part of the radical vanguard of nascent second-wave feminism in the mid-1960s. Nor were they among the pioneering feminists who labored at the grassroots with little or no public recognition. Instead, stewardesses in the mid-1960s helped to shape and propel the advent of second-wave feminism by staking highly visible, relatively uncontroversial ground in growing struggles against gender discrimination in the United States. They presented themselves as both photogenic representatives of femininity and victims of blatant sex discrimination by their employers. If not exactly radical, their efforts to secure greater respect and equality for themselves in the mid-1960s worked more broadly to raise consciousness of "women's issues"—and in a way that did not necessarily threaten traditional ideals of femininity. Stewardesses were well positioned to secure conservative as well as liberal sympathy for women's rights, and did so with all the feminine appeal they could muster.

The press only rarely departed from irreverent and salacious coverage of flight attendants' protests against the airlines. The news media had difficulty taking feminism in general seriously in the 1960s and well into the 1970s, when feminist ideas had taken firm hold in many quarters. Male-dominated news outlets typically greeted women's demands for change by at once trivializing and sensationalizing them. Similarly, many government officials' predilection for flattery and chivalry when confronted with stewardesses' grievances played upon and perpetuated patronizing stereotypes. The media and public officials were only beginning to figure out how to respond to the resurgence of women's rights activism in the mid-1960s. Stewardesses assisted them in doing so. In return, the press and governmental authorities offered flight attendants unprecedented opportunities to air long-standing complaints publicly.[14]

PUBLICIZING THE AGING STEWARDESS'S PLIGHT

The initial public relations strategy was simple: it was, as a writer for the New York *Sunday News* surmised, "Hey, Look Us Over!" In a series of public protests in the mid-1960s, stewardesses purposefully withstood and indeed invited objectification to force public scrutiny of discriminatory treatment by the airlines. Stewardesses' "look us over" strategy was not without precedent. Decades earlier, stage actors and actresses put their prodigious cultural resources to work in labor activism, blending theatricality with protest in a strike that darkened theaters across the United States in 1919. Stewardess unionists themselves were well versed in media outreach from past disputes with the airlines and bids for the attention of federal regulators. But as of 1963, stewardesses enlisted the media in a frontal assault on the airlines' age and marriage rules.

At their press conference in New York City on 17 April 1963, eight stewardesses for American Airlines had pioneered the "look us over" strategy to great effect. Dusty Roads, ALSSA lobbyist since 1958, had put the stewardesses' protest in perhaps the most plaintive and newsworthy terms when she asked whether she looked like "an old bag." Theo Wilson of the New York *Daily News* answered with more prurient flourish than others, but his affirmation of Roads's attractiveness typified coverage of the event. Wilson's report opened with a breathless description of how Roads spoke with "fire flashing from her big baby blues, and the rest of her poured elegantly into a form-fitting uniform (measurements, 36–24–36)." "Dusty," Wilson deadpanned, "is considered three years overripe by American Airlines."[15]

Some commentators delighted in questioning, with tongue in cheek, whether stewardesses ought to be attractive at all. The editors of the *New Yorker* declined to judge whether the airlines were right or wrong in retiring women, however attractive, at thirty-two; instead they proposed to resolve the "age problem" by revising stewardesses' image altogether. By their account the right age for stewardesses was seventy: passengers ought to be fearful for their lives in any circumstances at thirty thousand feet, and a grandmotherly type could best reassure them. While the *New Yorker* offered cold comfort for "overage" stewardesses, it did question, albeit facetiously, whether airlines should so prize youth and nubility in the first place. Roads and her colleagues had succeeded in making long-unquestioned airline policies a matter of public debate, if also snickering.[16]

As interest grew during the mid-1960s in bolstering the American ideal of equal opportunity, flight attendants seized on repeated opportunities to parlay the attention of the media and lawmakers into public disfavor toward airline discrimination. While flight attendants criticized both age and marriage restrictions, age discrimination became the more visible issue, because of lawmakers' interest in the subject and because of its appeal for journalists. In September 1965 a congressional subcommittee held hearings on the problems of aging workers, offering stewardesses who attended and testified a unique chance to garner national attention. A few months later, stewardesses again made the news when they appeared before the New York State Commission for Human Rights. Hearings in 1967 in the U.S. House of Representatives and Senate on bills to ban age discrimination in employment afforded stewardesses the national spotlight twice more. More than the prohibition against marriage, age policies offered ready fodder for reporters and editorialists to muse about women's attractiveness over the life cycle. Only some bothered to discuss discrimination against stewardesses as a serious matter in its own right. Nonetheless, sporadic waves of media attention and policy debate in the mid-1960s over aging stewardesses' plight showed to their advantage that female attractiveness was a matter of opinion—and perhaps not one with which airlines should be so much concerned.

On 2 September 1965 three male members of the U.S. House of Representatives Subcommittee on Labor looked over a group of "aging" stewardesses and liked what they saw. Stewardesses' appearance before Congress, and the press coverage and public debate that the event inspired, vividly demonstrated stewardesses' ability to muster the power of the media and the state to publicize airline discrimination, but also the trivialization they had to negotiate in the process. The president of ALSSA, Colleen Boland, thirty-six, testified before the House Labor Committee, accompanied by sixteen stewardesses faced with early retirement. Boland began by outlining the early retirement of ALSSA members on American, TWA, Northwest, and Southern. She charged that all but Southern were violating Executive Order 11141 of 1964, which banned age discrimination by federal contractors. But since the executive order lacked enforcement procedures, she suggested a more forceful measure, incorporating "age" into the classifications protected from employer discrimination in Title VII.[17]

Boland's carefully prepared statement and legislative proposal were not what most interested the lawmakers, as immediately became clear. Representative James H. Scheuer, Democrat of New York, asked Boland to have her entourage stand, so that he and his colleagues could "visualize the dimensions of the problem." "Would the airlines tell us," Scheuer asked, "that these pretty young ladies are ready for the slag heap?" "Apparently so," Boland affirmed. Boland inspired more questions, quips, and expressions of sympathy from the committee members after another lengthy statement on airline age policies. She then added a prurient note to the proceedings by quoting an anonymous airline executive concerning age rules: "It is the sex thing, pure and simple. Put a dog on an airplane and 20 businessmen are mad for a month." The quotation provoked a momentarily trenchant reflection on airlines' labor needs and marketing messages. Representative James G. O'Hara, Democrat of Michigan and the committee chairman, observed that according to his own extensive experiences flying, stewardesses worked at "breakneck" speeds and clearly were not employed merely to "stand or sit around looking beautiful." "The gist of this problem," according to Representative William D. Hathaway, Democrat of Maine, was "the notion that airlines are flying bunny clubs." "The services in question can be performed by people who are 40, 50, and perhaps 60 years old."[18]

After Hathaway's blunt comment on "bunny clubs," the hearings reacquired their alternately irreverent and chivalrous tone. To Representative Scheuer, who questioned Boland next, the more interesting matter was not stewardesses' function in commercial aviation but the age at which women ceased to be attractive: "I for one would oppose to my

Stewardesses at Capitol Hill to protest retirement at the age of thirty-two, 2 September 1965. The union president Colleen Boland, whose testimony before Congress drew national media attention, is at far left, front row.

© Bettmann/CORBIS.

dying breath the principle that a woman is less attractive, less alluring, and less charming after age 29 or 32 or 35. I think my colleagues on this committee will agree." "Especially if we want to be reelected," O'Hara added, drawing laughter again from the lawmakers and observers. In closing, O'Hara thanked Boland "for adding some beauty and grace" to the hearing through her presence, and that of her colleagues.[19]

Boland's appearance on Capitol Hill with several stewardesses in tow offered the news media a welcome spectacle. Some newspapers did note that the hearings had earnestly considered age discrimination in the employment of stewardesses, as well as racial discrimination, the speed-up on jets and resultant strain on flight attendants, and why airlines saw fit to have women as young as eighteen serve liquor. But it was the banter quoted above that captured the press's attention. Headlines alone spoke volumes: "Stewardesses Pushing 32 Stack Up Well in Age Plea" (*Baltimore Sun*); "Aging (31) Air Hostesses and Gallant Lawmakers" (*New York Herald Tribune*); and "Airline Stewardess Over the Hill at 32? Congressional Girl-Watchers Say 'No!'" (*Atlanta Constitution*). Industry insiders apparently found the matter less humorous. A headline in *Aviation Daily* soberly noted, "Stewardesses Accuse Carriers of Discrimination."[20]

With "women's issues" appearing more prominently on the political and cultural landscape in the mid-1960s and a historic sexual revolution under way, stewardesses' plight inspired broader discussion of the relationship of youth and feminine allure. Significantly, the editorialists and inspired citizens who weighed in generally rejected the airlines' presumption that feminine allure was marketable only in a youthful form. The eminent columnist Russell Baker penned a lengthy, lighthearted take on the matter for the *New York Times* editorial page on 5 September 1965. "In the present enlightenment," he wrote, "few people will be shocked to hear that the airlines have been subtly trading in sex. Where the modern spirit of tolerance rebels, however, is the point at which the flying industry starts trying to dictate their clients' taste in women." Baker charged the airlines with failing to consider the desires of many male passengers, like him, who prefer "the fuller hip and more worldly eye" of women over thirty-five: "The airlines' suggestion that the older woman is a 'dog' is as insulting to the tastes of these men as it is to the women." "Aging" stewardesses found more straight-faced defenders too. Verse by the amateur poet Tom Hilor expressed sympathy for the airlines' "aging dolls" in the *Chicago Tribune*, and the veteran air traveler E. L. Austin wrote to the editor of the *Washington Evening Star* echoing Baker's defense of more mature women's appeal. Some editorialists and outspoken citizens failed to find any fault with the airlines. But most criticized the age limits and what they saw as the misguided association of female attractiveness exclusively with youth.[21]

When stewardesses appeared a few months later on 7 December before the New York State Commission for Human Rights, Leonard Shecter of the *New York Post* slyly captured the politics of glamour at work in the anti-discrimination efforts of flight attendant activists in the mid-1960s. He at once publicized and trivialized their grievances, as many others had—but he also admired what he considered their canny mobilization of femininity. Reporting the next day on the state hearing, Shecter opined, "We are now engaged in a great civil debate" over whether women should have to be under thirty-five for "careers as jet-propelled waitresses." Shecter then evocatively described what he saw as stewardesses' well-planned invasion: "The stewardesses moved up their heavy artillery yesterday," he wrote, "showing up with a head-turning phalanx of trim, attractive women, all still flying and all over 35." With likely poetic license, Shecter sketched for readers the official response to the stewardesses' protest: "'Amazing,' commented Commissioner J. Edward Conway as the ladies stood up to be noticed. The Commissioner poured himself a cup of water and his hand shook."[22]

However silly and sexist such responses to stewardesses' protests may seem in retrospect, the airlines' discrimination found few defenders. Stewardesses' "hey, look us over!" strategy succeeded in serving notice to the airlines that they could no longer presume their age and marriage restrictions reflected public preference. For pundits, policymakers, and the proverbial "man on the street" confronted with changing sexual mores and new clamor for women's rights, stewardesses were not merely pleasing to look at and fun to discuss. To men and women confused or threatened by the resurgence of feminism in the mid-1960s, supporting stewardesses' protests offered a way to uphold equality in principle, while not necessarily questioning familiar notions of femininity. While all but buried in witty banter and journalistic pith, stewardesses' indictments of airline policies also inspired some serious questioning of how airlines exploited their bodies and labor. With his indignant quip that the airlines were "not bunny clubs," Representative Hathaway declared that the titillation provided by attractive women had no place in the business of air travel. Similarly, Representative Martha Griffiths, Democrat of Michigan, who took up stewardesses' cause in the mid-1960s, famously challenged a top official at United about the carrier's ban on married stewardesses in 1966. "What are you running," Griffiths asked in a widely quoted letter, "an airline or a whorehouse?" Few others so directly challenged the deeply engrained notion that feminine allure was a vital, legitimate qualification for cabin service. But such comments, if merely sound bites, evidenced how stewardesses' protests invited others to criticize the airlines for sexual exploitation.[23]

As for stewardesses themselves, it should not surprise us that activists would ask, "Do I look like an old bag?" instead of declaiming airlines as exploiters of female flesh. At least some did feel that airlines were too like "bunny clubs" in trading in young, single women's sex appeal. Nita Baum, a flight attendant for Northwest, wrote as much to Representative Scheuer in protesting age ceilings in late 1965, just after she had been forced into retirement upon turning thirty-two. Northwest apparently "could care less about the efficiency and capability of their stewardess as long as she is very young and attractive to the businessmen. This all leads us back to the old American way of using sex and womanhood for the advancement of big business," Baum declared. But for flight attendant leaders to air such profoundly critical sentiments was another matter. Whatever they personally thought of stewardesses' glamorized image, they risked alienating co-workers and the public by demystifying it. Many stewardesses saw nothing wrong with employment restrictions. As Dusty Roads recalled, "Some of our own flight attendants would say, 'I don't think you should fly when you're fat or old.'" It was more expedient to ask why women who married or passed the age of thirty-two should not be able to keep their jobs as long as they upheld the stewardess image than to ask why youth and availability mattered so much to start. So steward-ess activists made their demands in the liberal language of fairness and sugarcoated them with feminine flourish.[24]

WRITING LABOR, SKILLS, AND SAFETY INTO THE AIRLINES' "HOSTESS" IDEAL

In the mid-1960s, stewardesses added to the invitation "Hey, look us over!" the polite but firm request to respect the hard, exacting work that they did. Protests against airline discrimination generated unprecedented opportunities for stewardesses to let lawmakers and the public know what their work really entailed. The care that union representatives often took in describing the job and its qualifications indicated how important it was to stewardesses to publicize not only the discrimination they suffered but also their distinct skills and intensive labor. In particular, flight attendants embraced the opportunity to emphasize their role in passenger safety, the least recognized part of their job. Congress had rejected flight attendants' bid for safety licensing in 1962, but hearings on airline discrimination provided flight attendants' leaders with new opportunities to advertise their own occupational ideology of safety professionalism. By explaining why they deserved respect as skilled, hard-working hostesses who ensured passengers' safety and comfort, stewardesses found another way to indict exploitation by the airlines without debunking their celebrated image.

When Iris Peterson, regional vice-president of the ALPA-SSD, testified before the Senate Labor Committee about age discrimination on 17 March 1967, she outlined in exacting detail the "unseen" work of becoming a successful stewardess. After six weeks' training, she explained, the stewardess had to be prepared not only to serve passengers but to allay their fears. She had also to "recognize and care for any number of various ills, care for completely incapacitated or semi-incapacitated passengers, care for unaccompanied children and recognize and evaluate emergencies in order to effect immediate and rapid action for the safety of the passenger." And she had to know those emergency routines and procedures as they applied over land or water, and in as many as seventeen cabin configurations.[25]

Peterson added to "these unseen qualifications" the labor and skills required in stewardesses' on-stage performance as "hostesses." Working on a jet-age flight meant "acting as a gracious and considerate hostess for a house party of 100 guests or more," which included advance preparation, mingling with and serving the guests, cleaning up after them, and then submitting a written report of it all. The premise for Peterson's testimony before Congress was airline age discrimination, so she concluded simply by pointing out the folly of age ceilings. A stewardess's job performance required "capability, alertness, discernment, and evaluation of situations as well as graciousness and empathy toward her passengers . . . qualifications that once learned and practiced do not suddenly disappear at age 32." By imposing arbitrary age limits, airlines were only robbing themselves of the time-tested employees who should be their most valued flight attendants. In the process of making the point, Peterson provided an exceedingly detailed view of how much training, skill, initiative, and juggling of duties was required in what airlines euphemistically called "hostessing."[26]

Yet the more stewardesses tried to translate the power of glamour into the power of self-representation, the more they grew frustrated when their labor and skills remained undervalued—and the more critical they became of the airlines for emphasizing service exclusively instead of safety. On 15 August 1967, when ALPA-SSD's vice-president Marge Cooper testified before the House General Labor Subcommittee on age discrimination, she indicted the airlines not only for trouncing stewardesses' rights but for undermining passenger safety with wrongheaded marketing. Before Cooper's testimony, flight attendant leaders had carefully toed a line in such proceedings, criticizing airlines' emphasis on youth but accepting their demand for charm and attractiveness. Cooper continued to toe that line, but apparently she felt that the time had come for flight attendants themselves to make perfectly clear that airlines were not "bunny clubs." She informed the legislators that the "preoccupation with sex and beauty above all other considerations" in stewardess employment "is more consistent with show business theatrics than with responsible and conservative air transportation services." Airlines, she reminded them, "are certificated by public authority for one purpose and one purpose only; to sell safe air transportation service, not sex, not fantasies of sex, or to run beauty contests or fashion shows or dating bureaus."[27]

Cooper argued further that the airlines' "preoccupation with sex and beauty" carried possibly dire consequences. To replace "an experienced, competent, efficient, and indeed attractive stewardess, whose only failing is her date of birth," with "one who is less experienced, less competent, less efficient, and probably no more attractive—only younger—is not only a flagrant abuse of civil rights, but also a disservice to airline passengers and a potentially dangerous impairment of the highest possible degree" of cabin safety. In the event of an emergency, "nothing is less important than her age, her sexual allure, her measurements—and nothing is more important than her ability to function with calm efficiency when others are unable to do so." Airline discrimination, she concluded, "could well be tragic." By Cooper's account, the need for an age discrimination law to protect female flight attendants from early forced retirement was "even more compelling" than the need for other civil rights legislation, because public safety was implicated as well as equal opportunity.[28]

Such increasingly critical rhetoric did not mean that activists had given up on making the most of their glamorized image before the public and their colleagues. Indeed, when the newsletter of Cooper's union reprinted excerpts from her statement to the House subcommittee, it notably omitted her remarks on the relationship between sex and safety. Only a few months earlier, the newsletter of the other national flight attendants' union informed members that its lobbyists were "doing a terrific job helping to convince Senate Labor Committee members in Washington that charm does not cease at 32." The report ran under a photo of the smiling lobbyists in front of the Capitol building in Washington, captioned "Pulchritude on Capitol Hill!" Cooper nonetheless articulated what would become a basic refrain of flight attendant feminism in the 1970s: that airlines marketed and manipulated feminine allure in violation of stewardesses' civil rights and of the public's right to be sold the safest possible air travel. As for the media, at least some journalists took perceptive note of Cooper's profoundly critical sentiments. Front-page headlines the day after her testimony included "Stewardess' Role Strictly Business" and "Sex Deflated."[29]

THE SEARCH FOR LEGAL TOOLS

Though stewardesses succeeded in the mid-1960s in provoking widespread disfavor toward airline discrimination, public relations victories alone did not bring the job security for which they hoped. Stewardesses also needed the regulatory weight of the state to fall against airline employment practices. But as flight attendants knew all too well from experiences with federal officials and politicians in failed bids for safety licensing, government was an uncertain ally at best. Title VII, the subject of chapter 6, ultimately provided the federal legal breakthrough that flight attendants needed. But how and to what ends the new ban on sex discrimination could be used was far from certain when Title VII passed on 2 July 1964, or when it became effective a year later. As flight attendants began to take action under Title VII, they sought additional ways to challenge the legality of airline policies through state-level and other federal means. Stewardesses found public officials willing to consider and sometimes take action on their behalf, but airline discrimination proved quite durable.

Perhaps most frustrating for flight attendants, Congress failed to answer their calls for protection through age discrimination laws. Beginning in the late 1950s, Dusty Roads had lobbied several congressmen to back some kind of bill redressing the anomalous requirement that stewardesses must retire at thirty-two. She found many willing to listen, but to pass federal legislation pertaining to only one occupation in one industry struck most as "kind of preposterous," Roads later explained. "Eventually, the bill became a joke," she recalled. "They called it 'the old broads' bill.' " By the mid-1960s lawmakers were interested in, and did eventually pass, legislation banning age discrimination in employment more broadly. Stewardesses, as we have seen, were invited to present their case and were given some serious consideration, along with ogling and mirth. But under the Age Discrimination in Employment Act of 1967, only workers "at least forty years of age but less than sixty-five years of age" received statutory protection from age discrimination. Neither the House of Representatives nor the Senate amended the legislation to address stewardesses' unique dilemma, as their leaders had requested. The age discrimination in employment bill that Congress passed in 1967 was virtually useless to flight attendants.[30]

Stewardesses had also hoped that some relief from age ceilings could be secured under Executive Order 11141, signed by President Johnson on 12 February 1964, which barred federal contractors and subcontractors from engaging in employment discrimination on the basis of age. Several large airlines were federal contractors by virtue of Military Air Transport Service (MATS) agreements, through which commercial carriers provided air transport for military personnel and cargo. The executive order only declared policy, however, and specified no mechanisms for enforcement. It merely directed heads of federal departments and agencies to "take appropriate action to enunciate this policy." At flight attendants' request in 1965, the chairman of the House Subcommittee on Labor, Representative James O'Hara, contacted the Departments of Labor and Defense to inquire about MATS airlines' compliance with Executive Order 11141. By the spring of 1966, after several rounds of correspondence between O'Hara and officials at the departments, an Air Force official promised efforts to ensure that airlines would no longer discriminate on the basis of age. Continental dropped its age rule in response, officials reported a few months later, but other carriers refused. By February 1967 union representatives concluded that no additional help should be expected from the Air Force.[31]

Flight attendants also used state laws against discrimination, especially in New York. They focused on New York for essentially the same reasons that aspiring African American stewardesses and civil rights groups had done so in desegregating the airlines. New York offered a model law barring employment discrimination and, more generally, a liberal and pro-labor political establishment. Also, New York drew a disproportionate share of commercial air traffic in the United States: as of 1965, twenty of the thirty-eight airlines with government-certified routes, including all of the largest carriers, operated in New York. Late in 1964 ALSSA officials approached the New York State Commission for Human Rights (NYSCHR, formerly the New York State Commission against Discrimination) to solicit an investigation of airline age ceilings under the state's statute banning age discrimination, and the NYSCHR obliged. Over a year later, in March 1966, the investigation resulted in the finding that airlines with age ceilings were illegally discriminating against stewardesses under the state law.[32]

The NYSCHR acted as flight attendants had hoped, but making use of its ruling required a protracted process of individual charges and hearings before judicial action could commence, just as flight attendants would find at the federal level with Title VII. Resistance from the airlines slowed the process considerably. A federal suit filed by the industry's lobbying group, the Air Transport Association (ATA), challenged the state commission's jurisdiction over the practices of interstate carriers. The court found that the NYSCHR did have jurisdiction, but the airlines had succeeded in halting any progress on stewardesses' individual cases for seven months in 1966. By the spring of 1967, when the first four cases that stewardesses had filed were accorded hearings by the NYSCHR, twenty-five more cases were already on file, waiting to be processed.[33]

Worse for stewardesses than the snail's pace of testing the New York State law against age discrimination was the outcome. The first case to get through various hearings and findings and go to trial, *Soots v. American Airlines*, brought defeat in the Appellate Division of the New York Supreme Court. On 25 January 1968 the court found that the airline's age policy could not be legally overturned, because the state law on age discrimination only protected workers from forty to sixty-five years of age. The NYSCHR had wrongly assumed, according to the court, that the law implicitly covered workers under forty. After more than three years' time, effort, and expense, flight attendants ultimately found that New York State's ban on age discrimination was as meaningless for them as the federal law.[34]

Flight attendants not surprisingly grew ever angrier at the airlines' ability to avoid or at least delay accountability for sex-biased employment restrictions. But while the flight attendants found that the material results of their anti-discrimination efforts were frustratingly meager at first, they had taken the first crucial steps on a historic path. Stewardesses had promoted their own cause and the cause of women's rights more generally by making the public and lawmakers take notice of the age and marital restrictions that airlines imposed on their celebrated hostesses. As their activism showed, the discriminatory practices to which the airlines subjected them were more formal and extreme than what most Americans considered acceptable treatment of white, female wage-earners by the mid-1960s. The "aging" stewardess's plight may not have inspired much weighty public reflection in a nation struggling with profound racial strife, social and political turmoil of many kinds, and a deepening war in Southeast Asia. But by the same token, the levity and sensationalism that met stewardesses' protests against age rules lent their fight greater visibility and popular appeal, even for those disinclined to support feminist demands. For a brief time in the mid-1960s, stewardesses succeeded in using feminine glamour to popularize women's rights to better treatment as wage-earners.

It was not long, however, before the airlines' resistance, and the limitations of the strategy of swathing the progressive goal of workplace equality in a traditional cloak of femininity, heightened stewardesses' discontent and militancy. Their glamour image afforded them plenty of public attention at a propitious moment for feminist activism, but served poorly, if at all, to secure them the respect they wanted as workers. Even worse, the attention of lawmakers failed initially to provide any truly effective means of forcing the airlines to change their ways. Activist flight attendants nonetheless had declared a public war on airline discrimination in the mid-1960s, and they would ultimately see it through to historic victories in the courts under Title VII.

6

"YOU'RE WHITE, YOU'RE FREE, AND YOU'RE 21—WHAT IS IT?"
Title VII

In the late 1990s Barbara "Dusty" Roads recalled for an interviewer on public television her historic role in initiating federal action against the airline industry for sex discrimination under Title VII of the Civil Rights Act of 1964—literally at the very moment when it became possible to do so. The interviewer broached the subject of stewardesses' struggles against sex discrimination, asking Roads, "When [President] Johnson signed the civil rights act did you think the problem was solved?" Roads responded, "I was naive. I thought, ho, ho, no problem now. And so we were the first case."[1]

Roads, the same activist who protested age ceilings in 1963 by asking reporters rhetorically whether she looked "like an old bag," reconstructed in striking detail what it was like to file what she believed was the first case against sex discrimination under Title VII. She recalled, "The bill said that the Equal Employment Opportunity Commission would begin operating on July 1st, 1965. We were on their doorstep." Roads explained that the EEOC, charged with interpreting and administering Title VII of the Civil Rights Act, was both administratively and politically ill prepared to receive a complaint of discrimination from two stewardesses. The arrival of Roads and her American Airlines colleague Jean Montague at the barely opened commission offices engendered mutual surprise. "We walked in and looked around at a sea of black faces. Their typewriters were still in boxes. This woman came up to us, two blondes in stewardess uniforms, and she said, 'What are you doing here?' And I said, well, we have a problem. She said, 'You're white, you're free, and you're 21. What is it?' I said, 'Honey, sit down, I got a long story to tell you. So we helped unpack the typewriters, and she started typing away." Roads elaborated, "Most of the women in the office were very intelligent, well-educated black ladies who figured that most of the discrimination was going to be against black women. What a big jolt this was for them. We sat down and told them the story of discrimination in the airline industry and they just, oh, they couldn't believe it." Over the din of the typewriter, Roads and Montague informed the EEOC staffer of various airline policies that had cost thousands of stewardesses their jobs over the years, yet had never been imposed on male airline employees, including the pursers and stewards who did the same work as stewardesses. Roads and Montague offered their initially dubious audience a compelling tale of pervasive sex bias in the airline industry. But what neither the stewardesses nor sympathetic EEOC staffers could have foreseen was how many practical and political obstacles would confront working women who immediately made a bid for federal attention under Title VII.[2]

With Title VII the federal government suddenly invited women to demand equal access to labor markets and equal treatment in the workplace. But in practice, Title VII's designers and implementers were at first concerned primarily, if not exclusively, with racial discrimination. The surprise that Roads recalled among female African American staffers at the EEOC that she might have a complaint was a comparatively benign reflection of the new agency's equation of Title VII with racial equality. Only through women's hard-fought efforts would Title VII become an effective legal weapon against employers' habit of undervaluing and exploiting female labor.

Stewardesses were exceptionally well positioned among female wage-earners to push quickly for action under Title VII. But their battles with airlines evidenced how much more than a formal change in law it took to fight the entrenched patterns of sex discrimination in American workplaces. As unionized workers and popular icons, stewardesses had organizational as well as distinct cultural resources with which to mobilize government support for their claims of sex discrimination. That airline employment restrictions on stewardesses' age and marital status were gender-biased was not a difficult case to make. But the airline industry proved a powerful and resourceful adversary. American carriers had invested millions of dollars over the years in creating a marketable image of stewardesses as uniformly "young, attractive, and unencumbered," as one executive put it. Perhaps no less important, they had grown accustomed to the cost-effectiveness of employing young, single, healthy women for a short term at moderate wages. As stewardesses found too, the legal processes for pursuing charges of any kind of discrimination under Title VII were protracted and complicated, even in the best of circumstances. But sex discrimination cases were especially difficult to pursue in the later 1960s. Stewardesses were only one group among the thousands of white women and women and men of color who quickly put Title VII to the test of implementation. Nonetheless, their high-profile struggles to use the new law offer a revealing case study of working women's political mobilization—and of how effectively employers countered feminist demands for change.[3]

TESTING TITLE VII IN LABOR RELATIONS

Title VII's mere existence as of 2 July 1964 provided an opening for the flight attendant unions to begin chipping away at age and marriage rules at the bargaining table and in grievance proceedings. Even minor policy alterations were victories, for they saved some stewardesses from imminent termination and promised more job security for others. But because flight attendants' success in challenging discrimination through contract negotiations and grievances was piecemeal and tenuous, what progress they achieved tested their own and the airlines' resolve. The more the managers and union officials haggled and compromised over the details of age and marriage rules, the more imperative it became that their basic dispute—whether airlines could continue to demand only young, single women for passenger service—should be resolved permanently as a matter of law. Labor relations struggles over airline discrimination in the immediate wake of Title VII's passage were thus a prelude to and catalyst for an ultimate face-off in the courts.

American Airlines and the Air Line Stewards and Stewardesses Association (ALSSA) signed a new contract in October 1965 that exemplified the shifting negotiations terrain of the mid-1960s. Management was newly willing to cede ground on the disputed issues of age and marriage rules, yet resisted any fundamental change to the stewardess ideal. After years of futile protests, union negotiators took whatever concessions they could get. According to section 27(c) of the contract, "Stewardesses may be released any time following the expiration of six months after her marriage or upon pregnancy." So marriage did not mean automatic termination, but the threat of delayed termination at company whim; pregnancy, as always, meant immediate dismissal. American also tried to sweeten the bitter pill of early retirement by amending the "Age 32 Agreement" to provide that the company would "make every effort" to find new ground jobs for stewardesses that would not require relocation. Alternatively, stewardesses who had reached the age of thirty-two could put off retirement for up to a year and still claim severance pay of $250 for each year of service. But as soon as their thirty-third birthday arrived, stewardesses lost their job and their claim to any severance pay. American conceded that federal law might well trump the agreement: "If Federal legislation or ruling of Federal administrative agency renders the Agreement invalid (and such is found to be applicable by final judicial determination) stewardesses terminated between 10/1/65 and 12/31/67 will be rehired."[4]

That airlines not only recognized but feared the prospect of legal intervention in their employment practices was more strikingly evident in a final "Special Agreement" in the contract between American and ALSSA in 1965. Management offered a generous bribe to the most senior stewardesses simply to go away. Under the Special Agreement stewardesses who held "grandmother" exemptions from the age ceiling were offered an extra $4,500 lump payment, along with whatever severance pay, accrued salary, and benefits they were due, if they resigned. American was at least financially generous in its effort to dispatch veteran stewardesses before the full weight of Title VII fell on the industry. In difficult contract negotiations between ALSSA and TWA in early 1965, which saw stewardesses nearly strike, the only ground that the carrier gave on age rules was a new option of limbo: hostesses who reached retirement age under the new two-year contract could request an indefinite leave instead of transferring or resigning. Remarkably, the group in question that benefited from this grudging concession comprised a mere four hostesses out of two thousand.[5]

Smaller airlines proved just as reluctant to ease employment restrictions in the mid-1960s. In early 1966 Allegheny Airlines' head of personnel notified flight attendants of a change in the carrier's age ceiling. He explained that age and marriage restrictions were believed necessary, "and certainly beneficial to all concerned." But considering "the current

TWA flight
attendants in
San Francisco,
February 1965,
protesting the
age ceiling and
demanding
better wages and
shorter hours.
© Bettmann/
CORBIS.

environment," the airline decided to raise its age limit from thirty-two to thirty-five. There would, however, be no change in the carrier's mutually "beneficial" no-marriage rule, "for reasons that are obvious to all concerned." The stewardesses were also warned that relaxing the age rule did not mean any lowering of appearance, attitude, or productivity standards. On Frontier Airlines the attitude was basically the same, but management's stance less paternalistic. The carrier attempted to harass its two "grandmothered" stewardesses out of in-flight service in late 1965 with forced transfers to ground jobs and threats of termination if they complained to the union.[6]

Perhaps most damaging to stewardesses' anti-discrimination efforts was the fierce resistance of two of the largest employers in the industry, American and especially United. A lawyer for United later recalled, "The very thought of changing the rules was reprehensible. It was like heresy." In 1966, when flight attendants had already begun federal legal action against various airlines under Title VII, United adopted a new age ceiling of thirty-two. Four thousand stewardesses suddenly found themselves facing formalized age discrimination as well as the no-marriage rule. The Steward and Stewardess Division of the Air Line Pilots Association refused to allow the new age policy to be included in the stewardesses' contract, so the company imposed it unilaterally. It was not until late 1970 that United gave up on its belated age restriction.[7]

Grievance proceedings provided unionized flight attendants with another route of attack against airline discrimination when progress in union contracts fell short. After Title VII as before, grievance proceedings were a slow, risky way to seek redress for stewardesses who fell victim to age and marriage rules. But filing grievances also afforded flight attendants an important means to test the new law's implications, and could right past wrongs with reinstatement, back pay, and restoration of seniority rights.

Title VII did in fact allow flight attendants to secure the first successful grievance against the no-marriage rule after almost two decades of defeats. In September 1965 ALPA-SSD won a landmark grievance award against Braniff, which had terminated Betty Green Bateman in November 1964 when her supervisor learned that she had been secretly married for over a year and a half. Bateman's was no ordinary grievance. Not only did it turn on the long-disputed subject of marital restrictions around the very moment when Title VII took effect in mid-1965, but the grievant herself was the highest-ranking official in the flight attendants' union at Braniff. Whether provoked more by Bateman's role as a union leader or by the weightiness of the marriage policy at stake, Braniff refused to cooperate in seeing the grievance to a conclusion. It denied Bateman's request for arbitration of her deadlocked grievance three times. Only after the union obtained a federal court order was Braniff forced to accept adjudication of the matter by a referee.[8]

In the final hearing of Bateman's case before Walter L. Gray in August 1965, Braniff offered the same rationale for firing Bateman that other airlines had successfully used to defend marriage terminations previously. Braniff argued that Bateman had signed an individual contract when she was hired in 1959, agreeing to resign if she married. Furthermore, Braniff protested, Bateman was certainly aware of the no-marriage rule, since she led the negotiating team that in 1963 had presented—but then withdrawn—a union demand for the policy to end. Bateman's counsel likewise presented the same counterargument that union representatives had used, to no avail. The union claimed that company policies on stewardesses' continued employment required the union's assent in the collective bargaining agreement. But in Bateman's case, the union also argued that her termination must be reversed because of Title VII. The union asserted that because Title VII forbade discrimination based on sex, Braniff's no-marriage policy, imposed exclusively on stewardesses, was obviously now illegal. Thanks to the tie-breaking opinion of Gray, Bateman won her grievance on 14 September 1965 and was reinstated.[9]

Gray ruled in Bateman's favor in part because he rejected the prevailing logic of previous years in interpreting the absence of the no-marriage rule from the collective bargaining agreement. Whereas earlier referees had found the silence of contracts on the marriage restriction to mean that the union tacitly consented to the policy, Gray came to the opposite conclusion. If Braniff wanted "a valid employment understanding" on stewardesses' marital status, it needed a formal agreement "with the certified bargaining agent . . . and not with the individual." Gray also broke new ground in finding the "recent trend of thought," as embodied in Title VII and in airlines' own recent contract concessions, more compelling than prior grievance decisions. The victorious flight attendants' union cheered Bateman's grievance award as a "precedent-setting breakthrough." Although the decision was "only one step forward after a long series of setbacks," the union felt that it finally had the ammunition to fight no-marriage rules throughout the industry.[10]

After the landmark Braniff case, members of both ALPA-SSD and ALSSA began filing marriage and age grievances in droves—and won several. In the first eight months of 1966, ALSSA filed no fewer than twenty-five grievances against American Airlines' no-marriage rule. In May 1967 Nancy Wheelock finally succeeded in challenging American's no-marriage policy, the most important grievance breakthrough since the Bateman case in 1965. At the time American employed nearly one-tenth of the total flight attendant workforce in the United States and was still holding fast to basic restrictions on stewardesses' employment by age and marital status. The referee found that American's concession in 1965 on the no-marriage rule, allowing a six-month grace period to newly married stewardesses, did not establish the carrier's right to fire them after that without other cause. As a result, all American stewardesses grounded for marrying since 1965 were reinstated.[11]

Arbitrators who ruled in stewardesses' favor soon after the Braniff victory did not, however, consider Title VII directly as a factor in their rulings, as Gray had done in Bateman's case. Most arbitrators felt it was not for them to decide whether airline policies conflicted with Title VII before the Equal Employment Opportunity Commission did. Gray complained bitterly to an official of the flight attendants' union in 1967 that his pioneering ruling in the Bateman case had ruined his arbitration career, as airlines and colleagues thereafter viewed him as too controversial. But several arbitrators seem to have been influenced by what Gray called the "modern trend of thought" within what they considered their jurisdiction. Stewardesses began to win age and marriage grievances because arbitrators ruled that airline management had not bargained for the right to fire stewardesses solely on the basis of age or marital status. Yet other arbitrators continued to find that until union contracts or the EEOC said otherwise, airlines remained free to impose age and marriage restrictions at will. Only a month before Wheelock's victory, Terry Van Horn Baker lost her grievance against United's no-marriage rule. The denial of Baker's grievance, flight attendant activists believed, only stiffened United's resolve to defend both its no-marriage rule and its newly established age ceiling.[12]

While flight attendants' progress in fighting airline discrimination through contract concessions and grievances was generally two steps forward, one step backward, they welcomed any progress as a hopeful sign of a new era. At ALSSA's ninth biennial convention in April 1967, the union's president, Colleen Boland, noted, "We have had more upholding of our positions in the last two years than we have had in the entire eighteen previous years." By the time the EEOC unequivocally declared airline marriage and age restrictions illegal in mid-1968, the flight attendant unions had nearly succeeded in suspending terminations for marriage industry-wide. While the unions fought both age and marriage restrictions, it was the latter that had been more pervasive and far more effective in cutting short the careers of stewardesses. In August 1968, as American Airlines stewardesses were on the verge of striking, the airline agreed to ALSSA's demand to end its rule against marriage. Three months later ALPA-SSD signed a new contract that halted terminations for marriage with its Goliath, United. Age rules similarly fell by the wayside in collective bargaining.[13]

The compromises that negotiators made along the way were sometimes costly. It may be little wonder that union officials, faced with intransigence on the part of the airlines, accepted only slight alterations of age and marriage restrictions in the mid-1960s. But Title VII required nondiscrimination of labor organizations as well as employers. With some temporary settlements on age or marriage rules, negotiators enabled airlines to move employment restrictions from individual pre-employment pledges into collective bargaining agreements. Unions could no longer say that at least they had done their best to keep discriminatory policies out of their contracts. In other cases, the unions merely continued to brook airline discrimination in collective bargaining agreements, though in watered-down form. In any event, union negotiators gave a fleeting seal of approval to policies that as of July 1965, when Title VII took effect, illegally robbed members of their rights. This would come back to haunt the unions in the 1970s, when increasingly militant stewardesses occasionally dragged them to court alongside the companies. More important in the short run, the unions' advances in collective bargaining only went so far as the next round of negotiations. Flight attendants still ultimately needed federal action under Title VII to ensure that airlines would not turn back the clock on their progress in fighting sex discrimination.[14]

SEIZING ON "SEX" IN TITLE VII

Stewardesses were not the only group to file complaints of sex discrimination as soon as Title VII took effect. Within three months of opening its doors in July 1965, the EEOC received 143 charges of sex discrimination. By the end of its first year of operation, women had submitted nearly 2,500 sex discrimination charges, more than a quarter of the total filed. By mid-December 1966 stewardesses alone had over one hundred complaints on file with the EEOC, some already in litigation in federal district courts.[15]

The avid interest of working women in a more just workplace was crucial in deterring the new EEOC from concentrating on racial discrimination to the neglect of women's rights. As designed by Congress, the EEOC operated under five bipartisan commissioners, presidential appointees subject to Senate confirmation who served five-year terms. According to Aileen Hernandez, the lone female and one of two African Americans in the first slate of commissioners, discussion of sex discrimination engendered "boredom" or "virulent hostility" among nearly all her male colleagues. Sonia Pressman Fuentes, a high-level staff lawyer in the EEOC general counsel's office, was nicknamed the "sex maniac" by her boss because she took sex discrimination just as seriously as racial bias. The EEOC's executive director, Herman Edelsberg, pronounced the inclusion of "sex" in Title VII "a fluke" and told reporters in November 1965, "There are people on this commission that think that no man should be required to have a male secretary and I am one of them." The press treated the inclusion of sex in Title VII as a laughable diversion from the sober matter of racial discrimination. When journalists bothered to note Title VII's ban on sex discrimination, it was generally to muse about Playboy Clubs being forced to hire male "bunnies," or "matronly vice-presidents" making passes at their male secretaries. The apathy of the early EEOC toward women's rights was a major spur for veteran activists, including Hernandez and Pressman, to form the National Organization for Women in 1966, in an effort to press for Title VII enforcement and more generally for "a fully equal partnership of the sexes" in American life. To Betty Friedan looking back a decade later, Title VII's prohibition of sex discrimination, a law "never meant to be enforced," "ignited the organization of the women's movement."[16]

In joining the feminist push to make the early EEOC attentive to gender along with racial discrimination, flight attendant activists themselves were guilty of privileging one form of discrimination to the relative neglect of another. After the unions approached the new EEOC requesting action on their charges of sex discrimination, the chairman of the commission quickly urged them to consider race at least as important as sex in anti-discrimination efforts against the airlines. On 7 October 1965 the EEOC chairman, Franklin Roosevelt Jr., wrote to the president of ALPA, "We are glad that you share our concern with the fact that there has apparently been racial discrimination in the hiring of stewardesses and other flight crew personnel . . . We will be diligent in our action against unlawful discrimination based on sex. But we must be at least equally diligent in our efforts to combat racial discrimination." Beyond pursuing contract clauses against racial discrimination, however, activists in the flight attendants' unions took no real additional action to incorporate race in their increasingly militant anti-discrimination agenda. It was perhaps only logical that they should have focused their resources and energy on the discrimination suffered by the white women who predominated in airline passenger service. Flight attendants nonetheless, if unintentionally, perpetuated in reverse the separation and unequal valuing of discriminatory practices with which feminists charged the EEOC. In so doing flight attendants also contributed to the building of a mass movement for women's rights that implicitly understood the category of women as white and that was ill equipped to address the compounding effects of racial and gender discrimination for women of color.[17]

Whatever the EEOC's priorities, structural limitations hampered its ability to fight discrimination of any kind. While the sex amendment to Title VII engendered little debate in Congress, the proposed authority of the EEOC to fight racial discrimination with cease-and-desist orders and litigation met formidable opposition among Republicans and conservative southern Democrats. What helped the Civil Rights Act pass in mid-1964 was the elimination of much of the EEOC's power. Congress thus charged the EEOC with interpreting and administering Title VII in an advisory manner only. The EEOC's interpretive duties were essentially twofold: to issue employment guidelines and opinions on whether a given practice violated the Act; and to investigate individual complaints and determine whether there was "reasonable cause" to believe that illegal discrimination had occurred. When an individual complaint resulted in a finding of reasonable cause, the commission was to approach the employer in question to seek compliance with Title VII "by informal methods of conference, conciliation, and persuasion." If "conciliation" failed, the EEOC could recommend legal action to the attorney general, who was empowered to sue where "patterns or practices" of systematic discrimination were found. But involvement of the attorney general in most complaints was unlikely. For the most part, when conciliation failed the EEOC advised the aggrieved employee of her right to file a civil suit within thirty days. With the Equal Employment Opportunity Act of 1972, Congress expanded the EEOC's powers and transferred the authority to initiate legal action from the attorney general to the commission itself. From 1965 to 1972 EEOC findings were not legally binding in and of themselves.[18]

Congress also failed to provide the EEOC with adequate resources to investigate, let alone conciliate, a growing flood of worker complaints. In its first year, the EEOC received 8,854 complaints of discrimination; within five years it had received some 52,000. By 1970 the annual volume of new cases topped 17,000, and the commission fell increasingly behind in addressing them. After a decade, in 1975, the backlog of unprocessed complaints numbered 100,000. The EEOC fared poorly, moreover, in efforts to seek voluntary compliance from employers in cases where it found evidence of unlawful discrimination. In 1970 the EEOC only managed successful conciliation in 225 cases, slightly more than 1 percent of the charges filed that year (not to mention the backlog).[19]

The already formidable feat of securing a finding of "reasonable cause" from the overburdened EEOC was only the first step in using Title VII against employers that persisted in sex discrimination. The next step was litigation in the federal courts. As flight attendants found, federal courts at first were considerably more confused and divided than the EEOC on what exactly constituted unlawful sex discrimination. Because "sex" had been added to Title VII at the last minute only the day before the Civil Rights Act passed in the House—there was little substantive debate to show the legislators' intent. Federal courts had largely to decide for themselves what specific goals Congress had in mind and what practices it hoped to end by adding "sex" to Title VII. What they could do is look to the findings of the EEOC as the federal authority that Congress established to interpret and administer Title VII. In 1971 the U.S. Supreme Court made clear that EEOC findings were "entitled to great deference." Before then, judges were not bound nor were they necessarily willing to defer to the EEOC in determining Title VII's implications.[20]

Finally, Title VII included a potential loophole for employers in the "bona fide occupation qualification" (BFOQ) clause. The clause allowed employers to treat job applicants and employees differently on the basis of sex, religion, or national origin (but *not* race) if the classifications were "reasonably necessary" to "normal" business operations. Airlines were among many employers who cited the BFOQ clause in defense of their discriminatory policies. Title VII placed the burden on the employer to prove the business "necessity" of discrimination. Even so, the statutory possibility of the BFOQ exception added considerably to the legal complexities and conflicting opinions among courts that women faced when their Title VII cases began entering litigation. Sex discrimination claims in particular required extensive proceedings to define what employers could and could not legally do under Title VII. For flight attendants, it was a protracted and costly process that included some disheartening defeats.

STEWARDESSES AND THE EEOC

Only a few months after requesting investigations of airline policies as the EEOC opened its doors, stewardesses got what they considered a promising indication of support for their most pressing claim of discrimination: the airlines' no-marriage rules. On 10 September 1965 the EEOC issued employment guidelines specifying that any rule banning or restricting married women's employment but not married men's was sex discrimination prohibited by Title VII. While the EEOC's generic guidelines did not address airline practices specifically, flight attendants took them to mean that airlines were now clearly flouting federal law.[21]

An EEOC representative indicated otherwise to nervous airline lawyers, however. Legal counsel for the Air Transport Association (ATA), the airline industry's lobbying group, quickly asked the EEOC whether the ruling on marital restrictions would apply to stewardesses' employment. On 22 September 1965 the EEOC general counsel replied that he did not believe the ruling would apply. He explained what he considered the very real possibility of a "BFOQ" exception to Title VII for the airlines: "If an airline may give preference to females only as stewardesses,"—if sex were found to be a BFOQ—then it "could impose further qualifications with respect to such jobs and require that the employee be single and under a certain age." He concluded that airlines would be "safe" in assuming that the ruling could not apply to stewardesses until the commission first decided on the BFOQ.[22]

While a determination of the BFOQ clause's applicability would prove central to stewardesses' struggles with the airlines, the EEOC general counsel was wrong to suggest that the airlines need not worry in the interim. Stewardesses had already filed a number of individual complaints against specific airlines by September 1965, which according to the fine print in Title VII required a response from the EEOC within just a few months. The commission of necessity began to investigate specific carriers' age ceilings and no-marriage rules in the fall of 1965. By December the EEOC had handed a stewardess a formal finding of "reasonable cause" that an airline had engaged in unlawful sex discrimination. Thankfully for flight attendants, it was Commissioner Aileen Hernandez who handled the first preliminary ruling by the EEOC on their complaints against the airlines. Though overt champions of women's rights were few at the early EEOC, Hernandez and Sonia Pressman Fuentes, third in command in the general counsel's office, were feminists who became centrally involved in stewardesses' cases.[23]

On 16 December 1965 Hernandez issued her finding on the complaint of the stewardess Judith Evenson against Northwest Airlines. Evenson had filed her charge on 25 October 1965, contending that her termination for marriage violated Title VII because Northwest's male flight attendants could marry and keep their jobs. Hernandez agreed. She also noted that the company employed only men in higher-paid purser positions, without apparent justification. While only a finding of reasonable cause, Hernandez's decision was a promising first step in stewardesses' relationship with the commission. While the EEOC bungled its conciliation duties in Evenson's case (it declared conciliation efforts to have failed before any were actually made), it authorized Evenson to file suit against Northwest, which she did on 20 January 1966. Northwest quickly responded with a motion to dismiss, based in part on the allegation that the EEOC had failed in its statutory duty to seek compliance. The court eventually denied Northwest's motion on 17 March 1967, but Evenson never received a ruling on the merits of her case alone; apparently she settled with the carrier.[24]

Though the first Title VII lawsuit brought by a stewardess ultimately fizzled in the courts, it brought progress of a different kind. Evenson's suit prompted the airlines to request, and the EEOC to agree to conduct, a general investigation of airline age and marriage rules in the spring of 1966, which would then govern decisions on individual complaints. On 10 May four of the five commissioners presided over a five-hour public hearing at which stewardess and airline representatives debated whether sex was a BFOQ for the flight attendant occupation. Jesse Freidin, who presented the airlines' case as counsel for the Air Transport Association, argued that the airlines had invested millions of dollars to hire and train young, single women because they were uniquely valuable in attracting and serving passengers. Men could handle the manual aspects of the job, he admitted, but not the non-manual challenges of making flying pleasant. He contended that since employing female flight attendants was essential to successful business operations, sex was a bona fide occupational qualification for flight attendant work. And because sex was a BFOQ for flight attendant work, it followed that sex-related restrictions on stewardesses' employment by age and marital status were not in conflict with Title VII. Because of the BFOQ exception, Freidin argued that no gender-based policies concerning flight attendants' employment violated Title VII. In conclusion, he suggested that hiring only "girls" was the best policy for everyone, even the nation: "As an acceptable and useful job for young girls, as a training ground for future wives and mothers, as a steppingstone from school to a lifetime career, as a happy assistance to innumerable passengers, the stewardess corps serves an important social purpose and is universally recognized throughout the nation as being a very good thing."[25]

United Airlines contributed significantly to the airline industry's defense before the EEOC by preparing a hefty brief. The document outlined in nearly eighty pages the tangible and intangible reasons why United and the airline industry had come to believe that "attractive, young females" were uniquely able to fulfill passengers' social and psychological needs and desires aloft—and were thus crucial to airlines' business. Among the section headings in the United brief: "This Is a Female Job," "Stewardesses Have Effectively Produced the Desired Results and Have Done So Because of Their Inherent Female Make-up," and "Title VII Was Not Intended to Prohibit Airlines from Exclusively Hiring Girls as Flight Attendants." The theme that United repeated amid "expert" psychological testimony, excerpts from flight reports, and detailed descriptions of the job and its supposedly inherently feminine nature was basically this: "Men *can* carry trays, and hang up coats and assist in the rare event of an emergency—they *cannot* convey the charm, the tact, the grace, the liveliness that young girls can—particularly to men, who comprise the vast majority of airline passengers . . . . [Men] cannot create for the passenger the psychological impression of a memorable occasion . . . add to the pleasure of the trip, the loveliness of the environment or the ego of the male passenger." These objectives, United reassured, were all "legitimate" business concerns of the airlines. Lest the EEOC suspect the airlines of covertly selling sexual allure, United added that "the stewardess is not a 'bunny' nor does the job reflect, as some say, a supposed 'playboy syndrome' of airline managers."[26]

Flight attendants countered that the airlines' own practices belied their arguments. Arguing the stewardesses' case were the ALSSA president Colleen Boland and legal counsel from the two international unions representing flight attendants, the Transport Workers Union and Air Line Pilots Association. The representatives of the flight attendants' unions rejected the notion that sex was a BFOQ for flight attendant work, flatly stating that there were no job duties involved that men could not perform as well as women. Airlines had demonstrated as much by employing male cabin attendants in the past and present. Despite the decision by several airlines to stop hiring male attendants in the 1950s and 1960s, some carriers continued to employ men in the cabin to no apparent harm. "While the ratio of men to women steadily declines," Boland told the EEOC, "still the Royal Ambassador service provided by TWA places emphasis on the white dinner jacketed maître d' type role of male pursers." Airlines, the flight attendants' representatives argued, violated Title VII in limiting stewardesses' employment by age and marital status while not applying comparable restrictions to male cabin crew. That many airlines had never bothered to impose age ceilings and that marital restrictions were no longer industry-wide, moreover, controverted the business "necessity" of such rules in stewardesses' employment.[27]

On 9 November 1966 the EEOC issued its general opinion on airline policies. The commission ruled that airline age and marriage rules categorically violated Title VII and that sex was not a "bona fide occupational qualification" for flight attendants. Whatever the early EEOC's failings in making Title VII an accessible remedy for working women who suffered discrimination, the commission had taken a firm stance early on in narrowly interpreting the BFOQ clause. It had held in 1965 that the BFOQ could justify classification of employees by sex only "where it is necessary for the purpose of authenticity or genuineness, e.g., an actor or actress." And so the commission ruled regarding flight attendants' employment, providing stewardesses with a sweeping finding of airline discrimination. It was "the great pleasure and privilege" of Sonia Pressman Fuentes, the EEOC lawyer and founder of NOW, to draft the decision, as she later recalled in her autobiography.[28]

With the EEOC's ruling that sex-based classifications in the employment of flight attendants violated Title VII, the personnel policies of virtually the entire industry came under potential legal fire. Fewer than half of American carriers had imposed age ceilings on stewardesses, and the no-marriage rule was no longer industry-wide—but more and more airlines in the 1950s and 1960s had stopped hiring male flight attendants altogether. Of eighteen thousand flight attendants in the United States in 1966 fewer than eight hundred were male (4.4 percent), and they were concentrated on only a handful of airlines out of nearly forty. As of 1967, a federal court found, no airline in the United States was hiring male candidates as stewards. At the same time, airlines would not hire or promote women to more senior and better-paid purser positions. Even the very few carriers that employed men and women at equivalent levels, and did not impose age or marriage restrictions, engaged in other gender-biased practices concerning benefits, layover accommodations, and weight and grooming rules. By the EEOC's account, as of 9 November 1966 almost no airline could escape the charge of violating Title VII by failing to hire men as flight attendants, or employing them as a minority who received preferential treatment (or both).[29]

The airline industry's counteroffensive began immediately, grinding flight attendants' progress under Title VII to an immediate halt. Before the EEOC was even able to release the full decision of 9 November 1966, the ATA filed suit in federal court against the four commissioners involved in the EEOC decision: Aileen Hernandez, the vice-chairman Luther Holcolm, Stephen Shulman, and Samuel Jackson. In a historic irony, the ATA charged the EEOC with feminist partiality because of the role of Hernandez, the foremost internal critic of the federal agency's lack of concern over gender bias. The airlines persuaded a District Court judge to enjoin the commission from releasing its decision, or processing any individual stewardesses' complaints based on the contested ruling, as long as the matter was being litigated. The airlines claimed that the EEOC ruling was biased because Hernandez had voted on it on 9 November 1966 while also serving as an officer of the new National Organization for Women, which had publicly attacked the airline industry less than two weeks before. (The alleged conflict of interest was chronologically ambiguous, since Hernandez had officially resigned her position at the EEOC before the vote and had not yet accepted the post at NOW.) Hernandez's overlapping involvement with the EEOC and NOW on 9 November was enough for a federal court in Washington to suspect partiality on the part of the commission. On 21 February 1967 it enjoined the EEOC permanently from releasing its decision on airline discrimination from 9 November 1966. The court directed the commission either to rehear the airlines' and flight attendants' arguments and issue a new decision, or else drop the general investigation of airline policies. When an overburdened EEOC proposed simply to issue a new ruling based on the hearings and the memoranda on file, the ATA filed suit again and won again. On 23 May 1967 another federal district judge granted the airlines' call for the EEOC investigation to start over at square one.[30]

The airlines' delaying tactics could not prevent the inevitable. On 12 September 1967 the EEOC held another public hearing on whether sex was a BFOQ for flight attendants, as required by the courts. The airlines and flight attendants repeated basically the same arguments—and produced the same result. On 24 February 1968 the EEOC released a new blanket ruling that denied sex as a BFOQ for the flight attendant occupation and declared age and marriage rules to be violations of Title VII. This time, the airlines had no smoking gun of apparent partiality with which to challenge the EEOC's decision making. With guidelines thus in place, the EEOC proceeded to issue rulings on 20 June 1968 in three specific cases, thus setting permanent precedents for any individual actions on file or yet to be filed against age or marriage rules. In *Colvin v. Piedmont Aviation* the EEOC found that the carrier's marriage restriction, applied to its female flight attendants but not its male attendants, violated Title VII. More important was the second marriage case, *Neal v. American Airlines*. In *Neal* the EEOC rejected the carrier's claim that because it employed only women as flight attendants there could be no gender bias in how it treated them. The EEOC explained that sex discrimination was not only "an actual disparity of treatment among male and female employees in the same job classification," but also the consequence of an employment rule "applied to a class of employees because of their sex, rather than because of the requirements of the job." Here was a definitive statement from the EEOC that to charge discrimination under Title VII, stewardesses need not suffer inequality in direct comparison to male stewards or pursers—a condition that did not exist on most airlines in the late 1960s. In the third ruling, *Dodd v. American Airlines*, the commission similarly failed to find any legal justification for the grounding of American's all-female flight attendants at thirty-two.[31]

With the rulings in *Neal, Colvin,* and *Dodd,* the airlines' age and marriage rules were a settled matter at the EEOC. Flight attendants were thus past the first hurdle in taking legal action against the airlines under Title VII. But EEOC determinations merely authorized stewardesses to look to the federal courts for findings of discrimination and remedial measures, like reinstatement, back pay, and restoration of seniority rights. While the airlines' resistance on age and marriage rules had broken down at the bargaining table by the late 1960s, many carriers were more than willing to fight on in the courts, where the costs of remedying past discrimination could prove staggering. After almost three years of struggling to establish firm precedents at the EEOC by mid-1968, stewardesses had little choice but to press on with lawsuits. Charges by flight attendants and defenses by the airlines would remain much the same, but federal courts' views on sex discrimination and Title VII proved far more complicated and variable than the EEOC's.

STEWARDESSES AND TITLE VII IN THE COURTS

The major stumbling blocks that flight attendants had encountered in enlisting the EEOC's support for their charges of sex discrimination were essentially procedural. When flight attendants' Title VII cases began entering litigation, the new and more difficult obstacle they faced was juridical. The courts had virtually no historic record of supporting working women's claims to any legal rights other than special protection for their supposedly weaker physical constitutions and maternal obligations. Most notably, federal courts since the turn of the century had upheld state laws restricting hours for female wage-earners, while striking down any similar protections for men as constraints of the right to buy and sell labor freely. With Title VII, Congress dictated a new but ambiguous policy of gender blindness in private employment policies, except where sex was a bona fide occupational qualification. Advocates of African American civil rights had a venerable history of legal activism, and the NAACP Legal Fund, for one, was well funded and prepared to act when Title VII passed. The same cannot be said of feminists. Despite an inauspicious start, the EEOC became the leading advocate in a new legal coalition that emerged by the 1970s and helped convince the courts that many forms of sex discrimination in the workplace existed and were illegal. But the federal judiciary was at first unwilling to recognize sex discrimination in employment beyond obvious cases of differential treatment in precisely the same job, and yet willing to grant employers much latitude in claiming BFOQ exceptions to Title VII. Like other claimants of sex discrimination under Title VII, flight attendants had to wait while federal judges approached some consensus on what sex discrimination was and how Title VII prohibited it.[32]

In *Cooper v. Delta Airlines*, flight attendants got their first and most disheartening ruling from a federal district court on the legality of the airlines' no-marriage rules. The case, decided on 19 October 1967, not only brought the first opinion on airline practices, but more broadly established the first Title VII case law on no-marriage policies. Eulalie Cooper filed a charge with the EEOC after Delta had fired her as a stewardess on 1 April 1966, when it discovered she was married. By the fall of 1966 she had taken Delta to court in the Eastern District of Louisiana, where she was based, with the EEOC's authorization to claim sex discrimination under Title VII. Cooper had neither official backing from a union (since Delta flight attendants were then, as now, unorganized) nor a definitive general ruling on the illegality of airline marriage policies from the EEOC to help her fight Delta. The judge's ruling suggested, however, that she would have lost no matter what.

In the *Cooper* case Delta put on an elaborate BFOQ defense, with psy-

chological experts and airline personnel officials testifying that successful passenger service required young, single female attendants. The trial
judge was apparently impressed, for his ruling affirmed the airline's right
to restrict flight attendants' employment by sex, age, and marital status—
and the related criteria that Delta added, from physical size to education
and "moral character." Because Delta employed only women as flight
attendants, the court held that the discrimination charged by Cooper was
merely between married and single persons and thus not a violation of
Title VII's ban on "sex" discrimination. The judge went further, questioning whether sex discrimination was even a real concern of public
policy or law. He noted that only a few states had bothered to legislate
against sex bias to date; as for Title VII, he contended, the word sex had
"just sort of found its way into the equal employment opportunities
section of the Civil Rights Bill." Cooper appealed, but when Delta soon
after dropped its no-marriage rule and offered to reinstate her, she returned to work and dropped her suit. While Cooper lost what was a
crucial test case for flight attendants, at least she helped pressure her own
airline toward voluntary compliance with Title VII. Cooper was also
luckier in one sense than some flight attendants who subsequently lost
Title VII cases: the Louisiana court spared her from having to reimburse
Delta for its legal costs.[33]

It would take another defeat in the courts before flight attendants got a
legal ruling against marriage bans in 1970. In *Lansdale v. United Air Lines*
(1969) the federal court was again in the South (the Southern District of
Florida), but unlike in *Cooper*, the court at least took the inclusion of
"sex" in Title VII seriously. The plaintiff lost instead because of a new
legal theory of Title VII's limits, validated earlier in 1969 by a higher
court. The theory was the so-called sex-plus exemption, and the precedent was *Phillips v. Martin Marietta*, a case that turned on whether the
employer could reject female, but not male, job applicants with school-
age children. In *Phillips* the Fifth Circuit Court of Appeals (the appellate
court for the Southern District of Florida, among others) reasoned that
the restrictive policy was based on sex "plus" an additional factor, paren-
tal status, and because it was not discrimination based on sex alone, did
not violate Title VII. The court in *Lansdale* followed the same logic in its
ruling of 2 December 1969: "As in Phillips there is a coalescence here of a
two-pronged qualification, i.e., sex plus marriage. United did not discharge plaintiff because she was a woman nor because she was married.

Her discharge came about because she was a woman and married. It is clear that the Civil Rights Act of 1964 does not prohibit discrimination in employment because of marital status." The court ordered Marion Lansdale to pay United's legal tab.[34]

The sex-plus theory threatened to undermine entirely stewardesses' sex discrimination claims against no-marriage rules and age ceilings. Employers had to persuade the court of the business "necessity" of a discriminatory practice to claim a BFOQ exception from Title VII, but sex-plus policies were by very definition excluded from Title VII scrutiny according to some courts. In 1971, however, the Supreme Court overturned *Phillips v. Martin Marietta*, bringing an effective end to sex-plus exemptions from Title VII. As a result, Marion Lansdale's defeat on the basis of the sex-plus theory was soon after vacated on appeal.[35]

Only two months after Lansdale's defeat in trial court, another United stewardess found the federal district court in Chicago willing to hold the carrier's no-marriage policy up to stricter Title VII scrutiny. In *Sprogis v. United* (decided on 21 January 1970 and affirmed on 16 June 1971), the trial and appellate courts adopted essentially the same approach to Title VII as the EEOC. That is, the courts read Title VII to mean that any policy targeting a group of employees *because* of sex was discriminatory, regardless of whether the policy hinged on a "plus" condition (such as marriage) or whether men and women or just one sex made up the group in question. Since the *Sprogis* courts flatly rejected the idea that sex-plus policies were automatically exempt from Title VII, the burden of proof was on United to defend the no-marriage policy. United's arguments, the trial judge wrote in his brief ruling, did not show either sex or single status to be a bona fide occupational qualification for flight attendants. The appellate court refined the point. Even if the BFOQ exception to Title VII justified women-only hiring, "that conclusion would not automatically legitimate the no-marriage rule imposed exclusively upon stewardesses." United failed "to offer any salient rationale" for its single-only policy. The trial court granted Mary Burke Sprogis reinstatement, all the back pay and seniority she would have accrued, and legal costs. For flight attendants and the airlines, *Sprogis* set a crucial precedent by which age ceilings as well as no-marriage rules could be challenged—even if courts believed it legal for airlines to employ women only for passenger service. More broadly, the case also suggested that some federal courts were beginning to catch up with the EEOC in seeing sex discrimination as a deep-seated problem in the workplace and one that Title VII was meant to combat.[36]

GETTING TO THE HEART OF THE MATTER:
DIAZ AND THE BFOQ QUESTION

The EEOC had definitively denied that sex was a BFOQ for flight attendants by 1968. The trial court in *Sprogis* had agreed in effect in January 1970 but had not ruled directly on the matter. In *Diaz v. Pan American Airways*, a federal court (yet again in the South) did rule directly on whether it was legal under Title VII for airlines to hire only women for flight attendant positions. In the *Diaz* case, filed in Miami where the male plaintiff had been denied employment by Pan Am, there were no sex-plus complications of marital status or age—the case boiled down to whether airlines could hire one sex to the exclusion of the other. The key question for the court was whether Pan Am's female-only hiring policy met the standard for the BFOQ exception as outlined by Congress in Title VII: "those certain instances where religion, sex, or national origin is a bona fide occupational qualification reasonably necessary to the normal operation of that particular business or enterprise."

By the time the district court in Florida heard the *Diaz* case, the higher court of appeals for the region, the Fifth Circuit, had recently ruled on the first major case to test the BFOQ clause, *Weeks v. Southern Bell* (1969). The standard used by the appellate court in *Weeks* was the first sign that federal courts would follow the EEOC's policy of interpreting the BFOQ clause narrowly. In seeming contradiction, it was the same appellate court that in 1969 had established the sex-plus exemption in *Phillips* undercutting the efficacy of Title VII. According to the Fifth Circuit's ruling in *Weeks*, however, a BFOQ exception to Title VII required the employer to show that "all or substantially all women" would be unable to perform the job in question safely and efficiently. To do otherwise would allow the BFOQ exception to swallow the rule of nondiscrimination in Title VII.[37]

In *Diaz v. Pan Am* the airline found the trial judge more easily persuaded than the appellate court above him that the BFOQ exception's stated parameters—discrimination must be "reasonably necessary" to "normal" business—were not so restrictive after all. Pan Am argued, and the trial court agreed, that employers did not have to engage in more

egalitarian hiring practices if they knew from experience that such practices would be less practical and profitable. Had the ruling stood on
appeal in *Diaz*, it might have set a precedent by which employers had
little reason to worry about discriminating on the basis of sex under Title
VII as long as they could show that doing so was good for business.

In a lengthy ruling of 8 April 1970 the trial court for the Southern
District of Florida carefully paraphrased and affirmed Pan Am's arguments in claiming a BFOQ exception. In crafting its elaborate defense, the
carrier benefited from several years' worth of industry experience at
fighting sex discrimination charges in various legal contexts. Pan Am first
of all outlined the changing business environment since the 1930s that led
it first to hire males only, then in 1944 to begin hiring men and women as
flight attendants, and finally, to hire only women during the jet age.
While conceding that it had once hired men exclusively, Pan Am argued
that men were no longer able to perform the job satisfactorily as it had
evolved by the 1960s. In the early days flight attendant work included
heavy physical labor (such as baggage handling) and exceedingly long
hours, to which Pan Am believed men were better suited. With the jet age,
passenger service had come to focus almost exclusively on ensuring passengers' comfort and well-being—it had become "women's work." As the
trial court noted in its decision, Pan Am was not alone in revising its sex
preference: 96 percent of more than 23,000 U.S. flight attendants employed in 1967 were women, and no carrier was hiring men as stewards.[38]

Pan Am then elaborated on why women were better suited for jet-age
passenger service and why carriers thus needed to hire women exclusively. First and foremost, passengers preferred female attendants. The
carrier claimed this largely on the basis of experience, but also offered a
survey as confirmation. The Air Transport Association had commissioned the Opinion Research Corporation of Princeton, New Jersey, to
conduct an independent study in June 1966 of passengers' views on the
sex of flight attendants. The survey included the responses of five hundred passengers flying TWA, American, Eastern, and United, who were
interviewed in New York, Los Angeles, and Chicago. The passengers were
a "balanced sample" of "1/3 first class to 2/3 coach, and 2/3 men to 1/3
women." The survey found that 79 percent of those queried preferred to
be served by a stewardess; 18 percent had no preference and only 3 percent
would rather be served by a male steward.[39]

Pan Am offered expert psychological testimony too on the unique value of women in passenger service. The psychiatrist Eric Berne testified that the physical conditions of flight produced three emotional states in passengers: apprehension, boredom, and excitement. Berne argued that passengers experiencing any of the three emotional states were better handled by stewardesses because of the "nature" of females' relationship to members of both sexes, and that femininity was especially effective in taming the most important of the emotional states, apprehension. Berne explained that a male passenger would either be threatened or repulsed by a male steward, depending on whether he perceived the steward as more or less masculine than he himself; but a female flight attendant, Berne argued, would necessarily affirm the male passenger's masculinity. As for a female passenger, Berne stated that she might find a male flight attendant's attempts to reassure her intrusive or inappropriate, but would welcome a fellow female's attention.[40]

Pan Am acknowledged that passengers' preferences did not alone justify denying all men the chance to work as flight attendants, but it contended that it was impossible in practice to seek out the few men who might have sufficient "feminine" traits to be successful in passenger service. Raymond Katzell, industrial psychologist and chairman of the department of psychology at New York University, testified that while both men and women could adequately perform the "mechanical" aspects of the flight attendant job, women as a group were far better equipped for the all-important "interpersonal" aspects. He explained that the motivation and ability needed for a high level of performance in the "intangibles" of the job required various characteristics that together formed "femininity" as commonly understood. In particular, Katzell cited as "feminine" traits benevolence, a genuine interest in the comfort of others, and a lack of apparent aggressiveness. While some men might be exemplars of one of these distinguishing traits, "It would be quite infrequent to find a man possessing each of these traits to at least as high a degree as the average woman." More important for Pan Am's case, Katzell argued that any man who did possess a sufficient aggregate of feminine traits would be a proverbial needle in the hiring haystack. To eliminate sex as a qualification, Katzell concluded, would rob the airlines of the best means to screen out applicants unlikely to be satisfactory flight attendants.[41]

The *Diaz* trial court was amply persuaded by Pan Am's historical, psychological, and practical justifications for its female-only hiring. In the decision, handed down on 8 April 1970, the court held that Pan Am's policy was the result of "a pragmatic process" based on the carrier's considerable experience, which in the current business climate yielded "better average performance for its passengers than would a policy of mixed male and female hiring." The court ruled that sex was a bona fide occupational qualification for flight attendants and Pan Am's females-only hiring policy was "not an unlawful discrimination on the grounds of sex" under Title VII. The trial judge had thus accepted from Pan Am exactly the kinds of BFOQ arguments that the EEOC determined in 1965 should be rejected: blanket assumptions about women's or men's employability as a group and customers' preferences.[42]

When Diaz appealed the ruling, however, the Fifth Circuit imposed a much stricter standard of what was "reasonably necessary" to justify discrimination, which did not necessarily accommodate what was "normal" or desirable for employers. The appellate court, the same court that in *Weeks* had required employers seeking a BFOQ exception to show that "all or substantially all" members of one sex could not adequately perform the job in question, added another hurdle for employers in its ruling in *Diaz*: employers had to prove that excluding one sex from the job was essential to their core business, not just a profitable strategy.

In the end the Fifth Circuit determined that the necessary business of airlines was ultimately nothing other than safely transporting passengers, which did not require that flight attendants be female. "We begin with the proposition that the use of the word 'necessary' . . . requires that we apply a business necessity test, not a business convenience test." The court conceded that it could well be important to Pan Am's profits to provide "a pleasant environment," enhanced by "the obvious cosmetic effect that female stewardesses provide" and their "apparent ability to perform the non-mechanical functions of the job" better than most men. But such services "are tangential to the essence of the business involved. No one has suggested that having male stewards will so seriously affect the operation of an airline as to jeopardize or even minimize its ability to provide safe transportation from one place to another." After all, the court noted, airlines had employed both men and women in the past and Pan Am, even then, had nearly three hundred male attendants working on some of its foreign flights. Because the appellate court denied that the sex of flight attendants had anything to do with Pan Am's essential business, it left aside the rest of the carrier's arguments about the difficulty of finding qualified male applicants and the preferences of its customers. "While we recognize that the public's expectation of finding one sex in a particular role may cause some initial difficulty, it would be totally anomalous if we were to allow the preferences and prejudices of the customers to determine whether the sex discrimination was valid. Indeed, it was, to a large extent, these very prejudices the [Civil Rights] Act was meant to overcome."[43]

The Fifth Circuit reversed the lower court decision in *Diaz* on 6 April 1971, and declared that Pan Am's female-only hiring policy had resulted in unlawful discrimination. It rejected the carrier's request for a rehearing a month later, and the U.S. Supreme Court turned down Pan Am's petition in November 1971. With its ruling in *Diaz*, the Fifth Circuit settled the legal question of whether sex was a BFOQ for the flight attendant occupation. It was not. *Diaz* also more broadly restricted the ability of any employer to justify sex discrimination with the BFOQ clause, a strategy that would continue to be the primary defense of employers in Title VII lawsuits.[44]

BEYOND DIAZ AND THE BFOQ

After *Diaz* airlines had little choice but to make good-faith efforts to open entry-level cabin positions to male applicants. In 1972 the *New York Times* reported that there was suddenly a large number of men in training to become flight attendants. In some cases, previously all-female classes had almost overnight become about half male, half female. Thanks to the *Sprogis* ruling of 1971, no airline could dismiss female flight attendants simply for marrying. There was no comparable federal lawsuit that tested the legality of age ceilings in the late 1960s or early 1970s. But the outlawing of no-marriage rules in *Sprogis*, by logical extension, forestalled any "sex-plus" or BFOQ defense for airlines' forced retirement of female flight attendants in their mid-thirties. Together, stewardesses who had been fired for marrying, and Celio Diaz and other male applicants barred from airline cabin service, had secured a sweeping legal mandate from the federal courts by the early 1970s to force dramatic changes in the employment of flight attendants.[45]

The victory in *Sprogis* and the historic *Diaz* case still left untouched numerous other forms of sex discrimination against flight attendants. As more men entered the occupation and women began to stay longer, other discriminatory practices on the airlines became more obvious targets for legal action under Title VII. If stewardesses could get married, why could they not also have children and keep their jobs? Why should the small but growing number of men in the occupation enjoy preferential treatment in benefits and promotional opportunities—and face laxer weight and appearance standards?

Not long after *Diaz* and *Sprogis*, flight attendants scored another major legal success, in this case challenging policies that favored male cabin attendants. In *Laffey v. Northwest*, the federal trial court in the District of Columbia awarded Northwest's only female purser at the time, Mary P. Laffey, a stunning victory against the carrier in 1973. The case documented in careful detail the various ways Northwest had discriminated against female flight attendants, first by blocking them from promotion to more senior, better-paid purser positions, then by providing unequal benefits, despite equal pay scales, to stewardesses and their male equivalents in the category of "flight service attendants." Moreover, Northwest imposed a ban on eyeglasses and weight monitoring only on the women, and more generally showed a pattern of inflicting harsher discipline on women for infractions of company rules. The *Laffey* court determined that despite the classifications and slightly varying duties, male pursers, female stewardesses, and male flight service attendants all did the same job, with equivalent levels of skill, supervisory responsibilities, and required training. As a result, unequal treatment of men and women across the three categories was held to violate Title VII and the Equal Pay Act of 1963. The court's means of ending discrimination at Northwest were strict: the carrier could not equalize treatment on some middle ground but had to extend its highest pay scales and best promotional opportunities and benefits to all flight attendants. Northwest also had to do away with all restrictions on corrective eyewear and weight, except where an employee's physical ability to perform safety duties might be in question. The court awarded back pay and costs of litigation totaling an estimated $24 million to Laffey and the other stewardesses who had joined her in a class action. An editorial in the *Washington Post* heralded the ruling as not only the broadest yet against airline bias but also "another in the lengthening series of decisions which insist that corporations abolish the obsolete, artificial distinctions between men's professions and women's work."[46]

As *Laffey* suggested, enforcement of Title VII was gathering steam in the 1970s. After the EEOC gained prosecutorial powers in 1972 and courts generally grew more sympathetic, the commission increasingly launched intentionally sweeping attacks on racial and gender discrimination, targeting some of the nation's largest employers. Such efforts resulted in several high-profile agreements: with AT&T in 1973, then the nation's largest private employer; General Electric in 1978; the Associated Press in 1983; and General Motors in 1984. These agreements brought aggrieved workers millions of dollars in back pay and provided for affirmative action plans to move more women and minorities up the employment ladder and out of blue- and pink-collar ghettoes. Title VII was still not a fix-all for discrimination in the workplace. One scholar's review of more than six hundred cases in the 1970s and 1980s found that women more often lost than won their lawsuits alleging sex discrimination. Indeed, as the most blatant and quantifiable forms of sex discrimination ended, more subtle forms persisted that were harder for women to prove to the courts' satisfaction. Still, Title VII victories were important in and of themselves, and losses could promote action in other arenas. Women workers' protests that pregnancy-based employment restrictions were discriminatory, for example, ran into a quagmire of medical and social debates in the courts. But women's complaints and feminist pressure pushed Congress to pass the Pregnancy Discrimination in Employment Act in 1978 as an amendment to Title VII, requiring that employers treat pregnancy the same as any other temporary disability.[47]

Title VII, in the historian Nancy MacLean's words, unleashed a "vast drama of public innovation." A reform won by the African American civil rights movement, the prospect of fair employment encouraged women and other racial minorities to mobilize their own civil rights struggles and, in turn, broadened the black freedom struggle. Title VII was of course not self-enforcing. It took workers willing to press complaints of discrimination and allies willing to help them to force change. Those who acted "were themselves setting national policy," MacLean contends. Eventually workers and their activist allies used Title VII often enough and successfully enough to work a virtual revolution in workplace expectations and values in the United States. A nation that once unthinkingly accepted the subordination and exclusion of nonwhite and female workers came instead to prize diversity and inclusion across lines of race, gender, and ethnicity. Flight attendants were among the thousands of women and people of color who, by seizing on their new right to lodge charges of discrimination with the EEOC, helped launch this revolution in the mid-1960s.[48]

For flight attendants themselves, it would be hard to overstate the historic importance of Title VII. By immediately availing themselves of the new law as soon as it passed in mid-1964 in whatever ways they could, they brought a definitive end by the close of the decade to the airlines' no-marriage rules and age limits. Other employment restrictions were eliminated as well, such as "no-divorce" policies and age limits at the time of hire. Into the 1970s and 1980s activist flight attendants forced airlines to grant stewardesses maternity rights and loosen extraordinarily strict weight rules. Together age, marriage, maternity, and weight restrictions— all applied exclusively to stewardesses among airline employees—had made long-term careers virtually unthinkable for most female flight attendants. Changes in airline policies wrought by flight attendants' vigorous use of Title VII led to an abrupt drop in turnover. In 1971 only one-ninth of all stewardesses left their jobs. By 1976 stewardesses' average job tenure was six and a half years, and climbing. By the end of the 1970s, moreover, more than half of female flight attendants were married, with no need to keep it a secret. Female flight attendants collectively reaped more dramatic benefits from Title VII than perhaps any other single occupational group. As the sociologist Frieda Rozen argues, the Civil Rights Act "had a strikingly greater proportional impact in this occupation than in others because it changed the most important of working conditions, the right to stay on the job, for almost all the individuals already *in* the occupation."[49]

Title VII also effected more moderate changes in the flight attendant occupation, as in many others, by forcing open more jobs to previously excluded or underrepresented groups. After *Diaz v. Pan Am* men secured a firmer foothold. At the start of the 1980s they accounted for as much as 17 percent of the flight attendant workforce, a fourfold increase from when Pan Am rejected Celio Diaz's application in 1967. While a handful of pioneering African American women had forced airlines into piecemeal racial integration before Title VII, the new law's ripple effects in promoting equal opportunity helped women of color boost their presence in what had once been a lily-white field. African American women accounted for 15 percent of all flight attendants by the 1980s.[50]

Although legal activism under the aegis of Title VII began in the mid-

1960s to reverse more than three decades of airline discrimination, and although the airlines had already moderately liberalized their definition of hostess appeal in response to stewardesses' demands, in other respects the airlines resisted fundamental change to entrenched marketing ideals and employment practices. Airlines also began by the mid-1960s to evidence growing fondness for sexually provocative uniforms and ad campaigns laced with innuendo. The trend would only intensify during the decade after 1965, even as flight attendants progressively dismantled airlines' discriminatory policies. The swinging stewardess who enlivened airline marketing, along with popular novels and adult films, in the later 1960s and early 1970s embodied male, heterosexual fantasies of more sexual freedom for women—and drew critiques from feminists who found the fantasies degrading and exploitative. Angered female flight attendants would become leading critics of efforts by the airlines to cash in on the sexual revolution through provocative images of stewardesses.

"FLY ME? GO FLY YOURSELF!"

Stewardess Liberation in the 1970s

In 1974 the former stewardess Paula Kane published a memoir, *Sex Objects in the Sky: A Personal Account of the Stewardess Rebellion*, which captured the spirit of feminist militancy among many flight attendants by the early 1970s. Kane opened with pointed questions to an imaginary male passenger: "What is that pretty young stewardess thinking as she walks gracefully down the aisle to get you your third drink?" "Is she anxious, as much of the airlines' advertising says, to 'Make You Feel Good All Over,' to be asked 'Almost Anything'?" "Or is she perhaps musing about last night's orgy, as films such as *The Swinging Stewardesses* and *Come Fly with Me* would suggest?" Kane then informed her fictive "typical" passenger, "If she is a stewardess who has been flying for some time, the chances are very good that she is only hoping that you won't make a pass at her or get drunk or make a scene."[1]

In the late 1960s and early 1970s commercial expressions of the sexual revolution had cast stewardesses in a newly provocative role. In airline advertisements and popular novels and films, the "swinging stewardess" represented a male, heterosexual vision of a new era in which women eagerly embraced opportunities for overt flirtation and sexual adventure. Yet for Kane, sexy images in airline marketing and popular culture amounted to an invitation for unprecedented sexual harassment. "Pinching and patting" of stewardesses by drunken and lecherous male passengers had noticeably increased, she contended. But "pinching and patting" was not the only form of degradation that female flight attendants suffered in the early 1970s. They faced the patronizing attitudes of the

airlines, which subjected them to rigorous grooming and weight standards while offering them few prospects for career advancement. For
Kane, these were the exploitative realities that belied the glamorous, sexy
myths of the stewardess and that had made the real women who served
airline passengers ripe for feminist revolt.

To Paula Kane, Stewardesses for Women's Rights (SFWR) exemplified
the "stewardess rebellion" against popular stereotypes and airline exploitation. In 1972 two female flight attendants organized SFWR "to meet a
need created by the new consciousness among stewardesses." An inter-
airline association unaffiliated with a union, SFWR set out to improve the
working conditions of flight attendants and challenge "sexpot" images of
stewardesses by proclaiming them highly skilled safety professionals. In
bringing an explicitly feminist agenda to the labor activism of flight
attendants, SFWR represented, in its leaders' words, a "pioneer effort in
relatively unchartered territory." And they believed that their efforts carried symbolic weight for all women. Stewardess liberation, by SFWR's
account, was women's liberation.[2]

The self-consciously feminist zeal of SFWR was only one of the more
militant and well-publicized manifestations of the "stewardess rebellion."
From union independence campaigns, to health and safety activism, to
Title VII lawsuits against maternity policies and weight rules, to an unprecedented number of strikes, flight attendants of the 1970s evidenced
profound discontent with their celebrated occupation. For many flight
attendants in the 1970s, ending their exploitation was not necessarily the
broadly symbolic battle against gender inequity that SFWR activists envi-
sioned. But however flight attendants conceived of their activism in rela-
tion to the women's movement, their unprecedented militancy in the
1970s constituted a sweeping feminist challenge to the inequities they had
long confronted in the workplace and the labor movement; it was also a
challenge to how the public perceived and valued their labor. The stewardess rebellion was a historic culmination of decades of activism.

The stewardess rebellion was also one of the more dramatic manifestations of the upsurge in working women's resistance to sexual and racial
subordination in the 1970s. Women seized on affirmative action programs, organized workplace and union caucuses, and mobilized in numerous other ways to upgrade "women's work" and break into better-
paying male preserves in skilled trades, elite professions, and corporate
hierarchies. Working women refused en masse to accept gendered, sex-

ualized, and racialized stereotypes that had defined them as less deserving than male breadwinners of wages, benefits, and respect. As one of the most culturally visible and, by the 1970s, visibly sexualized of female occupational groups, flight attendants helped deal a particular feminist blow to the objectification, career limitations, and patronizing attitudes that beset privileged, white, female wage-earners. Their activist efforts, along with those of countless other women, demonstrated that one of the hardiest and most inclusive manifestations of the modern women's movement was workplace feminism.[3]

"HI, I'M CHERYL—FLY ME"

The stewardess rebellion was inspired in no small part by the increasing eroticization of airline marketing over the preceding decade. With ever-bolder innuendo, airlines invited passengers to consider titillation by stewardesses a main attraction of air travel. As we have seen, sexier airline advertising messages emerged in the 1960s as part of a larger competitive effort by carriers to sell fun and good feelings as well as the traditional ideal of gracious service. By the early 1970s invitations to sexual fantasy had become the overriding theme of the most visible and innovative airline marketing schemes. The hypersexualization of airline marketing unfolded in fits and starts and with economically and culturally driven variations among carriers. But the general trend of the late 1960s and early 1970s was to replace hints that stewardesses' sexual allure was but one, albeit important, visceral pleasure of jet travel with coy but clear indications that sexual provocation was the ultimate thrill aloft.

In January 1965 a newspaper advertisement for Continental Airlines offered a bold harbinger of a sexier era in marketing. The overwhelming visual component of the ad was a posterior view from the waist down of a slender, shapely stewardess bending slightly forward, wearing a snug, above-the-knee skirt and high heels. The accompanying boldface text explained with an implied wink and nudge, "Our first run movies are so interesting we hope you're not missing the other attractions abroad." In fine print, Continental declared itself "the one for fun."[4]

It was fitting that Continental should have helped to show the way to a spicier future in airline marketing. In the years to come, carriers like Continental, Braniff, and National that felt a particular squeeze in the industry's federally regulated market created the boldest and most visible of sexualized advertising campaigns. Continental, National, and Braniff were in the second tier of an oligopolistic industry. Above them were the historic "Big Four" airlines (United, American, TWA, Eastern) and the international specialist Pan Am, carriers which enjoyed the largest and most diverse government-granted route networks and the most stability. Lower down were numerous regional airlines, which the government protected from insolvency by allocating small but viable route networks to them and by providing subsidies when their routes proved unprofitable. Because of the regulatory structure and capital requirements, new entrants to the industry were effectively locked out. Among established airlines of various sizes, few wanted to compete much on price; the government regulated fares along with routes, and competitive price slashing, even if allowed, would simply reduce profits. Airlines competed as best they could with new technologies, but by the later 1960s even smaller carriers had acquired jet aircraft. Where airlines could—and did—compete most intensely for passengers was in service, which dominated marketing. Along with expensive jets came a new era of unprecedented spending on advertising in the 1960s and growing emphasis on securing the brand loyalty of passengers. When economic turmoil struck the entire industry in the late 1960s and worsened with skyrocketing fuel prices in the early 1970s, all American carriers suffered and searched for more effective means of advertising. The largest carriers had the biggest marketing budgets, but also had their reputability as industry leaders to uphold. So it was generally the mid-sized and small carriers that proved boldest with sexual messages, and National, Braniff, and Continental in particular whose campaigns had the most impact.[5]

In 1971, as economic troubles were growing for the airlines, National introduced the most famous and controversial airline slogan of the era, "Fly Me." The first signature print ad featured a photographic close-up of Cheryl Fioravante, a freckled National stewardess with a short, boyish coiffure, who smiled innocently. Above, in giant boldface, read, "Hi, I'm Cheryl—Fly Me." In subsequent ads National invited travelers to fly other fresh-faced stewardesses. The brainchild of the agency F. William Free and Co., the "Fly Me" campaign cost National more than $9 million annually to launch and sustain through the mid-1970s. But it was presumably worth the cost, since it raised the carrier's "brand" visibility, garnered advertising awards, and generated healthy sales of related "Fly Me" products. National offered t-shirts and mugs emblazoned with the slogan, a phonographic recording of the campaign's theme song, and even a Barbie-like "Fly Me" stewardess doll.[6]

The "Fly Me" campaign not only proved the most attention-getting of the provocative airline slogans but also exemplified the airlines' coyness about trading in stewardesses' sexual allure. From the start, National and its advertising agency professed innocence of sexual motives in anticipation of being accused otherwise. The invitation to "fly" Cheryl and her co-workers was part of a multifaceted promotion that the carrier and the Free agency claimed was merely intended to "personalize" the airline. National repeatedly explained in its employee publication that it sought to highlight the carrier's personalized service and shine a spotlight on staff, "visible or behind-the-scenes," with the use of real employees' first names. National's personnel department ascertained the sixty most common first names among female employees, which were then painted on National's fleet of aircraft. Technically, it was thus the aircraft so named that National was inviting passengers to fly. Moreover, the promotion incorporated male and female employees throughout the company, who donned buttons bearing their first names and the "Fly Me" slogan. National also ran lower-profile "Fly Me" ads in industry publications of a cheekier kind. In *Jet Cargo News*, for example, National's middle-aged, cigar-champing male chief of cargo operations beckoned, "I'm Foxy—Ship Me." Whatever the elaborate trappings of the campaign, however, "Fly Me" registered first and foremost with the public in the way National most often and visibly presented the phrase: as an invitation delivered by young, attractive, smiling stewardesses.[7]

The success of "Fly Me" pushed airline marketing to new heights of sexual innuendo. Continental, for one, offered "We Really Move Our Tails for You" in 1974. Publicists explained that this was merely a new spin on the carrier's older slogan celebrating its distinctly painted aircraft as "proud birds with the golden tails"—an explanation offered precisely because the new campaign implied that the moving tails were those of the stewardesses. Only a few months after Continental promised wiggling tails, National replaced its "Fly Me" invitations with the boast, "We'll Fly You Like You've Never Been Flown Before." Notably, airlines' move toward more erotically charged slogans was not unique to the United States, as indicated by Air Jamaica's "We Make You Feel Good All Over" and Air France's "Have You Ever Done It the French Way?"[8]

While second-tier carriers took the lead in hypersexualizing airline marketing, the trend was a spiraling one to which carriers of all sizes contributed, and which started well before "Fly Me." In 1967 United extended its "extra care" theme of recent years to include the advertised promise, "Everyone gets warmth, friendliness and extra care—and someone may get a wife." That same year, the small Midwestern carrier Lake Central revamped its image with the slogan "Love at First Flight," a phrase emblazoned on buttons that became part of the carrier's uniforms. In 1968 American pushed the envelope further with a national magazine advertisement that proclaimed with intended irony, "Think of Her as Your Mother." The ad pictured a typically young and attractive stewardess, but one whose atypical stare and casual posture conveyed smoldering sexuality rather than maternal concern. While industry leaders like United and American dabbled in such overtly sexualized marketing, one airline banked its future entirely on it: in 1971 Southwest began its meteoric rise from an upstart flying exclusively within Texas to one of the nation's top ten carriers by positioning itself as the "love" airline, with scantily dressed stewardesses serving "love bites" (snacks) and "love potions" (drinks).[9]

CHERYL WORE HOT PANTS

Southwest was not alone in pairing sexually charged marketing with complementary innovations in stewardesses' uniforms. For decades airlines had hired renowned designers to update stewardesses' uniforms periodically and keep them chic. But stewardess couture had evolved within relatively narrow boundaries. From the 1930s to the mid-1960s female cabin crew wore tailored skirt-suits and blouses, with few exceptions. Hemlines moved up and down and accessories changed with the styles of the day, but stewardesses were always garbed with a keen eye toward formality and respectability. Even when snug tailoring revealed their figures, they were covered from neck to at least knee, producing what United's designer once called "tailored restraint with youthful charm." By the later 1960s, however, restraint was suddenly passé. In but a few years, stewardesses' attire went from prim and proper ladies' suits to miniskirts, "wet-look" vinyl, and "hot pants" (minuscule, tight shorts).[10]

As the sexual revolution fired commercialized eroticism on Madison Avenue and in airline advertising, the transatlantic fashion industry in the 1960s also plunged into a new era of more provocative styles, which airlines eventually adopted. Amid growing youth-driven political protest and cultural radicalism in the United States and Europe, a new generation of designers boldly experimented with new materials, from paper to plastic to metal, and more flesh-revealing styles for daytime. The British designer Mary Quant, a pioneer in popularizing the miniskirt, explained her creations in bluntly sexual terms. "Mini-clothes," she declared in 1967, were "symbolic" of women like her who did not want "to wait until dark" to "go to bed with a man." While fashions of the later 1960s drew inspiration from numerous cultural sources beyond youth rebellion and sexual revolution, the general trend was to encourage women to dress more youthfully, casually, and revealingly, anytime and anywhere. For jet-age airlines hoping to lend more excitement to flying, it was only logical that stewardess couture should reflect the era's bolder fashion statements.[11]

In 1965, the same year that Continental advertised a stewardess's derriere as a main feature of its passenger service, another second-tier carrier, Braniff, inaugurated the fashion revolution on the airlines. Under the tutelage of the advertising executive Mary Wells, Braniff announced "an end to the plain plane": the carrier painted its jets in seven pastel colors and designed a high-fashion "air strip" to be performed by its hostesses. Braniff employed a rising star of the fashion industry, the Italian designer Emilio Pucci, who provided brightly colored, outlandishly accessorized "jet-age" fashion for the carrier's hostesses. During flights Braniff hostesses actually shed, or at least changed, components of their new Pucci wardrobes. The fashion show progressed from a coat with optional bubble helmet for inclement weather, through a bright raspberry skirt-suit for welcoming passengers and a "Puccino" shift for serving dinner, to a clingy mock turtleneck and knee-length "harem" pants for serving after-dinner drinks. Television and print advertisements portrayed the "air strip" literally as a striptease, though the fine print reassured travelers that the hostesses accomplished each sartorial transformation in "a flash," "to give you constant attention, from the time you take off to the time you land."[12]

Braniff had taken a bold risk, but it quickly paid off for almost everyone. By mid-1966 Braniff management reported a 50-percent increase in business over the past year, due to the heavily promoted "air strip" and the "End of the Plain Plane" campaign. Meanwhile, the campaign's success helped the creative director Mary Wells establish her own advertising agency, with Braniff as a top client. In late June 1966 Braniff announced that Pucci had designed even more eye-catching follow-up ensembles. With leopard- and geometric-print tunics and leotards and hooded fur coats, Pucci added more flair to the "air strip"—and two more outfit changes for Braniff hostesses to perform "in a flash" in the jet-age service rush.[13]

Braniff's triumph pushed the entire airline industry into new competition over who could claim the most fashionable stewardess uniforms. It was an expensive proposition. As *Newsweek* reported in September 1967, for American Airlines "the complex question of what women should wear in the air" required "a full year of policy discussions, executive-suite fashion shows, passenger surveys, frenzied shopping and designing and redesigning." American spent more than $2 million, including about $1 million on uniforms for the carriers' 2,500-plus stewardesses and another $750,000 on advertising the new look. The result of American's hefty spending and elaborate planning was the "American Beauty" uniform, a short-sleeved knit dress in white, red, or blue, ranging in length from just above the knee to mid-thigh, accessorized with bright scarves, belts, and white patent shoes or boots. Not to be outdone by American's modish look, United soon clad its stewardess workforce in an even more modish mini-dress with a jaunty, "kepi"-like hat in 1968, designed by Jean Louis for a record price of around $3 million.[14]

Some carriers mimicked Braniff not only in updating uniforms but in making stewardesses the hard-working mannequins in elaborate marketing schemes. In the most ill-fated instance, TWA sought in mid-1968 to highlight its cosmopolitanism by dressing hostesses in paper outfits that coordinated with special international menus. The styles included "British wench" and "French cocktail" dresses, a wrap-around "Roman toga," and "Manhattan penthouse" pajamas. TWA soon abandoned the paper uniforms after flight attendants complained of frequent tearing and the food often failed to match the costumes. Within less than two years American discarded its modish American Beauty dresses for a new uniform ensemble in early 1969 with frontier and colonial motifs, at a cost of about $1.2 million for the uniforms and $2 million more for advertising. New menus of regional cuisine from around the United States complemented the stewardesses' new "Daniel Boone" hats and "colonial" tartan miniskirts.[15]

Smaller airlines joined in the growing fashion competition despite

Braniff hostesses model their new, multilayered "Air Strip" uniforms by Pucci, October 1965. © Bettmann/CORBIS.

The American Airlines "American Beauty" uniform, designed at a cost of more than $2 million and modeled in all white (including fishnet stockings). © Bettmann/CORBIS.

Stewardesses at work on Southwest, the self-proclaimed "love" airline, in 1972. Courtesy of Alan Band/Hulton Archive/Getty Images.

their shallower pockets. Southern Airways tried to keep pace with relative conservatism but then plunged headlong into sexier, youthful styles. In 1967 it introduced a new uniform by the French designer Pierre Balmain that looked, compared to Braniff's Pucci wear, somewhat prudish. It featured an apricot-colored knee-length dress and a cowl-neck jacket, with pillbox hat. In its employee and passenger publication, Southern boasted that it was able to "respect femininity" and do what other airlines were "unable to do—give their stewardesses an outstanding look, while maintaining dignity." But three years later, in 1970, Southern boldly revised its vision of dignified femininity, this time with a casual black-and-white belted tunic that barely reached mid-thigh. The mini-dress could be worn alone or over "wet-look" black vinyl pants. In 1972 the carrier changed styles again, to an all-black ensemble of hot pants, short-sleeved tops, and lace-up "go-go" boots.[16]

By the early 1970s, after half a decade of rising hemlines, passengers could expect to see even more bare stewardess flesh aloft, as Southern was only one of several airlines whose uniforms consisted of hot pants and short sleeves. The heyday of hot pants aloft was not coincidentally when the advertising slogans of American carriers reached their high-water mark in sexual innuendo. The more casual and revealing uniforms of the later 1960s and early 1970s did have some important benefits for steward-esses. Many welcomed them as more comfortable and easier to launder than the starchier suits of earlier years, and more fun to wear. Several airlines allowed increased choice in styles, hemline lengths, and acces-sories, sometimes including pantsuit options. According to four steward-esses for American Airlines interviewed by the *Washington Post* in 1967, the vast majority of stewardesses loved their new "American Beauty" knit mini-dress; most were in their twenties and all their friends wore mini-skirts. Some carriers dressed their stewardesses with comparative mod-esty and kept their slogans relatively wholesome. But even Delta, then the most culturally conservative of major airlines, put its stewardesses in short-sleeved, above-the-knee dresses and offered a slogan, "Ready When You Are!" that could be read as merely a more subtle tease than "Fly Me." By the early 1970s airlines collectively had given passengers ample reason to think that stewardesses on any carrier would be "ready" for just about anything.[17]

COFFEE, TEA OR ME? THE SWINGING STEW IN POPULAR CULTURE

What airline marketing coyly left to the imagination of male passengers, films and novels about "swinging" stewardesses in the late 1960s and 1970s made increasingly explicit. In 1967 *Coffee, Tea or Me? The Uninhib-ited Memoirs of Two Airline Stewardesses* appeared as the first and most successful entry in what became a popular genre of "swinging" steward-ess literature. *Coffee, Tea or Me?* was not, as promoted, the memoirs of the stewardesses Trudy Baker and Rachel Jones, but a novel ghostwritten by a male airline publicist and then promoted by two flight attendants who posed as Baker and Jones. The book was marketed nonetheless as "au-thentic," "wacky," and "naughty." *Coffee, Tea or Me?* eventually sold more than one million copies and was followed by three more romps, *The Coffee, Tea or Me Girls' Round-the-World Diary* (1970), *The Coffee, Tea or*

Me Girls Lay It on the Line (1972), and *The Coffee, Tea or Me Girls Get Away from It All* (1974). A film adaptation of the original *Coffee, Tea or Me?* appeared on television in 1973.[18]

Compared to imitators, *Coffee, Tea or Me?* offered a relatively tame "insider" view of the occupation. The novel devoted plenty of pages to stewardesses' work culture along with romance, and left sexual activity to the reader's imagination. By 1974, when the last installment of the *Coffee, Tea or Me* series was published, a long list of other paperbacks and films featuring "swinging" stewardesses had appeared with more naughtiness and less authenticity. The cover of Cornelius Wohl's *How to Make a Good Airline Stewardess* from 1972 proclaimed, "First *Coffee, Tea or Me?*—Now this expert guide to the luscious stews of every airline you're likely to fly." In 1969 Bernard Glemser offered *The Fly Girls*, "the no-holds-barred novel of the stewardesses who swing in the sky—and on the ground!," followed in 1971 by *The Super-Jet Girls*, "a mile-high frolic with the playgirls of the air!" Bill Wenzel, a veteran illustrator of *Esquire*, sketched preposterously buxom stewardesses for many covers and chapter introductions. For *How to Make a Good Airline Stewardess*, Wenzel rendered thirty-seven "typical" stewardesses from various airlines in both their uniforms and completely unclothed. Films like *Swinging Stewardesses* and *Stewardesses 3-D* transferred the fantasy of the scantily attired, sexually adventuresome stewardess from print to screen with yet more explicitness.[19]

To the former stewardess Paula Kane, an encounter with a former Playboy bunny in the early 1970s dramatized stewardesses' new reputation for promiscuity, acquired thanks to the efforts of Wohl, Glemser, Wenzel, and others. The bunny, Kane wrote in 1974, "recalled that in the midst of her more ardent amorous exploits she always had in the back of her mind that this was nothing compared with what the stewardesses were up to." For stewardesses like Kane who found little of their realities in *The Super-Jet Girls* and *Stewardesses 3-D*, trumping Playboy bunnies in presumed sexual activity was hardly a welcome development. Even before some of the more salacious visions of flying swingers had appeared in print or on screen, a stewardess for American Airlines was moved to write a letter of protest to a local journalist in Chicago in 1969. She wanted to reassure the public: "most of us are serious, moral young women anxious to do a good job—because we like the work and flying, not 'making-out' with tired businessmen."[20]

Of course the airlines' own marketing played no small part in revising the image of stewardesses from that of the perfect brides-in-training of the postwar years to the ready and willing playmates of the swinging sixties and seventies. As a male editorialist for *Life* who had just observed the paper uniforms that TWA hostesses were wearing in mid-1968 quipped, "Never has aviation advertising had so little to do with aviation." Although he welcomed the change, many stewardesses resented it. Airlines had been glamorizing stewardesses for decades, but the more provocative marketing of the late 1960s and 1970s was newly offensive to many female flight attendants. Union leaders on Continental informed their management, "We like flirtations when we have the freedom of choice, but do not believe that just because we are Hostesses we must endure the reputation of professional flirts." Even stewardesses at American who waxed enthusiastically about their new mini-dress uniforms in 1967 explained that it was difficult "to keep their dignity" while bending and reaching at work. "A girl wants to attract a guy but not that way in public," one of them contended. Madison Avenue's vision of the sexual revolution, as seen so vividly on the airlines, was not the same as real sexual freedom and control for women. Just as flight attendants were increasingly finding their supposedly glamorous work to be a harried, grinding drudgery on crowded jets, airlines also managed to make many stewardesses view their celebrated status as equally unrewarding and alienating.[21]

SECOND-WAVE FEMINISM AND THE STEWARDESS REBELLION

By the time stewardesses found themselves wearing hot pants and "fly me" buttons, second-wave feminism was profoundly reshaping how many women viewed their lives, their jobs, and the images they saw of themselves in the media. While nurtured through the earlier activism of women in the labor, civil rights, and peace movements, among others, second-wave feminism first emerged as a definable movement unto itself by 1967 through the actions of two distinct groups. First were activists who had previously worked through government channels and liberal institutions to seek change, but had become increasingly disillusioned with establishment politics. Their frustration peaked with the inaction of the state on women's new right to equal treatment as workers under Title VII, and their response was to form pressure groups to agitate for greater enforcement efforts. In late 1966 a group of these disillusioned veteran activists formed the first and most important organization to embody second-wave feminists' demands for economic and legal equality, the National Organization for Women (NOW).[22]

Second-wave feminism also came to life through the efforts of young, white women who cut their activist teeth in civil rights and antiwar protests, but found that the lofty egalitarian ideals of these male-led movements did not extend to women's status. When women of the New Left began to decry their subordination in the division of activist labor and in the movement's sexual politics, they found their male colleagues generally indifferent or hostile. In 1967 disillusioned female veterans of the New Left began to organize separately as self-defined "women's liber-ationists." Soon a handful of radical women's groups in a few big cities were joined by other small groups across the nation. What united them was a drive to theorize women's oppression as not merely a byproduct of class oppression or a more benign counterpart to racial oppression but a fundamental organizing principle of American capitalism and society. Radicalized initially by the New Left but even more so by their analyses of their own lives, women's liberationists began producing political tracts and engaging in a range of public protests that indicted icons of tradi-tional femininity. When women's liberationists picketed the Miss Amer-ica pageant in 1968, to the derision and fascination of the media, second-wave feminism symbolically arrived as a national phenomenon with a visibly radical edge.[23]

Over time, however, second-wave feminism's radical and reformist trajectories blurred. By the early 1970s women's rights activism became a mass and increasingly diverse movement that attacked gender inequality in workplaces, the media, and social and legal institutions, from credit laws to the domestic division of labor. Women across the country mobi-lized to support an Equal Rights Amendment to the U.S. Constitution and organized in and outside unions to secure better treatment as female wage-earners. Activists picketed advertising agencies, "strip" bars, and other commercial sources of women's sexual objectification and lobbied for abortion on demand. Feminists set up a plethora of new institutions to empower women with information and services, including bookstores and publishing houses, health care clinics, and shelters for victims of domestic violence. From dramatic and well-publicized protests to count-less individual actions, women demanded respect and equal rights as never before and began questioning the received wisdom regarding gen-der difference and sexual relations.[24]

The advent of second-wave feminism profoundly influenced many female flight attendants. But as the historian Dorothy Sue Cobble has succinctly observed, flight attendants were "as much feminist leaders as followers." In the mid-1960s, as we have seen, flight attendant activists and their union leaders began an all-out struggle with the airlines over discriminatory work rules that helped set the legal wheels of Title VII in motion. In addition, veteran stewardess activists who had risen to the top ranks of union leadership were a feminist vanguard of sorts. They spoke out against airlines' sexual exploitation of stewardesses and forged alliances with other women's rights activists, even before there was much of a feminist movement. Colleen Boland, president of ALSSA, was a founding member of NOW, and NOW took up stewardesses' complaints of discrimination as one of its first causes.[25]

As the women's movement gained momentum, flight attendant unionists demonstrated a growing feminist consciousness that linked their workplace concerns to the larger project of women's liberation. On 26 August 1970 four ALPA-SSD officials from Continental Airlines dropped their work at the headquarters of the pilots' union in Washington to participate in a national "Women's Strike for Equality." The strike was organized by NOW and more radical liberationists to demand child care, abortion rights, and workplace equality for women. The Continental women marched in the "Women's Walk for Equality," with signs that read, "Storks Fly, Why Can't Mothers?," "We Want Our Babies and Our Wings," and "Mothers Are Still FAA Qualified." According to ALPA's national magazine, the stewardesses were invited by the event's organizers to march at the head of the parade and were interviewed by reporters from all three major television networks.[26]

Into the 1970s female flight attendants found even more cause for feminist militancy. Not only were the airlines trading in their sexual allure with unprecedented boldness but, as one flight attendant, Gene Reece, bitterly wrote in a feminist anthology in 1971, the job had become "the most strenuous, unrewarding, alienating concentration of housework and waitress-type drudgery to be found anywhere." While activists had managed to eliminate age ceilings and no-marriage rules, airlines continued to ground stewardesses upon pregnancy and subject them to petty harassment over their appearance, weight, and behavior on duty. Female flight attendants also watched more men enter the occupation as supposed equals who received more consideration from airlines and more deference from passengers. Despite the growing feminist sensibilities of many of their elected representatives, they had good reason to question whether their unions were doing enough to address their concerns. The ultimate power in setting contract priorities and choosing which grievances to back belonged to men. When Colleen Boland's five-year reign as president of ALSSA ended in 1969, one of the two flight attendant unions returned to its historic pattern of having a male officer in the top post representing a female workforce. Both unions remained subunits of male-dominated parent unions.[27]

Paula Kane recalled in her memoir that her growing frustration with the job and its cultural baggage prompted her to engage in subtle forms of resistance for a while. She wore a uniform two sizes too big and "couldn't find" her name tag so as to remain as anonymous as possible among passengers. "I wasn't too charming either," she wrote. Eventually breaking the rules was not enough to enable Kane to endure the affronts of demanding and lecherous passengers, offensive advertising, and patronizing airline policies. After five years' damage to her psyche, she quit in 1973. But Kane soon found a like-minded group of women in Stewardesses for Women's Rights (SFWR) who helped restore her self-esteem. In SFWR a small but committed corps of feminists attempted to redefine stewardesses as safety professionals and to make a singular contribution to the women's movement in the process.[28]

STEWARDESSES FOR WOMEN'S RIGHTS, 1972–1977

On 13 December 1972 a reporter for the *New York Times*, Laurie Johnson, warned readers, "The airline hostess who tells the departing passenger, 'It was nice to have you aboard, sir,' may be, behind her smile, a closet feminist on the verge of adding: 'And you acted like a male chauvinist pig.'" Johnson had attended a joint press conference that SFWR held with the Stewardess Anti-Defamation Defense League to protest stewardesses' "being 'sold' as sex symbols." Joanne Chaplin of the Defense League expressed particular concern over books and films like *Swinging Stewardesses* and airline slogans like "Fly Me." When one member of SFWR, Judi Lindsey, raised a workplace issue, her complaint sparked the kind of prurient response that the activists were trying to combat. Lindsey mentioned that according to regulations male as well as female supervisors were entitled to check whether stewardesses were wearing bras. According to Laurie Johnson's sardonic account in the *Times*, the mostly male reporters "leapt to life with probing, incisive questions." "You see what I mean?," the SFWR member protested. "It's just more of the same."[29]

Thus began SFWR's public fight to liberate stewardesses from degrading stereotypes and working conditions in December 1972. Despite some promising signs of interest from stewardesses in the New York area, Chaplin's Stewardess Anti-Defamation Defense League quickly disappeared. But SFWR received national media attention and foundation funding for its nationwide activities from 1972 to 1977. Those activities ranged from protests, conferences, and publications through which to vent anger and build feminist solidarity, to helping stewardesses file charges of discrimination against airlines, to health and safety advocacy on behalf of flight attendants and passengers. At its peak in 1974 and 1975 SFWR claimed one thousand members, which was less than 3 percent of the forty thousand flight attendants then working in the United States. But while relatively small in numbers, SFWR played a historically unique role in challenging stewardesses' sex-object status and fomenting feminist consciousness in the rapidly growing ranks of flight attendants.[30]

The first order of business for SFWR's two founders was to spread the gospel of women's liberation among stewardesses. Two former flight attendants for Eastern, Sandra Jarrell and Jan Fulsom, had had their own consciousnesses raised when Jarrell was fired for weighing a few extra pounds and Fulsom had a drunken passenger tear her skirt off, a trauma that drove her to quit. After deciding to organize, they sent a letter to union representatives announcing the group's formation and their purpose: "We hope to stimulate all stewardesses by raising their level of awareness of the women's rights movement." In retrospect, SFWR members described the vast majority of stewardesses as generally uninterested in women's liberation in the late 1960s and early 1970s. Cindy Hounsell, who had long considered herself a feminist before joining SFWR, remembered her fellow stewardesses on Pan Am as "not in any way feminist." Worse to Hounsell was that in her view, most rank-and-file stewardesses saw the legal and union challenges to airline employment policies in the late 1960s and early 1970s as of personal benefit to them, but not part of a larger political effort to claim women's rights.[31]

To the founders of SFWR, the unions could not provide an effective framework for mobilization. As Sandra Jarrell explained in her address at the group's first conference in March 1973, unions were the "most obvious tool available," but "unfortunately, unions do not have the reputation of representing the interests of women at the bargaining table." "It is not enough to blame the men who hold high positions in the union," because stewardesses had helped the men reach those positions and showed too little interest "in what is happening in our profession." Still, Jarrell predicted that the unions would engender rank-and-file loyalty and interest "only if they stop limiting their representation to economic issues." Significantly, Jarrell had struggled with her union over a grievance regarding her violation of Eastern's weight policy. Jarrell was eventually fired, and felt that she received no support from her union, the Air Line Stewards and Stewardesses Association, then a local of the Transport Workers Union. Some male officials in TWU showed intense hostility to SFWR as well. On at least one occasion, union officials stopped SFWR from distributing its newsletter to flight attendants' airport mailboxes. According to two former members who were active in their unions before joining the group, TWU officials charged SFWR with organizing a rival union. TWU officials eventually backed down from their attacks on SFWR. But the hostility of male unionists only reinforced early SFWR members' desire to provide "the women of the airline industry another way out (from the unions)."[32]

Charter members of SFWR discussed and debated a broad range of feminist goals and strategies that resulted in an ambitious agenda. Despite what they considered rampant apathy and "fear of organizing" among the nation's stewardesses, SFWR planned to mobilize to "end discrimination in the airline industry" and "create professionalism within the stewardesses corps." Members expressed their interest in seeking an endorsement from NOW and perhaps even affiliating with it. They also hoped "to have strong black membership and support," like many other white feminists who wanted the women's movement to be racially inclusive. While the historical evidence is sketchy, it seems they also wanted to reach out to lesbian flight attendants and promote their rights. SFWR members debated the usefulness of "consciousness raising," a feminist strategy for analyzing women's oppression through small-scale discussions of women's daily lives. Consciousness raising "goes on all the time on flights," one member, Marion Crawford, explained at the group's first press conference. Still, SFWR members worried whether declaring "consciousness raising" a prime objective was too difficult and perhaps too radical. As Paula Kane later recorded, members worried that the typical stewardess would respond, "Is that one of those groups where you

sit around and call each other sister?" The group elected to include consciousness raising as part of a broader program of social and economic
empowerment in the workplace. A recruiting pamphlet declared their
intent: "to raise the consciousness of stewardesses to their 'slut-in-
service-to-America' status . . . to fight the demeaning treatment to which
35,000 stewardesses are subjected by airlines, crews, and male passengers . . . to enforce airline compliance with Federal affirmative action
guidelines . . . to improve the economic status of stewardesses . . . to
increase the promotional opportunities for stewardesses."[33]

By 1973 SFWR began to publish a regular newsletter and organize semiannual national conferences, activities that put a premium on enabling
stewardesses to share and vent their anger and drawing stewardesses and
other feminists together. At SFWR's first national conference and work-
shop in New York City in March 1973, the group lined up an impressive
roster of feminist speakers for an audience of about eighty stewardesses. Included were Gloria Steinem, the editor of *Ms.* and media-favored
spokeswoman for the women's movement; Kathie Sarachild, a radical
feminist pioneer of consciousness raising; and the feminist labor attorney
Betty Southard Murphy, who provided pro bono counsel to SFWR. Subsequent conferences would feature other feminist luminaries, such as
Betty Friedan, Alix Kates Shulman, and Erica Jong, as well as repeat
appearances by Steinem. By contrast, SFWR included few labor organizers
on its semiannual conference programs. When Peggy McGuire, a national officer from the flight attendants' union affiliated with the TWU,
spoke at an SFWR conference, she was reportedly laughed at. Audience
members warned her not to think that her "salvation" lay with "male-
dominated unions."[34]

Importantly, SFWR quickly found an influential friend in Steinem, who
took the stewardesses seriously when other feminists did not. A former
SFWR member recalled that Steinem had been approached on a flight by
one of the flight attendants who would become active in SFWR. She
helped organize SFWR's first meetings, and under her editorship *Ms.* ran
a feature on stewardesses in January 1973 that highlighted the group's
efforts. The former SFWR member claimed, "She was real interested in
flight attendants . . . she was on airplanes all the time" and "thought, God,
this is a ripe group to be organized," and SFWR members "loved her" for
taking up their cause. Unlike Steinem, some other feminists were patronizing, unwittingly or not, and even hostile to women whose job and

image they perceived as degrading. Only a few months before flight attendants were profiled in *Ms.*, the radical feminist Kate Millett off-handedly belittled them in the same magazine by mocking a woman as "sugar cute—a 'stewardess' type." Far worse, Gloria Whitman remembered being hissed at by audience members when she and her fellow SFWR activists took the stage at a women's movement event. Steinem's and other high-profile feminists' support was thus not only of practical benefit to SFWR's efforts, but also legitimized them vis-à-vis the women's movement as a whole.[35]

As SFWR gathered force and secured funding, it homed in on tangible ways to improve stewardesses' working conditions and image. In June 1973 the group received a $25,000 grant from the Stern Fund, a small foundation based in New York that generally funded social studies. The fund, which a former member recalled was "looking for something unusual to contribute to," approached SFWR and offered a grant. SFWR gratefully accepted the money and agreed that it would go toward research on safety issues and racial and sex discrimination in the airline industry; legal services for individual stewardesses; and an effort to encourage the airlines to develop programs to end discrimination.[36]

SFWR began to investigate what members told *Newsweek* in March 1974 were "scandalous health and safety standards on the job." Occupational health and safety was the subject of a growing reform movement among workers in the 1970s, but for SFWR stewardesses' health and safety was above all a feminist issue. SFWR members believed that flight attendants' right to a safe and healthy work environment had been neglected by employers and regulators because of the basic lack of respect that stewardesses suffered. (In truth, the flight attendants' unions had long paid considerable attention to occupational health and safety issues and commissioned surveys and studies of their own.) SFWR discovered one safety threat to stewardesses only incidentally: members set fire to discarded items of their uniforms to protest the degrading image that the clothes represented, only to find that the synthetic fabrics melted and burned with shocking rapidity. SFWR members spoke out to the press about their uniforms, as well as their suspicion, based on anecdotal evidence, that stewardesses and their offspring suffered high rates of miscarriages and birth defects because of improperly packaged radioactive cargo on flights. More routinely, they charged that stewardesses suffered from excessive fatigue due to overlong shifts and high rates of hypoglycemia induced by irregular eating during flights. Airlines generally dismissed their complaints, only reinforcing the group's sense that stewardesses were exploited and belittled. One airline spokesperson told *Newsweek* that stewardesses' ailments were "primarily self-inflicted and psycho-somatic." He explained that "the girls" chose to eat "junk food" on flights and suffered jet lag because they sacrificed adequate rest for recreation.[37]

In 1974 and 1975 sfwr focused much of its activist energy on one particular health issue, hazardous cargo, and helped bring about significant change in airline safety regulations. Having not accomplished much on stewardesses' behalf in health and safety other than publicity, the group found that pegging its demands to the traveling public's well-being was a more successful strategy. Its research determined that radioactive cargo was aboard one of every ten passenger flights in the United States, and that the vast majority of the cargo contained some kind of hazardous material. Most shipments were found to be improperly packaged, exposing both passengers and crew to unsafe doses of radiation and other dangers. Working with a nuclear engineer from Arizona State University and the flight attendants' unions, sfwr arranged for one hundred stewardesses to wear radiation badges for eight weeks during flights to gather evidence of exposure. Members also passed out leaflets at airports and airline ticket offices and spoke out in television, radio, and newspaper interviews. In 1975 sfwr triumphantly reported to its main funder that it believed it "had played a significant role in bringing about the current, vastly improved situation." The Federal Aviation Administration ruled in February 1975 that no radioactive cargo other than properly packaged radioactive pharmaceuticals could be carried on passenger or cargo flights originating in the United States, and significantly increased fines for violations.[38]

While legal challenges to employment discrimination and health and safety issues were important to sfwr's goal of empowering stewardesses, the group's efforts to debunk stewardesses' sexy image ranked highest. In this endeavor the group received considerable help from other feminists. In early 1972, when the founders of sfwr were only beginning to contemplate their goals and strategies, now led an assault on the airline slogans it considered most exploitative of stewardesses and offensive to women. now members demonstrated on the street in New York City outside the offices of the advertising agency responsible for National's "Fly Me" campaign. Pickets appeared at National's ticket offices in New

York and Washington. NOW asked members to write letters of protest about the offending ads and to collect ticket stubs to exert economic pressure on the airlines. In 1974, when news leaked of National's plan for even bolder follow-up ads in which stewardesses in bathing suits would promise, "I'm going to fly you like you've never been flown before," SFWR joined NOW's Media Task Force in filing complaints with the Federal Communications Commission and the National Association of Broadcasters (NAB). Offensiveness aside, they argued that the ads were deceptive because cabin attendants did not pilot the planes themselves. As a result, the NAB required National to include other employees in the new ads and to clothe the stewardesses other than in swimwear. NOW and SFWR also assailed Continental's "We Really Move Our Tails for You" and similar slogans.[39]

SFWR activists in particular extended the fight against airline advertising by linking sexy images to the realities of their workplace. By SFWR's account, sex-oriented airline advertising was not only deceptive and degrading to stewardesses and other women, it was also dangerous. As an SFWR funding report explained in 1975, "In emergency situations, passengers want a professional, not a 'sex object' to depend on . . . [Yet] some airlines spend millions of dollars to ensure that a portion of the flying public will never take stewardesses seriously, and may even actively interfere with . . . their primary duty . . . of ensuring the safety of passengers." SFWR's charge that the airlines' emphasis on stewardesses' sexual allure posed a threat to passengers' safety had been made before by other flight attendants, including in the public statements of their union leaders as early as 1967. But as with occupational health and safety, SFWR drew unprecedented public attention. And SFWR threatened Continental and National with lawsuits, claiming that their advertising created unsafe working conditions.[40]

Through skillful relations with the news media, SFWR members repeatedly scored airline advertising and how it obscured and hindered flight attendants' safety work in newspapers nationwide and on television. One widely reported phrase became a virtual motto for the group: "I don't think of myself as a sex symbol or a servant. I think of myself as somebody who knows how to open the door of a 747 in the dark, upside down and in the water." SFWR members could be more blunt too, as when the group's executive director Cynthia Glacken wrote in a letter to *Time* in 1974, "We're in the business of saving tails, not serving them." SFWR's sex-versus-safety media campaign culminated in a "counter commercial" produced in September 1974, in which an actress posing as a stewardess explained the safety threat of sexist advertising in a sober, measured tone. She advised that "one of the *least* advertised facts" in the airline industry was stewardesses' primary duty, the enforcement of federal safety regulations. "Exhaustive training" and subsequent testing and retraining in safety assured their proficiency in "seldom used—but terribly important skills." The stewardess-actress asserted, "I am a highly trained professional with a serious job to do. Should an emergency situation arise, I urgently need the respect, confidence and cooperation of all my passengers . . . Fantasies are fine—in their place—let's be honest, the 'sexpot stewardess' image is unsafe at any altitude! Think about it." Several networks agreed to air the spot on news or documentary programs. SFWR hoped that the counter-commercial and related media efforts would be enough to discourage the airlines from perpetuating their exploitive advertising. If it were not enough, the group threatened the worst airline offenders with legal action in which it would provide evidence from stewardesses' experiences that the advertising resulted in endangering passengers' lives.[41]

In its sex-versus-safety campaign, SFWR felt it had struck on a link between the cultural and material that was crucial to achieving more dignity not only for stewardesses but for all women. As the group explained to its major funding source, "If SFWR can drive sexist advertising out of the airline industry, it will be the *first* major victory for the Women's Movement in this area. . . . All previous efforts by other groups have ended in frustration and failure because the women had no counter threat which gave their demands any clout. The National Organization of Women (NOW) and enlightened women and men working in the media agree with SFWR that we have the leverage to win this battle and feel that such a success will do much to improve the image and self-esteem of all women." For the members of SFWR, demanding that stewardesses be taken seriously as safety professionals was the capstone of all their efforts as workplace feminists and contributors to women's liberation.[42]

By 1977 financial difficulties, conflicts among members, and a lack of focused campaigns led SFWR's members to drift away, and the organization became defunct. But within the space of a few years SFWR members had empowered themselves and influenced their colleagues by taking on the airlines in a militant, avowedly feminist, and well-publicized way. When former members gathered for a reunion in 1987, they shared their assessments of what participation in the group had meant to them. Tommi Hutto Blake explained, "[SFWR] pushed me into my union and as long as I'm a flight attendant I will be an active rank-and-file member, officer, whatever of my union, thanks to SFWR." Blake was not alone. Many SFWR members transferred their activist energy and the organizing skills they had developed to union work. As the unions became more independent and feminist, as we will see, SFWR members found more appeal in union activism. Kathleen Heenan recalled an equally important if more intangible effect: "SFWR helped us hold our heads up high during this terrible advertising blitz. We fought back in an articulate and intelligent way. We gave ourselves some dignity."[43]

Other stewardesses took notice. Although SFWR never represented more than 3 percent of all flight attendants, when Heenan was later asked how stewardesses generally had viewed the group, she replied, "they were very positive about us." As a high-profile activist group that forged the closest links between flight attendants and the women's movement, SFWR encouraged other stewardesses to assert themselves as never before. SFWR was both a symbol and a catalyst of a larger change. Female flight attendants were growing numerous enough, staying on the job long enough, and becoming angry enough with how they were stereotyped as docile sex objects to push for far-reaching changes in their occupation.[44]

THE UNION REVOLT

With the arrival of wide-bodied "jumbo" jets at the end of the 1960s, flight attendants' numbers skyrocketed, from about fifteen thousand in 1965 to forty thousand less than a decade later, in 1974. On three- to four-hundred-seat jumbos, flight attendants were far more numerous on each flight. The sociologist Frieda Rozen found that a much stronger sense of "occupational community" developed as flight attendants had more contact with each other and looked less to pilots and other groups for a sense of workplace community. Feminist sensibilities blended with demographic change, and flight attendants no longer wanted or had to brook decades-old patterns of male oversight in their union affairs. Female flight attendants were hardly all "libbers" like the women of SFWR, but they were more than ready to take control of their own destinies as trade unionists.[45]

Over the course of the 1970s flight attendants transformed their extant unions and established new and independent unions as well. As in the early 1960s, activists plunged into intense and often bitter union politicking. But the union struggles of the 1970s played out in a new era of feminist consciousness among both the rank and file and the leadership, in which the older, elusive goal of autonomy took on special meaning and impetus. Flight attendants wanted to have and run their own unions and had the collective will and numerical strength to make that happen in many cases. Their "autonomy movement," as Rozen has called it, provided one of the decade's greatest success stories of women achieving self-determination in the American labor movement.

The first major chapter in the union autonomy movement saw another break from the Air Line Pilots Association, but this one more successful and amicable than that of 1960. By the early 1970s pilots had growing reason to worry about stewardesses' expanding presence in their shared union. As an ALPA handout for pilots bluntly explained, the "girls can vote for the ALPA president and, with wide body jets, 10 and 20 girls per plane soon will outnumber pilots 2 to 1." If the "girls" were to remain in ALPA, they would "have to be willing to give up votes for president." In fact the demographics remained vastly in pilots' favor; about 31,000 pilots and 12,000 flight attendants belonged to ALPA as of 1971. But what mattered more was that stewardesses' docility in joint union matters could no longer be taken for granted. Pilots were also growing tired of subsidizing the stewardess division. Stewardesses, for their part, increasingly wondered why ALPA should have control over their contract negotiations and other crucial matters. The chief of the stewardess division, Kelly Rueck, contended, "We have been parasites on the Pilot Division for a long time, and we still are, essentially." "I think it is about time that we tried to look at this thing as responsible people in charge of a business, and do something about it." By 1973 the pilot and stewardess divisions were ready to part ways officially. Factions in both unions differed on how to separate, but after some tense negotiations the pilot and flight attendant leaders reached an agreement.[46]

As of 1 January 1974 the stewardess division of ALPA became the Association of Flight Attendants (AFA), an independent affiliate of the pilot union. Both the pilots' and stewardesses' boards of directors, consisting of all local and national officials, quickly and overwhelmingly approved the spin-off agreement. Among other provisions it allowed AFA to continue to use ALPA resources at reduced or no cost for several years, waived the former SSD's debt, and provided both unions with equal power to alter the new affiliation arrangement. All that remained was the transfer of legal bargaining rights for flight attendants from ALPA to AFA. To the surprise of both unions and the chagrin of the new AFA, the National Mediation Board required representation elections to effect the transfer. While dissension in the AFA ranks caused a few airline groups to go elsewhere, elections between 1975 and 1979 generally confirmed AFA's right to negotiate contracts for fourteen thousand flight attendants on thirteen carriers, including the industry giant United. In a final, historic confirmation of AFA's independent status, the union received its own international charter from the AFL-CIO in 1984, the same charter that had eluded postwar flight attendants.[47]

For the other major union of flight attendants, ALSSA, Local 550, TWU, securing increased autonomy was a more complicated, contentious process. The gender politics in ALSSA were far more complex than the relationship of subordination between the pilots' and stewardesses' divisions of ALPA. In addition to the TWU male hierarchy, many elected officials in ALSSA, including the president and vice-president from 1969 to 1973, were male pursers and stewards. As the union that represented most of the male minority in the occupation, ALSSA also faced divisiveness engendered by stewardesses' use of Title VII and their growing expectations of equal treatment. Some male flight attendants worried that stewardesses' progress came at their expense, such as the merging of seniority lists and the opening of purser positions to women. The men on Northwest formed a "Purser Defense League" in 1971 in response to their stewardess co-workers' legal actions. Many female flight attendants felt that the union still fell short in addressing their concerns as women. When the Eastern stewardess Bernice Dolan ran unsuccessfully for ALSSA president in 1971, she accused the incumbent male leadership of ignoring the gendered issue of weight rules: "This union is approximately ninety percent women, being 'led' by two men," Dolan declared in campaign literature. "How well do they represent the interests of the majority? Are we being well served?" Dolan invited stewardesses to judge for themselves from the experience of stewardesses at Eastern, where she claimed that without any union protest, a clampdown on weight rules left hundreds "harassed and threatened including yours truly."[48]

In June 1973 the increasingly restive ALSSA membership elected a fe-

male president for the first time since 1967, Martha O'Rourke, a stewardess at American. O'Rourke would be the last ALSSA president, because
male and female flight attendants' desire for more local autonomy soon
drove the union, almost three decades old, out of existence. In early 1974
the airline groups then within ALSSA—Eastern, Southern, TWA, and
American—began formalizing plans to establish their own locals, which
neither the national officers of ALSSA nor TWU officials tried to prevent.
TWA flight attendants initiated the breakup of ALSSA. More than the
other groups in the union, TWA attendants were split between overseas
and domestic operations and included a large number of male pursers in
the international section. Both characteristics led TWA's hostesses, but
especially the pursers, to feel ill served by ALSSA, which they believed was
dominated in priorities as well as numbers by domestic stewardesses at
American. As it happened, flight attendants for American, Eastern, and
Southern were not necessarily any happier with the current union structure. As the first newsletter put out by the new TWA local explained with
emphasis in March 1975, the local remained affiliated to the Transport
Workers, but "we now have *our own* Local representing *only* TWA Flight
Attendants." Flight attendants wanted their own locals in part because of
their long-standing belief that their union concerns varied widely across
airlines. But the break up of ALSSA also reflected flight attendants' unprecedented willingness to reject union business as usual and insist on
local autonomy.[49]

The new AFA and the new airline-based locals in TWU still left many
flight attendants dissatisfied with their union representation. In some
cases flight attendants changed affiliations in pursuit of a better home in a
large international union. National attendants left AFA for TWU in 1975,
after a long and bitter strike, while Northwest attendants moved from
ALSSA to AFA's predecessor in 1971, and then to the Teamsters in 1976,
where they were reportedly no happier. But in other cases, many flight
attendants decided that the risks of forgoing any protective links to the
AFL-CIO were worth complete self-governance. The autonomy movement thus culminated in movements for union independence on several
carriers. Four independence campaigns succeeded that were led variously
by flight attendants' elected leaders, dissident local officials, and rank-
and-filers. Others failed. In nearly every case the prospect of independence saw flight attendant activists divide, sometimes personally and
bitterly. Though tumultuous, independence campaigns all made clear

how widespread and deeply felt the desire for local autonomy had become among flight attendants.[50]

While the male-run TWU would be hit far harder by flight attendants' defections than the female-led AFA, it was AFA that suffered the first loss in an independence battle when Continental flight attendants bolted in 1976. Having ended its subordination as a division of ALPA only a few years earlier, AFA was wracked by growing pains and internal conflicts. As local representatives in AFA began to do their contract bargaining on their own, they grew more ambitious and thus more vulnerable to disappointment. Continental flight attendants were not the only group within AFA to feel that their national union had failed to support them adequately in struggles with management in the mid-1970s. But Continental flight attendants' leaders were among the most insistent on local control. Continental's head of labor relations later explained that the carrier's flight attendants "felt they were controlled by AFA but not supported . . . the membership became disillusioned . . . and [the leaders] did run a good campaign against AFA—emphasizing new freedom and independence." In November 1976 Continental flight attendants voted three to one to have a new and fully independent union, the Union of Flight Attendants, Local 1. Rather than call themselves an "association," the designation that flight attendants had long chosen because of its professional ring, the Continental attendants intentionally chose a name that bespoke a commitment to trade unionism as such and a break from the past.[51]

The vast majority of the flight attendants in TWU soon departed too. While the airline groups who dismantled ALSSA in 1974 were not enamored of TWU, they hoped to get better support from the international by eliminating the middle layer of hierarchy. What they got instead was a direct dose of TWU oversight that many found less palatable. When ALSSA disappeared, TWU quickly assigned what the president of the TWA group, Art Teolis, later described as "watchdogs" to the three new flight attendants' locals, singling them out for "help" that no other airline locals in TWU apparently needed. TWU also pushed the TWA and American flight attendant locals into "accelerated negotiations" in 1976 for new contracts, which meant that they were to bargain with management only over a short list of issues presented by each side. Flight attendant negotiators thus had to scrap longer lists of bargaining goals based on members' input. Even worse in TWA's case, the negotiations did not go well, flight attendants threatened to strike, and TWU officials moved to settle the dispute without the involvement of flight attendant leaders. While the contract struggle at American was not as ugly, the members, as at TWA, voted to reject the contracts produced by TWU's "accelerated negotiations" at least once before finally accepting them. Within a year the TWA local's leaders had convinced a majority of its more than five thousand members that they would be better off on their own. In March 1977 TWA flight attendants officially became the membership of the Independent Federation of Flight Attendants.[52]

At American Airlines the drive for independence had started even earlier than at TWA or Continental, but because dissidents led it, it took longer to build in the face of the elected leaders' opposition. But more important, unlike at TWA, both the pro- and anti-independence factions at American were led by women who symbolized flight attendants' growing militancy. The leaders of the American local opposed independence largely because more than half of the rest of American's employees were TWU members too, unlike at TWA, which promised strength in numbers across crafts. But the dissident leaders of the independence drive eventually persuaded a majority of their co-workers that labor solidarity was less important than complete control over their own treasury. In May 1977 American flight attendants elected to break from TWU. The name of their new union, the Association of Professional Flight Attendants, symbolically connected more directly than ever before the flight attendants' union militancy to the occupation's long-standing ideal of professionalism.[53]

The last major chapter in the flight attendant autonomy movement of the 1970s unfolded at Pan Am, where the flight attendants' union was in a historically unique position and the members had fallen into a distinct rut of apathy. Since the late 1940s they had resided in an umbrella Pan Am local in TWU with a variety of other ground workers. In earlier years, their anomalous representation in TWU perhaps served them well; other flight attendants envied the Pan Am group's contracts. But by 1976 Pan Am flight attendants were widely considered to have the worst contract in the industry for a large airline group. By the mid-1970s, one Pan Am attendant later explained, "We could have dominated our local, we were forty-five percent of the membership. But we didn't know how." Alice Flynn, one of a handful of rank-and-filers who led the independence campaign at Pan Am, first agitated merely to increase the membership's role in upcoming negotiations. But after TWU officials responded with hostility, she and like-minded rank-and-file activists began campaigning for union independence. Officers of the new independent unions elsewhere encouraged them. According to Flynn, they hoped at least to push TWU into offering Pan Am flight attendants a local of their own. But the international, she contended, "did nothing during this entire campaign to appease" the flight attendants or "to change anything." "It was unfortunate for them," Flynn added, "[since] we ended up winning by the largest margin the National Mediation Board had ever seen." Pan Am's new flight attendant union, named the Independent Union of Flight Attendants, won bargaining rights in October 1977 and entered negotiations for what would be a new and much better contract.[54]

The union revolt swept aside decades-old structures of subordination in just a few years. All told, over 15,000 flight attendants were in unaffiliated unions by 1978: an estimated 1,630 at Continental, 5,000 at TWA, 5,100 at American, and 3,400 at Pan Am. Nearly 14,000 had been members of TWU only a year earlier. Another 14,000 in AFA had finally become fully self-governing members of the labor movement, affiliated to, but no longer ruled by, their former parent union, ALPA. Whatever their organizational status, the more than 37,000 unionized flight attendants in the United States were more combative and demanding than ever before. One manager complained in *Airline Executive* of "an over-supply of militancy" among cabin crew. When United Airlines sat down to bargain with AFA for the first time in 1974, the flight attendants presented the longest, most expensive list of initial contract demands that the carrier had ever seen from any union. Leaders across unions, moreover, began to lobby aggressively for federal safety licensing of flight attendants in the later 1970s, breathing new life into an effort started in the 1950s but moribund for more than a decade.[55]

What SFWR set out to do in the early 1970s was in effect taken up by many thousands of flight attendants in union autonomy movements (with some SFWR veterans as leaders among them): fighting the inseparable problems of working conditions and patronizing, degrading stereotypes. In 1974, as SFWR members were speaking out repeatedly to the media about sexist airline advertising and its potential threat to passenger safety, the AFA's president, Kelly Rueck, issued her own public warning to the offending airlines. "If airlines such as National and Continental do not realize that their ads are degrading to women, their flight attendants may soon find an effective way to educate them . . . . A spontaneous loss

of enthusiasm is not inconceivable." Rueck also, like SFWR, threatened to
file suit over ads of the "Fly Me" variety. In an interview in 1979, Rueck
looked back on the union transformations of the decade and attributed
about "eighty or ninety percent" of the inspiration to the women's movement; she also remembered agreeing with SFWR on many issues.[56]

Unlike SFWR, however, the unions were responsible to memberships
united by occupation and not necessarily by politics. Some stewardesses
found nothing wrong with practices and ads that others found sexist, and
occasionally charged their unions with being too feminist. When Continental Airlines introduced its "We Really Move Our Tails for You" campaign in early 1974, *Advertising Age* reported that many of the carrier's
stewardesses liked the slogan and hoped that it would boost business;
some were also angry with their union for protesting the campaign and,
they believed, paying some of their colleagues for time off to complain to
reporters about the slogan. One Continental attendant who had flown
for ten years called it "absurd" to suggest that the ads inflicted emotional
distress on stewardesses. She added, "When a flight attendant acts professionally and like a lady, she is treated with respect."[57]

Not all the union autonomy drives appear as feminist battles against
stewardesses' exploitation either, when viewed separately. Indeed one
former member of SFWR, Kathleen Heenan, felt that the insurgents who
ran the independence campaign at her carrier, TWA, were not very competent and "certainly were not feminists." "They were all these men that
were very, very sexist. . . . It was just to take over and run their own
union." Yet their insurgency, like others, could not have succeeded without backing from members and local representatives who were mostly
female. An officer of the newly independent TWA union explained to a
reporter in 1978 that the groups who left TWU did so because the international had not only allowed insufficient wages but ignored flight attendants' health and safety concerns and more generally treated them at best
as "stepchildren" and at worst as "dumb broads." Whether male or female, flight attendants had suffered too long the patronizing attitudes of
airlines and male union overseers toward them because they were mostly
women. Taken together, the union revolts were ultimately a collective
feminist protest against the exploitation and undervaluing of flight attendants' labor and skills, even though many participants did not consider
themselves feminists, nor were they all women.[58]

For some flight attendants, the feminist implications of their union activism were obvious. In 1977 Pat Fink, an Eastern attendant and negotia-

tor for her local in TWU, informed her members, "What we are trying to negotiate for is a change of attitude and opinion of our worth." Flight attendants, because they were predominantly female, "have been regarded as subservient for eons." Times had changed, "and we have changed . . . Women are liberating themselves." But flight attendants were still left behind. "Everyone you see on this airline makes more than we do." "We are grounded immediately if we get pregnant, gain weight . . . wear the wrong shoes, get a complaint letter . . . etc. . . . What other employee group puts up with that kind of treatment? . . . Respect is a not a gift, it has *not* been given—we must demand it!" Fink was frustrated to be sure. But whether she realized it or not, she was preaching to the converted. She was writing not in an official newsletter approved by the TWU but rather in *Labor Speaks*, an independently produced "forum for the rank and file" of Eastern and Southern that promoted union-based feminism. Stewardesses were already working hard at liberating themselves in, and outside, their unions.[59]

"NO MORE STEWARDESSES—WE'RE FLIGHT ATTENDANTS"

While SFWR's high-profile activism and the union revolts were the most dramatic manifestations of flight attendants' activism in the 1970s, discontent registered in countless other ways. It was evident in the raft of union grievances and legal actions that stewardesses filed on maternity policies and weight and other appearance rules. By 1974 the Association of Flight Attendants had maternity and weight complaints on file with the EEOC against no fewer than twenty airlines. The shift in flight attendants' anti-discrimination targets from age ceilings and no-marriage rules to maternity and weight policies was revealing in itself. As flight attendants had argued in the mid-1960s, stewardesses' age and marital status were hardly detectable to passengers and did not affect their image of allure. A visibly pregnant flight attendant, however, obviously undermined the fantasy of stewardesses' sexual availability that the airlines worked so hard to promote, while resistance to weight rules struck at the heart of the airlines' control over stewardesses' appearance. As a TWA flight attendant asked rhetorically in 1980, "By allowing a 'preggie' on board, management would obviously have to waive the weight restriction, right? And that would give away the name of the game, wouldn't it?" By the end of the 1970s flight attendants had not yet ended airline discrimination in maternity and weight policies, but they could return to work after bearing children, could keep their seniority and benefits while on extended maternity leaves, and had pushed many carriers into easing weight restrictions.[60]

Stewardesses also rebelled en masse with more informal means of resistance in the 1970s. The sociologist Arlie Hochschild recorded that five stewardesses at American staged what she called a "shoe-in": they decided to show up for work one day in flat, crepe-soled shoes of their own choosing, rather than regulation high heels. When their supervisor said nothing, the woman adopted the more comfortable footwear permanently. To Hochschild, the "shoe-in" was symbolic of a larger change that she witnessed in the 1970s. From breaking appearance rules to refusing to smile as often and "genuinely" as management wanted, flight attendants rebelled, in Hochschild's terms, "against the costumes, the script, and the general choreography" of their hostess role on the airlines' "commercial stage." Perhaps the most basic sign of the stewardess rebellion was that many began to insist on the less culturally freighted, gender-neutral term "flight attendant," rather than "stewardess" or "hostess."[61]

Flight attendants had taken occupational struggles for respect and recognition to new heights in the 1970s and succeeded where earlier generations had fallen short. Their collective militancy was unprecedented, but it also played out in a more conducive era. Flight attendants were far more numerous and able to protest more effectively against working conditions and stereotypes that they found degrading. Feminists in general had revised the broader social and political context to provide more legitimacy for women as workers. Working women, from elite professionals to female pioneers in male trades to pink-collar workers in offices and service industries, declared that their economic needs were as real as those of male breadwinners and their skills as valuable. The stewardess rebellion was but one part of a larger female rebellion in workplaces across the United States. Finally, as stewardesses' image evolved from that of the perfect wife- and mother-to-be of the postwar years to what SFWR denounced as "slut-in-service-to-America," stereotypes that had once been flattering to many had grown alienating and offensive and only brought worse working conditions. Many female flight attendants no longer would accept their glamour-girl image as anything other than exploitive in its supposed rewards as well as its burdens.

As the 1970s drew to a close, female flight attendants' unprecedented militancy had worked to change their image as well as their unions and working conditions. When the feminist writer Louise Kapp Howe profiled stewardesses in the traditional women's magazine *Redbook* in 1979, she followed the path of earlier reporters in portraying them as exemplary women. But unlike countless earlier profiles of stewardesses that mused over their romantic exploits, unusual lives of travel, and attractiveness, hers presented flight attendants as symbols of women's new assertiveness in the workplace. In Howe's report, titled "No More Stewardesses—We're Flight Attendants," she wrote, "The women whom the airlines have tried to portray as docile, flighty sex bunnies, whose weight and hair styles they still seek to control, have become the least docile and most independent of all female occupational groups." Howe's portrayal was stereotypical in its own way—flight attendants were feminist heroines for her. Subsequent years would show that older stereotypes had not disappeared, nor were flight attendants immune from new ones less flattering than Howe's. Yet as Howe and others made clear in the national media, "stewardesses" had become "flight attendants" and began to muster more respect as workers.[62]

Flight attendants did not necessarily recognize that the extraordinary militancy of the 1970s flowed from an older legacy of activism. In 1973 one of the two founders of SFWR told *Ms.*, "I've always thought it was ironic that we have this docile image. Maybe in the past that's been true, but most of the women I know began to fly because they were just too independent and curious about the world to sit around in a nine-to-five job getting cramps in their shoulders." Stewardesses as a group have always been independent, curious women. Traveling for a living, after all, requires adventurousness. As airlines found repeatedly to their chagrin, high turnover and the flattery of glamour hardly ensured stewardesses' docility in earlier eras. From unionizing in the 1940s, to seeking safety certification and protesting against male domination in the postwar labor movement, to asking whether female allure suddenly evaporated at the age of thirty-two in 1963, stewardesses organized for greater respect as workers and professionals for many years before Title VII and second-wave feminism. Their efforts helped create the "flight attendants" of the 1970s and the women's movement, even as they drew strength from the broader upsurge in women's activism.[63]

In the flight attendant occupation and its history of activism throughout the mid-twentieth century, we can see how paid labor that is meant first and foremost to produce an ideal of femininity can be both exploitative and potentially empowering. On the one hand, the occupation throws into high relief how women's labor and skills have been rendered invisible as such. In jobs that blend ideals of female self-sacrifice and domesticity with demands for charm and attractiveness—a common mix in the growing world of public-contact service work—white women have been valued for meeting cultural expectations of femininity, but not for performing work of distinct skill or economic worth. As the airlines' glamorized hostesses demonstrate particularly well, such jobs may bring admiration and envy but generally do not offer good wages, job security, or respect for the discrete work involved. Stewardesses enjoyed wages of glamour that others did not, but also toiled especially hard to earn them. In airline passenger service, where the point of production and consumption were one and the same, concealing the labor involved demanded an additional, crucial effort to deliver the promised charm and attractiveness, along with the service that customers expected and the safety they were encouraged not to notice.

On the other hand, flight attendants' historic struggles also suggest how women have sought to turn the labor of representing femininity to their own dignifying ends. Flight attendants leveraged their cultural visibility to draw the attention of lawmakers and the press to their grievances, and then insisted that they be recognized as public-safety professionals. Nurses used formal credentials and technology over the course of the twentieth century to define their work as highly skilled and distinct, rather than a female duty. Playboy bunnies "bit back," as their union leader quipped, with complaints to the EEOC and union grievances when they felt that management's view of the "bunny image" was too aggressively youthful in the 1960s and 1970s. Women workers did not have to be popular icons of allure or domesticity to put their employers' demands for femininity to their own uses. Taking pride and enjoyment from the cultivation of appearance and personality on the job and in the union hall, even while challenging management on what attractiveness required, has been a common thread across many women's work cultures and activism—from telephone operating, to waitressing, to factory labor.[64]

While reclaiming femininity from employers' use may have been pleasurable and even empowering, it rarely enabled women workers to effect radical changes in the basic gender, class, and race hierarchies that governed their place in the workforce and the labor movement. Flight attendants were relatively high on the pink-collar ladder, had more ability than most women to capture public and state attention, and enjoyed union resources. But that still did not enable them to claim professional status on the terms they desired, nor to win a charter of their own from the AFL-CIO for several decades. Nurses and social workers were more successful in their professionalizing projects, yet still suffered in status and pay from the devaluation of feminized care work. Others, such as nursing assistants and Pullman maids, had little to no cultural or professional privilege to mitigate their exploitation. Indeed, the relatively privileged, although also exploited, positions of white women in jobs like airline passenger service depended on the greater subordination of other, often nonwhite women in even lower-wage, lower-status work.[65]

Flight attendants' historic activism reflected how they were caught between the elitism of glamour and white-collar work and the low wages and denial of skills typical of pink-collar work. In their union struggles flight attendants emphasized craft autonomy and professionalizing goals over industrial solidarity. Stewardesses for Women's Rights, though keen to collaborate with other feminists, viewed women's issues nearly exclusively through the lens of white stewardesses' concerns and put even more stress than unionists did on achieving a professional identity. These strategies may have suited flight attendants' particular class and gender consciousness, but they limited their ability to make common cause with others in creating a more just labor movement and service economy. Drives for union autonomy in the early 1960s and the 1970s also brought fragmentation and union competition among flight attendants themselves. Though many finally achieved long-desired independence by the later 1970s, flight attendants spread themselves thinly across several unions just as the looming deregulation of the industry in 1978 was about to wreak economic havoc for airline workers.

Flight attendants' activism cannot offer a perfect blueprint of what pink-collar protest has been or should be, nor should we expect it to do so. But flight attendants' history does tell us much about the rewards and costs of representing femininity for a living. And it also shows us how much those who have undertaken that labor to an employer's profit want—and ought—to be respected for doing real work and using real skills.

EPILOGUE

After Title VII and Deregulation

When World Wings International, a philanthropic group of former flight attendants for Pan Am, held a reunion in New York City in the fall of 2003, the *New York Times* took a nostalgic look back at air travel with the airline alumnae. The women who attended "all worked the skyways before stewardesses became flight attendants, before the women's movement, before airborne luxury was edged out by low fares and frequent flier miles. Then, flying commercial was elegant, elite. Passengers were well dressed and well coiffed and left their crying babies at home, and the stewardesses who pampered them were glamorous." In the pre-feminist era the job imposed now-unthinkable requirements as to age, marital status, weight, and looks, readers learned. Despite the stringent rules, the reunion attendees remembered that they "were overjoyed to have the job . . . Suddenly they had the prestige and cachet approaching that of a model or actress today." The stewardess alumnae "preferred the good old sexist days" to "hawking headsets and minibottles of liquor and keeping the peanuts-per-passenger ratio as low as possible. The days before the concerns were shoe bombs and stun guns." Such paeans to a luxurious past have become a staple of aviation reporting in recent years, as passengers and the crew who serve them have struggled with economic turmoil and service cutbacks resulting from deregulation, and, worse, the current climate of escalated terrorist threats aloft.[1]

Much as African American women forced their way into stewardessing just as the jet age eroded its benefits and added to its burdens, flight attendants managed to make the job less sexist and more permanent in the 1970s, only to find it an even harder and perhaps less rewarding career than before. When "stewardesses" became "flight attendants," the cultural baggage of their glamour-girl image became less weighty, but respect as service workers and safety professionals remained all too elusive. Deregulation and terrorist attacks posed fundamental challenges to the business of air travel, worsening the working conditions and threatening the very livelihoods—and lives—of flight attendants. Yet the flight attendants' unions still managed to be a rather prominent thorn in the side of airline management, with some impressive victories from strikes and in court. Affronts to flight attendants' dignity continue to the present, but so do their activist efforts.

DEREGULATION

Above all else in the late twentieth century, flight attendants found their world of work changed by deregulation. The move to end federal control of airline routes and fares reflected a broad, bipartisan critique of regulation as it had evolved in the airline industry. Economists argued and lawmakers agreed that regulation had come to benefit airlines at consumers' expense by inflating fares and dampening competition in lucrative travel markets. In the fall of 1978 Congress passed and President Jimmy Carter signed the Airline Deregulation Act, which mandated the immediate scaling back of federal limits on routes and fares, with an eventual phasing out of economic regulation altogether. Despite some second thoughts in Congress over the chaos initially created by deregulation, the generally anti-regulatory Republican administration of President Ronald Reagan ensured the complete end of regulation, as scheduled, in 1985.[2]

Spiraling energy prices in the 1970s had already posed an economic challenge to airlines, but deregulation sent most reeling and some into bankruptcy. Fare wars slashed profits and airlines scrambled to snap up new routes and planes that they could ill afford. The leveraged buyout frenzy of the 1980s hit the airline industry hard, and many carriers' debt burdens soared. Braniff folded and Continental filed for bankruptcy in just a few years; within a decade and a half, the venerable giants Eastern, Pan Am, and TWA collapsed under the weight of staggering financial obligations. Many smaller carriers, long sustained by regulation and subsidies, were swallowed up in often awkward mergers. Deregulation also encouraged an unprecedented number of upstarts. Among them were some notable stories of meteoric rise followed by swift collapse, as with the low-fare, no-frill pioneer People Express in the early 1980s and ValuJet in the mid-1990s. While Southwest, the industry's cinderella of low-fare carriers, got its start several years before deregulation, it took full advantage of the new competitive climate and climbed into the top ten of American carriers by the end of the century.[3]

For flight attendants and other airline workers, the consequences of deregulation were often devastating. Many were laid off, while others held on to their jobs by accepting deep pay cuts, increased productivity demands, and other concessions. In this heavily unionized industry, workers newly confronted a fiercely anti-union environment. President Reagan's breaking of an air traffic controllers' strike in 1981 evidenced the ascendance of conservatism and "free market" values, and their significant impact on labor relations. The flight attendant union publication *Flightlog* reported in 1983, "While companies tried to put unions in their place before deregulation, it was nothing like the all-out assault we are seeing today across the industry. Companies are trying to stop unions from forming, and trying to bust them after they have. Union-busting comes in a variety of forms," from pushing grievances into arbitration so as to drain union resources, to demanding alterations to contracts, to engaging in corporate maneuvers such as forming holding companies and declaring bankruptcy to weaken unions and break contracts. Continental filed for bankruptcy in the early 1980s largely to void its union contracts and reorganize with far lower labor costs. Flight attendants were particularly vulnerable in some ways to the pressures of deregulation. One study found that deregulation had depressed their real earnings by as much as a third as of 1985, significantly more than for pilots or mechanics. As always, flight attendants held less power than their licensed counterparts to devastate an airline with strikes, and fewer funds to support strikers in their ranks. Unlike pilots and mechanics, moreover, cabin crew were spread across several unions, some quite small and unaffiliated. Flight attendants in an independent union at TWA walked out in a long and bitter strike in 1986 that showed their militancy and tenacity, but also management's willingness to replace them permanently with strikebreakers and pretend that the union no longer existed. Many TWA attendants were reinstated and their union bounced back, but only after three more years of protracted struggle and litigation, going all the way to the U.S. Supreme Court.[4]

Flight attendants could take heart that more public concern with airline safety since the 1970s encouraged greater recognition for what they had long defined as their essential role in cabin safety. Union lobbying helped persuade government regulators to ban smoking on all domestic flights in 1990, and to introduce long-sought-after limits on duty hours for flight attendants in 1994. In a significant gesture, President George H. W. Bush signed a proclamation declaring a "Flight Attendant Safety Professionals' Day" on 19 July 1990 to honor cabin crew for their contributions to "enhancing the safety and convenience of our Nation's air transportation system." Still, many flight attendants would have preferred to see the president sign a licensing bill. As the union president Susan Bianchi-Sand contended that same year, "It is no accident that the only safety profession that is not certified is the one made up primarily of women." Union leaders repeatedly described flight attendants as "second-class citizens" in the aviation industry because of not only the failure of campaigns for licensing but the FAA's inattention to their occupational health. A growing number of health studies on flight attendants in recent years have shown that they do indeed suffer a disproportionate number of work-related illnesses and injuries, yet enjoy less government protection than most workers in the United States.[5]

Although flight attendants won more recognition for their safety work, the service that consumed most of their working hours grew harder and more hazardous with deregulation. Flight attendants occupied the front lines of customer service in a struggling industry that gave passengers many reasons to be disgruntled. The result was not only crankier customers but more verbal abuse and even physical assaults. What the news media called "air rage" in the 1990s was not new to flight attendants, but it was on the rise. At the start of the twenty-first century, the FAA declared that tougher enforcement of federal laws against assaults on airline crews were finally beginning to reverse what had been increasing reports of such incidents. Both the pilot and flight attendant unions, however, continued to charge that "air rage" remained a serious problem that neither federal authorities nor the airlines had sufficiently addressed. At least a few flight attendants managed to turn passengers' misbehavior into fodder for briskly selling memoirs. With *Plane Insanity: A Flight Attendant's Tales of Sex, Rage, and Queasiness at 30,000 Feet, Around the World in a Bad Mood! Confessions of a Flight Attendant,* and other true-life tales from above, flight attendants let air travelers know just how poorly behaved some of them were.[6]

"THE NEW FACE OF LABOR"

By the 1990s flight attendants had largely recovered from the setbacks of the 1980s to become model "new" unionists in a struggling labor movement. The largest flight attendant union, the Association of Flight Attendants, AFL-CIO, doubled its membership, from 22,000 attendants at eighteen carriers in 1982, to 46,000 at twenty-six carriers by 1999, lessening union fragmentation among cabin crew. In 1993 some twenty thousand flight attendants at American Airlines, who belonged to the independent Association of Professional Flight Attendants, nearly shut down the nation's largest carrier at the time with an eleven-day strike during the peak Thanksgiving travel season. American's management wrongly assumed that the attendants would relent and did not bother to train strikebreakers. That same year, AFA members at Alaska Airlines successfully tested a new strike strategy: intermittent, unannounced work stoppages aimed at specific flights. The flight attendants at Alaska struck only seven flights over the course of several months, but the threat of disruption cost the carrier 20 percent of its normal business. A federal court ruling prevented the airline from firing the strikers. AFA thought the campaign at Alaska so successful that it trademarked the strategy as "CHAOS," for "Creating Havoc around Our System," and has since threatened to use it against several other airlines. With labor relations in turmoil on the deregulated airlines, the news media began to pay more attention to flight attendants as unionized workers with great potential for militancy, rather than as staple subjects for "human interest" stories. When American's flight attendants launched their successful walkout in 1993, *Time* and *U.S. News and World Report* both portrayed them as the "new face of labor." In flight attendants they saw representatives of the increasingly feminized workforce and growing service sector, and workers whose pugnacity might revamp the labor movement for the postindustrial age.[7]

Flight attendants in other nations fared similarly well in using strikes to challenge cost cutting and union busting, as well as stereotypes, in an era of globalization and deregulation. Perhaps nothing better belied presumptions of flight attendants' docility than when cabin crew crippled Cathay Pacific with a seventeen-day strike at the start of 1993. Like Singapore Airlines, known for its iconic "Singapore Girls," Cathay Pacific, based in Hong Kong, promised superlative service with ads depicting demure, young hostesses who offered "traditional" Asian hospitality. One Cathay Pacific attendant told a reporter, "They are always telling us that we are pretty and intelligent and that we are a very important part of the company and they treat us as if we clean the toilets AND no matter what happens we must always SMILE." Management attempted to slash labor costs by increasing hours and job duties, though Cathay Pacific ranked as the world's third-most profitable airline at the time. When negotiations stalled, most of the carrier's 3,500 flight attendants walked off the job. As the management studies scholar Stephen Linstead argues, the Cathay Pacific women used the feminine allure for which they were hired, and then further trained in, as a weapon to win media support, and threw management off guard in the process. Cathay Pacific attendants did not get everything they wished for in the strike settlement, but they shook up the corporate culture at the carrier and won widespread support in Hong Kong and among airline workers around the world.[8]

In 1997 cabin crewmembers at British Airways resisted management's attempt to scale back union power with another largely effective strike. Here the mobilization of the global airline labor community was crucial in sustaining the walkout. Airline workers worldwide feared the precedent that an unsuccessful strike might set at British Airways, an international industry leader and a bellwether of privatization (the British government sold off the airline to private investors in the 1980s, making it the first of several flag carriers to be privatized). The union's adept public relations campaign helped by alleging management bullying at what was seen as a model corporation in Britain. While management's cost-cutting agenda weathered the strike, its anti-union hopes were dashed. Not only did the strikers' union survive, but unionization among British cabin crew increased in the wake of the dispute.[9]

By the beginning of the twenty-first century, flight attendants around the world faced new pressures as globalization, deregulation, and privatization heightened competition and made airlines increasingly sensitive to labor costs and hostile to unions. But as the strikes at American, Alaska, Cathay Pacific, and British Airways all evidenced, flight attendants' unions adapted with creative strike techniques, savvy image management, and considerable militancy. The geographer Drew Whitelegg argues that globalization and deregulation have in some ways increased flight attendants' leverage in labor relations. With delicately calibrated route networks spread across continents and branding efforts dependent

on the level of service that their frontline employees provide, giant airlines in an intensively competitive age can suffer mightily when their
flight attendants rebel.[10]

PLUS ÇA CHANGE

Although flight attendants represented the "new face of labor" in the
1990s, their demographic profile was surprisingly unchanged. After Title
VII cabin crews did become more diverse, with women and men of
nearly all ages, races, and socioeconomic backgrounds represented. (The
new diversity was pruriently signaled by the publication in 1980 of *Stewardess with the Moustache!*, which tweaked the *Coffee, Tea or Me?* formula
to chart the heterosexual adventures of a male flight attendant.) Yet the
occupation remained filled with young, white women. The main change
was that many were married mothers in their thirties accruing considerable seniority, instead of single women in their twenties soon to depart.
An economist found in the late 1990s that the proportion of women in
the flight attendant occupation remained relatively steady after the 1970s
at around 85 percent, while nationwide service work became less thoroughly feminized. The same researcher found that the underrepresenta-
tion of African Americans in the flight attendant occupation had diminished only slightly in recent decades. Compared to other service workers,
flight attendants were therefore more likely to be female and less likely to
be black after second-wave feminism and the civil rights movement. Male
flight attendants, however, were more likely to be African American than
their female colleagues. This latter development suggests, like the continued predominance of women, that hoary biases regarding who should
serve, care for, and clean up after others (white women and people of
color, but not white men) still influence customer and managerial expectations and delimit workers' job choices, especially in high-profile service
occupations.[11]

Male flight attendants regardless of race remained subject to stereotyping as effeminate or homosexual. As a male flight attendant explained,
"People just assume that if you are a man, and you are in this job you
must be gay." But there was at least more demographic truth behind the
stereotyping than in earlier years. Gay men became numerous enough to
have made the occupation one that attracts gay applicants and provides a
relatively favorable environment for coming out and staying out com-

fortably. Most of a group of nearly ninety gay flight attendants surveyed in the mid-1990s considered their heterosexual co-workers generally supportive of gay colleagues. But they also made clear that the favorable environment overall did not amount to the disappearance of homophobia among passengers and co-workers. Sexual harassment remained a problem for gay men along with women in the job. At least with passengers, flight attendants have had the protection in recent years of increasingly stringent federal laws against interference with flight crewmembers. Some gay male flight attendants, as well as their female co-workers, have had particularly aggressive harassers arrested.[12]

While airlines proved themselves gay-friendly, or at least tolerant, they continued to manage female flight attendants' appearances in ways that harkened back to the days before Title VII. Controlling female cabin crew's weight remained a central pillar in airlines' "appearance" regimes. Though flight attendants repeatedly sought to end weight policies under anti-discrimination law, the policies proved uniquely difficult to challenge. Despite some considerable victories for flight attendants from the 1970s to the 1990s, several courts ruled that weight restrictions are merely appearance standards and thus not a matter for Title VII scrutiny. In other cases, courts found that female flight attendants failed to show enough of a disparate impact between the sexes for the weight rules to be declared illegal.[13]

Though Northwest and Continental adopted a "weight in proportion to height" standard without regular checks, and many smaller airlines dropped weight rules altogether, some of the largest carriers continued to impose specific limits. "When are we finally going to do away with this degrading, humiliating weighing in?," an angry USAir flight attendant wrote to the union magazine *Flightlog* in 1990. "I find it most offensive and embarrassing. . . . Just because my hips are on the full side doesn't mean I stop being a valuable flight attendant." Three years later USAir forfeited its weigh-ins in the largest legal victory to date for a flight attendant union on weight policies. After the EEOC filed suit against the carrier's weight program in 1992, USAir and the Association of Flight Attendants entered a settlement in 1994 that replaced weight monitoring with a proficiency test ensuring that flight attendants were physically fit enough to do their job. Most other weight cases were less successful. In 1991 American agreed to ease its maximum allowable weights but maintained its right to enforce a standardized chart. Weight restrictions, which tend disproportionately to affect older flight attendants, provide a pretext to replace more senior workers in the highest salary brackets with lower-paid, entry-level workers—a particularly effective way to trim costs at a carrier like American, which pioneered the use of lower "B-scale" wages for new workers in 1983.[14]

In what must be a bitter irony for many flight attendants, airlines like American, United, and Delta have defended their weight policies in recent years as necessary to ensure a "professional" look. American's flight attendant manual stated in 1991, "A firm, trim, silhouette, free of bulges, rolls, or paunches, is necessary for an alert, efficient image." As Anna Quindlen quipped in 1993 in a column in the *New York Times*, "In other words, svelte equals professional. So much for telling girls . . . that it is performance and not appearance that counts." The tenacity with which some airlines clung to an older ideal of stewardess slenderness, repackaged as "professional" appearance standards (along with required use of cosmetics), suggests just how little perhaps changed in management attitudes after the tumult of the 1970s.[15]

SEPTEMBER 11

While deregulation was the defining event of the late twentieth century for air travel in the United States, the terrorist attacks of September 11, 2001, seem destined to be the most tragically momentous turn of events of the early twenty-first century. The terrorist attacks that have since become known simply by their date saw two hijacked airliners smash into the World Trade Center in New York City and a third into the Pentagon in Washington, killing thousands and turning New York's iconic "Twin Towers" into rubble within hours. A fourth plane, presumed to be destined for a second target in the capital, crashed in a remote field in Pennsylvania after passengers and crew fought their captors. Hijackings of commercial airliners, or "skyjackings," had occurred for decades. But the attacks of 2001, which used airplanes to cause death and destruction on an unprecedented scale, inaugurated a new era of threat and anxiety.

In the wake of the attacks, beefing up airline safety and security ranked high on the list of concerns for both policymakers and the public. Many of the initial reactions could hardly have been reassuring to flight attendants. A writer for the typically conservative editorial page of the *Wall Street Journal* argued three weeks after the attacks that "airlines need guards, not stewards." To Edward Jay Epstein, flight attendants were merely one of many frills to be eliminated as frivolous distractions. Thankfully for cabin crew, neither the federal government nor airlines agreed. Instead, flight attendants finally achieved the federal safety certification they had sought for half a century. In a far-ranging aviation bill, Congress in late November 2003 dictated that flight attendants should be issued licenses by the FAA, just as pilots, mechanics, and others had been for decades, certifying their safety training under extant government standards. The AFA trumpeted, "Our lack of certification allowed us to be categorized as second-class employees" and viewed "as merely 'waitresses in the sky.' But no more." "We have finally been recognized for our safety roles and will forever be considered primarily as safety professionals." In addition to overdue respect, flight attendants welcomed certification for standardizing credentials and encouraging the hiring of experienced flight attendants over other applicants. But as union officials noted, it was a "bittersweet" victory. Regulators declined to codify the security training that flight attendants were required to receive at a time when responding to hijacking attempts no longer meant automatically cooperating with assailants, and flight attendants could no longer expect help from pilots, who would now remain locked in the cockpit.[16]

The victory of licensing must indeed have been more bitter than sweet for the many thousands of flight attendants who lost their jobs after September 11. The terrorist attacks in New York and Washington sparked an abrupt economic decline in the airline industry that dwarfed earlier ones. Congress stepped in and prevented the widespread collapse of airlines with a $15 billion aid package, including $5 billion cash in emergency funds and $10 billion in loan guarantees. Even so, some of the largest carriers were unable to survive without drastic measures. United and US Airways filed for bankruptcy in 2002, while American only narrowly avoided doing so in 2003. What kept struggling airlines afloat in large part, as in the early days of deregulation, were employee concessions and layoffs. More than 20 percent of the flight attendants employed in the United States were laid off within two years of September 11. Scaling back on amenities also helped to stem fatal losses once again, and it disappointed and angered passengers again. Some airlines, like Southwest and JetBlue, managed to prosper, but only because they had kept service simple and costs low by design. As an aviation reporter surmised in September 2004, "For decades, an airline job was a coveted plum," thanks to good pay and benefits, strong unions, and the allure of travel. But now "there are two airline industries, one that created those attractive jobs but can no longer afford them, and another that is thriving in large part because it has avoided creating them." "Ask any flight attendant; when we all took this job, it was for the lifestyle, the freedom," Louis Rudy, who began flying in 1986, told the *New York Times* in 2003 in a feature on rising stress for cabin crew. "But it's changed so much, with mergers and layoffs and concessions and service reductions and waiting for pay cuts. The thrill is gone."[17]

The bleak economic context created by airline restructuring pushed the main flight attendant union in the United States once more into an affiliation with a more powerful union within the AFL-CIO. But the future looked brighter this time for the Association of Flight Attendants. In a historic merger of pink-collar labor, AFA, with just under 50,000 members, joined forces as of 1 January 2004 with the Communication Workers of America, a union 700,00 members strong with roots in telephone operator organizing in the early twentieth century. Union activists at United Airlines campaigned against the merger, warning that their union's independence was too precious to forfeit. But AFA's national leadership successfully persuaded enough members that a merger with CWA was the best course for the future. Unlike in earlier days, AFA members had less reason to worry that the leaders of their new parent union would be patronizing or domineering. "In terms of the modern battle for women's rights in society and the workplace, the history of CWA parallels the history of the AFA," AFA's magazine contended. What the combined forces of AFA and CWA will allow flight attendants to accomplish remains to be seen. But perhaps flight attendants will come to value labor solidarity at least as much as union autonomy in their activist formula for the twenty-first century.[18]

What is clear is that the sexual folklore attached to flight attendants remains alive and well after the tragedy of September 11 and perhaps even thrives, helped by nostalgia for bygone glamour, ease, and comfort aloft. Feature films released in the past few years (*Catch Me If You Can, View from the Top, Soul Plane*) suggest the durability of prurient fascination with the airlines' "glamour girls." *Coffee, Tea or Me?* (1967), the fictional memoir that spawned so many raunchy portrayals of flight attendants, was reissued in 2003 with retro styling and a foreword by its newly acknowledged male ghost author. It is not likely to help dispel the "coffee, tea, or me" myths that Hooters, Inc., the restaurant chain famous for buxom waitresses in tight t-shirts and shorts, started an airline in 2003 serving the resort area of Myrtle Beach, South Carolina. At least Hooters Air has taken the novel step of splitting the historic components of stewardesses' work: while "Hooters Girls" adorn flights as scantily clad hostesses, flight attendants in more modest garb fulfill federal safety mandates and serve snacks and beverages.[19]

Out of recent wistfulness for stewardesses' glamorous past has come one intriguing instance of popular revisionism. "Plane Crazy," a musical that opened at the New York Musical Theatre Festival in September 2005, covers the familiar ground of the loves and adventures of a pair of stewardesses circa 1965, with the trademarked tagline, "When stews were sexy and the world was sexist." But more surprisingly, one of the "stews" turns out to be a budding feminist activist. The historical details may be a little shaky for professional historians' comfort, but this Helen-Gurley-Brown-meets-Betty-Friedan tale of stewardess life in the 1960s celebrates flight attendants' glamour and activism together, as popular culture almost never has. One can only hope that stewardess feminism will make it on Broadway.[20]

NOTES

INTRODUCTION

1. Traveler quoted in Nielsen, *From Sky Girl to Flight Attendant*, 20. "Glamor Girls of the Air," *Life*, 25 August 1958, 68–76. The phrase "workplace feminism" is from Cobble, "'A Spontaneous Loss of Enthusiasm.'" I use "stewardess(es)" or "hostess(es)" along with "flight attendant(s)" for historical discussion through the 1970s, when cabin crew began to prefer the gender-neutral title.

2. Quotation from "Fifty Years of Flight Attendants," *Flightlog*, winter 1980, 6.

3. Quotation from "Labor Speaks Statement of Purpose," *Labor Speaks* 2, no. 1 (May 1977): 8, in "Items from the TWU Bulletin Board" folder, box 5, accession date 13 August 1981, Association of Flight Attendants Collection, Archives of Labor and Urban Affairs, Wayne State University [hereafter cited as AFA Collection].

4. The literature exploring the marginalization of female wage earners and their struggles to be taken seriously is large and growing. For overviews see Kessler-Harris, *Out to Work*; Baron, ed., *Work Engendered*; Milkman, ed., *Women, Work and Protest*; Cobble, *The Other Women's Movement*. On the labor movement's male orientation see Faue, *Community of Suffering and Struggle*. On "work," its meanings, and the consequences of how it is defined see Castel, "Work and Usefulness to the World"; Kessler-Harris, *In Pursuit of Equity*.

5. I am indebted to the insightful analyses of flight attendants' work as emotional labor in Hochschild, *The Managed Heart*, and, among responses to her pioneering book, Whitelegg, "Cabin Pressure," and Williams, "Sky Service"; and on the aesthetic as well as emotional labor demanded of flight attendants as unacknowledged and unremunerated, Tyler, "Women's Work as the Labour of Sexual Difference"; Tyler and Abbott, "Chocs Away"; Tyler and Taylor, "The Exchange of Aesthetics"; Taylor and Tyler, "Emotional Labour and Sexual Differ-

ence in the Airline Industry." On the labor of femininity see also Skeggs, *Forma-tions of Class and Gender*; Dooley, "Battle in the Sky," 79–80.

6. Quotation from Joan Beck, "25 Years Ago: Birth of the Air Line Stewardess Idea," *Chicago Daily Tribune*, 5 May 1955, D, 1. The phrase "wages of glamour" is adapted from David Roediger's formulation of the "wages of whiteness," drawing on W. E. B. Du Bois's insights (discussed more in chapter 2). Roediger, *The Wages of Whiteness*; W. E. B. Du Bois, *Black Reconstruction*, 700.

7. Fields, "The Production of Glamour," 9; Gundle, "Hollywood Glamour and Mass Consumption in Postwar Italy," 97. Gundle continues: "Its forms change but it is always available to be consumed vicariously by the masses who see in it an image of life writ large according to the criteria of a market society. As a language it is a hybrid that mixes luxury, class, exclusivity, and privilege with the sexuality and seduction of prostitution, entertainment, and the commercial world. Aristocratic forms and styles persist within modern glamour; but without the beauty, color, and sexual enticements of the popular theater and high-class prostitution, the drama, dynamism, scandal, and feminine display that are central to glamour would be absent." See also Bailey, "Parasexuality and Glamour," 148–72; Gundle, "Mapping the Origins of Glamour," 269–95; Mizejewski, *Ziegfeld Girl*; Glenn, *Female Spectacle*; Banner, *American Beauty*. Both Stephen Gundle and Lois Banner are working on book-length studies that promise to shed more historical light on glamour.

8. Mizejewski, *Ziegfeld Girl*, 12 and *passim*; Fields, "The Production of Glamour"; Banet-Weiser, *The Most Beautiful Girl in the World*; Peiss, *Hope in a Jar*; Marling, *Debutante*; Barbas, *Movie Crazy*; Berry, *Screen Style*; Latham, *Posing a Threat*; Howard, "'At the Curve Exchange.'" On desire for glamour see also Enstad, *Ladies of Labor, Girls of Adventure*; Steedman, *Landscape for a Good Woman*; Schrum, *Some Wore Bobby Socks*. Cf. McLean, *Being Rita Hayworth*, which argues that Hayworth's labor in transforming herself into America's favorite glamour girl of the 1940s was widely recognized and admired at the time.

9. Mrs. William A. Corkran (née Janet M. Blanchfield), e-mail to author, 11 June 2004.

10. Boydston, *Home and Work*, 146 and *passim*; Strasser, *Never Done*; Glenn, "From Servitude to Service Work"; Reverby, *Ordered to Care*.

11. Quotation from Cobble, *Dishing It Out*, 46. Howe, *Pink Collar Workers*; Macdonald and Sirianni, eds., *Working in the Service Society*; Norwood, *Labor's Flaming Youth*; Benson, *Counter Cultures*; Strom, *Beyond the Typewriter*; Kwolek-Folland, *Engendering Business*; Glenn, "From Servitude to Service Work"; Green, *Race on the Line*; Kirkby, *Barmaids*; Willett, *Permanent Waves*; Pringle, *Secretaries Talk*; Hughes and Tadic, "'Something to Deal with'"; Folgerø and Fjeldstad, "On Duty Off Guard."

12. Blackwelder, *Now Hiring*, 3, 6; Macdonald and Sirianni, eds., *Working in the Service Society*, 1. See also Kessler-Harris, *Out to Work*, chapters 8–11; Goldin,

Understanding the Gender Gap; Oppenheimer, *The Female Labor Force in the United States.*

13. See sources in note 11. Howe coined the term "pink collar."

14. Cockburn, *Machinery of Dominance*, 167–68; MacLean, "The Hidden History of Affirmative Action"; Baron, "Gender and Labor History: Learning from the Past, Looking to the Future," in *Work Engendered*, 1–46. Judith Butler's theory of gender as performance has been an important influence on many historians of gender and labor. Butler, *Gender Trouble.* For a similar formulation in sociology of gender as produced recurrently in social interactions see West and Zimmerman, "Doing Gender."

15. Hochschild, *The Managed Heart*; Tyler, "Women's Work as the Labour of Sexual Difference"; Tyler and Abbott, "Chocs Away"; Nielsen, *From Sky Girl to Flight Attendant.* See also Whitelegg, "Cabin Pressure" and "Touching Down." The most historically illuminating studies in addition to Nielsen's include Lessor, "Unanticipated Longevity in Women's Work" and "Social Movements, the Occupational Arena and Changes in Career Consciousness"; Rozen, "Turbulence in the Air" and "Technological Advances and Increasing Militance"; Kolm, "Women's Labor Aloft" and "Stewardesses' 'Psychological Punch'"; Dooley, "Battle in the Sky." Flight attendants' place in a larger trajectory of working women's activism is most effectively captured in Cobble, "'A Spontaneous Loss of Enthusiasm'" and *The Other Women's Movement.* See also Boris, "Desirable Dress," on flight attendants' embodiment and use of femininity as a case study in the doubled-edged politics of appearance for women in the workplace.

There is as yet little historical scholarship on flight attendants in other national contexts or in international comparison. The most helpful concerns Australia, Britain, and Canada: Williams, *Blue, White and Pink Collar Workers in Australia* and "Sky Service"; Mills, *Sex, Strategy and the Stratosphere.*

CHAPTER 1: "PSYCHOLOGICAL PUNCH"

1. "Sky Stewardesses Take Times Reporter for a Ride—or Why Girls Want to Leave Home for Work in the Clouds," quoted in "Happy 45th Birthday to Flight Attendants," *Flightlog*, June–July 1975, 8.

2. Scharf, *To Work and to Wed*; Wandersee, *Women's Work and Family Values*; Kessler-Harris, "Gender Ideology in Historical Reconstruction"; Faue, *Community of Suffering and Struggle*; Hapke, *Daughters of the Great Depression.*

3. Perata, *Those Pullman Blues*, xix and *passim*; Santino, *Miles of Smiles, Years of Struggle.* On race, gender, and technology see Richter, *Home on the Rails*; Green, *Race on the Line*; Cockburn, *Machinery of Dominance*; Sandelowski, *Devices and Desires.* On early airlines' use of racialized images of progress and modernity in marketing see Kolm, "Women's Labor Aloft," 109–10.

4. On the racial and gender division of service work see especially Glenn,

"From Servitude to Service Work." See also Benson, *Counter Cultures*; Cobble, *Dishing It Out*; Green, *Race on the Line*.

5. "Putting Luxury in the Air," *Literary Digest*, 9 January 1932, 32. On early aviation and its cultural meanings see Davies, *Airlines of the United States since 1914*; Corn, *The Winged Gospel*; Solberg, *Conquest of the Skies*; Bilstein, *Flight in America*; Smith, *Airways*; Kelly, *The Sky's the Limit*; Paris, *From the Wright Brothers to "Top Gun."* More surplus military aircraft, government subsidies, and devastated rail systems after the First World War contributed to Western European leadership in early passenger transport. Hudson, *Air Travel*; Allen, *The Airline Builders*.

6. Early federal legislation is discussed in many aviation histories. See especially Smith, *Airways*; van der Linden, *Airlines and Air Mail*. On Lindbergh's flight see Corn, *The Winged Gospel*, 17–27; Solberg, *Conquest of the Skies*, chapter 6.

7. Davies, *Airlines of the United States since 1914*, chapter 4 and 582–606; Bilstein, *Flight in America*, 52; "Growth in the Air," *New York Times*, 6 June 1931, 16; "Big Gain in Air Travel," *Literary Digest*, 16 December 1933, 38; "American Air Travel Quadrupled," *Literary Digest*, 20 December 1930, 16; Davies, *Airlines of the United States since 1914*, 56–57.

8. Smith quoted in William Vassallo, "The Ageless Airliner: Venerable DC-3 Still Airborne," *American History Illustrated* 19, no. 4 (June 1984): 47. On airplane comfort see e.g. Reginald M. Cleveland, "Air Transport Becomes Luxurious," *Scientific American*, December 1933, 264–65; "Transcontinental Flying Pullmans," *Literary Digest*, 16 November 1935, 28; "12-Ton Flying Hotel Has 16 Berths," *Popular Mechanics* 65 (February 1936): 232; Willis, *Your Future Is in the Air*, 60–61.

9. Solberg, *Conquest of the Skies*, 215. See also recollections in McLaughlin, *Footsteps in the Sky*; Vecsey and Dade, *Getting off the Ground*, 272.

10. On European stewards see Mills, "Cockpits, Hangars, Boys and Galleys" and "Strategy, Sexuality and the Stratosphere." On American stewards see McLaughlin, *Footsteps in the Sky*, 2–8; Bilstein, *Flight in America*, 101; Steele et al., *Wings of Pride*, 16; Serling, *The Only Way to Fly*, 72–73. On steamship travel see Fox, *Transatlantic*; Coons and Varias, *Tourist Third Cabin*.

11. Perata, *Those Pullman Blues*; Santino, *Miles of Smiles, Years of Struggle*; Chateauvert, *Marching Together*; Bates, *Pullman Porters and the Rise of Protest Politics in Black America*. As Chateauvert argues, the Brotherhood of Sleeping Car Porters' investment in "manhood rights" effectively barred maids from any substantive role in union politics or goals; they were encouraged to join the BSCP's ladies' auxiliary.

12. Quotation from Segrave, *Tipping*, 11. Santino, *Miles of Smiles*; Coons and Vargas, *Tourist Third Cabin*; Richter, *Home on the Rails*, chapter 5.

13. Quotations in Follet, *Careers in Aviation*, 101; Hall and Merkle, *The Sky's the Limit!*, 132. Though these sources are from the 1940s and refer to stewardesses, the

no-tipping rule began with the first stewards, as did the racial "fellowship" between employee and customer. For a similar argument see Kolm, "Women's Labor Aloft," 63–65. Former American Airlines employees explained the racial screening process, based on residential addresses, in Serling, *Eagle*, 288. When African Americans did fly, airlines mimicked racial segregation in other means of transport by assigning black passengers to seats in the back of the cabin. Quindry, "Airline Passenger Discrimination." For descriptions of stewards as "good-looking" and "alert" or "professional" see sources in note 10; and "Rodney" and "1,000,000 Silent Salesmen," *Pan American*, March 1933, 2–3, 14. On career mobility for stewards see McLaughlin, *Footsteps in the Sky*, 5; Steele et al., *Wings of Pride*, 15; Rickenbacker, *Rickenbacker*, 247.

14. C. B. Allen, "The Airline Attendant's Job," *Aviation*, April 1931, 245. See also Mills, "Strategy, Sexuality and the Stratosphere," 81.

15. Bilstein, *Flight in America*, 101; Solberg, *Conquest of the Skies*, 215; Allen, "The Airline Attendant's Job," 244–45. See also " 'Hush, Baby, Hush' Sings Helpful Steward," *Pan American Air Ways* 3, no. 3 (July 1932): 15, which suggests that stewards, in contrast to stewardesses, were not necessarily expected to be able to help mothers calm children.

16. In late 1934 Central Airlines hired Helen Richey, a celebrity "aviatrix," as a co-pilot. She quickly resigned in protest when concerns about female "weakness" (mostly voiced by male pilots) prompted the Aeronautics Bureau of the Department of Commerce to restrict her to fair-weather duty. She was the only woman pilot hired by a commercial airline until the 1970s. "First Woman Airline Co-pilot Flies Plane from Capital to Detroit with 7 Passengers," *New York Times*, 1 January 1935, 22; "Feminist Stirred over Woman Flier," *New York Times*, 8 November 1935, 25; Corn, *The Winged Gospel*, chapter 4; Ware, *Still Missing*.

The story of Church approaching Stimpson, and how he became the "father" of stewardess service, has been recounted many times, often with excerpts from his memo proposing the idea. See e.g. "Practicing Paragons: Profession of Stewardess 15 Years Old This Month," *National Aeronautics*, May 1945, 18; Joan Beck, "25 Years Ago: Birth of the Air Line Stewardess Idea," *Chicago Daily Tribune*, 5 May 1955, D, 1; Horace Sutton, "Isle-Hoppers, Aisle-Walkers," *Saturday Review*, 15 May 1965, 37–38. Why Stimpson's initial thought of hiring Filipino attendants never took hold is not clear in contemporary or historical sources. On Filipino men's employment by Pullman in the 1920s and 1930s see Posadas, "The Hierarchy of Color and Psychological Adjustment in an Industrial Environment."

17. Quotations from Stimpson's memo as reprinted in "Stewardesses Mark 40th Year," *Air Line Pilot*, May 1970, 36.

18. Peckham, *Sky Hostess*, 5; Taylor, *High Horizons*, 70–71; Harriet Fry Iden in Vecsey and Dade, *Getting off the Ground*, 271; Inez Keller Fuite in McLaughlin, *Footsteps in the Sky*, 19; Reginald M. Cleveland, " 'Contact,' " *New York Times*,

28 May 1933, VIII, 8. For popular cultural images see e.g. Wheeler, *Jane, Stewardess of the Air Lines*; Hurst, *Air Stewardess*; Graf, *Air Stewardess*; George Shaffer, "Studio to Pick Air Hostess to Star in Movie," *Chicago Daily Tribune*, 23 September 1932, 20; Paris, *From the Wright Brothers to "Top Gun,"* 75. *Air Hostess* (1933), from Columbia Pictures, was the first Hollywood feature to focus on an airline stewardess.

19. On TWA's use of "hostess" see Serling, *Howard Hughes' Airline*, 51; Peckham, *Sky Hostess*, 2. Employment estimates in Oakes, *United States Women in Aviation*, 22; "The Typical Air Hostess," *U.S. Air Services* 17 (May 1932): 40; Marie Elwell Onions, "Welcoming the Nation," *Independent Woman* 17 (February 1938): 41; Rozen, "Turbulence in the Air," 70.

20. Peckham, *Sky Hostess*, 11; "Contact," *New York Times*, 11 July 1937, XI, 6; Brad Williams, "NAL's First Stewardess Remembers . . . ," *National NOW*, 24 April 1972, 6. On Eastern see "Hostesses Soon to Be Replaced by Men on Eastern Air Lines," *Washington Post*, 18 October 1936, M, 6; "Where We Came From . . . Where We're Going," *Flightlog*, March 1978, 23; Solberg, *Conquest of the Skies*, 215; Rickenbacker, *Rickenbacker*, 246–47.

21. On gender and labor costs see Kolm, "Women's Labor Aloft," 53–54. Ware, *Still Missing*, especially chapter 2; Corn, *The Winged Gospel*, chapter 4; J. C. Furnas, "Mr. Milquetoast in the Sky," *Scribner's Magazine* 104, no. 3 (September 1938): 7–11, 60; Alice Rogers Hager, "More Women Take to Air," *New York Times*, 11 July 1937, XI, 6; Willis, *Your Future Is in the Air*, 37.

22. "Air Hostess Finds Life Adventurous," *New York Times*, 12 April 1936, II, 1; Francis Vivian Drake, "Air Stewardess," *Atlantic Monthly* 151 (February 1933): 190.

23. Richter, *Home on the Rails*, 60 and *passim*.

24. See e.g. Onions, "Welcoming the Nation," 41; W. B. Courtney, "High-Flying Ladies," *Collier's*, 20 August 1932, 30. On hospital efforts to create a "homely" environment see Rima D. Apple, "Image or Reality? Photographs in the History of Nursing," Jones, ed., *Images of Nurses*, 48–49; Sandelowski, *Devices and Desires*, 3, 5.

25. Quotations from Jones, ed., *Images of Nurses*, xix, xxii; Drake, "Air Stewardess," 188. Chateauvert, *Marching Together*, 22, 24; Melosh, *"The Physician's Hand"*; Reverby, *Ordered to Care*.

26. Many historians have examined how sex segregation in industrial, clerical, and service work was codified and how difficult employers' discrimination was to challenge once legitimized by ideologies of "appropriate" gender roles; they have also emphasized workers' participation and resistance in occupational sex-typing. For a sampling of exemplary scholarship see Baron, ed., *Work Engendered*. Ruth Milkman's analysis in *Gender at Work* remains an influential model.

27. Stimpson quoted in "Happy 45th Birthday to Flight Attendants," *Flightlog*, June–July 1975, 8. Catherine MacKenzie, "Hostess of the Sky," *New York Times*,

28 March 1933, XII, 1; Peckham, *Sky Hostess*, 12; Joseph Kastner, "Joan Waltermire: Air Stewardess," *Life*, 28 April 1941, 110; "Sky School," *Trained Nurse and Hospital Review* 104, no. 1 (January 1940): 37; "Hostess Instruction Letter No. 177," signed Ruth K. Rhodes, Chief Air Hostess, 8 April 1937, reprinted in Steele et al., *Wings of Pride*, 41; Robert W. Hambrook, "Airline Hostesses," *Air Commerce Bulletin*, 15 August 1939, 32.

28. TWA manager quoted in Steele et al., *Wings of Pride*, 31; Planck, *Women with Wings*, 197. Norwood, *Labor's Flaming Youth*; Scharf, *To Work and to Wed*; Kessler-Harris, *Out to Work*, chapter 9; Blackwelder, *Now Hiring*, chapter 4.

29. Quotations from Onions, "Welcoming the Nation," 41; Catherine Mac-Kenzie, "Hostess of the Sky," *New York Times*, 28 March 1933, XII, 1; "Flying Supermen and Superwomen," *Literary Digest*, 14 November 1936, 23; Walter L. Avery to Ruth Kathryn Rhodes, n.d. [1935], repr. in Steele et al., *Wings of Pride*, 30. See also Peckham, *Sky Hostess*, 14; Willson, *Hostess of the Skyways*, 32. Airlines expressed concern that passengers might interpret scars, regardless of what caused them, as evidence of a previous crash.

30. Hiring statistics in "U.S. Airway Lists 135 Stewardesses," *New York Times*, 9 March 1935, 13; "5,000 Seek 20 Jobs as Air Stewardesses," *New York Times*, 17 October 1939, 27. Willson, *Hostess of the Skyways*, 170; Peckham, *Sky Hostess*, 14.

31. "5,000 Seek 20 Jobs as Air Stewardesses," *New York Times*, 17 October 1939, 27. Reverby, *Ordered to Care*, 81–82.

32. Quoted in Steele et al., *Wings of Pride*, 77.

33. "Flying Supermen and Superwomen," *Literary Digest*, 14 November 1936, 22–23. Benson, *Counter Cultures*; Reverby, *Ordered to Care*; Cobble, *Dishing It Out*; Willett, *Permanent Waves*.

34. Quotations from Rhodes in Steele et al., *Wings of Pride*, 44; "Air Hostess Finds Life Adventurous," *New York Times*, 12 April 1936, II, 1; Margaret Scully, "She's a Trained Nurse Who Has Taken to Flying," *Chicago Daily Tribune*, 16 August 1936, D, 7. See also McLaughlin, *Footsteps in the Sky*, 74 and passim; Bomar and Bankston, *Birdie*.

35. Marjorie Gibson Howe quoted in Kolm, "Women's Labor Aloft," 114. Nurses too would presumably have found abundant opportunities for upwardly mobile marriages through their regular contact with doctors. But for those who wished to work past marriage, becoming a doctor's wife could mean social marginalization within nurses' work culture. Melosh, *Introduction*, "*The Physician's Hand.*"

36. Wage comparisons in Kolm, "Women's Labor Aloft," 88–89; see also Hambrook, "Airline Hostesses," 33. Flight attendants earned better pay than Pullman porters, whose wages were about $75 to $90 in the 1930s. Posadas, "The Hierarchy of Color and Psychological Adjustment in an Industrial Environment," 356; Chateauvert, *Marching Together*, 156.

37. Quotation from "Contact," *New York Times*, 11 July 1937, XI, 6. Peckham,

Sky Hostess, 27–28 and Appendix; Hager, *Wings to Wear*, "Housekeeping in the Clouds," *Popular Mechanics*, November 1937, 120A.

38. Follet, *Careers in Aviation*, 97.

39. "Air Hostess Finds Life Adventurous," *New York Times*, 12 April 1936, II, 1; poem by "Hugh R. Porter, Chicago," repr. in McLaughlin, *Footsteps in the Sky*, 29; "The Air Hostess Carries On," *New York Times*, 19 April 1936, X, 12. See also "Tact and Heroism on U.S. Air-Lines," *Literary Digest*, 18 April 1936, 6.

40. Wheeler, *Jane, Stewardess of the Air Lines*; Paris, *From the Wright Brothers to "Top Gun*," 75 and chapter 4.

41. Courtney, "High-Flying Ladies," 29; Drake, "Air Stewardess," 187–88; "Stewardess on an Air-Liner," *Literary Digest*, 18 February 1933, 35.

42. Joan Thomas, "What about That Hostess Job?," *Popular Aviation*, May 1933, 290; Drake, "Air Stewardess," 187.

43. Melosh, *"The Physician's Hand*," 20 and *passim*; Reverby, *Ordered to Care*, chapter 7; Sandelowski, *Devices and Desires*; Cott, *The Grounding of Modern Feminism*, chapter 7; Murphy, *Blackboard Unions*; Walkowitz, *Working with Class*. For critical scholarship on professionalization generally see Larson, *The Rise of Professionalism*; Macdonald, *The Sociology of the Professions*.

44. Quotations from Onions, "Welcoming the Nation," 60; "Women on Wheels," *Time*, 10 August 1937, 32. Coons and Varias, *Tourist Third Cabin*, chapter 4; "Stewardesses Replace Maids on Los Angeles Limited Cars," *Washington Post*, 6 October 1935, F, 1; Eunice Peterson Hoevet, R.N., "Nurse Stewardesses: Nursing Takes to the Railroad," *American Journal of Nursing* 37, no. 1 (January 1937): 18–21; Kathryn Cogley, "Girl on the Train," *American Magazine*, June 1942, 45, 102–3; Willson, *Hostess of the Skyways*; "Stewardesses Walk Long, Smile Plenty," *Washington Post*, 13 July 1947, L, 6; Mimi Conway, "The Bus Hostess: Down to Earth," *Washington Post*, 7 May 1972, L, 1.

45. Jeanette Lea, "We *Don't* Fly for Love," *Popular Aviation*, September 1938, 24–25; Parker quoted in Peckham, *Sky Hostess*, 80. See also "Stewardess Airs Views on Marriage," *United Air Lines News* 6, no. 12 (December 1937): 6.

46. Quotations from Courtney, "High-Flying Ladies," 30; Sally Knapp, *New Wings for Women* (New York: Thomas Y. Crowell, 1946), 78. Reverby, *Ordered to Care*, 42.

47. Ellis K. Baldwin, "Ocean Hoppers," *Independent Woman*, December 1943, 363.

CHAPTER 2: "GLAMOR GIRLS OF THE AIR"

1. "Glamor Girls of the Air," *Life*, 25 August 1958, 68–76 [quotations from 68].

2. See e.g. "Why Airlines Run a Bride School," *Business Week*, 11 December 1965, 164–66, 169; "Practicing Paragons," *National Aeronautics* 23 (May 1945): 25. Bailey, *From Front Porch to Back Seat*; May, *Homeward Bound*.

3. On the "wages of whiteness" see Roediger, *The Wages of Whiteness*, and W. E. B. Du Bois, *Black Reconstruction*, 700 and *passim*. See also Lipsitz, *The Possessive Investment in Whiteness*.

4. Civil Aeronautics Act quoted in Solberg, *Conquest of the Skies*, 200. See also Kelly, *The Sky's the Limit*, 85–96; Davies, *Airlines of the United States since 1914*, 114–203, 200–209; Smith, *Airways*, 305–10.

5. Burkhardt, CAB: *The Civil Aeronautics Board*; Jordon, *Airline Regulation in America*; Fruhan, *The Fight for Competitive Advantage*; Bender and Altschul, *Chosen Instrument*. In 1955 the CAA listed fifteen airlines based in the United States as engaged in international operations, including the "Big Four" (TWA, Eastern, American, and United), none of which flew overseas before the Second World War. U.S. Civil Aeronautics Administration, CAA *Statistical Handbook of Civil Aviation, 1956*, 67.

6. Lewis C. Sorrell, "Air Transport in Wartime," in Thorsten Sellin and Donald Young, eds., *Transportation: War and Postwar; The Annals of the American Academy of Political and Social Science* 230 (November 1943): 82–86; Solberg, *Conquest of the Skies*, 251–344. From the start of 1943 through 1946, scheduled passenger traffic increased fourfold, a growth rate not matched before or since. Davies, *Airlines of the United States*, 324–25.

7. Bilstein, *Flight in America*, 233, 286; "The Important Passengers," *Air Line Pilot*, September 1962, 14; CAA *Statistical Handbook of Civil Aviation, 1956*, 64–65, 73, 76, 82, 87; Jordon, *Airline Regulation in America*, 37, 45–46; "Air Fare vs. Rail," *Business Week*, 1 September 1945, 46; "Bargains in Air Travel," *Consumer Reports*, February 1949, 73–75; "Air Coach," *Fortune*, December 1949, 18; "Low Cost Air Travel Is Possible," *New Republic*, 18 June 1951, 14–16; "Travel Tourist," *Time*, 7 September 1953, 87; "Travel on Credit," *Business Week*, 17 April 1954, 66.

8. Heppenheimer, *Turbulent Skies*, 108–30; Davies, *Airlines of the United States since 1914*, 324–35; Lester, *Fasten Your Seat Belts!*, 97.

9. TWA promised coach passengers "prompt service by ever-attentive hostesses" in full-page, color "Bargain Fares" advertisements, which ran in national magazines including *Time* in 1953 and 1954. Lester, *Fasten Your Seat Belts!*, 103; Davies, *Airlines of the United States since 1914*, 380; James H. Winchester, "Glamor on Wings," *American Mercury*, November 1956, 146; Mahler, *Wings of Gold*, 60. For an overview see Bilstein, "Air Travel and the Traveling Public."

10. Gill and Bates, *Airline Competition*, 135–37; see also Solberg, *Conquest of the Skies*, 377; Bilstein, "Air Travel and the Traveling Public."

11. Willis, *Your Future Is in the Air*, 66–67; "Dry Blue Yonder: Liquor-Pouring Airlines," *Time*, 19 September 1955, 102; "Airlines Warned on Serving Liquor," *Christian Century*, 28 September 1955, 1107; "Low Altitude: Drinking on Planes," *Newsweek*, 16 July 1956; "Alcohol and Airplanes Don't Mix," *Service Aloft* 4, no. 1 (October–December 1949): 2. See also Bilstein, "Air Travel and the Traveling Public," 102–3. On the changing culture of drinking see Rotskoff, *Love on the Rocks*.

12. Mahler, *Wings of Gold*, 58; "Always a Long Walk," *Service Aloft* 2, no. 2 (January–March 1948): 2; "Figures Don't Lie," *Service Aloft* 4, no 3 (April–June 1950): 2; "Planes Branded 'Saloons' in Air Steward Complaint," *Christian Science Monitor*, 10 October 1955, 14; "Favor Liquor Ban on Airlines," *Service Aloft* 10, no. 3 (fall 1957).

13. Murray, *Skygirl*, 94 [emphasis in original].

14. Quotation from 1961 American Airlines advertisement reprinted in Mahler, *Wings of Excellence*, 154. Dooley emphasizes how the extensive guidance that airlines provided in manuals on passenger care and service routines showed the work to be hardly "natural," "but learned behavior that had to be reinforced continually." "Battle in the Sky," 98; see also 101–6 on training programs. On interviewing see Murray, *Skygirl*; Airline Stewardess Information Bureau, *How to Become an Airline Stewardess*; Smith, *How to Be a Flight Stewardess*. On large carriers' training see also, e.g., "UAL Family Album," *United Air Lines News*, May 1949, 2.

15. Quotations from Delta recruiting literature reprinted in Murray, *Skygirl*, 227–29; "School for Air Hostesses," *Life*, 8 December 1947, 83–87; McLaughlin, *Footsteps in the Sky*, 237. "De Paul Course for Stewardesses," *Chicago Daily Tribune*, 20 March 1942, 9; "University of Denver to Train Hostesses," *School and Society*, 1 February 1947, 80; McLaughlin, *Footsteps in the Sky*, 167, 212; Mahler, *Wings of Gold*, 80. See also Edward S. Kitch, "Based Her Empire on a Charm School," *Washington Post*, 9 July 1953, 27; "Hard Selling Stewardesses," *Dun's Review and Modern Industry*, July 1964, 49–50.

16. Quotations from McLaughlin, *Footsteps in the Sky*, 162; Rich, *Flying High*, 73; Mahler, *Wings of Gold*, 80.

17. Quotation from Toni Carpenter in McLaughlin, *Footsteps in the Sky*, 125–26. Torn uniform incident described by a former Eastern flight attendant in e-mail to the author, 1 June 2004. Weight programs are described in many sources, e.g. Rich, *Flying High*, 77–78, 189. See also Barry, "Lifting the Weight."

18. Murray, *Skygirl*, 107–8 [emphasis in original]; "Stewardess Flight Observation Report," 6 May 1957, repr. in Mahler, *Wings of Excellence*, 134.

19. "Glamour Girl of the Zoo," *New York Times Magazine*, 5 January 1947, 14; Harry V. Forgeron, "Railroad Barge Becomes Glamor Girl," *New York Times*, 5 May 1963, 47. Delano, "Making Up for War"; Anderson, *Wartime Women*; Honey, *Creating Rosie the Riveter*.

20. Susan McLeland, "Elizabeth Taylor: Hollywood's Last Glamour Girl," in Radner and Luckett, eds., *Swinging Single*, 227–51; Banet-Weiser, *The Most Beautiful Girl in the World*; Watson and Martin, eds., *"There She Is, Miss America"*; Marling, *Debutante*; Lovegrove, *Pageant*; Robbins, *From Girls to Grrlz*, 15–17. See also the documentary produced for the PBS series "American Experience," *Miss America* (Alexandria, Va.: Clio Inc. and Orchard Films, 2001).

21. See e.g. "Why Airlines Run a Bride School," *Business Week*, 11 December 1965, 164–66, 169; "Glamor Girls of the Air"; Oney Fred Sweet, "Stewardesses Also Make Good Homemakers," *Chicago Daily Tribune*, 23 April 1944, W, 2. Changing uniform styles can be tracked in McLaughlin, *Footsteps in the Sky*; Omelia and Waldock, *Come Fly with Us!*; Lovegrove, *Airline*. The women's branches of the military strove to glamorize their postwar uniforms as well, though the goal there was to modify, not abandon, military traditions with feminine flourishes. Virginia Pope, "New Outfit Adds Glamour to WAC," *New York Times*, 24 February 1950, 20; Anna Petersen, "The 'New Army' Offers Attractions to Wacs, Too," *New York Times*, 19 April 1961, 41.

22. The "Vicki Barr, Flight Stewardess" Series was published by Grosset and Dunlap, publisher also of Carolyn Keene's Nancy Drew mystery stories. The Vicki Barr series began with Wells, *Silver Wings for Vicki* (1947), and included at least ten sequels by Wells and Julie Tatham (also known as Julie Campbell). Playtex advertisement, #AT88: 1621, Ted Bates Historical Reel, Museum of Television and Radio, New York City.

23. Paula Christian, *Edge of Twilight* (1959) and *The Other Side of Love* (1963), both reprinted in *Twilight Girls*.

24. "Hollywood's Stars Shine for Dona Lee," *Service Aloft* 4, no. 2 (January–March 1950): 2; Lucy Key Miller, "Front Views and Profiles: Hollywood's New Star," *Chicago Daily Tribune*, 26 September 1950, A, 2; Albert D. Hughes, "Airline Hostess Gets Job of Promoting Own Movie," *Christian Science Monitor*, 7 February 1951, 14. Postwar stewardesses' public relations work is extensively recorded in the union publication *Service Aloft*; see also McLaughlin, *Footsteps in the Sky*; Steele et al., *Wings of Pride*.

25. Air India official quoted in " 'World's Best,' " *Service Aloft* 3, no. 2 (January–March 1949): 2. "The Girl Behind the Smile," *World Airports*, November 1960, 119–23; Melita Spraggs, "Girl Stewardesses, Late-comers with British Air Lines, Qualify Rapidly," *Christian Science Monitor*, 6 January 1947, 14; Mills, "Cockpits, Hangars, Boys and Galleys" and "Duelling Discourses."

26. For the gender breakdown of the workforce see Rozen, "Turbulence in the Air," 82 n. 140; ALSSA "Fact Sheet," n.d. [ca. December 1965], Transport Workers Union of America: Records of Locals, Wagner 234, box 108, folder 9, Tamiment Library / Robert F. Wagner Labor Archives, New York University [hereafter cited as TWU Collection]; Dooley, "Battle in the Sky," 161. On male attendants in international flying see Lester, *Fasten Your Seat Belts!*

27. Quotations from former Eastern flight attendant, e-mail to author, 18 June 2004; Mrs. William A. Corkran (née Janet M. Blanchfield), e-mail to author, 11 June 2004; former Eastern flight attendant, e-mail to author, 28 June 2004 [names of correspondents withheld unless they gave express permission to be identified].

28. Quotations from Corkran, e-mail to author, 11 June 2004; Eastern flight attendant, e-mail to author, 18 June 2004; former Eastern flight attendant, e-mail to author, 28 May 2004; former Eastern flight attendant, e-mail to author, 1 June 2004. On men doing "women's work" see Segal, "Male Nurses"; Evans, "Men Nurses"; Williams, *Gender Differences at Work*; Young and James, "Token Majority"; Willett, *Permanent Waves*, chapter five.

29. Quotation from Corkran, e-mail to author, 11 June 2004. Judson, *Carol Trent, Air Stewardess.* For portrayals of male flight attendants as "family men" within flight attendants' work culture see e.g. "Veteran Cabin Attendants Honored," *Service Aloft* 10, no. 3 (fall 1957): 4; Michael O. Kevany to Matthew Guinan, 9 June 1969, box 109, folder 3, TWU Collection. Cf. Orason, *Plight of a Flight Attendant*, in which the author recalls his experiences as a bachelor flight attendant during the postwar era as in large part a string of heterosexual conquests.

30. Kolm, "Women's Labor Aloft," especially chapter 4; Howard, " 'At the Curve Exchange,' " 596.

CHAPTER 3: "LABOR'S LOVELIEST"

1. "Lake Central Pact Provides Big Gains," *Service Aloft* 11, no. 4 (winter 1958): 6; news clippings in box 108, folder 1, TWU Collection; Rowland K. Quinn, ALSSA president, to Patricia Crews Watts, 4 February 1959, "ALSSA—5th Biennial Convention, April 1959—Chicago" folder, box 16, accession dates 13 December 1972, 8 December 1972, Records of the Steward and Stewardess Division, Air Line Pilots Association Collection, Archives of Labor and Urban Affairs, Wayne State University [hereafter cited as ALPA-SSD Collection]. For press coverage see "Strike-Bound Airlines," *Time*, 8 December 1958, 94; "TWA Settles," *Time*, 15 December 1958, 68; "What Happens When Strikes Ground the Airlines," *U.S. News and World Report*, 5 December 1958, 50; "Issues in Airline Disputes," *New York Times*, 25 November 1958, 27. On earlier strike threats and walkouts see Frederick Graham, "Arbitration Ends Strike on Airline," *New York Times*, 14 May 1950, 65; "Plane Groups at Work," *New York Times*, 20 December 1951, 36; "Authorize Vote by Stewards on Air Line Strike," *Chicago Daily Tribune*, 8 November 1952, 7; "Airline Union Votes to Authorize Strike," *Washington Post*, 31 August 1955, 2; "Stewardesses Strike Delayed," *Los Angeles Times*, 15 November 1957, 18.

2. Important revisionist works include Meyerowitz, ed., *Not June Cleaver*; Cobble, *The Other Women's Movement* and *Dishing It Out*; Deslippe, *"Rights, Not Roses"*; Gabin, *Feminism in the Labor Movement*; Crawford, Rouse, and Woods, eds., *Women in the Civil Rights Movement*; Kennedy and Davis, *Boots of Leather, Slippers of Gold*; Harrison, *On Account of Sex*; Rupp and Taylor, *Survival in the Doldrums*; Hartmann, *The Other Feminists*; Horowitz, *Betty Friedan and the Making of the Feminine Mystique.* For a parallel argument about postwar masculinity

see Ehrenreich, *The Hearts of Men*. For an influential view that emphasizes the power of domestic ideals see May, *Homeward Bound*.

3. Kessler-Harris, *Out to Work*, 300–11 [figures from 301]; Blackwelder, *Now Hiring*, 147–76; Goldin, *Understanding the Gender Gap*, chapter 6; Leighbow, *Nurses' Questions / Women's Questions*.

4. Nielsen, *From Sky Girl to Flight Attendant*, 30.

5. Quotations from "Flight Attendant History: The First Stewardess Union," *Flightlog*, September–November 1993, 13. Nielsen, *From Sky Girl to Flight Attendant*, 26–28; "You and the Railway Labor Act," *Air Line Employee* 2, no. 1 (June 1956): 3–7; Rehmus, ed., *The Railway Labor Act at Fifty, The Railway Labor Act and the National Mediation Board*, 15 (full text of the RLA of 1926 and 1934 amendments on 44–76).

6. Nielsen, *From Sky Girl to Flight Attendant*, 26–49; "Merger Strengthens Largest ALPA Affiliate," *Air Line Pilot*, December 1949, 14; "ALSSA Now Represents 16 Air Lines," *Service Aloft* 4, no. 1 (October–December 1949): 1; Rozen, "Turbulence in the Air," 134.

7. Victor J. Herbert quoted in Nielsen, *From Sky Girl to Flight Attendant*, 48. Lipsitz, *Rainbow at Midnight*; Lichtenstein, *Walter Reuther*.

8. Union officials' frequent urgings to members to provide updated addresses attest to the high degree of mobility: "On the Go? Let Us Know," *Service Aloft* 2, no. 2 (January–March 1948): 3; "Where Are YOU Living Now?," *Service Aloft* 5, no. 1 (October–December 1950): 8. On high costs of representation see Rozen, "Turbulence in the Air," 148 n. 279.

9. U.S. Civil Aeronautics Administration, CAA *Statistical Handbook of Civil Aviation, 1956*, 71; U.S. Department of Labor, Bureau of Labor Statistics, *Handbook of Labor Statistics 1969*, 185; "Ellen Church, First Airline Stewardess," *Air Line Employee* 1, no. 1 (June 1955): 18. The no-marriage rule prompted Ada Brown, who initiated the unionization of stewardesses in late 1944, to resign her post as ALSA president and her position at United in the fall of 1947. She later told the historian Georgia Nielsen that she would have continued flying had she been able to do so. *From Sky Girl to Flight Attendant*, 46–47.

10. Lauterbach quoted in "Through the Eyes of Our Founders," *Flightlog*, summer 1995, 13. Jeanne H. Notaro, interview with author, New York City, 5 August 2004. Notaro went to work for Colonial Airlines in July 1949 and joined the union six months later, as soon as the expiration of her probationary period allowed her to do so. When she called a point of order at her first union meeting (everyone had been gossiping, she recalled), she was immediately elected to office simply for knowing parliamentary procedure. On manliness and the labor movement see especially Faue, *Community of Suffering and Struggle*, chapter 3; Martha May, "Bread before Roses: American Workingmen, Labor Unions and the Family Wage," in Milkman, ed., *Women, Work and Protest*, 1–21. On anti-communist

purges see Labor Research Association, *Labor Fact Book 10*, 93–111; Zieger, *American Workers, American Unions*, 100–136.

11. Statistics from Labor Research Association, *Labor Fact Book 8*, 76, 125; U.S. Department of Labor, Bureau of Labor Statistics, *Handbook of Labor Statistics 1969*, 351; Peterson, *American Labor Unions*, 80–81; Labor Research Association, *Labor Fact Book 9*, 65; "Women in Labor Unions," *Monthly Labor Review* 94, no. 2 (February 1971): 43.

12. Norwood, *Labor's Flaming Youth*; Schacht, *The Making of Telephone Unionism*; Cobble, *Dishing It Out*; Murphy, *Blackboard Unions*; Walkowitz, *Working with Class*; Sharon Hartman Strom, " 'We're No Kitty Foyles': Organizing Office Workers for the Congress of Industrial Organizations, 1937–1950," in Milkman, ed., *Women, Work and Protest*, 206–34; Opler, " 'For All White-Collar Workers' "; Melosh, *"The Physician's Hand."* For an overview see Cobble, *The Other Women's Movement*, 17, 19–22. On actors' and actresses' "uneasy compromise between professional pretension and trade-union practice" in the Progressive Era see Holmes, "All the World's a Stage!"

13. ALPA pamphlet from 1946 excerpted in an open letter to ALSSA members from Colleen Boland, ALSSA chairman, TWA, 10 June 1961, box 107, folder 13, TWU Collection [emphasis added]; unidentified union president quoted in Blum et al., *White-Collar Workers*, 32. "Negotiating Sincerity," *Service Aloft* 2, no. 1 (October–December 1947): 2; "Guard Our Peace," *Service Aloft* 3, no. 2 (January–March 1949): 2; "Good Labor Relations from Good Planning," *Service Aloft* 4, no. 2 (January–March 1950): 2.

14. Editorial, *Service Aloft* 1, no. 1 (October 1946): 2.

15. Quoted in "Through the Eyes of Our Founders," 13 [ellipsis in original].

16. Hopkins, *The Airline Pilots* and *Flying the Line*; Baitsell, *Airline Industrial Relations*; Northrup, "Collective Bargaining by Air Line Pilots"; Solberg, *Conquest of the Skies*, 327.

17. "Air Line Pilots Association International Permanent Charter of Affiliation of the Air Line Stewards and Stewardesses Association, International," in "Organization" folder, box 9, accession dates 30 September 1971, 23 August 1972, ALPA-SSD Collection; Baitsell, *Airline Industrial Relations*, 211; Northrup, "Collective Bargaining by Air Line Pilots," 537–38, 544. Other subordinate affiliates included the Air Carrier Flight Engineers Association, Air Carrier Communication Operators Association, Air Carrier Mechanics Association, Air Line Agents Association, and Air Line Employees Association (mostly clerical workers).

18. On the history of the TWU see Freeman, *In Transit*; Lichtenstein, "Putting Labor's House in Order." On Pan Am flight attendants see Lester, *Fasten Your Seat Belts!*; Nielsen, *From Sky Girl to Flight Attendant*, 46. On flight engineers and their turf wars with pilots see Baitsell, *Airline Industrial Relations*, 186–225; Hopkins, *Flying the Line*, 175–86.

19. Lauterbach quoted in "Breaking New Ground," *Flightlog,* fall 1995, 13. On romances between flight attendants and pilots see e.g. McLaughlin, *Footsteps in the Sky*; Bomar and Bankston, *Birdie.*

20. Joyce Richardson Austin quoted in McLaughlin, *Footsteps in the Sky,* 122.

21. "Merger Strengthens Largest ALPA Affiliate," *Air Line Pilot,* December 1949, 14; "ALSSA Now Represents 16 Air Lines," *Service Aloft* 4, no. 1 (October–December 1949): 1; Nielsen, *From Sky Girl to Flight Attendant,* 49.

22. "Charts, Tables Show Big Gains Won by Association since 1952," *Service Aloft* 11, no. 1 (spring 1958): 4–5; Rowland K. Quinn, ALSSA president, to the AFL Executive Council, n.d. [ca. 1960], box 107, folder 11a, TWU Collection; Rozen, "Turbulence in the Air," 134; Hart, "The Effect of Union Shop on the Contracts of the Airline Stewards and Stewardesses Association," 5, 58–59.

23. Ronald L. Oakman, "Crossing the Rubicon" and "First Convention Marks Solo Flight of Group," *Service Aloft* 5, no. 3 (April–June 1951): 1, 2, 4, 9; "ALSSA Becomes Autonomous at Meet," *Air Line Pilot* 20, nos. 4–6 (May–July 1951): 13; "Air Stewards and Stewardesses Hold Banquet," *Chicago Daily Tribune,* 7 June 1951, B, 8; "Officers of Air Association," *Chicago Daily Tribune,* 15 June 1951, 15; Nielsen, *From Sky Girl to Flight Attendant,* 56. Jeanne Notaro recalled that Koos failed to win reelection because she was considered a "puppet" of ALPA. Interview with author, New York City, 5 August 2004. For more on Koos's tenure see Nielsen, *From Sky Girl to Flight Attendant,* 55, 58–59.

24. Congress on 10 January 1951 amended the Railway Labor Act to allow union shop agreements and dues check-offs (another important ALSSA achievement in the later 1950s). "You and the Railway Labor Act," *Air Line Employee* 2, no. 1 (June 1956): 7. Hart, "The Effect of Union Shop on the Contracts of the Airline Stewards and Stewardesses Association," 2; "Union Shop: What It Means," *Service Aloft* 6, no. 1 (October–December 1951): 2; "Big Victory on TWA; Other Gains Reported," *Service Aloft* 11, no. 1 (spring 1958): 2; Nielsen, *From Sky Girl to Flight Attendant,* 57.

25. Quotation from George Carroll, "Stewardesses Want License . . . But Not of the Marrying Kind," *New York Journal American,* 11 September 1961, 21. Jeanne Notaro emphasized the importance of certification to early union organizers in an interview with the author, New York City, 5 August 2004. Nielsen notes that Mary Alice Koos ran on a platform stressing safety certification when she won the ALSSA presidency in 1951. *From Sky Girl to Flight Attendant,* 55.

26. See e.g. "Cabin Attendants Have Terrible Responsibility: Their Safety Is Important," *Service Aloft* 10, no. 3 (fall 1957): 5; "For Greater Safety," *Service Aloft* 11, no. 2 (summer 1958): 5; "Heroines—All," *Service Aloft* 5, no. 2 (January–March 1951): 2; "High Degree of Professional Skill," *Service Aloft* 11, no. 4 (winter 1958): 10; "Their Skill Paid Off in Lives," *Service Aloft* 3, no. 2 (summer 1959): 7 [publication numbering system changed as of 1959].

27. Phyllis F. Young, ALSSA official, quoted in Carroll, "Stewardesses Want License," 21. See also "It's Your Department of Education," *Service Aloft* 4, no. 1 (summer 1961): 6.

28. "Skyways Limited," *Scholastic*, 26 October 1949, 25; Mahler, *Legacy of the Friendly Skies*, 89; William Barry Furlong, "Fustest with the Hostess," *New York Times Magazine*, 15 May 1960, 73. Ruth Weyand, "Air-line Stewardess: Glamour Isn't Enough . . . ," *Nation*, 22 September 1962, 156–60; "All 33 Aboard Escape Blazing Air Line Wreck; Stewardess Shepherds Them to Safety," *Chicago Daily Tribune*, 28 February 1951, 17.

29. Burkhardt, *The Federal Aviation Administration*, chapter 7; U.S. Congress, House Committee on Interstate and Foreign Commerce, *To Include Flight Attendants within the Definition of "Airman"* (Washington: U.S. Government Printing Office, 1962). See also various documents concerning certification lobbying in box 108, folder 6, TWU Collection.

30. *To Include Flight Attendants within the Definition of "Airman"*; Rowland K. Quinn Jr., "Weekly Report of ALSSA-TWU, Local 550 for the Period December 18, thru December 28, 1961," 29 December 1961, 2, box 108, folder 5, TWU Collection.

31. ALSSA Press Release, 5 December 1961, box 108, folder 5, TWU Collection; statements of Rowland Quinn, ALSSA president, to Congressional committees on 7 June 1960 and 1 May 1962, box 108, folders 1 and 6, TWU Collection; Weyand, "Air-line Stewardess," 156–60.

32. ATA report quoted in Weyand, "Air-line Stewardesses," 160. *To Include Flight Attendants within the Definition of "Airman."*

33. On the criteria for "real" professions see Larson, *The Rise of Professionalism*; Macdonald, *The Sociology of the Professions*. Studies of professionalization generally carry a teleological bias toward groups whose efforts succeeded to some degree, even if gender stereotyping devalued feminized professions. Ignored generally are groups like flight attendants, who attempted to professionalize but failed to secure state or public recognition. For a view of "partial professionalization" in real estate brokerage see Hornstein, *A Nation of Realtors*.

34. "Statement of Rowland K. Quinn Jr., President Air Line Stewards and Stewardesses Association, International, before the Aviation Subcommittee on Interstate and Foreign Commerce on the Subject of Certification of Airmen," 7 June 1960, 4–5, box 108, folder 1, TWU Collection. Quinn made the same argument almost verbatim at Congressional hearings in 1962. The sociologist Claire Williams similarly argues in her work on Australian flight attendants that their safety work is invisible and subsumed by "gendered cultural performance." *Blue, White and Pink Collar Workers in Australia* and "Sky Service."

35. Quotations from Captain R. C. Robson, "License Attendants?," *Aviation Week*, 8 December 1952. "The CAB and Liquor in the Air," *Christian Science Monitor*, 10 August 1955, 18; Catherine Johnson, "ALSSA Creates Safety Board," *Air*

Line Employee, September 1955, 9; "ALSSA Is Represented on New AFL-CIO Aviation Legislation Committee," *Service Aloft* 10, no. 1 (spring 1957): 2; "ALSSA Active on Safety Front," *Service Aloft* 10, no. 2 (summer 1957): 3, 7; "Favor Liquor Ban on Airlines," *Service Aloft* 10, no. 3 (fall 1957): 2.

36. Quotations from Phyllis Young, "ALPA or ALSSA-TWU?" [pamphlet], n.d. [ca. June 1961], box 107, folder 13, TWU Collection; former Eastern flight attendant, e-mail to author, 28 June 2004. See also "Report of Joint ALPA Executive Committee: ALSSA Officer Meeting, May 18, 1960," in "Transcripts, ALSSA—Legal Dispute" folder, box 16, accession dates 13 December 1972, 8 December 1972, ALPA-SSD Collection; Nielsen, *From Sky Girl to Flight Attendant*, 57; "Statement of Air Line Stewards and Stewardesses Association, International, in Support of its Application for a Charter of Affiliation from the AFL-CIO," n.d. [ca. 1960], 28, box 107, folder 11a, TWU Collection.

37. "Flight Attendants Recognized In Proposed Part 40 of C.A.R.," *Service Aloft* 6, no. 3 (April–June 1952): 4; Nielsen, *From Sky Girl to Flight Attendant*, 18. Phyllis F. Young, "Board of Directors' Weekly Newsletter," 4 May 1962; and Rowland K. Quinn Jr. to Hon. Jack Brooks, 10 October 1962; "ALSSA-TWU" folder, box 16, accession dates 13 December 1972, 8 December 1972, ALPA-SSD Collection.

38. "ALSSA Becomes Autonomous at Meet," *Air Line Pilot* 20, nos. 4–6 (May–July 1951): 13; "First Convention Marks Solo Flight of Group," *Service Aloft* 5, no. 3 (April–June 1951): 1, 4, 9. In the fall of 1951, when ALSSA made its first bid for a charter, the "assistant to the president" of the union, who had been appointed by ALPA, abruptly withdrew the request, apparently without consulting ALSSA's elected officers. Three years later, in October 1954, a renewed plea from ALSSA and follow-up letters drew a response from George Meany, president of the AFL. Meany expressed concern over the pilots' practice of subchartering affiliates for other workers, but explained that no action could be taken on ALSSA's behalf "until a final decision is made regarding the standing of ALPA" in the federation. ALPA earned the AFL's enmity not only for the subchartering but also for ongoing disputes with the flight engineers and a refusal to support other unions' strikes. An additional charter request in 1957 failed. Victor J. Herbert to William Green, 13 September 1951 and 30 October 1951, box 107, folder 11a, TWU Collection; "Statement of Air Line Stewards and Stewardesses Association, International, in Support of Its Application for a Charter of Affiliation from the AFL-CIO," n.d. [ca. 1960], box 107, folder 11a, TWU Collection; George Meany to Rowland K. Quinn Jr., 26 October 1954, box 107, folder 13, TWU Collection; Nielsen, *From Sky Girl to Flight Attendant*, 58.

39. Ada J. Brown to All ALSA Members, 17 July 1947, repr. in "Opening Remarks to the Sixth Biennial Convention of the Air Line Stewards and Stewardesses Association, International," n.d. [April 1961], box 107, folder 12, TWU Collection; Rowland K. Quinn to AFL-CIO Executive Council, n.d. [November 1960], 5, 31–32,

and "Statement of Air Line Stewards and Stewardesses Association, International, in Support of its Application for a Charter of Affiliation from the AFL-CIO," n.d. [ca. 1960], 30–32, box 107, folder 11a, TWU Collection. Copy of telegram, Nancy Silverthorn to Captain Neal Payton, n.d. [November 1958], and Nancy Silverthorn to Betty [Purcell], 30 March 1959, "ALSSA—5th Biennial Convention, April 1959—Chicago" folder, box 16, accession dates 13 December 1972, 8 December 1972, ALPA-SSD Collection; Clarence N. Sayen to Robert Reardon, 15 September 1960, 2–3, "ALSSA General" folder, box 16, accession dates 13 December 1972, 8 December 1972, ALPA-SSD Collection. Nielsen, *From Sky Girl to Flight Attendant*, 63; William R. Clabby, "Stock-holding Pilots of Lake Central Keep Flying Despite Strike," *Wall Street Journal*, 28 November 1958, 3; "Strike-bound Airlines," *Time*, 8 December 1958, 94.

40. On the Mohawk "raid" see Clarence N. Sayen to Robert Reardon, 15 September 1960, 2, "ALSSA General" folder, box 16, accession dates 13 December 1972, 8 December 1972, ALPA-SSD Collection; "Statement of Air Line Stewards and Stewardesses Association, International, in Support of Its Application for a Charter of Affiliation from the AFL-CIO," n.d. [ca. 1960], 34–35, box 107, folder 11a, TWU Collection. On the implications of the jets see Nielsen, *From Sky Girl to Flight Attendant*, 64–65; Hopkins, *Flying the Line*; "Association Presses for Jet Pay, Conditions," *Service Aloft* 3, no. 3 (fall–winter 1959): 3; "Jet Girls Set to Strike over Medical Woes," *Washington Post*, 9 October 1959, A, 2; "Report of Joint ALPA Executive Committee: ALSSA Officer Meeting," 1 September 1959, 2–3, "Transcripts, ALSSA—Legal Dispute" folder, box 16, accession dates 13 December 1972, 8 December 1972, ALPA-SSD Collection; "Opening Remarks to the Sixth Biennial Convention," 4. At the 5th Biennial Convention ALSSA's top officials warned that the union's already limited autonomy was under growing threat from pilot leaders, and rumors flew on the convention floor that ALPA representatives were intimating delegates behind the scenes in an attempt to quash any disaffiliation move. Nielsen, *From Sky Girl to Flight Attendant*, 66–67; ALSSA *News Bulletin 6*, no. 2 (March–April 1959): 1–4, "ALSSA—5th Biennial Convention, April 1959—Chicago" folder, box 16, accession dates 13 December 1972, 8 December 1972, ALPA-SSD Collection; "Delegates Support Autonomous ALSSA by an Overwhelming Vote," *Service Aloft* 3, no. 1 (spring 1959): 3, 11.

41. Dubofsky, *State and Labor in Modern America*, 220–23; Labor Management Reporting and Disclosure Act, Public Law 86-257, 86th Congress, 1st sess. (14 September 1959). As Dubofsky cautions, the designers and main proponents of the act did not intend to advance civil rights, despite its egalitarian implications.

42. George Meany to Clarence Sayen, 17 November 1959, reprinted in "Statement of Air Line Stewards and Stewardesses Association, International, in Support of Its Application for a Charter of Affiliation from the AFL-CIO," n.d. [ca. 1960], 16–17, box 107, folder 11a, TWU Collection [emphasis added]; Nielsen, *From Sky Girl to Flight Attendant*, 67–68.

43. Lauterbach quoted in Nielsen, *From Sky Girl to Flight Attendant*, 60 (on male flight attendants as "mature" family men see 59–60); Michael O. Kevany to Matthew Guinan, 9 June 1969, box 109, folder 3, TWU Collection. On postwar breadwinner ideology, labor organizing, and manliness see Ehrenreich, *The Hearts of Men*; Faue, *Community of Suffering and Struggle*. I have been unable to locate precise figures tracking the gender breakdown of union membership and local office holding over time. But the imperfect method of categorizing names as male or female in union rosters of convention delegates, candidates for local offices, etc. suggests that men accounted for 20 to 40 percent of active union workers at the local level, but only about 10 percent of the membership in ALSSA in the 1960s (comparable records for the 1950s are not available).

44. Nancy Silverthorn to Betty [Purcell], 30 March 1959, correspondence in "ALSSA—5th Biennial Convention, April 1959—Chicago" folder, box 16, accession dates 13 December 1972, 8 December 1972, ALPA-SSD Collection. The Lake Central strike occurred amid an unprecedented wave of strikes in the airline industry sparked by the arrival of jet aircraft; other unions' walkouts caused temporary layoffs of up to several weeks for other flight attendants, including those at TWA. TWA hostesses were already facing financial hardships, which made many feel particularly burdened by the assessment. A. H. Raskin, "Strikes Threaten to Halt Half of Nation's Airliners," *New York Times*, 24 November 1958, 1, 22; "What Happens When Strikes Ground the Airlines," *U.S. News and World Report*, 5 December 1958, 50–51; "Strike-bound Airlines," *Time*, 8 December 1958, 94–95; "New Strikes Hit Major Airlines," *Business Week*, 29 November 1958, 107–8.

45. Joyce Hills to Mr. Quinn, 31 December 1958, and Shirley Johnson to Mr. R. K. Quinn, December 1959, "ALSSA—5th Biennial Convention, April 1959—Chicago" folder, box 16, accession dates 13 December 1972, 8 December 1972, ALPA-SSD Collection. On ALSSA's union shop drive see Lee Liebik, "Labor Law and You," *Service Aloft* 10, no. 2 (summer 1957): 8; "Big Victory on TWA; Other Gains Reported," *Service Aloft* 11, no. 1 (spring 1958): 2; Nielsen, *From Sky Girl to Flight Attendant*, 62, 65; Hart, "The Effect of Union Shop on the Contracts of the Airline Stewards and Stewardesses Association."

46. Alanna [Schenkosky] to Betty [Purcell], 28 March 1959; ALSSA *News Bulletin* 6, no. 2 (March–April 1959); Memo, Betty Purcell to All United Stewards and Stewardesses, May 1959; Geraldine A. Dwyer to Rowland K. Quinn Jr., 25 April 1959; Geraldine A. Dwyer to Rowland K. Quinn Jr., 12 June 1959; Geraldine A. Dwyer to Phyllis F. Young, 11 January 1961, all in "ALSSA—5th Biennial Convention, April 1959—Chicago" folder, box 16, accession dates 13 December 1972, 8 December 1972, ALPA-SSD Collection. Roscoe Born, "Hoffa's Combine," *Wall Street Journal*, 22 April 1959, 1, 13; "If Hoffa's Dreams Come True . . . ," *U.S. News and World Report*, 9 January 1959, 84–86; "Hoffa Offers Air Stewardesses Special Division in Teamsters," *New York Times*, 21 February 1961, 29; Nielsen, *From Sky Girl to Flight Attendant*, 67. On the history of the Teamsters see Brill, *The Team-*

sters; La Botz, *Rank and File Rebellion*; Witwer, *Corruption and Reform in the Teamsters Union.*

47. Quotation from "Airline Girls Meet, and Harsh Words Fly," *Chicago Daily Tribune*, 12 August 1960, 1. "ALSSA is Now Free!!!!!," open letter to ALSSA membership, n.d. [mid-August 1960]; "Hostesses and Pilots End Romance on Union Front in Abrupt Move," *Chicago Sun-Times*, 10 August 1960, news clipping; "Stewardesses Lead Fight to Stay with Pilot Union," *Chicago American*, 12 August 1960, news clipping, all in "S&S General" folder, box 14, accession date 18 August 1972, ALPA-SSD Collection. "Airlines: Girls against the Boys," *Newsweek*, 22 August 1960, 73.

48. Nielsen, *From Sky Girl to Flight Attendant*, 69–70; "Stewardesses Break with Pilots' Union," *Miami Life*, 4 March 1961, news clipping, box 107, folder 12, TWU Collection; "Pilot Union Sued by Stewardesses," *New York Times*, 30 September 1960, 53. Copies of many of the legal documents are in boxes 107 and 108, TWU Collection, and variously in the ALPA-SSD Collection.

49. On the final charter request see "Statement of Air Line Stewards and Stewardesses Association, International, in Support of its Application for a Charter of Affiliation from the AFL-CIO," n.d. [ca. 1960], box 107, folder 11a, TWU Collection; Rowland K. Quinn, "Opening Remarks to the Sixth Biennial Convention of the Air Line Stewards & Stewardesses Association, International," n.d. [April 1961], box 107, folder 12, TWU Collection; "Air Hostess Union Barred by Meany," *New York Times*, 28 February 1961, 67; Rozen, "Turbulence in the Air," 151; Nielsen, *From Sky Girl to Flight Attendant*, 73–75. On TWU affiliation see Michael J. Quill to Rowland K. Quinn Jr., 6 March 1961; Memo, Rowland K. Quinn Jr. to ALSSA Board of Directors and General Membership, 7 March 1961; ALSSA *News Bulletin*, February, March, April 1961, all in box 107, folder 12, TWU Collection. See also "Plane Hostesses Join Quill Union," *New York Times*, 8 March 1961, 66.

50. "Flight Attendants of Other Lines Urge Unity in ALSSA-TWU," *TWU Express*, special ATD edition, June 1962, 3, and ALSSA-TWU pamphlet, "Progress thru Unity," 6, box 107, folder 12, TWU Collection. For "ladies auxiliary" references see e.g. ALSSA Press Release, 30 June 1961, box 107, folder 13, TWU Collection; "Confidential" letter, Bev Nelson to "Girls," n.d. [1961], box 108, folder 1, TWU Collection.

51. Quotations from ALPA memo to All Western Air Line Stewardesses, 14 July 1961, 1, box 108, folder 1, TWU Collection; MEC Newsletter, "To All Northwest Airlines Pilots," 5 June 1961, 1, box 107, folder 13, TWU Collection. Sally Gibson to Gerald M. Maeser, 18 May 1961, 3, "Correspondence—General—S&S Div., 1961, 1962, 1963" folder, box 8, accession date 18 August 1972, ALPA-SSD Collection; Ernest M. Mitchell, "Confidential Report—ALSSA-TWU," 20 May 1961, 3, box 107, folder 12, TWU Collection; "Affidavit of Colleen Boland," n.d. [September 1961], 2, box 108, folder 2, TWU Collection; ALPA flyers and Braniff Hostesses [signed Virginia Curran] to All TWA Hostesses, 24 October 1961, 1, in exhibits to "Weekly

Report of ALSSA, Local 550, for the period October 14, 1961 thru October 31, 1961," box 108, folder 3, TWU Collection; Phyllis F. Young, "Board of Directors' Weekly Newsletter," 16 October 1961, box 108, folder 3, TWU Collection; Rowland K. Quinn Jr., "Weekly Report of ALSSA, Local 550, for the period September 23, 1961 thru October 13, 1961," box 108, folder 3, TWU Collection; Memo, Rowland K. Quinn Jr., president, to ALSSA-TWU Membership, 16 October 1961, box 108, folder 3, TWU Collection; open letter to members from Local Council 47, ALSSA-TWU-SEA [Seattle], 9 June 1961, box 107, folder 13, TWU Collection.

52. Quotation from William Grogan to James F. Horst, 21 May 1961, 4–5, box 107, folder 12, TWU Collection; ALSSA-TWU pamphlet, "Progress thru Unity," n.d. [ca. 1961], box 107, folder 12, TWU Collection.

53. See e.g. Sandra Strang to All Non-Members [American Airlines, LaGuardia], 27 December 1961, box 108, folder 5, TWU Collection; Margie Cooper to All Trans International Flight Attendants, 3 June 1966, "201.2—1966" folder, box 8, accession date 18 August 1972, ALPA-SSD Collection.

54. Elections eventually took place on most small and mid-sized carriers and on every large airline in the United States, except two: Delta, whose flight attendants to this day remain unorganized, and Pan Am, where TWU's bargaining rights for 1,200 flight attendants went unchallenged. The results and breakdown of voting of most (but not all) relevant elections are recorded in press releases from ALPA and ALSSA, certification notices from the National Mediation Board, internal communications in boxes 107 and 108 of the TWU Collection, and issues of the *Air Line Pilot* and *TWU Express*. For a summary table see appendix B in Barry, "Femininity in Flight," 609–10.

55. Quotation from Ernest M. Mitchell, "Confidential Report—ALSSA-TWU," 20 May 1961, 3, box 107, folder 12, TWU Collection. See also Rowland K. Quinn Jr., "Weekly Report of ALSSA, Local 550, for the Period Sunday, July 16, 1961 thru Saturday, July 30, 1961," 28 July 1961, box 108, folder 1, TWU Collection; Rowland K. Quinn Jr., "Weekly Report of ALSSA, Local 550, for the Period Sunday, June 25, 1961 thru Saturday, July 1, 1961," 30 June 1961, box 107, folder 13, TWU Collection.

56. On "wining and dining" see handwritten letter, Fred Simpson to Michael [Quill], 3 July 1961, box 108, folder 1, TWU Collection; William Grogan to James F. Horst, 21 May 1961, box 107, folder 12, TWU Collection; "Confidential" letter, Bev Nelson to "Girls," n.d. [1961], and "Your Local *Elected* Council" to All Kansas City-Based Hostesses [TWA], 21 August 1961, box 108, folder 1, TWU Collection; Colleen Boland, "Quotations from ALPA—What They Are Saying about Us," n.d. [October 1961], box 108, folder 3, TWU Collection. Several pursers at TWA launched a movement to join the International Guild of Flight Attendants, a minuscule Teamster affiliate, but they did so before ALSSA's break from ALPA. After the break, the movement for the IGFA at TWA fizzled and male flight attendant activists at TWA, Northwest, and Eastern helped ALSSA-TWU's campaign. "Comments by Fran Holmes, TWA Stewardess, regarding ALSSA Meeting at the

New York Hotel, New York City, August 24, 1960"; Carole Dalley to All TWA La Guardia Based Hostesses, 25 August 1960; Clarence N. Sayen to Robert Reardon, 15 September 1960, all in "ALSSA General" folder, box 16, accession dates 13 December 1972, 8 December 1972, ALPA-SSD Collection. Mel Pearce, "An Open Letter to Capt. Fontaine," 19 July 1961, box 108, folder 1, TWU Collection; Michael Haag to All T.W.A. Hostesses, 6 October 1961, box 108, folder 3, TWU Collection.

57. Quotations from Douglas [McMahon] to Mike [Quill], 22 May 1961, and Fred Simpson to Michael J. Quill, 16 May 1961, 2, box 107, folder 12, TWU Collection. See also handwritten letter, Bill Grogan to Mike [Quill], 2 June 1961, box 107, folder 13, TWU Collection.

58. Quotations from Rowland K. Quinn Jr. to All [ALSSA] chairmen, 6 August 1963, box 108, folder 7, TWU Collection; Fredric A. Simpson to James F. Horst, n.d. [February 1964], box 108, folder 8, TWU Collection. Michael J. Quill to Rowland K. Quinn Jr., 27 June 1963; Michael J. Quill to Rowland K. Quinn Jr., 10 July 1963; "Quinn Removed From Office," TWU flyer to ALSSA membership, n.d. [August 1963]; Frederic Simpson to ALSSA Membership, 2 August 1963; Rowland K. Quinn Jr. to All [ALSSA] chairmen, 6 August 1963; various legal documents and Master Executive Council resolutions, all in box 108, folder 7, TWU Collection. See also Nielsen, *From Sky Girl to Flight Attendant*, 78; "Quinn Denies Charge He Mishandled Funds," *New York Times*, 5 August 1963, 36.

59. Rozen, "Turbulence in the Air," 151–56, 162; Nielsen, *From Sky Girl to Flight Attendant*, 71–74, 79–80.

60. Nielsen, *From Sky Girl to Flight Attendant*, 77.

61. Chateauvert, *Marching Together*; Majorie Penn Lasky, "'Where I Was a Person': The Ladies' Auxiliary in the 1934 Minneapolis Teamsters' Strike," in Milkman, ed., *Women, Work and Protest*, 181–205; Foner, *Women and the American Labor Movement*; Baron, ed., *Work Engendered*; Lichtenstein, *State of the Union*; Dubofsky, *The State and Labor in Modern America*; Murphy, *Blackboard Unions*; Walkowitz, *Working with Class*; Strom, "'We're No Kitty Foyles'"; Opler, "'For All White-Collar Workers.'" When ALSSA made its last ill-fated charter request to the AFL-CIO in late 1960, Quinn argued that the federation would be doing itself a favor in creating a showcase white-collar, female union and demonstrating its progressiveness to other women and white-collar workers. "Statement of Air Line Stewards and Stewardesses Association, International, in Support of Its Application for a Charter of Affiliation from the AFL-CIO," n.d. [ca. 1960], box 107, folder 11a, TWU Collection.

62. Editorial, *Service Aloft* 1, no. 4 (January–March 1947): 1; "Meet Our Cover Girl: Miss Hawaii" and *passim* in *Service Aloft* 10, no. 4 (winter 1957): 2. On the centrality of beauty culture in the work culture of postwar women workers at the undergarment manufacturer Maidenform see Howard, "'At the Curve Exchange.'"

CHAPTER 4: "NOTHING BUT AN AIRBORNE WAITRESS"

1. "Stewardess Claims Job Becomes Chore," *Dallas Morning News*, 18 August 1961, news clipping in box 108, folder 1, TWU Collection.

2. Solberg, *Conquest of the Skies*, chapter 6; Bilstein, *Flight in America*, 227–39; Boyne and Lopez, eds., *The Jet Age*.

3. Solberg, *Conquest of the Skies*, 406; statistical estimates from Bilstein, *Flight in America*, 286; Bilstein, "Air Travel and the Traveling Public," 108; "54% of Adult Americans Have Flown with the Airlines," *Air Line Pilot*, December 1973, 42. On airline expansion generally see Solberg, *Conquest of the Skies*, 406.

4. Solberg, *Conquest of the Skies*, 406; Joseph G. Smith, TWA consultant, quoted in Bruce Haxthausen, "How and Where Airlines Will Sell Seats in 1973," *Airline Management* 4 (October 1972): 11.

5. Estimates from "A.M. & M. Airline Reference Chart: Marketing," *Airline Management and Marketing* 2 (March 1968): 26–27, cited in Kolm, "Women's Labor Aloft," 200 n. 5. Kolm astutely analyzes airline marketing trends in successive eras and their relationship to broader economic developments. See "Women's Labor Aloft," 197–214 (on the jet age) and *passim*, "Stewardesses' 'Psychological Punch.'"

6. Fox, *The Mirror Makers*, 218–71.

7. Bailey, *Sex in the Heartland*; Grant, *Sexing the Millennium*; Douglas, *Where the Girls Are*, chapter 3. On the Playboy Clubs as a cultural institution and workplace see Scott, *The Bunny Years*. Cf. Gloria Steinem's "diary" of her brief stint as a Bunny in 1963 in her memoir, *Outrageous Acts and Everyday Rebellions*, 32–75. On *Playboy* Magazine see Ehrenreich, *The Hearts of Men*, chapter 4.

8. "More Blue in Braniff's Yonder," *Business Week*, 21 January 1967, 106.

9. Eastern Airlines advertisement, "Presenting the Losers," *Time*, 29 September 1967, 41.

10. United Airlines advertisement, "The Boys with the Friday Night Faces," *Los Angeles Times*, 20 March 1967, 25.

11. Delta Airlines advertisement, "No Floor Show, Just a Working Girl Working," *Wall Street Journal*, 25 February 1969, 17. On Delta's distinctive culture of "southern hospitality" and conservatism in marketing amid the sexual revolution see Whitelegg, "From Smiles to Miles."

12. Mel Pearce, "The E.A.L. Flight Attendants Trade-Union Heritage," *Dance Program and Directory, Annual Welfare Fund Ball, Stewardesses & Stewards, L.E.C. No. 2 ALSSA-TWU* No. 550, 29 November 1963, 29, box 108, folder 7, TWU Collection. See also, e.g., " . . . Flight Attendant A Will Serve the First 100 . . . Flight Attendant B the Second 100 . . . *Good Gracious, No!* . . . ," *Intercom* 4, no. 6 (November 1967): 4.

13. Eastern attendant quoted in Stephen C. Rogers, "Bigger Cut of That Pie in

the Sky Demanded by Air Stewardesses," *Washington Post*, 25 March 1965, A, 2. "Jet Girls Set Strike over Medical Woes," *Washington Post*, 9 October 1959, A, 2; "Left on the Ground, They Picket," 5 June 1964, and "After Protests, Fly," 6 June 1964, news clippings from unidentified newspapers in Kansas City, box 108, folder 8, TWU Collection.

14. Edward Hudson, "Big Planes' Short Trips Compound Hostesses' Service Problems," *New York Times*, 6 May 1968, 94.

15. Lessor, "Unanticipated Longevity in Women's Work," 181–87 and chapter 5 *passim*. Hochschild, *The Managed Heart*, 119–20.

16. Braverman, *Labor and Monopoly Capital*; Lessor, "Unanticipated Longevity in Women's Work," 182; Hochschild, *The Managed Heart*, 120–21. Influential analyses of innovations in managerial control and organization of work, and how workers experienced and resisted "deskilling," include Nelson, *Managers and Workers*; Montgomery, *Workers' Control in America*; Gordon, Edwards, and Reich, *Segmented Work, Divided Workers*. For an insightful view of deskilling with careful attention to race and gender see Green, *Race on the Line*.

17. Quotation from Hudson, "Big Planes' Short Trips Compound Hostesses' Service Problems," 94. As other historians of service work have shown, the de-skilling paradigm has limited applicability to work involving customers, in which feminized "people skills" have never been well valued. Benson, *Counter Cultures*; Cobble, *Dishing It Out* and "'A Spontaneous Loss of Enthusiasm,'" 24. Still, service employers have striven to routinize service exchanges with a variety of techniques. Leidner, *Fast Food, Fast Talk*.

18. "Coffee, Tea—But Not Me!," *Newsweek*, 1 January 1968, 55. See also Hochschild, *The Managed Heart*, 135.

19. Anne Keegan, "High-Flying Brawlers Headache for Airlines," *Chicago Tribune*, 22 October 1978, news clipping in "Pat Margrave, SOU/ATL" folder, box 5, accession date 13 August 1981, AFA Collection.

20. Quotations from Sally Doyle, "Lovely Girls Fly to Jobs on Soaring Spirits," *Chicago Daily Tribune*, 13 September 1953, A, 13; "Coffee, Tea—But Not Me!," *Newsweek*, 1 January 1968, 55. Mills, *White Collar*, 173–74. See also James Calogero, "Romance Rarely Buds above the Clouds," *Washington Post*, 4 January 1966, A, 16.

21. Lessor, "Unanticipated Longevity in Women's Work," 203–5; Response to Memo/Questionnaire from Evelyn Aycock, National Safety Committee, to all ALSSA-TWU Southern Stewardesses, 5 April 1972, "Correspondence" folder, box 4, accession date 13 August 1981, AFA Collection.

22. Quotation from Bratt, *Glamour and Turbulence*, 14. Notes from Executive Board Meeting, ALSSA Local 550, TWU, 18 September 1968, box 109, folder 2, TWU Collection; Godfrey Sperling Jr., "Union Raps Airline Liquor Serving," *Christian Science Monitor*, 12 December 1955, 8; "Members Submit Reports of Intoxicated Passengers," *Intercom* 9, no. 4 (April 1972): 8.

23. "Carry-On Baggage Rules, A Required Change," *S & S Division News* 5, no. 12 (December 1967): 3–4; FAA report, "Safety Aspects of Flight Attendant's Environment," 24 May 1972, excerpted in "FAA Admits Cabin Safety Hazards," *Intercom* 9, no. 6 (June 1972): 4. In 1972 the Federal Aviation Administration ruled that all carry-on baggage must be stowed in overhead bins, in closets, or under seats. Subsequent complaints by flight attendants suggest that the regulations were not very effective, at least at first.

24. *Transcript of Proceedings, Air Line Pilots Association, Steward and Stewardess Division, Second Executive Board Meeting, May 18–19, 1971, Washington, D.C.*, 63–64, box 15, accession dates 30 September 1972, 25 June 1972, 24 July 1972, ALPA-SSD Collection; "Coffee, Tea—But Not Me!," *Newsweek*, 1 January 1968, 55. On the history of commercial (as opposed to military) charters see Solberg, *Conquest of the Skies*, 409–10; Lyth and Dierikx, "From Privilege to Popularity." The years following the Second World War saw the rise of so-called nonskeds, entrepreneurial airlines that survived exclusively on charters, thereby getting around federal control on routes and fares. But by the 1960s growing tourist and corporate traffic made charters an increasingly large-scale business for which scheduled airlines competed along with nonskeds. Large airlines like United and Pan Am came to depend on charters for as much as 10 percent of their passenger traffic.

25. Judy Klemesrud, "Meet the Girl Who Wears Those Silver Wings and a Big Smile," *Des Moines Register*, 18 October 1965.

26. "From the Hostesses," *S & S Division Shop Talk* 5, no. 6 (July 1967): 3.

27. For employment totals see table 6.28, FAA *Statistical Handbook of Aviation*, 153.

28. Goldin, *Understanding the Gender Gap*, chapter 6; quotation from 174–75 [emphasis added]. As Goldin explains, married women were once maligned as transient, inefficient workers but became coveted employees to many employers by the 1950s, praised as more mature, reliable, and productive than single women. The rise of part-time work in the postwar era, especially in retail sales, was a catalyst for, and an accommodation to, married white women's increasing participation in the labor force. See also Leighbow, *Nurses' Questions / Women's Questions*, chapter 2; Harrison, *On Account of Sex*; Cobble, *The Other Women's Movement*.

29. ALSSA "Fact Sheet," n.d. [ca. November 1965], box 108, folder 9, TWU Collection.

30. See e.g. Shirley H. Beck to Colleen Boland, 6 February 1965, box 108, folder 9, TWU Collection; ALSSA, "Four Latest Contracts Negotiated," n.d. [ca. October 1967], box 109, folder 1, TWU Collection.

31. "'Stewardesses Old at 32,' Says American," *Service Aloft* 8, no. 1 (October–December 1953): 1–2; Catherine Harrington, "Union Fighting New Policy," *Washington Post*, 21 February 1954, S, 18. See also "No Fury like a Woman Scorned,"

Business Week, 3 April 1954, 50–51; "Stewardesses Up in Air over Retirement at 32," *Christian Science Monitor*, 16 February 1954, 1.

32. "Reported Age Ceilings for Continued Employment as Airline Stewardess," November 1965; ALSSA "Fact Sheet"; Shirley H. Beck to Colleen Boland, 6 February 1965, all in box 108, folder 9, TWU Collection. Frederic C. Appel, "Unions Want Airlines to Break Age Barrier for Stewardesses," *New York Times*, 8 December 1965, 49.

33. "Casey and Congress: Age Limits Stewardesses Serving America," *Intercom* 2, no. 6 (November 1965): 3; Heenan, "Fighting the 'Fly-Me' Airlines," 49; Leonard Shecter, "Flying High," *New York Post*, 8 December 1965, news clipping in Box 108, folder 9, TWU Collection.

34. "Marriage Now No Bar to Hostesses on TWA," *Service Aloft* 10, no. 3 (fall 1957): 7. The major exception regarding marriage bans and age rules was Pan American, which never instituted an age ceiling and decided in 1949, not long after it began adding women to its cabin crews, to allow stewardesses to marry and stay on (albeit with probationary status). Minor exceptions were some small carriers, whose employment relations were more paternalistic and individualized.

35. O'Connor, *Flying Mary O'Connor*, 118–19; Raycroft, "An Occupational Study of Airline Hostesses," 17–20; Colleen Boland, president of ALSSA, paraphrased in "Stewardesses Accuse Carriers of Discrimination," *Aviation Daily*, 3 September 1965, news clipping in box 108, folder 9, TWU Collection.

36. "The Origin and Limited Number and Use of Stewards," *Sex as a Bona Fide Occupational Qualification for Stewardesses: Statement of United Air Lines, Inc.*, 14 April 1966, 44–48, box 13, accession date 18 August 1972, ALPA-SSD Collection; Gwen Mahler, *Legacy of the Friendly Skies: A Pictorial History of United Airlines Stewardesses and Flight Attendants* (Marceline, Mo.: Walsworth, 1991): 125–26; "Aloha Scores a 'First': In-Flight Entertainment," *Service Aloft* 11, no. 3 (fall 1958): 6. Notably, the job description that United provided in its statement in 1966 indicated that it ironically limited the Hawaiian stewards' visibility to passengers by assigning them to more menial, behind-the-scenes duties, such as food preparation, baggage handling, supplies maintenance, and cleaning of the cabin and lavatory.

37. "Airline Integration Project: Stewardesses," group II, box A-9, part 18, Special Subjects, 1940–1955, series B, Papers of the National Association for the Advancement of Colored People (Bethesda, Md.: University Microforms, 1993). The correspondence in this slim file indicates that the NAACP's "airline integration project" foundered with regard to stewardess positions for a lack of qualified applicants willing to participate. Richard Witkin, "Aviation: Stewardess," *New York Times*, 29 December 1957, II, 25; "First Negro Hired as a Stewardess," *New York Times*, 23 December 1957, 25; "Airline Hires First Negro Stewardess," *Washington Post*, 22 December 1957, B, 3; "TWA Will Hire a Negro Hostess," *New York*

Times, 10 February 1958, 44; "Negro Awarded Stewardess Job," *Washington Post*, 12 May 1958; "Protest Airlines' Employment Bias," *Chicago Defender*, 3 October 1959, 1. On an earlier, unsuccessful case in New York in which a black male purser applicant charged Pan Am with discrimination see "No-Bias Ruling Fought," *New York Times*, 15 December 1955, 20; Jeanpierre v. Arbury, 2 A.D.2d 514, 162 N.Y.S.2d 506 (7 May 1957). For a critical history of New York State employment equity legislation and enforcement see Biondi, *To Stand and Fight*.

38. "The Right to Equal Treatment: Administrative Enforcement of Antidiscrimination Legislation," *Harvard Law Review* 74, no. 3 (January 1961): 539; Patricia Banks Collection, Schomburg Center for Research in Black Culture, New York Public Library; "Desegregating the Airlines," *Time*, 21 March 1960, 92, 94; details of *Banks v. Capital Airlines* reported in *Civil Liberties Docket* 4, no. 4 (August 1959), and 5, no. 3 (June 1960); "Query Airline on Hiring Bias," *Chicago Daily Defender*, 20 July 1959, 4; "Negro Stewardess Hired," *New York Times*, 7 May 1960, 46.

39. Quotations from Marlene White to Michael J. Quill, 14 May 1963, box 108, folder 7, TWU Collection. Additional correspondence between White and TWU International officials in same source; "Northwest Is Cited," *New York Times*, 14 January 1962, 86; "Order Air Line to O.K. Negro Stewardess," *Chicago Daily Tribune*, 21 June 1962, A, 10; "Airline Hires Second Negro Stewardess," *Chicago Defender*, 18 August 1962, 1; "Stewardess Fired by Airline; Union Blasts Race Bias," *Chicago Defender*, 9 April 1963, 1, 3, 18; "Airline Stewardess Wins Her Job Back," *Chicago Defender*, 21 December 1963, 1. White resigned in August 1964, when she decided to make public that she had secretly married in January 1964. Theresa Fambro Hooks, "Teesee's Topics," *Chicago Defender*, 17 August 1964, 14. See also, on alleged discrimination against black trainees at United, Walter E. Hall, "Says Airlines Snub Negro Stewardesses," *Chicago Defender*, 11 April 1964, 9.

40. "LBJ Sets Fast Pace on Equality," *Chicago Defender*, 14 January 1963, 13; Laurence Stern, "'60 'Reach' Disclaimed by Johnson," *Washington Post*, 27 March 1963, A, 4; Robert Serling, "Negro Hostesses Aloft—With No To-Do," *New York World-Telegram* 21 July 1965, 18; "Negro Pilots Gain but Pace Is Slow," *New York Times*, 11 December 1966, V, 22; Mahler, *Wings of Excellence*, 167; "Hostesses Wanted!," *Amsterdam News*, 16 October 1965, news clipping in box 108, folder 9, TWU Collection; Patterson with Friskey and Klinger, *I Reached for the Sky*; "Two African-American Experiences," Lester, *Fasten Your Seatbelts!*, 157–63; Sandra Haggerty, "Black Airline Stewardesses," *Los Angeles Times*, 4 January 1972, C, 7; "American Airlines Quiet Revolution in Employment," *Chicago Defender*, 11 March 1967, 27; Paul J. C. Friedlander, "Blacks Are Ready to Travel, but—," *New York Times*, 26 April 1970, 39. Parallel struggles by African American men and civil rights groups forced airlines to begin integrating cockpit crews as well. For an overview see Northrup et al., *The Negro in the Air Transport Industry*, 45–49.

41. Quotation from decision by the EEOC (1975) in Dooley, "Battle in the Sky," 110. "Labor Letter," *Wall Street Journal*, 28 December 1965, 1; "Delta Faces Rights Boycott," *New York Times*, 3 September 1970, 9.

42. New York State investigator quoted in "Velvalea Smith Hammer v. American Airlines, Inc., Velvalea Smith Hammer v. Mohawk Airlines, Inc.," *Race Relations Law Reporter* 2 (spring 1966): 505–6, as cited in Kolm, "Women's Labor Aloft," 218–19. Fletcher quoted in McLaughlin, *Footsteps in the Sky*, 178–79. See also Lester, *Fasten Your Seat Belts!*, 157–63.

43. Quotations from McNutt in Lester, *Fasten Your Seat Belts!*, 161; Haggerty, "Black Airline Stewardesses"; Kathleen Heenan interview, conducted by Sara Rapport, 21 November 1985, Stewardesses For Women's Rights Oral Histories, 1985–1987, Robert F. Wagner Labor Archives, New York University [hereafter cited as SFWR Oral Histories]. " 'Natural' Hair Style Grounds Stewardess," *New York Times*, 23 September 1969, 93.

44. "Open Skies for Negro Girls," *Ebony*, June 1963, 43; Lillian S. Calhoun, "Confetti," *Chicago Defender*, 1 August 1963, 13; flight attendant quoted in Haggerty, "Black Airline Stewardesses."

45. Northrup et al., *The Negro in the Air Transport Industry*, 50–51; "Up, Up, and Away: Racial Barriers Falling but Airlines Choose Stewardesses with Care Regardless of Color," *Manpower* 3 (December 1971): 10, as cited in Kolm, "Women's Labor Aloft," 219 n. 47.

46. Quotation from Richard Witkin, "Aviation: Stewardess," *New York Times*, 29 December 1957, II, 25. When the flight attendant union was seeking a charter from the AFL-CIO amid the struggle over its future in early 1961, a stewardess union leader suggested an exchange of favors with the pioneering black labor leader A. Philip Randolph, head of the Brotherhood of Sleeping Car Porters and a member of the AFL-CIO executive committee: her union would seek to boost black employment on the airlines if Randolph intervened in the charter dispute. Randolph politely declined, and nothing in the union's records suggests any greater commitment to increasing black employment then or for several years after. Correspondence between Iris Peterson and Randolph discussed and cited in Chateauvert, *Marching Together*, 189–90, 256 n. 7. On racial nondiscrimination clauses see contract summaries in various folders in box 108, TWU Collection; Nielsen, *From Sky to Flight Attendant*, 87.

CHAPTER 5: "DO I LOOK LIKE AN OLD BAG?"

1. "Four of These Stewardesses Are over 32—Which Four?," *Herald Tribune*, 19 April 1963, 23, and additional news clippings in box 108, folder 7, TWU Collection; "32 Skidoo," *Newsweek*, 8 April 1963, 56; "Labor: A Kiwi at 32," *Time*, 26 April 1963, 84; Davis, *Moving the Mountain*, 20–21. In "Desirable Dress" Eileen Boris makes an argument similar to that made in this chapter concerning flight atten-

dants' use of their airline-managed image and uniformed appearance in their challenges to gender discrimination, as part of a broader analysis of the politics of appearance in the workplace. My thanks to her for generously sharing her work before its publication.

2. "Does Hostess Appeal Fade at Beauty Peak—32–35 Too Old?" *Intercom* 1, no. 2 (August 1964): 2; "Fact Sheet: Airline Industry—Maximum Age Requirements (Stewardesses), Inv. 1851-65," November 1965, 1, box 108, folder 9, TWU Collection.

3. Cobble, *The Other Women's Movement*; Deslippe, *"Rights, Not Roses"*; Gabin, *Feminism in the Labor Movement*; Meyerowitz, ed., *Not June Cleaver*; Harrison, *On Account of Sex*; Rupp and Taylor, *Survival in the Doldrums*; Hartmann, *The Other Feminists*.

4. " 'Stewardesses Old at 32,' Says American," and editorial, "About Stewardess Retirement," *Service Aloft* 8, no. 1 (October–December 1953): 1–2; "Too Old to Fly? 'Propwash,' " *Service Aloft* 8, no. 2 (January–June 1954): 2; "No Fury like a Woman Scorned," *Business Week*, 3 April 1954, 50–51.

5. Quotations from Quinn interview in Nielsen, *From Sky Girl to Flight Attendant*, 84; "Eastern Council Meets to Form Proposals," ALSSA *News Bulletin* 8, no. 3 (October–December 1961): 2. See also Dooley, "Battle in the Sky," 210–12; Davis, *Moving the Mountain*, 18–20.

6. "Opinion of the Referee, in the Matter of the Dispute between [Terminated Flight Attendant] and ALSSA, Local 550, TWU, AFL-CIO, and Northwest Airlines, Inc.," 8 January 1965; and ALPA S&S Case no. 394, Betty Green Bateman and Air Line Pilots Association, International v. Braniff Airways, Incorporated, 14 September 1965, "Discrimination" folder (1st of 2), box 13, accession date 18 August 1972, ALPA-SSD Collection; Deloros Kidder to Carol Carraro, 17 September 1965, "101.1, 1965" folder, box 8, accession date 18 August 1972, ALPA-SSD Collection. Dooley, "Battle in the Sky," 210–12; Nielsen, *From Sky Girl to Flight Attendant*, 84–85. As Dooley notes, the failed Pan Am grievance did help persuade the carrier to ease its no-marriage rule the following year.

7. See e.g. Crawford, Rouse and Woods, eds., *Women in the Civil Rights Movement*; Ransby, *Ella Baker and the Black Freedom Movement*; Lee, *For Freedom's Sake*; Evans, *Personal Politics*.

8. Cobble, *The Other Women's Movement*; Harrison, *On Account of Sex*, 109–37; Rosen, *The World Split Open*, chapter 3. The PCSW also increased common ground among women's rights activists by finessing the long-divisive question of an Equal Rights Amendment to the U.S. Constitution. While many feminists had championed the ERA since the 1920s, advocates of working women's interests had long opposed it for fear that it would invalidate state labor laws protecting female wage earners. The latter were better represented on the PCSW. The commission did not endorse the ERA but argued for some firmer guarantee of women's equality before the law.

9. On the Equal Pay Act see Harrison, *On Account of Sex*, 89–105; Kessler-

Harris, *A Woman's Wage*, chapter 4. Gender wage gap estimates in Goldin, *Understanding the Gender Gap*, 60.

10. Maschke, *Litigation, Courts, and Women Workers*, 7–21; Harrison, *On Account of Sex*, 176–82; Deitch, "Gender, Race, and Class Politics and the Inclusion of Women in Title VII of the 1964 Civil Rights Act"; Freeman, "How 'Sex' Got into Title VII"; Brauer, "Women Activists, Southern Conservatives, and the Prohibition of Sex Discrimination in Title VII of the 1964 Civil Rights Act"; Cobble, *The Other Women's Movement*, chapter 6. The "sex" amendment did encounter opposition, notably from what Harrison calls the "Women's Bureau" coalition, which included the Women's Bureau of the U.S. Department of Labor, the pcsw, and the American Association of University Women. These groups argued that the Civil Rights Act should remain focused on racial discrimination and that gender discrimination should be treated in separate statutes. Advocates of working women who opposed the bill were also concerned that like the era, it would jeopardize protective state laws.

11. Civil Rights Act of 1964, Public Law 88-352, 88th Congress, 2d sess., 2 July 1964.

12. Brown, *Sex and the Single Girl*; Friedan, *The Feminine Mystique*; Rosen, *World Split Open*, 4–8, 51; Douglas, *Where the Girls Are*, 68–69 and chapters 3–6 *passim*; Horowitz, *Betty Friedan and the Making of the Feminine Mystique*. On tensions in earlier popular cultural messages see Meyerowitz, "Beyond the Feminine Mystique."

13. Evans, *Personal Politics*; Echols, *Daring to Be Bad*.

14. Rosen, *World Split Open*, esp. chapter 9; Douglas, *Where the Girls Are*; Echols, *Daring to Be Bad*.

15. Christina Kirk, "Skidoo at 32? No! Say 'Mature' Hostesses to Airline That Wants to Clip Their Wings," *New York Sunday News*, 19 May 1963, 90 (subtitle "'Hey, Look Us Over' Girls Tell the Press"); Theo Wilson, "She's 36–24–36, Alas 32-Plus: Air Hostesses Fighting Retirement Age," *Daily News*, 18 April 1963, 3. On the labor activism of actors and actresses see Holmes, "All the World's a Stage!"

16. "The Talk of the Town," *New Yorker*, 4 May 1963, 33.

17. *Employment Problems of the Older Worker (The Airline Stewardess Case)*, 2 September 1965, U.S. House of Representatives, Subcommittee on Labor of the Committee on Education and Labor, 389–91, box 108, folder 9, twu Collection.

18. *Employment Problems of the Older Worker*, 397, 401–402, 404.

19. *Employment Problems of the Older Worker*, 405, 409.

20. News clippings, box 108, folder 9, twu Collection.

21. Russell Baker, "Observer: Up in the Air with the Girls," *New York Times*, 5 September 1965, IV, 8; Hilor poem repr. in "Aging Dolls," *Intercom* 2, no. 6 (November 1965): 3; Austin letter in *Evening Star*, 9 September 1965, A, 18, news clipping in box 108, folder 9, twu Collection. Cf. "The Tragic Yearning for

Youth," *Daily News*, n.d. [ca. September 1965], news clipping, box 108, folder 9, TWU Collection.

22. Leonard Shecter, "Flying High," *New York Post*, 8 December 1965, news clipping, box 108, folder 9, TWU Collection.

23. See e.g. David Kraslow, "Congresswoman Says Airlines Are Too Sexy," *Los Angeles Times*, 27 October 1966, 26. When Griffiths died in 2003, her question to the United official was cited in several obituaries as evidence of her directness and commitment to women's rights.

24. Nita L. Baum to Hon. James Scheuer, U.S. House of Representatives, 15 November 1965, repr. in *Employment Problems of the Older Worker*, 475–76; Roads quoted in Davis, *Moving the Mountain*, 18. See also TWU News Release, 4 May 1964, box 108, folder 8, TWU Collection.

25. Testimony by Iris Peterson to Senate Committee on Labor and Welfare, n.d. [17 March 1967], 2–3, "Discrimination" folder (1st of 2), box 13, accession date 18 August 1972, ALPA-SSD Collection. See also "ALPA Stewardesses Push Age Discrimination Fight," *Air Line Pilot*, May 1967, 15.

26. Peterson testimony, 4.

27. Transcript of Proceedings, H.R. 3651, H.R. 4221, and H.R. 3768, Age Discrimination in Employment, 15 August 1967, U.S. House of Representatives, General Subcommittee on Labor of the Committee on Education and Labor, 172–73, "Discrimination" folder (1st of 2), box 13, accession date 18 August 1972, ALPA-SSD Collection.

28. Transcript of Proceedings, 173.

29. "ALPA Asks No Female Flight Attendant Age Discrimination," *S & S Division News* 5, no. 8 (August 1967): 3; "Barbara Speaks . . . 'We Have a Good Chance,'" *Intercom* 4, no. 2 (April 1967): 5; headlines from front pages of *Oregonian* and *Seattle Times*, 16 August 1967, news clippings, "Discrimination" folder (1st of 2), box 13, accession date 18 August 1972, ALPA-SSD Collection.

30. Roads quoted in Davis, *Moving the Mountain*, 20. Age Discrimination in Employment Act of 1967, Public Law 90-202, 90th Congress, 1st sess., 15 December 1967; Francis A. O'Connell to James F. Horst, 12 December 1968, box 109, folder 2, TWU Collection; "Senate Votes Age Discrimination Ban," *Washington Post*, 7 November 1967, A, 2. The bill did direct the secretary of labor to study airline age limits and report back to Congress in six months. On the act and its subsequent history see Gregory, *Age Discrimination in the American Workplace*.

31. Text of Executive Order 11141, signed 12 February 1964, included as exhibit 7 in *Employment Problems of the Older Worker*, 395–96, correspondence between O'Hara and officials at the Departments of Labor and Defense at 490–93; John G. Loomos [ALPA] to Marge Cooper, 1 February 1967, "400.5—1967" folder, box 13, accession date 18 August 1972, ALPA-SSD Collection. See also "Age Discrimination-

Airline Stewardesses" (2 folders), box 10, James G. O'Hara Papers, Bentley Historical Library, University of Michigan.

32. "Report of Findings after Investigation, in the Matter of Airline Industry: Maximum Age Requirements (Stewardesses)," NYSCHR Investigation 1851–65,
signed J. Edward Conway, Investigating Commissioner, 23 March 1966, 1, box 108,
folder 10, TWU Collection.

33. "News Release: New York State Commission for Human Rights," 18 December 1966, box 108, folder 10, TWU Collection. For a more detailed discussion see
Barry, "Femininity in Flight," 393–98.

34. American Airlines v. State Commission for Human Rights, 286 N.Y.S.2d
493, 29 A.D.2d 178 (25 January 1968); "Age Limit on Air Hostesses Upheld," *New
York Times,* 26 January 1968, 94; Dooley, "Battle in the Sky," 217–18, 238–39, 244–
45; Harry Bernstein, "Do Women Age Faster on Airplanes?," *Washington Post,*
26 June 1968, C, 2.

CHAPTER 6: "YOU'RE WHITE, YOU'RE FREE, AND YOU'RE 21"

1. "Interview with Barbara 'Dusty' Roads," edited transcript, "Half the People,
1917–1996" episode, *People's Century* series, Public Broadcasting System web site,
http://www.pbs.org/wgbh/peoplescentury/episodes/halfthepeople/roadstranscript.
html (26 June 2001). Many thanks to Dave Kinkela for pointing out this source.
Roads recounted much the same story in an earlier interview for Davis, *Moving
the Mountain,* 22.

2. Officials of both national flight attendant unions were preparing in advance
of July 1965 to approach the EEOC as soon as possible. Colleen Boland to Honor-
able Franklin D. Roosevelt Jr., 24 June 1965, and enclosure, box 108, folder 9, TWU
Collection; Deloros Kidder to J. Meals, 24 June 1965, "400.5—1965" folder, box 13,
accession date 18 August 1972, ALPA-SSD Collection. According to Cathleen Dooley, Montague's was the first case ever filed with the EEOC by a flight attendant, but
it was never investigated because she had not yet been fired for aging when she
made her complaint. Roads had a "grandmother" exemption from the age ceiling
and so did not file a complaint herself. "Battle in the Sky," 239–40.

3. Southern Airlines used "young, attractive, and unencumbered" in a grievance case on its no-marriage rule in 1966. Decision of System Board of Adjustment, Grievance: Termination of [names of grievants withheld], Southern
Airways, Inc. and ALSSA-TWU, 14 September 1966, box 108, folder 10, TWU Collection. See Dooley, "Battle in the Sky," for more detailed treatment of many of the
Title VII cases, legal arguments, and issues discussed in this chapter. On the
broader history of anti-discrimination battles under Title VII see MacLean, *Freedom Is Not Enough.*

4. "Summary of Agreement—American Airlines, Inc.," n.d. [contract signed

12 October 1965], 6, box 108, folder 9, TWU Collection. For other contracts with marriage bans modified by three- or six-month grace periods see "Summary of Agreement, Pacific Air Lines, Inc.," 18 March 1965; "Eastern Airlines, Inc., Tentative Agreement Reached April 10, 1965"; "Highlights of Caribair Contract," n.d. [1 August 1965], all in box 108, folder 9, TWU Collection.

5. "Summary of Agreement—American Airlines, Inc.," 6; Shirley H. Beck to Colleen Boland, 6 February 1965; "Trans World Airlines, Inc. Tentative Agreement Reached February 26, 1965," all in box 108, folder 9, TWU Collection. "Stewardesses Strike Called on T.W.A.," *New York Times*, 26 February 1965, 58.

6. W. L. Wickham, director of personnel, Allegheny Airlines, to Flight Attendants, 28 January 1966, "101.1, 1965" folder, box 8, accession date 18 August 1972, ALPA-SSD Collection; Helen Etzel to Deloros Kidder, 19 October 1965, "400.5—1965" folder, box 13, accession date 18 August 1972, ALPA-SSD Collection.

7. John R. Hill, retired United legal counsel, quoted in Nielsen, *From Sky Girl to Flight Attendant*, 87, 147 n. 6; *Transcript of Proceedings: Air Line Pilots Association, Steward and Stewardess Division, Second Executive Board Meeting, May 18–19, 1971, Washington, D.C.*, 18, box 15, accession dates 30 September 1972, 25 June 1972, 24 July 1972, ALPA-SSD Collection.

8. ALPA S&S Case N. 394, Betty Green Bateman and ALPA, International v. Braniff Airways, 14 September 1965, "Discrimination" folder (1st of 2), box 13, accession date 18 August 1972, ALPA-SSD Collection; "Job Loss Because of Marriage Subject to Arbitration, Court Rules," *S & S Division News* 3, no. 5 (May 1965): 2; "ALPA Wins Preliminary Order from Appellate Court in Stewardess Marriage Case," *S & S Division News* 3, no. 7 (July 1965): 4; "Stewardess Keeps Job—And Husband," *AFL-CIO News*, 2 October 1965, 1.

9. Bateman v. Braniff; "Stewardess Keeps Job—And Husband."

10. Bateman v. Braniff [quotation from 5]; "Arbitrator Orders Braniff to Reinstate Married Stewardess," *S & S Division News* 3, no. 8 (September 1965): 3.

11. "Marriage Case to Be Heard Oct. 10," *Intercom* 3, no. 5 (September 1966): 3; "American Marriage Award," *Intercom* 4, no. 3 (June 1967): 3–4; Colleen Boland to All American Chairman, 9 June 1967, box 109, folder 1, TWU Collection.

12. Decision of System Board of Adjustment, Grievance: Termination of [names of grievants withheld], Southern Airways, Inc. and ALSSA-TWU, 14 September 1966, box 108, folder 10, TWU Collection; Walter L. Gray to Marge Cooper, 26 May 1967, "101.1, 1967" folder, box 8, accession date 18 August 1972, ALPA-SSD Collection; "No-Marriage Rule Held Unreasonable in ALPA S&S Case N. 572," *S & S Division News* 5, no. 3 (March 1967): 2; "Neutral Rules Marriage Grounds for Discharge," *S & S Division News* 5, no. 4 (April 1967): 1; "We Thought We Couldn't Lose This One . . . but, We Did," *S & S Division News* 5, no. 12 (December 1967): 3; McKelvey, "Sex and the Single Arbitrator"; Nielsen, *From Sky Girl to Flight Attendant*, 87; Binder, "Sex Discrimination in the Airline Industry," 1102 n. 61.

13. Quotation from "ALSSA-TWU President Boland Reports to Ninth Biennial Congress," *Intercom* 4, no. 2 (April 1967): 2. "Hostesses Agree to an Airline Pact," *New York Times*, 11 August 1968, 7; Harry Bernstein, "Airline Battle Ends—Stewardesses Will Wed," *Los Angeles Times*, 12 November 1968, 3.

14. For Title VII cases in the 1970s in which unions as well as airlines were defendants see Binder, "Sex Discrimination in the Airline Industry," and on unions charged with discrimination generally see Kessler-Harris, *In Pursuit of Equity*, 256.

15. Blackwelder, *Now Hiring*, 182; Deslippe, *"Rights, Not Roses,"* 121; Memorandum, Colleen Boland to All Representatives Re: Age and Marriage, 6 December 1966, 3, and Colleen Boland to Currently Unemployed [ALSSA] Member[s], 7 December 1966, box 108, folder 10, TWU Collection.

16. Hernandez quoted in Harrison, *On Account of Sex*, 187; Edelsberg and NOW founding statement quoted in Rosen, *The World Split Open*, 72, 78; Friedan, *It Changed My Life*, 80. Fuentes, *Eat First, You Don't Know What They'll Give You*, 124–42; Harrison, *On Account of Sex*, 188–89; Mezey, *In Pursuit of Equality*, 41; Kessler-Harris, *In Pursuit of Equity*, chapter 6; Graham, *The Civil Rights Era*, chapter 8.

17. Franklin D. Roosevelt Jr. to Charles H. Ruby, 7 October 1965, "400.5—1965" folder, box 13, accession date 18 August 1972, ALPA-SSD Collection. White second-wave feminists' poor record on dealing with race and racism is addressed in most histories of the women's movement. See e.g. Echols, *Daring to Be Bad*, chapter 5; Rosen, *The World Split Open*, 278–80. But as Nancy MacLean argues, the women's movement generally looks less racially and class-insensitive when workplace-oriented activists are placed at center stage. *Freedom Is Not Enough*, 118.

18. Maschke, *Litigation, Courts, and Women Workers*, 21–23; Hamilton, "From Equal Opportunity to Affirmative Action," chapter 1. EEOC powers, duties, and procedures are outlined in sections 705 through 711 and 713 of Title VII, Civil Rights Act of 1964, Public Law 88-352, 88th Congress, 2d sess., 2 July 1964.

19. Figures from Mezey, *In Pursuit of Equality*, 39; Kessler-Harris, *In Pursuit of Equity*, 355 n. 26. See also Hamilton, "From Equal Opportunity to Affirmative Action."

20. That the EEOC was "entitled to great deference" was established in Griggs v. Duke Power Co., 401 U.S. 424 (1971). Binder, "Sex Discrimination in the Airline Industry," 1092–93; Harrison, *On Account of Sex*, 178; Kessler-Harris, *In Pursuit of Equity*, 241–46.

21. "TWU Presses Stewardess Discrimination Fight," *Aviation Daily*, 25 October 1965, 314; "Commission Outlaws Marriage, Sex as Bases for Hiring, Firing," *S & S Division News* 3, no. 8 (September 1965): 2.

22. The EEOC general counsel's letter of 22 September 1965 is quoted at length by Judge C. J. Stevens in his dissent in Sprogis v. United Air Lines, 444 F.2d 1194, 1204, 1206 (7th Cir. 1971).

23. Both Hernandez and Sonia Pressman Fuentes would be instrumental in the launching of NOW. See Fuentes's autobiography, *Eat First, You Don't Know What They'll Give You.*

24. Commissioner Decision, Case N. 5-10-2153, Judith W. Evenson v. Northwest Airlines, Inc., signed Aileen C. Hernandez, 16 December 1965, box 108, folder 9, TWU Collection; Herman Edelsberg to Judith Evenson and Edelsberg to Northwest Airlines, Inc., 3 January 1966, box 108, folder 10, TWU Collection; Evenson v. Northwest Airlines, 268 F. Supp. 29 (E.D. Va. 1967); Binder, "Sex Discrimination in the Airline Industry," 1103 n. 72. See also Francis A. O'Connell to Aileen C. Hernandez and O'Connell to James F. Horst, 7 January 1965 [*recte* 1966], box 108, folder 9, TWU Collection.

25. Freidin quoted in Dooley, "Battle in the Sky," 164. See also EEOC press release, 11 May 1966, box 108, folder 10, TWU Collection; "A Pillow, Please, Miss . . . er, Mister," *New York Times*, 29 May 1966, V, 20; Robert Serling, "Pretty Stewardesses Find Themselves in Jeopardy," *Washington Post*, 19 June 1966, G, 10.

26. *Sex as a Bona Fide Occupational Qualification for Stewardesses: Statement of United Air Lines, Inc.,* 22 April 1966, box 13, accession date 18 August 1972, ALPA-SSD Collection [quotations from 11–12, 10, 19].

27. Statement of Colleen Boland before the Equal Employment Opportunity Commission, 10 May 1966, 6, "400.5—1966" folder, Box 13, accession date 18 August 1972, ALPA-SSD Collection.

28. *EEOC Guidelines on Discrimination Because of Sex* (1965), quoted in Reed, "Flight Attendant Furies," 277. Binder, "Sex Discrimination in the Airline Industry," 1094–95; Fuentes, *Eat First, You Don't Know What They'll Give You*, 124–42.

29. "Fact Sheet: Airline Industry—Maximum Age Requirements (Stewardesses), Inv. 1851–65," November 1965, box 108, folder 9, TWU Collection; Margie Cooper to Tamara Danish, 25 April 1966, "101.1, 1966" folder, box 8, accession date 18 August 1972, ALPA-SSD Collection; Dooley, "Battle in the Sky," 161; Diaz v. Pan American World Airways, 311 F. Supp. 559, 564 (S.D. Fla. 1970); Laffey v. Northwest Airlines, 366 F. Supp. 763 (D.D.C. 1973).

30. Air Transport Association of America v. Aileen C. Hernandez, 1966 U.S. Dist. LEXIS 6954 (D.D.C. 21 November 1966); Air Transport Association of America v. Hernandez, 264 F. Supp. 227 (D.D.C. 1967); Air Transport Association of America v. Hernandez, 1967 U.S. Dist. LEXIS 7706 (D.D.C. 23 May 1967). See also "Judge Bars Ruling on Stewardesses," *New York Times*, 25 February 1967, 54; Dooley, "Battle in the Sky," 170–73. Material on the case in Betty Friedan Papers, box 44, folder 1547, Schlesinger Library, Radcliffe Institute.

31. Dooley, "Battle in the Sky," 175–76; Binder, "Sex Discrimination in the Airline Industry," 1103.

32. On the courts, gender ideology, protective legislation, and women workers see e.g. Purcell, "Ideology and the Law"; Boris, *Home to Work*; Kessler-Harris, *Out to Work*, 180–214. On the relative lack of preparation of feminists to act on Title

VII and the EEOC's eventual leadership on sex discrimination see Maschke, *Litigation, Courts, and Women Workers*, 83–99; MacLean, *Freedom Is Not Enough*, chapter 4; Herr, *Women, Power, and AT&T*.

33. Cooper v. Delta Air Lines, 274 F. Supp. 781, 782–83 (E.D. La. 1967); Nielsen, *From Sky Girl to Flight Attendant*, 85–86; Dooley, "Battle in the Sky," 173–75," 39; Binder, "Sex Discrimination in the Airline Industry," 1104 n. 74.

34. Lansdale v. United Air Lines, 1969 U.S. Dist. LEXIS 9522 (S.D. Fla. 2 December 1969). On the landmark case of Phillips v. Martin Marietta and the Supreme Court's reversal in 1971, as well as "sex-plus" theory in general and cases involving stewardesses and the airlines see Binder, "Sex Discrimination in the Airline Industry," 1099–1100.

35. Lansdale v. United Air Lines, 437 F.2d 454 (5th Cir. 1971); Mezey, *In Pursuit of Equality*, 47–48, on Phillips.

36. Sprogis v. United Air Lines, 308 F. Supp. 959 (N.D. Ill. 1970); Sprogis v. United Air Lines, 444 F.2d 1194 (7th Cir. 1971) [quotation from 1199].

37. Weeks v. Southern Bell Telephone & Telegraph, 408 F.2d 228 (5th Cir. 1969).

38. Diaz v. Pan American World Airways, 311 F. Supp. 559, 562–64 (S.D. Fla. 1970). For a more detailed summary of the case see Dooley, "Battle in the Sky," 178–88.

39. "Airline Passengers' Preferences between Women Stewardesses and Men Stewards: A Survey for the Air Transport Association, Opinion Research Corporation, Princeton, New Jersey, July 1966," "Discrimination" folder, box 13, accession date 18 August 1972, ALPA-SSD Collection; Diaz v. Pan American World Airways, 311 F. Supp. 559, 564–65 (S.D. Fla. 1970).

40. Diaz v. Pan American World Airways, 311 F. Supp. 559, 565–66 (S.D. Fla. 1970).

41. Diaz v. Pan American World Airways, 311 F. Supp. 559, 566–68 (S.D. Fla. 1970).

42. Diaz v. Pan American World Airways, 311 F. Supp. 559, 561–62 (S.D. Fla. 1970).

43. Diaz v. Pan American World Airways, 442 F.2d 385, 388–89 (5th Cir. 1971).

44. Diaz v. Pan American World Airways, 346 F. Supp. 1301 (S.D. Fla. 1972). On the continuing use of the BFOQ clause and the importance of the rulings in *Diaz* (and *Sprogis*) see Babcock, Freeman, Norton, and Ross, *Sex Discrimination and the Law*, 230–43.

45. Robert Lindsey, "U.S. Airlines Seek Stewards to Work Aloft," *New York Times*, 7 April 1972, 37.

46. Laffey v. Northwest Airlines, 366 F. Supp. 763 (D.D.C. 1973); Laffey v. Northwest Airlines, 1974 U.S. Dist. LEXIS 7378 (1974); "Equality on the Wing," *Washington Post*, 21 November 1973, A, 18. For a detailed analysis of *Laffey* in historical context see Dooley, "Battle in the Sky," chapter 1.

47. Hamilton, "From Equal Opportunity to Affirmative Action"; U.S. Equal Employment Opportunity Commission, "EEOC History: 35th Anniversary: 1965–2000," http://www.eeoc.gov/abouteeoc/35th/index.html (2000–); Herr, *Women, Power, and AT&T*; Maschke, *Litigation, Courts, and Women Workers*, 83 (review of cases) and 39–80 *passim*; Mezey, *In Pursuit of Equality*, chapters 3, 5, 6, 8; Edwards, "Pregnancy Discrimination Litigation."

48. MacLean, *Freedom Is Not Enough*, 9, 77, and *passim*.

49. Quotation from Rozen, "Turbulence in the Air," 170 [emphasis in original]. Binder, "Sex Discrimination in the Airline Industry," 1101 n. 59; Lessor, "Unanticipated Longevity in Women's Work," 236, 290; Heenan, "Fighting the 'Fly-Me' Airlines," 48. On flight attendants' Title VII challenges to maternity and weight restrictions see Reed, "Flight Attendant Furies"; Stolker, "Weigh My Job, Not My Body"; Weinlein, "Flight Attendant Weight Requirements and Title VII of the Civil Rights Act"; Whitesides, "Flight Attendant Weight Policies."

50. Lessor, "Unanticipated Longevity in Women's Work," 157.

CHAPTER 7: "FLY ME? GO FLY YOURSELF!"

1. Kane with Chandler, *Sex Objects in the Sky*, 1.

2. Quotations in "Proposal for Funding," n.d. [ca. 1973], 2, box 1, folder 9, Stewardesses for Women's Rights Collection, Robert F. Wagner Labor Archives, New York University [hereafter cited as SFWR Collection].

3. See especially MacLean, *Freedom Is Not Enough*, chapter 4, and "The Hidden History of Affirmative Action," and Cobble, "'A Spontaneous Loss of Enthusiasm.'"

4. Continental Airlines advertisement, *Los Angeles Times*, 13 January 1965, 7. See also Continental's advertisement with the heading "Not One Passenger Flirted with the Hostess," *Chicago Tribune*, 12 January 1965, 13.

5. Kolm, "Women's Labor Aloft," provides an insightful overview of the oligopolistic nature of the industry, airline competition, and changing marketing strategies.

6. The début "fly me" ad was featured in National's employee publication, *National NOW*, 27 September 1971, 3. "'Fly Me' Ads Win Top Award," *National NOW*, 9 October 1972, 1; "We Launch First-Name Campaign; Ads, Programs Feature YOU!" *National NOW*, 27 September 1971; "'Fly Me' Shirts Become Newest Fashion Craze," *National NOW*, 18 June 1973, 3; "A National Christmas," *National NOW*, 3 December 1973, 5.

7. "We Launch First-Name Campaign; Ads, Programs Feature YOU!" *National NOW*, 27 September 1971, 1–4 [quotation from 1]; "NAL Employees Play Key Role in Newest 'Fly Me' Campaign," *National NOW*, 25 November 1974, 1; "New Campaign Expands Fly Me Theme," *National NOW*, 11 September 1972, 3–5.

8. Henry R. Bernstein, "Continental's New Ad Campaign Spurs Stewardess Debate," *Advertising Age*, 4 February 1974, 2, 8; Bob Donath, "New National Ads Spark Attacks Against 'Sexist' Airline Campaigns," *Advertising Age*, 24 June 1974, 2, 74; Lindsy Van Gelder, "Coffee, Tea or Fly Me," *Ms.*, January 1973, 87, cites Air Jamaica's and other international airline slogans.

9. United and Lake Central slogans quoted in "Coffee, Tea—But Not Me!" *Newsweek*, 1 January 1968, 55; American Airlines advertisement, "Think of Her as Your Mother," reproduced in Omelia and Waldock, *Come Fly with Us!*, 98; Freiberg and Freiberg, *Nuts!* Notably, when Southwest was later sued under Title VII for accepting applications from male candidates but failing to hire any, the carrier argued that its carefully crafted image of sexiness, which it considered vital to its profitability, made it necessary to hire only attractive young women as flight attendants (and ticket counter staff), for only they could genuinely deliver the promised sex appeal. Recall that the EEOC had long defined the BFOQ as only applicable if authenticity or genuineness was at stake, as with an actor or actress. The court dismissed Southwest's defense. Wilson v. Southwest Airlines, 517 F. Supp. 292 (N.D. Tex. 1981).

10. Designer quoted in "Sky Girls Have New Uniform," *Christian Science Monitor*, 16 April 1941, 11.

11. Quant's comment was reported in *Newsweek*, 13 November 1967, 67, as quoted in D'Emilio and Freedman, *Intimate Matters*, 306. Steele, *Fifty Years of Fashion*; Peacock, *20th-Century Fashion*.

12. "The Wild Hue Yonder," *Life*, 3 December 1965, 76; Braniff advertisement, "Introducing the Air Strip," n.d. [ca. late 1965] reproduced in Omelia and Waldock, *Come Fly with Us!*, 102–3; for television advertisement see Jason Mojica, "Alexander Girard," *The Modernist*, terminal 2, 2003, http://www.themodern ist.com/terminal2/girard.html (29 September 2004).

13. Walter Carlson, "Advertising: Braniff, Pucci and 'Air Strips,'" *New York Times*, 28 June 1966, 70; Fox, *The Mirror Makers*, 268–70. Wells married the president of Braniff, but later, after they divorced, she forfeited the Braniff account, worth $10 million, for the TWA account, worth $14.6 million. Thanks to triumphs like the Braniff campaign, Wells became the most influential woman in the advertising industry and one of its most successful executives. Pucci continued to design Braniff's hostess uniforms through the early 1970s.

14. "Airlines: Up from Betty Grable," *Newsweek*, 4 September 1967, 58; "The New American Beauties," *Astrojet*, 22 March 1967; Lovegrove, *Airline*, cover and 33; "New Stewardess Uniforms," *New York Times*, 15 August 1967, 76; Diane Monk, "Airlines Take Highflier on Fashion," *Los Angeles Times*, 11 September 1967, C, 26; *The Air Line Pilot*, October 1971, 32. For photos of various uniforms see McLaughlin, *Footsteps in the Sky*, 135–47; Omelia and Waldock, *Come Fly with Us!*, chapter 4; Lovegrove, *Airline*; various histories of individual carriers by Gwen Mahler; Steele et al., *Wings of Pride*.

15. Kolm, "Women's Labor Aloft," 231, 237; Heenan, "Fighting the 'Fly-Me' Airlines," 58; "Here's Our New Americana Look," *Astrojet News*, 10 February 1969, 1; Jean Bennett, "Air Hostesses Going Colonial for American," *Record*, 6 February 1969, A, 20, news clipping in box 109, folder 3, TWU Collection; Tania Long, "Airways Turn to High Style in Bid for Business," *New York Times*, 2 April 1967, 199.

16. "The Industry Is Talking," *Southernaire* 18, no. 6 (June 1967): 7; "Color Shelved as Black and White Stewardess Look Appears," *Southernaire* 21, no. 6 (June 1970): 1, 4; cover, *Southernaire*, January 1972.

17. Nancy L. Ross, "Pretty Girls Are Standard Airline Equipment," *Washington Post*, 6 August 1967, H, 10; Julie Byrne, "Stewardesses Win Hemline Altitude Battle," *Los Angeles Times*, 7 August 1970, G, 1; "Summer Stewardess Uniforms," *Delta Digest*, May 1969, 2; advertisement, *Delta Digest*, November 1969, 12.

18. Baker and Jones, *Coffee, Tea or Me?*; Baker and Jones, *The Coffee, Tea or Me Girls' Round-the-World Diary*; Baker and Jones, *The Coffee, Tea or Me Girls Lay It on the Line*; Baker and Jones, *The Coffee, Tea or Me Girls Get Away from It All*. The recent reissue of *Coffee, Tea or Me?* newly credits, and includes a foreword by, the ghostwriter, Donald Bain. That *Coffee, Tea or Me?* was ghostwritten has long been common knowledge, but the author's identity was previously something of a mystery.

19. Wenzel and Wohl, *How to Make a Good Airline Stewardess*; Glemser, *The Fly Girls* and *The Super-Jet Girls*. *The Fly Girls* was a more provocatively marketed version of Glemser's earlier novel, *Girl on a Wing*. Film titles in Kane with Chandler, *Sex Objects in the Sky*, 28; Moles and Friedman, "The Airline Hostess," 306; Laurie Johnston, "Airlines Assailed by Stewardesses," *New York Times*, 13 December 1973, 21. More explicit films included *The Daisy Chain* (1969), *Spread Eagles* (1968), and *Fly Now, Pay Later* (1969).

20. Kane with Chandler, *Sex Objects in the Sky*, 1; letter quoted in "AA Stewardesses' 'Good Will' Worthy of Praise," *Intercom* 6, no. 3 (June 1969): 3.

21. William Zissner, "Worrisome Angles on Aging Angels," *Life*, 31 May 1968, 14; union letter quoted in Dooley, "Battle in the Sky," 124; Ross, "Pretty Girls Are Standard Airline Equipment."

22. Harrison, *On Account of Sex*; Hartmann, *The Other Feminists*; Deslippe, *"Rights, Not Roses"*; Hennessee, *Betty Friedan*; Davis, *Moving the Mountain*.

23. Echols, *Daring to be Bad*; Evans, *Personal Politics*.

24. Baxandall and Gordon, eds., *Dear Sisters*; Rosen, *The World Split Open*; Farrell, *Yours in Sisterhood*; Wandersee, *On the Move*; Ezekiel, *Feminism in the Heartland*.

25. Cobble, " 'A Spontaneous Loss of Enthusiasm,' " 27–28. Various documents in boxes 108 and 109, TWU Collection; "Discrimination" folders, box 13, accession date 18 August 1972, ALPA-SSD Collection; and various articles in the union newsletters *Intercom* and *S&S Division News* (later 1960s to 1973), and *Flightlog*

(1974–). See chapter 6 of this book on early NOW and stewardesses' complaints to the EEOC; Betty Friedan Papers, box 44, folders 1545–46, Schlesinger Library, Radcliffe Institute.

26. "Women's Lib," *Air Line Pilot*, November 1970, 37; Mahler, *Wings of Gold*, 96; Claudia Levy and Alex Ward, "Women Rally to Publicize Grievances," *Washington Post*, 27 August 1970, A, 1; Echols, *Daring to Be Bad*, 4.

27. Gene Reece, "Pie in the Sky," in *Women's Liberation Now: Writing from the Liberation Movement* (New York: Dell, 1971): 87, quoted in Kolm, "Women's Labor Aloft," 250; Lessor, "Unanticipated Longevity in Women's Work," 148–57. Boland resigned the ALSSA presidency upon marrying and moving away from Chicago, where ALSSA had its headquarters. Vice President J. D. Preston, an Eastern steward, was interim president until elected to the post in 1971. Colleen (Boland) Taylor, "Holiday Memo from Headquarters," 13 December 1968, box 109, folder 2, TWU Collection. "Membership Elects National Officers," *Intercom* 6, no. 3 (June 1969): 1.

28. Kane with Chandler, *Sex Objects in the Sky*, 73.

29. Laurie Johnston, "Airlines Assailed by Stewardesses," *New York Times*, 13 December, 1972, 21.

30. Johnston, "Airlines Assailed by Stewardesses"; Baker and Jones, *The Coffee, Tea or Me Get Away from It All*, 2; *Aviation Daily's Airline Statistical Annual 1974*, 22; U.S. Department of Transportation, Federal Aviation Administration, *FAA Statistical Handbook of Aviation 1972*, 154. SFWR repeatedly claimed about 1,000 members in statements to funders and the press in 1974 and 1975.

31. Lindsy Van Gelder, "Coffee, Tea or Fly Me," *Ms.* 1, no. 7 (January 1973): 105; Jay Mathews, "Stewardesses Map Airline Rules Fight," *Washington Post*, 28 February 1973, C, 1; letter to union representatives, March 1972, box 1, folder 1, SFWR Collection; tape 1B, Heenan interview by Sara Rapport, 21 November 1985, and tape 2A, Hounsell interview by Sara Rapport, 15 November 1985, SFWR Oral Histories 1985–87; Gloria Whitman, interview by author, New York City, 6 April 1996.

32. Conference address draft [untitled, undated], 5, box 2, folder 47, SFWR Collection. Excerpts reprinted in Sandra Jarrell, "Keynote Address at First SFWR Conference," *SFWR Newsletter* 1, no. 2 (May 1973). On lack of union support for Jarrell, Whitman interview with author, 6 April 1996; on TWU response, tape 2A, Hounsell interview and Heenan interview, SFWR Oral Histories; Whitman interview. "Another way out" quotation from "Planning, Co-ordinating Meeting," handwritten notes, n.d. [1972], box 1, folder 1, SFWR Collection.

33. "Planning, Co-ordinating Meeting" notes; tape 7, "SFWR Organizational Meeting," n.d. [ca. 1972], SFWR Oral Histories; Crawford quoted in Johnston, "Airlines Assailed by Stewardesses," 21; Kane with Chandler, *Sex Objects in the Sky*, 23; recruiting pamphlet quoted in Rozen, "Turbulence in the Air," 205, from

personal records of SFWR staff member Pat Conway Bass. The audiocassette recording is of an early group meeting, presumably the same meeting for which notes are cited. Unfortunately the tape is badly damaged and barely audible in many parts, but it seems to evidence discussion of the "need" for a "race case" to organize around and a similar discussion of the group's desire to reach out to lesbians. Cindy Hounsell told her interviewer Sara Rapport in 1985 that at least one lesbian stewardess had "come out" at an SFWR conference, or some other meeting. Tape 2A, Hounsell interview, SFWR Oral Histories.

34. Newsletters and conference files in boxes 1 and 2, SFWR Collection. Response to McGuire's remarks recalled by the former SFWR member Anne Sweeney at SFWR's reunion on 22 April 1987 at the Robert F. Wagner Labor Archives, New York University. Tape 4B, SFWR Oral Histories.

35. Quotation from Tape 2A, Hounsell interview, SFWR Oral Histories. Van Gelder, "Coffee, Tea, or Fly Me"; Rozen, "Turbulence in the Air," 203; Whitman interview with author, 6 April 1996; Lessor, "Unanticipated Longevity in Women's Work," 29. On Steinem's life and activist career see her memoir, *Outrageous Acts and Everyday Rebellions*; Heilbrun, *The Education of a Woman*.

36. Quotation from tape 1B, Heenan interview, SFWR Oral Histories. "Aviation: In a Stew," *Newsweek*, 18 March 1974, 100; correspondence between Stern Fund and SFWR and "Report to the Stern Fund—$25,000 Grant," n.d. [ca. 1975], box 1, folder 9, SFWR Collection. Regarding legal activism see Legal Right Task Force folders in box 1, SFWR Collection; tape 1B, Heenan interview, SFWR Oral Histories.

37. Funding proposals and reports in box 1, folder 9, and news clippings in SFWR Collection; Rich, *What It's Like to Be a Flight Attendant*, 107; "Aviation: In a Stew," *Newsweek*, 18 March 1974, 100. On the occupational health and safety movement generally see Stellman and Daum, *Work Is Dangerous to Your Health*; Messing, *One-Eyed Science*; Lessor, "Unanticipated Longevity in Women's Work," 34–38. While this chapter does not delve into health and safety activism beyond SFWR, it was an important manifestation of flight attendants' militancy and far-reaching activism in the 1970s. Lessor's work details how the flight attendant workforce became more attuned to occupational health and safety in the 1970s. Lessor, "Unanticipated Longevity in Women's Work," chapter 6, "Social Movements, the Occupational Arena and Changes in Career Consciousness," and "Consciousness of Time and Time for the Development of Consciousness."

38. Quotations from "Report to the Stern Fund," 2, 3. Betty Liddick, "Radioactive Shipments Alarm Stewardesses," *Los Angeles Times*, 10 June 1974, D, 1, 4.

39. "NOW Demonstration," *New York Times*, 1 March 1972, 49; "National on the Offensive," *Newsweek*, 15 November 1971, 96; "Feminist Airline Project" notices in box 2, folder 56, SFWR Collection; Henry R. Bernstein, "Continental's New Ad Campaign Spurs Stewardess Debate," *Advertising Age*, 4 February 1974, 2, 8; Bob

Donath, "New National Ads Spark Attacks against 'Sexist' Airline Campaigns," *Advertising Age*, 24 June 1974, 2, 74; Kolm, "Women's Labor Aloft," 279.

40. Quotation from "Report to the Stern Fund—$25,000 Grant," n.d. [ca. 1975], 4, box 1, folder 9, SFWR Collection [emphasis in original]. Box 1, folder 11, SFWR Collection; Cobble, " 'A Spontaneous Loss of Enthusiasm,' " 28; Dooley, "Battle in the Sky," 124–26.

41. Virtual motto noted in Kolm, "Women's Labor Aloft," 280–81; Van Gelder, "Coffee, Tea or Fly Me"; Glacken quoted in Cobble, " 'A Spontaneous Loss of Enthusiasm,' " 29. "Stewardesses for Women's Rights: Television Spot," n.d., box 2, folder 50, SFWR Collection; David Behrens, "Stewardesses Serving Spot of Safety," *New York Newsday*, 13 September 1974, news clipping in box 1, folder 8, SFWR Collection; untitled funding proposal, n.d. [ca. 1974], 6, box 1, folder 9, SFWR Collection. The "counter-commercial" aired as part of the feminist public affairs show "Woman Alive!" on 9 and 10 December 1975 on WNET-TV, New York, archived as T91:0090, Museum of Television and Radio, New York City.

42. "Report to the Stern Fund: $25,000 Grant," n.d. [ca. 1975], 4, box 1, folder 9, SFWR Collection [emphasis in original].

43. Blake and Heenan quotations from their remarks at SFWR's reunion on 22 April 1987 at the Robert F. Wagner Labor Archives, New York University, tapes 4A and 4B, SFWR Oral Histories. On the conflicts and financial problems that crippled SFWR see internal correspondence and memos in box 1, folders 5–8, SFWR Collection; tape 1B, Heenan interview, and tape 2A, Hounsell interview, SFWR Oral Histories.

44. Tape 1B, Heenan interview, SFWR Oral Histories. The sociologists Frieda Rozen and Roberta Lessor both found in interviews in the late 1970s with flight attendants that the group's influence was far-reaching. See Rozen, "Turbulence in the Air"; Lessor, "Unanticipated Longevity in Women's Work."

45. Occupational totals in FAA *Statistical Handbook of Aviation 1972*, 153; *Aviation Daily's Airline Statistical Annual 1974*, 22. *Newsletter: Eastern-MEC Council*, April 1973, 2, box 109, folder 9, TWU Collection. Rozen, "Turbulence in the Air" and "Technological Advances and Increasing Militance"; Nielsen, *From Sky Girl to Flight Attendant*.

46. "Las Vegas! MEC Convention Highlights" [ALPA flyer], n.d. [ca. December 1972–January 1973], "ALSSA Executive Board Meetings" folder, box 5, accession date 13 August 1981, AFA Collection. ALPA press release, 30 April 1971, "Organizing" folder, box 9, accession date 18 August 1972; *Transcript of Proceedings: Air Line Pilots Association, Meeting of the S. and S. Division Executive Board, June 14, 1972, Washington, D.C.*, 148–49 [Rueck quotation], 108–17, box 15, accession date 30 September 1972, 25 June 1972, 24 July 1972, ALPA-SSD Collection. Nielsen, *From Sky Girl to Flight Attendant*, 109–14; Rozen, "Turbulence in the Air," 230–40. While negotiating with ALPA, SSD leaders also quietly but seriously looked into

affiliating with TWU, despite the long history of conflicts, and the International Association of Machinists. Correspondence between Rueck and high-ranking TWU and Machinist officials in box 109, folder 9, TWU Collection.

47. "Flight Attendants OK Affiliate Status," *Air Line Pilot*, January 1974, 37; "S&S No Longer a Division of ALPA," *Air Line Pilot*, February 1974, 33; "Where We Came from . . . Where We're Going, 1974–1979," *Flightlog*, spring 1979, 23; Robert J. Serling, "Independent Flight Attendant Unions . . . Do They Pose Industry Menace?," *Airline Executive* 2, no. 6 (June 1978): 62; Rozen, "Turbulence in the Air," 240–42; Nielsen, *From Sky Girl to Flight Attendant*, 114–15.

48. Marty Brown to Kelly [Rueck], Memorandum re: NWA [Northwest], n.d. [ca. 1971], "Northwest Organizing" folder, box 9, accession date 18 August 1972, ALPA-SSD Collection; Bernice Dolan, "Vote ALSSA Election" flyer, n.d. [ca. 1971], "Northwest—ALSSA Publications" folder, box 9, accession date 18 August 1972, ALPA-SSD Collection.

49. Quotation from "Executive Board and Local 551," *Box 551* 1, no. 1 (March 1975): 1 [emphasis in original]. "National Officers & LEC Elected," *Intercom* 10, no. 3 (June 1973): 1; Martha L. O'Rourke to All ALSSA-TWU Eastern Airline and Southern Chairmen, 14 March 1974, "Executive Board Letters" folder, box 5, accession date 13 August 1981, AFA Collection; Notes from Local 550, TWU, AFL-CIO executive board meeting, 29 March 1974, 2, "ALSSA Executive Board Meetings" folder, box 5, accession date 13 August 1981, AFA Collection; Rozen, "Turbulence in the Air," 222, 251–53. Officially the new locals were 551 (TWA), 552 (American), and 553 (shared by the two smaller groups, Eastern and Southern). Not long before it dissolved, ALSSA had lost two other airline groups: Northwest attendants, who moved to ALPA-SSD in 1971, and Northeast attendants, who were absorbed into the larger, non-union Delta workforce when the two carriers merged in 1972.

50. On National and Northwest union changes see Rozen, "Turbulence in the Air," 244–47; various documents in box 109, folders 6 and 7, TWU Collection; various folders concerning Northwest and organizing generally in box 9, accession date 18 August 1972, ALPA-SSD Collection; and "NAL Raid 1976" folders, box 2, accession date 22 June 1983, AFA Collection.

51. Continental official quoted in Serling, "Independent Flight Attendant Unions," 61. Rozen, "Turbulence in the Air," 246–47, Nielsen, *From Sky Girl to Flight Attendant*, 126–27.

52. "Charges Spelled Out—Officers Suspended," *Box 551*, December 1976, 4; "TWU International Council Finds Teolis, Tuller and Frankovich Guilty and Orders Them Removed from Office," *Box 551*, January 1977, 3; IFFA newsletter *Inside Treachery and Truth*, December 1976, in "Unions IFFA" folder, box 1, accession date 22 June 1983, AFA Collection; Rozen, "Turbulence in the Air," 254–59.

53. Rozen, "Turbulence in the Air," 258–61; "President's Page," *Local 552 Newsletter* 3, no. 3 (April 1977): 2. Rozen notes that of all the participants of autonomy

and independence campaigns whom she interviewed in the late 1970s, Kathy Knoop, the key leader at American, more than others emphasized financial independence as the main appeal.

54. Lynn Egge, flight attendant, quoted in Rozen, "Turbulence in the Air," 262; Flynn quoted in Lester, 203–4, 207. See Lester's chapter, "An Independent Union," and Rozen, 262–63, for more detailed discussion, and for archival sources Star D. Hesse Papers, Wagner 85, Tamiment Library / Robert F. Wagner Labor Archives, New York University.

55. Robert J. Serling, "Independent Flight Attendant Unions . . . Do They Pose Industry Menace?," *Airline Executive* 2, no. 6 (June 1978): 61–62. Nielsen, *From Sky Girl to Flight Attendant*, 120.

56. Rueck quoted in Carolyn Childers, "Stewardesses Challenge Airlines," *Christian Science Monitor*, 30 July 1974, news clipping in box 2, folder 64, SFWR Collection [ellipsis in original]; Rozen, "Turbulence in the Air," 214. Joan Sweeney, "Stewardesses Take Off on Playmate," *Los Angeles Times*, 14 October 1974, D, 1, 8; "Fly Them! Stewardesses Say Buzz Off," *Los Angeles Times*, 26 June 1974.

57. Continental attendant quoted in Dooley, "Battle in the Sky," 126. Henry R. Bernstein, "Continental's New Ad Campaign Spurs Stewardess Debate," *Advertising Age*, 4 February 1974, 2, 8.

58. Tape 1B, Heenan interview, SFWR Oral Histories; Serling, "Independent Flight Attendant Unions," 61.

59. Pat Fink, "Negotiations Proceed: Union Determined to Fight Company Attitude," *Labor Speaks* 1, no. 3 (February 1977): 1, "Union Newsletters" folder, box 5, accession date 13 August 1981, AFA Collection. See also "Labor Speaks Statement of Purpose," *Labor Speaks* 2, no. 1 (May 1977): 8, and other issues from 1976 and 1977 in various folders, box 5, accession date 13 August 1981, AFA Collection.

60. TWA attendant quoted in Lett and Silverman, "Coffee, Tea and Dignity," 4. "EEOC Report," *Flightlog*, November–December 1974, 3; Dooley, "Battle in the Sky," chapters 5–6.

61. Hochschild, *The Managed Heart*, 126 and chapter 6 *passim*. Unions had long used "flight attendant" and "cabin attendant" as umbrella terms for stewardesses or hostesses, stewards, and pursers, but only secondarily. In the 1970s, with more men entering the occupation and the majority of women wanting to break from the past, "flight attendant" assumed primacy. As union records reflect, contracts in early 1970s were revised to replace the gendered terms "stewardess" and "hostess" with "flight attendant." The two historic flight attendant unions, the Air Line Stewards and Stewardesses Association and the Steward and Stewardess Division of ALPA, were superseded by new or re-formed unions whose names all used the new term.

62. Louise Kapp Howe, "No More Stewardesses—We're Flight Attendants," *Redbook*, January 1979, 75. See also, e.g., Letty Cottin Pogrebin, "The Working

Woman," *Ladies' Home Journal,* November 1976, 86; Anna Quindlen, "Flight Attendants: An Old Stereotype Is Given the Air," *New York Times,* 24 April 1978, 20; Patt Morrison, "Stewardesses Not Swingers of Yesteryear," *Los Angeles Times,* 18 June 1974, A, 1.

63. Sandra Ashworth [Jarrell] quoted in Van Gelder, "Coffee, Tea or Fly Me," 105.

64. Reverby, *Ordered to Care;* Sandelowski, *Devices and Desires;* Cobble, *Dishing It Out,* 127–31; Norwood, *Labor's Flaming Youth;* Enstad, *Ladies of Labor, Girls of Adventure;* Howard, " 'At the Curve Exchange.' "

65. Melosh, *"The Physician's Hand";* Walkowitz, *Working with Class;* Hine, *Black Women in White;* Glenn, "From Servitude to Service Work."

EPILOGUE

1. Corey Kilgannon, "When Flying Was Caviar," *New York Times,* 19 October 2003, 23. See also, e.g., Rick Marin, "When Flying Tourist Meant Going in Style," *New York Times,* 28 March 1999, 9, 1.

2. Airline Deregulation Act, Public Law 95-504, 95th Congress, 1st sess., 24 October 1978; "This Month's Feature: Controversy over Proposed Airline Deregulation," *Congressional Digest* 57 (June 1978): 163–92; Meyer and Oster, eds., *Airline Deregulation;* Petzinger, *Hard Landing.*

3. TWA would limp on to reorganize and file for bankruptcy twice more before being bought by American in 2001. For a lively overview of deregulation's impact on airlines see Petzinger, *Hard Landing.*

4. Quotation from "Issues of the '80s: Job Security, Having a Say, Union Busting," *Flightlog,* fall 1983, 5. Crémieux, "The Effect of Deregulation on Employee Earnings"; Cappelli and Harris, "Airline Union Concessions in the Wake of Deregulation"; McKelvey, ed., *Cleared for Takeoff;* Cappelli, *Airline Labor Relations in the Global Era.* On the TWA strike see Albrecht, " 'We Are on Strike!' "; Belcon, "Women and Labor-Management Conflicts in the Airline Industry."

5. Bianchi-Sand quoted in "Certification: What's Your View?," *Flightlog,* October–November 1990, 13. "AFA Members Celebrate Flight Attendant Safety Professionals' Day," *Flightlog,* October–November 1990, 21; Mahler, *Wings of Gold,* 165. Susan Bianchi-Sand, "Improving Our Profession," *Flightlog,* spring 1988, 2; Dee Maki, "Duty Time and Certification: Achieving the Dignity and Respect We Deserve," *Flightlog,* May–June 1993, 2; Friend, "Walking a Fine Line between Productivity and Exploitation." For an overview of occupational health and safety research see Boyd and Bain, " 'Once I Get You Up There, Where the Air Is Rarified.' "

6. Salinger, "Assaults against Airline Flight Attendants"; "Airline Unions Confer on Unruly Passengers," *USA Today,* 1 May 1997, A, 4; Christopher Reynolds,

"Misbehavior Aloft Less Likely to Go Unpunished," *Los Angeles Times*, 14 January 2001, L, 2; "Air Rage on the Rise, Union Says," *Houston Chronicle*, 7 July 2001, 19; Barry Estabrook, "A Paycheck Weekly, Insults Daily," *New York Times*, 15 February 2004, 10–12. Hester, *Plane Insanity*; Foss, *Around the World in a Bad Mood!*

7. Borer, "Doing Battle"; "A Half Century of Milestones," *Flightlog*, spring 1995, 13; "A Growing Itch to Fight," *Time*, 6 December 1993, 34–35; "The New Face of Labor Fights an Old Struggle," *U.S. News and World Report*, 6 December 1993, 8; Rose Ciotta, "A Perfect Strike: A Women's Union Flexes Its Muscle," *Ms.* 4 (March–April 1994): 88–91; "1993–2003: 10th Anniversary of the Strike against American Airlines," *Skyword*, November–December 2003 [special issue].

8. Linstead, "Averting the Gaze," 192–206 [quotations from 197]; Philip Shenon, "The Last Stewardess," *New York Times*, 25 October 1992, V, 3; Michael Mecham, "Attendants Strike Leaves Cathay Reeling," *Aviation Week and Space Technology*, 25 January 1993, 54.

9. Whitelegg, "Touching Down."

10. Whitelegg, "Touching Down" and "Cabin Pressure"; Gil, "Air Transport Deregulation and Its Implications for Flight Attendants."

11. Taylor, *Stewardess with the Moustache!*; Agesa, "The Impact of Deregulation on Racial and Gender Employment." See also Young and James, "Token Majority."

12. Male flight attendant quoted in Murphy, "Managing 'Nowhere,'" 103–4. Adams, "The Impact of Work on Gay Male Identity among Male Flight Attendants (Homosexual)," especially chapter 5. See also "The Flight Attendants," *Air and Space*, May 1993, 62; "Not Flying Right," *Advocate*, 4 March 1997, 14; Ted Gideonse, "Flying the Gay-Friendly Skies," *Advocate*, 14 September 1999, 34–36. On sexual harassment see Littler-Bishop, Seidler-Feller, and Opaluch, "Sexual Harassment in the Workplace as a Function of Initiator's Status"; Williams, "Sky Service"; Gary DiNunno, "The High Price of Sexual Harassment," *Air Line Pilot*, March 1988, 16–19.

13. Whitesides, "Flight Attendant Weight Policies"; Lynch, "The Heavy Issue"; Stolker, "Weigh My Job, Not My Body"; Weinlein, "Flight Attendant Weight Requirements and Title VII of the Civil Rights Act."

14. Quotation from Letter to the Editor, *Flightlog*, October 1990, 3. Mary Suh, "A Future Up in the Air: Flight Attendants Contest Weight Rules," *Ms.*, September 1989, 83–84; Molly Charboneau, "Beauty Backlash: AFA Fights Discriminatory Weight Program," *Flightlog*, July–August 1993, 4–5, 14; "United Union Balks on Plan," *New York Times*, 24 February 1994, 5; Walsh, "Accounting for the Proliferation of Two-Tier Wage Settlements in the U.S. Airline Industry," 58–59.

15. American manual quoted in Daniel Seligman, "Keeping Up," *Fortune*, 20 May 1991, 155; Anna Quindlen, "Public and Private: In Thin Air," *New York Times*, 16 May 1993, IV, 17. See also Murphy, "Managing 'Nowhere,'" 102–3; Tyler

and Abbott, "Chocs Away;" Taylor and Tyler, "Emotional Labour and Sexual Difference in the Airline Industry."

16. Edward Jay Epstein, "Airlines Need Guards, Not Stewards," *Wall Street Journal*, 3 October 2001, 22; "Flight Attendants Will Be Certified," Association of Flight Attendants-CWA, AFL-CIO web site, http://www.afanet.org (17 March 2004); "Certification at Last!," *Flightlog*, spring 2004, 6. Vision 100—Century of Aviation Reauthorization Act, Public Law 108-176, 108th Congress, 1st sess., 12 December 2003, section 814, "Flight Attendant Certification," 102.

17. Quotations from Micheline Maynard, "Coffee, Tea or Job? For Airline Workers, an Uncertain Future," *New York Times*, 3 September 2004, C, 1; Francine Parnes, "For Flight Attendants, Stress Comes with the Job," *New York Times*, 12 August 2003, C, 7. See also Joe Sharkey, "Coffee, Tea and Fatigue: Airline Job Loses Its Allure," *New York Times*, 20 April 2004, C, 6, and "Grilled Flight Attendant, Anyone?" *New York Times*, 27 April 2004, C, 9; Brooks Barnes, "The New Face of Air Rage," *Wall Street Journal*, 10 January 2003, W, 1. On the bailout and bankruptcies see Lizette Alvarez with Stephen Labaton, "An Airline Bailout," *New York Times*, 22 September 2001, A, 1; Edward Wong, "11th-Hour Union Vote Keeps American Afloat," *New York Times*, 26 April 2003, C, 1; Micheline Maynard, "Airline Bailout Fails to Do the Job, Some Experts Say," *New York Times*, 14 May 2004, C, 2; Susan Carey and Scott McCartney, "How Airlines Resisted Change for 25 Years, and Finally Lost," *Wall Street Journal*, 5 October 2004, A, 1.

18. "AFA-CWA: Higher Altitude, Same Direction," *Flightlog*, spring 2004, 8; "Edie Lauterbach," 13, in same issue. Edward Wong, "United's Flight Attendants' Union Opposes Merger," *New York Times*, 22 November 2003, C, 4; Susan Carey, "Union for Flight Attendants, Hit by Downturn, Seeks Partner," *Wall Street Journal*, 28 March 2003, B, 4.

19. Elizabeth Olson, "Hostesses in Shorts? This Is No Ordinary Flight," *New York Times*, 19 August 2003, C, 7; Sean Daly, "Leave It to Cleavage," *Washington Post*, 25 June 2003, C, 2; Susan Spano, "Hooters Air Girls are for 'Entertainment,'" *Chicago Tribune*, 9 June 2003, 36.

20. "Plane Crazy the Musical" web site, http://www.planecrazythemusical.com (12 December 2005).

BIBLIOGRAPHY

Adams, Kay Virginia. "The Impact of Work on Gay Male Identity among Male Flight Attendants (Homosexual)." Ph.D. diss., Loyola University of Chicago, 1997.

Agesa, Jacqueline. "The Impact of Deregulation on Racial and Gender Employment: The Case of the Airline Industry." Ph.D. diss., University of Wisconsin, Milwaukee, 1996.

Airline Stewardess Information Bureau. *How to Become an Airline Stewardess.* Minneapolis: Midwest Business Service, 1964.

Albrecht, Sandra L. " 'We Are on Strike!' The Development of Labor Militancy in the Airline Industry." *Labor History* 45, no. 1 (2004): 101–17.

Allen, Oliver. *The Airline Builders.* Alexandria, Va.: Time-Life, 1981.

Anderson, Karen. *Wartime Women: Sex Roles, Family Relations, and the Status of Women during World War II.* Westport, Conn.: Greenwood, 1981.

Aviation Daily's Airline Statistical Annual 1974. Washington: Ziff-Davis, 1974.

Babcock, Barbara Allen, Ann E. Freeman, Eleanor Holmes Norton, and Susan C. Ross. *Sex Discrimination and the Law: Causes and Remedies.* Boston: Little, Brown, 1975.

Bailey, Beth. *From Front Porch to Back Seat: Courtship in Twentieth-Century America.* Baltimore: Johns Hopkins University Press, 1988.

———. *Sex in the Heartland.* Cambridge: Harvard University Press, 1999.

Bailey, Peter. "Parasexuality and Glamour: The Victorian Barmaid as Cultural Prototype." *Gender and History* 2, no. 2 (summer 1990): 148–72.

———. *Popular Culture and Performance in the Victorian City.* New York: Cambridge University Press, 1998.

Baitsell, John M. *Airline Industrial Relations: Pilots and Flight Engineers.* Boston: Graduate School of Business Administration, Harvard University, 1966.

Baker, Trudy, and Rachel Jones. *Coffee, Tea or Me? The Uninhibited Memoirs of Two Airline Stewardesses.* New York: Bartholomew House, 1967; repr. New York: Penguin, 2003.

——. *The Coffee, Tea or Me Girls Get Away from It All.* New York: Grosset and Dunlap, 1974.

——. *The Coffee, Tea or Me Girls Lay It on the Line.* New York: Grosset and Dunlap, 1972.

——. *The Coffee, Tea or Me Girls' Round-the-World Diary.* New York: Grosset and Dunlap, 1970.

Balser, Diane. *Sisterhood and Solidarity: Feminism and Labor in Modern Times.* Boston: South End, 1987.

Banet-Weiser, Sarah. *The Most Beautiful Girl in the World: Beauty Pageants and National Identity.* Berkeley: University of California Press, 1999.

Banner, Lois W. *American Beauty.* Chicago: University of Chicago Press, 1983.

Barbas, Samantha. *Movie Crazy: Fans, Stars, and the Cult of Celebrity.* New York: Palgrave Macmillan, 2001.

Barnard, Malcolm. *Fashion as Communication.* New York: Routledge, 1996.

Baron, Ava, ed. *Work Engendered: Toward a New History of American Labor.* Ithaca: Cornell University Press, 1991.

Barry, Kathleen Morgan. "Femininity in Flight: Flight Attendants, Glamour, and Pink-Collar Activism in the Twentieth-Century United States." Ph.D. diss., New York University, 2002.

——. "Lifting the Weight: Flight Attendants' Challenges to Enforced Thinness." *Iris: A Journal about Women* 38 (winter–spring 1999): 50–54.

Bartky, Sandra Lee. "Foucault, Femininity, and the Modernization of Patriarchal Power." In *The Politics of Women's Bodies: Sexuality, Appearance, and Behavior,* ed. Rose Weitz, 25–45. New York: Oxford University Press, 1998.

Bates, Beth Tompkins. *Pullman Porters and the Rise of Protest Politics in Black America, 1925–1945.* Chapel Hill: University of North Carolina Press, 2001.

Baxandall, Roslyn Fraad, and Linda Gordon, eds. *Dear Sisters: Dispatches from the Women's Liberation Movement.* New York: Basic, 2000.

Belcon, Patricia E. D. "Women and Labor-Management Conflicts in the Airline Industry: Implications for the Future of Organized Labor in the United States." Ph.D. diss., City University of New York, 1991.

Bender, Marylin, and Selig Altschul. *Chosen Instrument: Pan Am, Juan Trippe, the Rise and Fall of an American Entrepreneur.* New York: Simon and Schuster, 1982.

Benson, Diana. *Mile High Club.* Los Angeles: Dove, 1997.

Benson, Susan Porter. *Counter Cultures: Saleswomen, Managers and Customers in American Department Stores, 1890–1940.* Urbana: University of Illinois Press, 1986.

Berry, Sarah. *Screen Style: Fashion and Femininity in 1930s Hollywood.* Minneapolis: University of Minnesota Press, 2000.

Bilstein, Roger E. "Air Travel and the Traveling Public: The American Experience, 1920–1970." In *From Airships to Airbus: The History of Civil and Commercial Aviation,* vol. 2: *Pioneers and Operations,* ed. William F. Trimble, 99–105. Washington: Smithsonian Institution Press, 1995.

——. *Flight in America: From the Wright Brothers to the Astronauts.* Rev. edn. Baltimore: Johns Hopkins University Press, 1994.

Binder, Denis. "Sex Discrimination in the Airline Industry: Title VII Flying High." *California Law Review* 59, no. 5 (1971): 1091–1112.

Biondi, Martha. *To Stand and Fight: The Struggle for Civil Rights in Postwar New York City.* Cambridge: Harvard University Press, 2003.

Blackwelder, Julia Kirk. *Now Hiring: The Feminization of Work in the United States, 1990–1995.* College Station: Texas A&M University Press, 1997.

Blum, Albert A., et al. *White-Collar Workers.* New York: Random House, 1971.

Bolton, Sharon C., and Carol Boyd. "Trolley Dolly or Skilled Emotion Manager? Moving on from Hochschild's Managed Heart." *Work, Employment and Society* 17, no. 2 (2003): 289–308.

Bomar, Birdie, and Kathryn Bankston. *Birdie: The True Story of Delta's First In-Air Stewardess.* Bloomington, Ind.: 1st Books, 2002.

Bordo, Susan. *Unbearable Weight: Feminism, Western Culture, and the Body.* Berkeley: University of California Press, 1993.

Borer, David A. "Doing Battle: Flight Attendant Labor Relations in the '90s." In *Handbook of Airline Economics,* ed. Darryl Jenkins and Cecilia Preble Ray, 563–68. Washington: Aviation Week Group, 1995.

Boris, Eileen. "Desirable Dress: Rosies, Sky Girls, and the Politics of Appearance." *International Labor and Working Class History* 69 (spring 2006): 123–42.

——. *Home to Work: Motherhood and the Politics of Industrial Homework in the United States.* New York: Cambridge University Press, 1994.

Boris, Eileen, and Sonya Michel. "Social Citizenship and Women's Right to Work in Postwar America." In *Women's Rights and Human Rights: International Historical Perspectives,* ed. Patricia Grimshaw et al., 199–219. New York: Palgrave, 2001.

Boyd, C., and P. Bain. "'Once I Get You Up There, Where the Air Is Rarified': Health, Safety and the Working Conditions of Airline Cabin Crews." *New Technology, Work and Employment* 13, no. 1 (1998): 16–28.

Boydston, Jeanne. *Home and Work: Housework, Wages, and the Ideology of Labor in the Early Republic.* New York: Oxford University Press, 1990.

Boyne, Walter J., and Donald S. Lopez, eds. *The Jet Age: Forty Years of Jet Aviation.* Washington: Smithsonian Institution Press, 1979.

Bratt, Aimée. *Glamour and Turbulence: I Remember Pan Am, 1966–91.* New York: Vantage, 1996.

Brauer, Carl M. "Women Activists, Southern Conservatives, and the Prohibition of Sex Discrimination in Title VII of the 1964 Civil Rights Act." *Journal of Southern History* 49 (February 1983): 37–56.

Braverman, Harry. *Labor and Monopoly Capital: The Degradation of Work in the Twentieth Century.* New York: Monthly Review, 1974.

Brill, Steven. *The Teamsters.* New York: Simon and Schuster, 1978.

Brody, David. *Workers in Industrial America: Essays on the Twentieth Century Struggle.* New York: Oxford University Press, 1980.

Brown, Helen Gurley. *Sex and the Single Girl.* New York: B. Geis, 1962.

Burkhardt, Robert. CAB: *The Civil Aeronautics Board.* Dulles International Airport, Va.: Green Hills, 1974.

——. *The Federal Aviation Administration.* New York: F. A. Praeger, 1967.

Butler, Judith. *Gender Trouble: Feminism and the Subversion of Identity.* New York: Routledge, 1990.

Cadogan, Mary. *Women with Wings: Female Flyers in Fact and Fiction.* Chicago: Academy Chicago, 1993.

Cameron, Ardis. *Radicals of the Worst Sort: Laboring Women in Lawrence, Massachusetts, 1860–1912.* Urbana: University of Illinois Press, 1993.

Cappelli, Peter. *Airline Labor Relations in the Global Era.* Ithaca: ILR, 1995.

Cappelli, Peter, and Timothy Harris. "Airline Union Concessions in the Wake of Deregulation." *Monthly Labor Review* 108, no. 6 (1985): 37–39.

Carden, Maren Lockwood. *The New Feminist Movement.* New York: Russell Sage Foundation, 1974.

Castel, Robert. "Work and Usefulness to the World." *International Labour Review* 135, no. 6 (1996): 615–22.

Chase, Lucille. *Skirts Aloft.* Chicago: Louis Mariano, 1959.

Chateauvert, Melinda. *Marching Together: Women of the Brotherhood of Sleeping Car Porters.* Urbana: University of Illinois Press, 1997.

Christian, Paula. *Twilight Girls.* New York: Kensington, 2003.

Clark-Lewis, Elizabeth. *Living In, Living Out: African American Domestics and the Great Migration.* Washington: Smithsonian Institution Press, 1994.

Cobble, Dorothy Sue. *Dishing It Out: Waitresses and Their Unions in the Twentieth Century.* Urbana: University of Illinois Press, 1991.

——. *The Other Women's Movement: Workplace Justice and Social Rights in Modern America.* Princeton: Princeton University Press, 2003.

——. " 'A Spontaneous Loss of Enthusiasm': Workplace Feminism and the Transformation of Women's Service Jobs in the 1970s." *International Labor and Working Class History* 56 (fall 1999): 23–44.

Cockburn, Cynthia. *Brothers: Male Dominance and Technological Change.* London: Pluto, 1983.

——. *Machinery of Dominance: Women, Men, and Technical Know-How.* London: Pluto, 1985.

Cohen, Colleen Ballerino, Richard Wilk, and Beverly Stoeltje, eds. *Beauty Queens on the Global Stage: Gender, Contests, and Power.* New York: Routledge, 1996.

Cohen, Lizabeth. *A Consumers' Republic: The Politics of Mass Consumption in Postwar America.* New York: Alfred A. Knopf, 2003.

——. *Making a New Deal: Industrial Workers in Chicago, 1919–1939.* New York: Cambridge University Press, 1990.

Coons, Lorraine, and Alexander Varias. *Tourist Third Cabin: Steamship Travel in the Interwar Years.* New York: Palgrave Macmillan, 2003.

Corn, Joseph J. *The Winged Gospel: America's Romance with Aviation, 1900–1950.* New York: Oxford University Press, 1983.

Cott, Nancy. *The Grounding of Modern Feminism.* New Haven: Yale University Press, 1987.

Crawford, Vicki L., Jacqueline Anne Rouse, and Barbara Woods, eds. *Women in the Civil Rights Movement: Trailblazers and Torchbearers, 1941–1965.* Brooklyn, N.Y.: Carlson, 1990; repr. Bloomington: Indiana University Press, 1993.

Crémieux, Pierre-Yves. "Does Strike Insurance Matter? Evidence from the Airline Industry's Mutual Aid Pact." *Journal of Labor Research* 17, no. 2 (spring 1996): 201–17.

——. "The Effect of Deregulation on Employee Earnings: Pilots, Flight Attendants, and Mechanics, 1959–1992." *Industrial and Labor Relations Review* 49, no. 2 (January 1996): 223–42.

Davies, Margery W. *Woman's Place is at the Typewriter: Office Work and Office Workers, 1870–1930.* Philadelphia: Temple University Press, 1982.

Davies, R. E. G. *Airlines of the United States since 1914.* Washington: Smithsonian Institution Press, 1972.

Davis, Flora. *Moving the Mountain: The Women's Movement in America since 1960.* New York: Simon and Schuster, 1991.

Deitch, Cynthia. "Gender, Race, and Class Politics and the Inclusion of Women in Title VII of the 1964 Civil Rights Act." *Gender and Society* 7, no. 2 (1993): 183–203.

Delano, Page Dougherty. "Making Up for War: Sexuality and Citizenship in Wartime Culture." *Feminist Studies* 26 (spring 2000): 33–68.

D'Emilio, John, and Estelle B. Freedman. *Intimate Matters: A History of Sexuality in America.* New York: Harper and Row, 1988.

Deslippe, Dennis A. *"Rights, Not Roses": Unions and the Rise of Working-Class Feminism, 1945–80.* Urbana: University of Illinois Press, 2000.

Dooley, Cathleen Marie. "Battle in the Sky: A Cultural and Legal History of Sex Discrimination in the United States Airline Industry, 1930–1980." Ph.D. diss., University of Arizona, 2001.

Douglas, Susan J. *Where the Girls Are: Growing Up Female with the Mass Media.* New York: Times, 1995.

Dubofsky, Melvyn. *The State and Labor in Modern America.* Chapel Hill: University of North Carolina Press, 1994.

Du Bois, W. E. B. *Black Reconstruction in America, 1860–1880.* New York: Harcourt, Brace, 1935; repr. New York: Simon and Schuster, 1992.

Dudden, Faye E. *Serving Women: Household Service in Nineteenth-Century America.* Middletown, Conn.: Wesleyan University Press, 1983.

Echols, Alice. *Daring to Be Bad: Radical Feminism in America, 1967–1975.* Minneapolis: University of Minnesota Press, 1989.

Edwards, Mark Evan. "Pregnancy Discrimination Litigation: Legal Erosion of Capitalist Ideology under Equal Employment Opportunity Law." *Social Forces* 75, no. 1 (1996): 247–68.

Ehrenreich, Barbara. *The Hearts of Men: American Dreams and the Flight from Commitment.* New York: Doubleday, 1983.

Eisenberg, Susan. *We'll Call You If We Need You: Experiences of Women Working Construction.* Ithaca: ILR, 1998.

Engeman, Jack. *Airline Stewardess: A Picture Story.* New York: Lothrop, Lee and Shepard, 1960.

Enstad, Nan. *Ladies of Labor, Girls of Adventure: Working Women, Popular Culture, and Labor Politics at the Turn of the Twentieth Century.* New York: Columbia University Press, 1999.

Etzioni, Amitai, ed. *The Semi-professions and Their Organization: Teachers, Nurses, Social Workers.* New York: Free Press, 1969.

Evans, Joan. "Men Nurses: A Historical and Feminist Perspective." *Journal of Advanced Nursing* 47, no. 3 (2004): 321–28.

Evans, Sara. *Personal Politics: The Roots of Women's Liberation in the Civil Rights Movement and the New Left.* New York: Vintage, 1980.

Ezekiel, Judith. *Feminism in the Heartland.* Columbus: Ohio State University Press, 2002.

Farrell, Amy. *Yours in Sisterhood: Ms. Magazine and the Promise of Popular Feminism.* Chapel Hill: University of North Carolina Press, 1998.

Faue, Elizabeth. *Community of Suffering and Struggle: Women, Men and the Labor Movement in Minneapolis, 1915–1945.* Chapel Hill: University of North Carolina Press, 1991.

Feldberg, Roslyn L. "'Union Fever': Organizing Among Clerical Workers, 1900–1930." *Radical America* 14, no. 3 (May–June 1980): 53–70.

Ferree, Myra Marx, and Beth B. Hess. *Controversy and Coalition: The New Feminist Movement.* Boston: Twayne, 1985.

Fields, Jill Susan. "Erotic Modesty: (Ad)dressing Female Sexuality and Propriety in Open and Closed Drawers, USA, 1800–1930." *Gender and History* 14, no. 3 (November 2002): 492–515.

——. " 'Fighting The Corsetless Evil': Shaping Corsets and Culture, 1900–1930." *Journal of Social History* 33, no. 2 (winter 1999): 355–84.

——. "The Production of Glamour: A Social History of Intimate Apparel, 1909–1952." Ph.D. diss., University of Southern California, 1997.

Filby, M. P. " 'The Figures, the Personality and the Bums': Service Work and Sexuality." *Work, Employment and Society* 6, no. 1 (1992): 23–42.

Fine, Lisa M. *The Souls of the Skyscraper: Female Clerical Workers in Chicago, 1870–1930*. Philadelphia: Temple University Press, 1990.

Folgerø, Ingebjorg S., and Ingrid H. Fjeldstad. "On Duty Off Guard: Cultural Norms and Sexual Harassment in Service Organizations." *Organization Studies* 16, no. 2 (1995): 299–313.

Follet, Ben B. *Careers in Aviation*. Boston: Waverly House, 1940.

Foner, Philip S. *Women and the American Labor Movement: From World War I to the Present*. New York: Free Press, 1980.

Foss, Rene. *Around the World in a Bad Mood! Confessions of a Flight Attendant*. New York: Hyperion, 2002.

Fox, Stephen. *The Mirror Makers: A History of American Advertising and Its Creators*. New York: William Morrow, 1984.

——. *Transatlantic: Samuel Cunard, Isambard Brunel, and the Great Atlantic Steamships*. New York: Harper Collins, 2003.

Frank, Dana. *Purchasing Power: Consumer Organizing, Gender, and the Seattle Labor Movement, 1919–1929*. New York: Cambridge University Press, 1994.

Freeman, Jo. "How 'Sex' Got into Title VII: Persistent Opportunism as a Maker of Public Policy." *Law and Inequality* 9 (March 1991): 163–84.

——. "The Origins of the Women's Liberation Movement." *American Journal of Sociology* 78, no. 4 (1973): 792–811.

——. *The Politics of Women's Liberation*. New York: Longman, 1975.

Freeman, Joshua B. "Hardhats: Construction Workers, Manliness, and the 1970 Pro-war Demonstrations." *Journal of Social History* 26, no. 4 (1993): 725–44.

——. *In Transit: The Transport Workers Union in New York City, 1937–1966*. New York: Oxford University Press, 1989.

Freiberg, Kevin, and Jackie Freiberg. *Nuts! Southwest Airline's Crazy Recipe for Business and Personal Success*. Austin: Bard, 1996.

Friedan, Betty. *The Feminine Mystique*. New York: W. W. Norton, 1963.

——. *It Changed My Life: Writings on the Women's Movement*. New York: Random House, 1976.

Friend, Patricia A. "Walking a Fine Line between Productivity and Exploitation: Flight Attendants and the Airline Industry in the 1990s." In *Handbook of Airline*

Economics, ed. Darryl Jenkins and Cecilia Preble Ray, 63–70. Washington: Aviation Week Group, 1995.

Fruhan, William E., Jr. *The Fight for Competitive Advantage: A Study of the United States Domestic Trunk Air Carriers*. Boston: Graduate School of Business Administration, Harvard University, 1972.

Fuentes, Sonia Pressman. *Eat First, You Don't Know What They'll Give You: The Adventures of an Immigrant Family and Their Feminist Daughter*. Philadelphia: Xlibris, 1999.

Gabin, Nancy F. *Feminism in the Labor Movement: Women and the United Auto Workers, 1935–1975*. Ithaca: Cornell University Press, 1990.

Garson, Barbara. *All the Livelong Day: The Meaning and Demeaning of Routine Work*. New York: Doubleday, 1975.

Garvey, William, and David Fisher. *The Age of Flight: A History of America's Pioneering Airline*. Greensboro, N.C.: Pace Communications, 2002.

Gerard, Jane. *Jet Stewardess*. New York: Messner, 1962.

Gerhard, Jane. *Desiring Revolution: Second-Wave Feminism and the Rewriting of American Sexual Thought, 1920–1982*. New York: Columbia University Press, 2001.

Gil, Avishai. "Air Transport Deregulation and Its Implications for Flight Attendants." *International Labour Review* 129, no. 3 (1990): 317–31.

Gill, Frederick W., and Gilbert L. Bates. *Airline Competition: A Study of the Effects of Competition on the Quality and Price of Airline Service and the Self-Sufficiency of the United States Domestic Airlines*. Boston: Graduate School of Business Administration, Harvard University, 1949.

Glemser, Bernard. *The Fly Girls*. New York: Bantam, 1969.

——. *Girl on a Wing*. New York: Random House, 1960.

——. *The Super-Jet Girls*. New York: Bantam, 1971.

Glenn, Evelyn Nakano. "From Servitude to Service Work: Historical Continuities in the Racial Division of Paid Reproductive Labor." *Signs* 18 (autumn 1992): 1–43.

Glenn, Susan A. *Daughters of the Shtetl: Life and Labor in the Immigrant Generation*. Ithaca: Cornell University Press, 1990.

——. *Female Spectacle: The Theatrical Roots of Modern Feminism*. Cambridge: Harvard University Press, 2000.

Goldin, Claudia. *Understanding the Gender Gap: An Economic History of American Women*. New York: Oxford University Press, 1990.

Gordon, David M., Richard Edwards, and Michael Reich. *Segmented Work, Divided Workers: The Historical Transformation of Labor in the United States*. New York: Cambridge University Press, 1982.

Graf, Nelly. *Air Stewardess*. New York: Gramercy, 1938.

Graham, Hugh Davis. *The Civil Rights Era: Origins and Development of National Policy, 1960–1972*. New York: Oxford University Press, 1990.

Grant, Linda. *Sexing the Millennium: Women and the Sexual Revolution.* New York: Grove, 1994.

Green, Venus. *Race on the Line: Gender, Labor, and Technology in the Bell System, 1880–1980.* Durham: Duke University Press, 2001.

Greene, Carla. *I Want to Be an Airline Hostess.* Chicago: Children's Press, 1960.

Gregory, Raymond F. *Age Discrimination in the American Workplace: Old at a Young Age.* New Brunswick: Rutgers University Press, 2001.

Gundle, Stephen. "Hollywood Glamour and Mass Consumption in Postwar Italy." *Journal of Cold War Studies* 4, no. 3 (summer 2002): 95–118.

——. "Mapping the Origins of Glamour: Giovanni Boldini, Paris and the Belle Époque." *Journal of European Studies* 29, no. 3 (1999): 269–95.

Gutman, Herbert G. *Work, Culture and Society in Industrializing America: Essays in American Working-Class and Social History.* New York: Vintage, 1977.

Hager, Alice Rogers. *Janice, Air Line Hostess.* New York: Julian Messner, 1948.

——. *Wings to Wear.* New York: Macmillan, 1939.

Hall, Charles Gilbert, and Rudolph A. Merkle. *The Sky's the Limit! Jobs in Commercial Aviation and How to Get Them.* New York: Funk and Wagnalls, 1943.

Hall, Elaine J. "Waitering/Waitressing: Engendering the Work of Table Servers." *Gender and Society* 7, no. 3 (1993): 329–46.

Hall, Jacquelyn Dowd. "Disorderly Women: Gender and Labor Militancy in the Appalachian South." *Journal of American History* 73 (September 1986): 354–82.

Hall, Jacquelyn Dowd, et al. *Like a Family: The Making of a Southern Cotton Mill World.* New York: W. W. Norton, 1989.

Halle, David. *America's Working Man: Work, Home, and Politics among Blue-Collar Property Owners.* Chicago: University of Chicago Press, 1984.

Hamilton, Konrad Mark. "From Equal Opportunity to Affirmative Action: A History of the Equal Employment Opportunity Commission, 1965–1980." Ph.D. diss., Stanford University, 1998.

Hanlon, Gerard. "Professionalism as Enterprise: Service Class Politics and the Redefinition of Professionalism." *Sociology* 32, no. 1 (1998): 43–63.

Hapke, Laura. *Daughters of the Great Depression: Women, Work, and Fiction in the American 1930s.* Athens: University of Georgia Press, 1995.

Harrison, Cynthia. *On Account of Sex: The Politics of Women's Issues, 1945–1968.* Berkeley: University of California Press, 1988.

Hart, James Francis. "The Effect of Union Shop on the Contracts of the Airline Stewards and Stewardesses Association." M.A. thesis, De Paul University, 1969.

Hartmann, Susan. *The Other Feminists: Activists in the Liberal Establishment.* New Haven: Yale University Press, 1999.

Hearn, Jeff, and Wendy Parkin. *Sex at Work: The Power and Paradox of Organisation Sexuality.* New York: St. Martin's, 1995.

Heenan, Kathleen. "Fighting the 'Fly-Me' Airlines." *Civil Liberties Review,* December 1976–January 1977, 48–59.

Heilbrun, Carolyn G. *The Education of a Woman: The Life of Gloria Steinem.* New York: Dial, 1995.

Hennessee, Judith Adler. *Betty Friedan: A Biography.* New York: Random House, 1999.

Heppenheimer, T. A. *Turbulent Skies: The History of Commercial Aviation.* New York: John Wiley and Sons, 1995.

Herr, Lois Kathryn. *Women, Power, and AT&T: Winning Rights in the Workplace.* Boston: Northeastern University Press, 2003.

Hester, Elliott. *Plane Insanity: A Flight Attendant's Tales of Sex, Rage, and Queasiness at 30,000 Feet.* New York: St. Martin's, 2003.

Hine, Darlene Clark. *Black Women in White: Racial Conflict and Cooperation in the Nursing Profession, 1890–1950.* Bloomington: Indiana University Press, 1989.

Hochschild, Arlie Russell. *The Managed Heart: Commercialization of Human Feeling.* Berkeley: University of California Press, 1983.

Hole, Judith, and Ellen Levine. *Rebirth of Feminism.* New York: Quadrangle, 1971.

Holmes, Sean. "All the World's a Stage! The Actors' Strike of 1919." *Journal of American History* 91, no. 4 (March 2005): 1291–1317.

Honey, Maureen. *Creating Rosie the Riveter: Class, Gender, and Propaganda during World War II.* Amherst: University of Massachusetts Press, 1984.

Hopkins, George E. *The Airline Pilots: A Study in Elite Unionization.* Cambridge: Harvard University Press, 1971.

———. *Flying the Line: The First Half Century of the Air Line Pilots Association.* Washington: Air Line Pilots Association, 1982.

Hornstein, Jeffrey M. *A Nation of Realtors: A Cultural History of the Twentieth-Century American Middle Class.* Durham: Duke University Press, 2005.

Horowitz, Daniel. *Betty Friedan and the Making of the Feminine Mystique: The American Left, the Cold War, and Modern Feminism.* Amherst: University of Massachusetts Press, 1998.

Howard, Vicki. " 'At the Curve Exchange': Postwar Beauty Culture and Working Women at Maidenform." *Enterprise and Society* 1, no. 3 (September 2000): 591–618.

Howe, Louise Kapp. *Pink Collar Workers: Inside the World of Women's Work.* New York: G. Putnam's Sons, 1977.

Hudson, Kenneth. *Air Travel: A Social History.* Totowa, N.J.: Rowman and Littlefield, 1972.

Hughes, Karen D., and Vela Tadic. " 'Something to Deal with': Customer Sexual Harassment and Women's Retail Work in Canada." *Gender, Work and Organization* 5, no. 4 (1998): 207–19.

Hunter, Tera W. *To 'Joy My Freedom: Southern Black Women's Lives and Labors after the Civil War.* Cambridge: Harvard University Press, 1997.

Hurst, Vida. *Air Stewardess.* New York: Grosset and Dunlap, 1934.

James, George W., ed. *Airline Economics.* Lexington, Mass.: Lexington, 1982.

Jones, Anne Hudson, ed. *Images of Nurses: Perspectives from History, Art, and Literature.* Philadelphia: University of Pennsylvania Press, 1988.

Jones, Jacqueline. *Labor of Love, Labor of Sorrow: Black Women, Work and the Family, From Slavery to the Present.* New York: Vintage, 1985.

Jordon, William A. *Airline Regulation in America: Effects and Imperfections.* Baltimore: Johns Hopkins University Press, 1970.

Joseph, Nathan. *Uniforms and Nonuniforms: Communication through Clothing.* New York: Greenwood, 1986.

Josephson, Matthew. *Empire of the Air: Juan Trippe and the Struggle for World Airways.* New York: Harcourt, Brace, 1944.

Judson, Jeanne. *Carol Trent, Air Stewardess.* New York: Bantam, 1957.

Kane, Paula, with Christopher Chandler. *Sex Objects in the Sky: A Personal Account of the Stewardess Rebellion.* Chicago: Follett, 1974.

Katzman, David M. *Seven Days a Week: Women and Domestic Service in Industrializing America.* New York: Oxford University Press, 1978.

Kelley, Robin D. G. *Race Rebels: Culture, Politics, and the Black Working Class.* New York: Free Press, 1996.

Kelly, Charles J., Jr. *The Sky's the Limit: The History of the Airlines.* New York: Coward-McCann, 1963.

Kennedy, Elizabeth Lapovsky, and Madeline D. Davis. *Boots of Leather, Slippers of Gold: The History of a Lesbian Community.* New York: Routledge, 1993.

Kerslake, Evelyn, and Janine Liladhar. " 'Jolly Good Reading' for Girls: Discourses of Library Work and Femininity in Career Novels." *Women's History Review* 8, no. 3 (1999): 489–504.

Kessler-Harris, Alice. "Gender Ideology in Historical Reconstruction: A Case Study from the 1930s." *Gender and History* 1 (spring 1989): 31–49.

——. *In Pursuit of Equity: Women, Men, and the Quest for Economic Citizenship in 20th-Century America.* New York: Oxford University Press, 2001.

——. *Out to Work: A History of Wage-Earning Women in the United States.* New York: Oxford University Press, 1982.

——. *A Woman's Wage: Historical Meanings and Social Consequences.* Lexington: University of Kentucky Press, 1990.

Kibler, M. Alison. *Rank Ladies: Gender and Cultural Hierarchy in American Vaudeville.* Chapel Hill: University of North Carolina Press, 1999.

King, M. C. "Black Women's Breakthroughs into Clerical Work: An Occupational Tipping Model." *Journal of Economic Issues* 27 (December 1993): 1097–1125.

Kirkby, Diane. *Barmaids: A History of Women's Work in Pubs.* New York: Cambridge University Press, 1997.

Knapp, Sally. *New Wings for Women.* New York: Thomas Y. Crowell, 1946.

Kolm, Suzanne Lee. "Stewardesses' 'Psychological Punch': Gender and Commercial Aviation in the United States, 1930–1978." In *From Airships to Airbus: The History of Civil and Commercial Aviation,* vol. 2: *Pioneers and Operations,* ed. William F. Trimble, 112–27. Washington: Smithsonian Institution Press, 1995.

——. "Women's Labor Aloft: A Cultural History of Airline Flight Attendants in the United States, 1930–1978." Ph.D. diss., Brown University, 1995.

Kwolek-Folland, Angel. *Engendering Business: Men and Women in the Corporate Office, 1870–1930.* Baltimore: Johns Hopkins University Press, 1994.

Labor Research Association. *Labor Fact Book 8.* New York: International, 1947.

——. *Labor Fact Book 9.* New York: International, 1949.

——. *Labor Fact Book 10.* New York: International, 1951.

La Botz, Dan. *Rank and File Rebellion: Teamsters for a Democratic Union.* New York: Verso, 1990.

Larson, Magali Sarfatti. *The Rise of Professionalism: A Sociological Analysis.* Berkeley: University of California Press, 1977.

Latham, Angela. *Posing a Threat: Flappers, Chorus Girls and Other Brazen Performers of the 1920s.* Hanover, N.H.: University Press of New England, 2000.

Leary, William M. *The Airline Industry: Encyclopedia of American Business History and Biography.* New York: Facts on File, 1992.

Lee, Chana Kai. *For Freedom's Sake: The Life of Fannie Lou Hamer.* Urbana: University of Illinois, 1999.

Leidner, Robin. *Fast Food, Fast Talk: Service Work and the Routinization of Everyday Life.* Berkeley: University of California Press, 1993.

Leighbow, Susan Rimby. *Nurses' Questions / Women's Questions: The Impact of the Demographic Revolution and Feminism on United States Working Women, 1946–1986.* New York: Peter Lang, 1996.

Lessor, Roberta. "Consciousness of Time and Time for the Development of Consciousness: Health Awareness among Women Flight Attendants." *Sociology of Health and Illness* 7, no. 2 (July 1985): 191–213.

——. "Social Movements, the Occupational Arena and Changes in Career Consciousness: The Case of Women Flight Attendants." *Journal of Occupational Behavior* 5 (1984): 37–51.

——. "Unanticipated Longevity in Women's Work: The Career Development of Airline Flight Attendants." Ph.D. diss., University of California, San Francisco, 1982.

Lester, Valerie. *Fasten Your Seatbelts! History and Heroism in the Pan Am Cabin.* McLean, Va.: Palawdr, 1995.

Lett, AlexSandra, and Harold Silverman. "Coffee, Tea and Dignity: Knocking Down Employment Barriers 37,000 Feet Up." *Perspectives: The Civil Rights Quarterly* 12, no. 1 (spring 1980): 4–11.

Lichtenstein, Alex. "Putting Labor's House in Order: The Transport Workers

Union and Labor Anti-Communism in Miami during the 1940s." *Labor History* 39, no. 1 (1998): 7–23.

Lichtenstein, Nelson. *State of the Union: A Century of American Labor.* Princeton: Princeton University Press, 2002.

——. *Walter Reuther: The Most Dangerous Man in Detroit.* Urbana: University of Illinois Press, 1997.

Linstead, Stephen. "Averting the Gaze: Gender and Power on the Perfumed Picket Line." *Gender, Work and Organization* 2, no. 4 (October 1995): 192–206.

Lipsitz, George. *The Possessive Investment in Whiteness: How White People Profit from Identity Politics.* Philadelphia: Temple University Press, 1998.

——. *Rainbow at Midnight: Labor and Culture in the 1940s.* Urbana: University of Illinois Press, 1994.

Littler-Bishop, Susan, Doreen Seidler-Feller, and R. E. Opaluch. "Sexual Harassment in the Workplace as a Function of Initiator's Status: The Case of Airline Personnel." *Journal of Social Issues* 38, no. 4 (winter 1982): 137–48.

Lovegrove, Keith. *Airline: Identity, Design and Culture.* New York: teNeues, 2000.

——. *Pageant: The Beauty Contest.* New York: teNeues, 2002.

Lynch, Dennis M. "The Heavy Issue: Weight-Based Discrimination in the Airline Industry." *Journal of Air Law and Commerce* 62 (1996): 204–42.

Lyth, Peter J., and Marc L. J. Dierikx. "From Privilege to Popularity: The Growth of Leisure Air Travel since 1945." *Journal of Transport History* 15, no. 2 (1994): 97–116.

Macdonald, Cameron Lynne, and Carmen Sirianni, eds. *Working in the Service Society.* Philadelphia: Temple University Press, 1996.

Macdonald, Keith. *The Sociology of the Professions.* Thousand Oaks, Calif.: SAGE, 1995.

MacLean, Nancy. *Freedom Is Not Enough: The Opening of the American Workplace.* Cambridge: Harvard University Press, 2006.

——. "The Hidden History of Affirmative Action: Working Women's Struggles in the 1970s and the Gender of Class." *Feminist Studies* 25, no. 1 (spring 1999): 43–78.

Mahler, Gwen. *Legacy of the Friendly Skies: A Pictorial History of United Airlines Stewardesses and Flight Attendants.* Marceline, Mo.: Walsworth, 1991.

——. *Wings of Excellence: American Airlines Flight Attendants, A Pictorial History, 1933–1993.* Marceline, Mo.: Walsworth, n.d.

——. *Wings of Gold: Continental Airlines Flight Attendants, Past, Present, and Proud.* Topeka: Jostens Printing, n.d. [199–].

Marling, Karal Ann. *Debutante: Rites and Regalia of American Debdom.* Lawrence: University Press of Kansas, 2004.

Maschke, Karen J. *Litigation, Courts, and Women Workers.* New York: Praeger, 1989.

May, Elaine Tyler. *Homeward Bound: American Families in the Cold War.* New York: Basic, 1988.

McKelvey, Jean T. "Sex and the Single Arbitrator." *Industrial and Labor Relations Review* 24, no. 3 (1971): 335–53.

——, ed. *Cleared for Takeoff: Airline Labor Relations since Deregulation.* Ithaca: ILR, 1988.

McLaughlin, Helen E. *Footsteps in the Sky: An Informal Review of U.S. Airlines In-flight Service.* Denver: State of the Art, 1994.

——. *Walking on Air: An Informal History of In-flight Service of Seven U.S. Airlines.* Denver: State of the Art, 1986.

McLean, Adrienne L. *Being Rita Hayworth: Labor, Identity, and Hollywood Stardom.* New Brunswick: Rutgers University Press, 2004.

Melosh, Barbara. *"The Physician's Hand": Work Culture and Conflict in American Nursing.* Philadelphia: Temple University Press, 1982.

Messing, Karen. *One-Eyed Science: Occupational Health and Women Workers.* Philadelphia: Temple University Press, 1998.

Meyer, Dickie. *Girls at Work in Aviation.* New York: Doubleday, Doran, 1943.

Meyer, John R., and Clinton Oster, eds. *Airline Deregulation: The Early Experience.* Boston: Auburn House, 1981.

Meyer, Stephen. "Workplace Predators: Sexuality and Harassment on the US Automotive Shop Floor, 1930–1960." *Labor* 1, no. 1 (2004): 77–93.

Meyerowitz, Joanne. "Beyond the Feminine Mystique: A Reassessment of Postwar Mass Culture, 1946–1958." *Journal of American History* 79, no. 4 (1993): 1455–82.

——, ed. *Not June Cleaver: Women and Gender in Postwar America, 1945–1960.* Philadelphia: Temple University Press, 1994.

Mezey, Susan Gluck. *In Pursuit of Equality: Women, Public Policy, and the Federal Courts.* New York: St. Martin's, 1992.

Milkman, Ruth. *Gender at Work: The Dynamics of Job Segregation by Sex during World War II.* Urbana: University of Illinois Press, 1987.

——, ed. *Women, Work and Protest: A Century of Women's Labor History.* Boston: Routledge and Kegan Paul, 1985.

Mills, Albert J. "Cockpits, Hangars, Boys and Galleys: Corporate Masculinities and the Development of British Airways." *Gender, Work and Organization* 5, no. 3 (1998): 172–88.

——. "Duelling Discourses: Desexualisation versus Eroticism in the Corporate Framing of Female Sexuality in the British Airline Industry, 1945–60." *Managing the Organizational Melting Pot: Dilemmas of Workplace Diversity*, ed. Pushkala Prasad et al., 171–98. London: Sage, 1997.

——. *Sex, Strategy and the Stratosphere: Airlines and the Gendering of Organizational Culture.* New York: Palgrave Macmillan, 2006.

——. "Strategy, Sexuality and the Stratosphere: Airlines and the Gendering of Organisations." In *Gender Relations in Public and Private: New Research Perspectives*, ed. Lydia Morris and E. Stina Lyon, 77–94. New York: St. Martin's, 1996.

Mills, C. Wright. *White Collar: The American Middle Classes.* New York: Oxford University Press, 1956.

Mills, Jean Helms. "Employment Practices and the Gendering of Air Canada's Culture during Its Trans Canada Airlines Days." *Culture and Organization* 8, no. 2 (2002): 117–28.

Mizejewski, Linda. *Ziegfeld Girl: Image and Icon in Culture and Cinema.* Durham: Duke University Press, 1999.

Moles, Elizabeth R., and Norman L. Friedman. "The Airline Hostess: Realities of an Occupation with a Popular Cultural Image." *Journal of Popular Culture* 7, no. 2 (1973): 305–13.

Montgomery, David. *The Fall of the House of Labor.* New York: Cambridge University Press, 1987.

——. *Workers' Control in America: Studies in the History of Work, Technology, and Labor Struggles.* New York: Cambridge University Press, 1979.

Murphy, Alexandra G. "Hidden Transcripts of Flight Attendant Resistance." *Management Communication Quarterly* 11, no. 4 (1998): 499–535.

——. "Managing 'Nowhere': The Changing Organizational Performance of Air Travel." Ph.D. diss., University of South Florida, 1998.

Murphy, Marjorie. *Blackboard Unions: The AFT and the NEA, 1900–1980.* Ithaca: Cornell University Press, 1990.

Murray, Mary F. *Skygirl: A Career Handbook for the Airline Stewardess.* New York: Duell, Sloan and Pearce, 1951.

Nelson, Daniel. *Managers and Workers: Origins of the New Factory System in the United States, 1880–1920.* Madison: University of Wisconsin Press, 1975.

Nelson, Marguerite. *Air Stewardess.* New York: Bouregy, 1961.

Newby, N. Jill. *The Sky's the Limit: The Story of the Canadian Air Line Flight Attendants' Association.* Vancouver: Canadian Air Line Flight Attendants Association, 1986.

Nielsen, Georgia Panter. *From Sky Girl to Flight Attendant: Women and the Making of a Union.* Ithaca: ILR, 1982.

Northrup, Herbert R. "Collective Bargaining by Air Line Pilots." *Quarterly Journal of Economics* 61, no. 4 (August 1947): 533–76.

Northrup, Herbert R., Armand J. Thieblot, and William N. Chernish. *The Negro in the Air Transport Industry.* Philadelphia: University of Pennsylvania Press, 1971.

Norwood, Stephen H. *Labor's Flaming Youth: Telephone Operators and Worker Militancy, 1878–1923.* Urbana: University of Illinois Press, 1990.

Oakes, Claudia M. *United States Women in Aviation, 1930–1939.* Washington: Smithsonian Institution Press, 1985.

O'Connor, Mary. *Flying Mary O'Connor: The Story of a Pioneer Stewardess*. New York: Rand McNally, 1961.

Omelia, Johanna, and Michael Waldock. *Come Fly with Us! A Global History of the Airline Hostess*. Portland, Ore.: Collectors, 2003.

Opler, Daniel Joseph. " 'For All White-Collar Workers': The Possibilities of Radicalism in New York City's Department Store Unions, 1934–1953." Ph.D. diss., New York University, 2003.

Oppenheimer, Valerie Kincade. *The Female Labor Force in the United States: Demographic and Economic Factors Governing Its Growth and Changing Composition*. Westport, Conn.: Greenwood, 1976.

Orason, Roy. *Plight of a Flight Attendant*. Sacramento: Sierra, 1994.

Palmer, Phyllis. *Domesticity and Dirt: Housewives and Domestic Servants in the United States, 1920–1945*. Philadelphia: Temple University Press, 1989.

Paris, Michael. *From the Wright Brothers to "Top Gun": Aviation, Nationalism and Popular Cinema*. New York: Manchester University Press, 1995.

Patterson, Betty, with Margaret Friskey and Gene Klinger. *I Reached for the Sky*. Chicago: Children's Press, 1970.

Peacock, John. *20th-Century Fashion: The Complete Sourcebook*. London: Thames and Hudson, 1993.

Peckham, Betty. *Sky Hostess*. New York: T. Nelson and Sons, 1941.

———. *Women in Aviation*. New York: T. Nelson and Sons, 1945.

Peiss, Kathy. *Cheap Amusements: Working Women and Leisure in Turn-of-the-Century New York*. Philadelphia: Temple University Press, 1986.

———. *Hope in a Jar: The Making of America's Beauty Culture*. New York: Metropolitan, 1998.

Perata, David D. *Those Pullman Blues: An Oral History of the African American Railroad Attendant*. New York: Twayne, 1996.

Percivall, Julia, and Pixie Burger. *High Flying*. New York: Avon, 1974.

Peterson, Florence. *American Labor Unions: What They Are and How They Work*. New York: Harper and Row, 1963.

Petzinger, Thomas, Jr. *Hard Landing: The Epic Contest for Power and Profits That Plunged the Airlines into Chaos*. New York: Three Rivers, 1996.

Planck, Charles E. *Women with Wings*. New York: Harper and Brothers, 1942.

Posadas, Barbara M. "The Hierarchy of Color and Psychological Adjustment in an Industrial Environment: Filipinos, the Pullman Company, and the Brotherhood of Sleeping Car Porters." *Labor History* 23 (summer 1982): 349–73.

Pringle, Rosemary. *Secretaries Talk: Sexuality, Power and Work*. New York: Verso, 1989.

Purcell, Susan Kaufman. "Ideology and the Law: Sexism and Supreme Court Decisions." In *Women in Politics*, ed. Jane J. Jaquette, 131–53. New York: John Wiley and Sons, 1974.

Quindry, Frank E. "Airline Passenger Discrimination." *Journal of Air Law and Commerce* 3, no. 4 (October 1932): 479–514.

Quisenberry, Phillip Neil. "Glamour and Glitter: The Social Construction of Enviable Careers." M.A. thesis, University of South Florida, 1992.

Rachlin, Marjorie B. "Training Rank and File Leaders: A Case Study." In *Labor Education for Women Workers*, ed. Barbara Mayer Wertheimer, 62–70. Philadelphia: Temple University Press, 1981.

Radford, Ruby Lorraine. *Patty O'Neal on the Airways*. Racine, Wis.: Whitman, 1946.

Radner, Hilary, and Moya Luckett, eds. *Swinging Single: Representing Sexuality in the 1960s*. Minneapolis: University of Minnesota Press, 1999.

The Railway Labor Act and the National Mediation Board. Washington: U.S. Government Printing Office, 1940.

Ransby, Barbara. *Ella Baker and the Black Freedom Movement: A Radical Democratic Vision*. Chapel Hill: University of North Carolina Press, 2003.

Raycroft, Maureen Cecile. "An Occupational Study of Airline Hostesses." M.A. thesis, University of Missouri, Kansas City, 1966.

Reed, Toni Scott. "Flight Attendant Furies: Is Title VII Really the Solution to Hiring Policy Problems?" *Journal of Air Law and Commerce* 58 (1992): 267–343.

Rehmus, Charles M., ed. *The Railway Labor Act at Fifty*. Washington: U.S. Government Printing Office, 1977.

Reverby, Susan M. *Ordered to Care: The Dilemma of American Nursing, 1850–1945*. New York: Cambridge University Press, 1987.

Rich, Elizabeth. *Flying High: What It's Like to Be an Airline Stewardess*. New York: Stein and Day, 1970.

——. *Flying Scared: Why We Are Being Skyjacked and How to Put a Stop to It*. New York: Bantam, 1972.

——. *What It's Like to Be a Flight Attendant*. New York: Stein and Day, 1982.

Richter, Amy G. *Home on the Rails: Women, the Railroad, and the Rise of Public Domesticity*. Chapel Hill: University of North Carolina Press, 2005.

Rickenbacker, Edward V. *Rickenbacker*. Englewood Cliffs, N.J.: Prentice-Hall, 1967.

Robbins, Trina. *From Girls to Grrlz: A History of Women's Comics from Teens to Zines*. San Francisco: Chronicle, 1999.

Roediger, David R. *The Wages of Whiteness: Race and the Making of the American Working Class*. New York: Verso, 1991.

Rosen, Ruth. *The World Split Open: How the Modern Women's Movement Changed America*. New York: Penguin, 2000.

Rotskoff, Lori. *Love on the Rocks: Men, Women and Alcohol in Post–World War II America*. Chapel Hill: University of North Carolina Press, 2002.

Rozen, Frieda S. "Technological Advances and Increasing Militance: Flight Attendant Unions in the Jet Age." In *Women, Work, and Technology*, ed. Barbara Drygulski Wright et al., 220–38. Ann Arbor: University of Michigan Press, 1987.

——. "Turbulence in the Air: The Autonomy Movement in the Flight Attendant Unions." Ph.D. diss., Pennsylvania State University, 1988.

Rupp, Leila J., and Verta Taylor. *Survival in the Doldrums: The American Women's Rights Movement, 1945 to the 1960s.* New York: Oxford University Press, 1987.

Ryan, Barbara. "Ideological Purity and Feminism: The U.S. Women's Movement from 1966 to 1975." *Gender and Society* 3, no. 2 (1989): 239–57.

Sacks, Karen Brodkin. *Caring by the Hour: Women, Work and Organizing at Duke Medical Center.* Urbana: University of Illinois Press, 1988.

Salinger, Lawrence M. "Assaults against Airline Flight Attendants: A Victimization Study." *Transportation Journal* 25 (fall 1985): 66–71.

Sánchez, George J. *Becoming Mexican-American: Ethnicity, Culture and Identity in Chicano Los Angeles, 1900–1945.* New York: Oxford University Press, 1993.

Sandelowski, Margarete. *Devices and Desires: Gender, Technology, and American Nursing.* Chapel Hill: University of North Carolina Press, 2000.

Santino, Jack. *Miles of Smiles, Years of Struggle: Stories of Black Pullman Porters.* Urbana: University of Illinois Press, 1989.

——. "The Outlaw Emotions: Narrative Expressions on the Rules and Roles of Occupational Identity." *American Behavioral Scientist* 33, no. 3 (1990): 318–29.

Saunders, Keith. *So You Want to Be an Airline Stewardess.* Rev. edn. New York: Arco, 1973.

Savage, Lydia Anne. "Negotiating Common Ground: Labor Unions and the Geography of Organizing Women Workers in the Service Sector." Ph.D. diss., Clark University, 1996.

Schacht, John N. *The Making of Telephone Unionism, 1920–1947.* New Brunswick: Rutgers University Press, 1985.

Scharf, Lois. *To Work and to Wed: Female Employment, Feminism, and the Great Depression.* Westport, Conn.: Greenwood, 1980.

Schrum, Kelly. *Some Wore Bobby Socks: The Emergence of Teenage Girls' Culture.* New York: Palgrave Macmillan, 2004.

Scott, Joan Wallach. *Gender and the Politics of History.* New York: Columbia University Press, 1988.

Scott, Kathryn Leigh. *The Bunny Years: The Surprising Inside Story of the Playboy Clubs, the Women Who Worked as Bunnies, and Where They Are Now.* Los Angeles: Pomegranate, 1998.

Segal, B. "Male Nurses: A Case Study in Status Contradictions and Prestige Loss." *Social Forces* 41 (1962): 31–38.

Segrave, Kerry. *Tipping: An American Social History of Gratuities.* Jefferson, N.C.: McFarland, 1998.

Serling, Robert J. *Eagle: The Story of American Airlines.* New York: St. Martin's / Marek, 1985.

——. *Howard Hughes' Airline: An Informal History of* TWA. New York: St. Martin's / Marek, 1983.

——. *The Only Way to Fly: The Story of Western Airlines, America's Senior Air Carrier.* Garden City, N.Y.: Doubleday, 1976.

——. *Stewardess.* New York: St. Martin's, 1982.

Sharma, Ursula, and Paula Black. "Look Good, Feel Better: Beauty Therapy as Emotional Labour." *Sociology* 35, no. 4 (2001): 913–31.

Skeggs, Beverly. *Formations of Class and Gender: Becoming Respectable.* London: Sage, 1997.

Smith, Henry Ladd. *Airways: The History of Commercial Aviation in the United States.* New York: Alfred A. Knopf, 1942; repr. Washington: Smithsonian Institution Press, 1991.

Smith, Johnni. *How to Be a Flight Stewardess: A Handbook and Training Manual for Airline Hostesses.* North Hollywood: Pan American Navigation Service, 1966.

Snell, Roy J. *Gypsy Flight.* Chicago: Reilly and Lee, 1935.

Sokoloff, Natalie J. *Black Women and White Women in the Professions: Occupational Segregation by Race and Gender, 1960–1980.* New York: Routledge, 1992.

Solberg, Carl. *Conquest of the Skies: A History of Commercial Aviation in America.* Boston: Little, Brown, 1979.

Spellman, Susan V. "All the Comforts of Home: The Domestication of the Service Station Industry, 1920–1940." *Journal of Popular Culture* 37, no. 3 (2004): 463–77.

Staggenborg, Suzanne. "Stability and Innovation in the Women's Movement: A Comparison of Two Movement Organizations." *Social Problems* 36, no. 1 (1989): 75–92.

Steedman, Carolyn Kay. *Landscape for a Good Woman: A Story of Two Lives.* New Brunswick: Rutgers University Press, 1986.

Steele, Donna, et al. *Wings of Pride:* TWA *Cabin Attendants: A Pictorial History, 1935–1985.* Marceline, Mo.: Walsworth, 1985.

Steele, Valerie. *Fifty Years of Fashion: New Look to Now.* New Haven: Yale University Press, 1997.

Steinem, Gloria. *Outrageous Acts and Everyday Rebellions.* New York: Henry Holt, 1995.

Stellman, Jeanne M., and Susan M. Daum. *Work Is Dangerous to Your Health: A Handbook of Health Hazards in the Workplace and What You Can Do about Them.* New York: Vintage, 1973.

Stolker, Paula B. "Weigh My Job, Not My Body: Extending Title VII to Weight-Based Discrimination." *Journal of Human Rights* 10 (1992): 223–50.

Strasser, Susan. *Never Done: A History of American Housework.* New York: Pantheon, 1982.

Strom, Sharon Hartman. *Beyond the Typewriter: Gender, Class, and the Origins of Modern American Office Work, 1900–1930.* Urbana: University of Illinois Press, 1992.

Stuckey, Mary Carlene. "The Determinants of Occupational Cynicism among Female Flight Attendants." M.A. thesis, Southern Methodist University, 1977.

Susman, Warren I. *Culture as History: The Transformation of American Society in the Twentieth Century.* New York: Pantheon, 1973; repr. Washington: Smithsonian Institution Press, 2003.

Taylor, Frank J. *High Horizons: Daredevil Flying Postmen to Modern Magic Carpet: The United Airlines Story.* New York: McGraw-Hill, 1951.

Taylor, Justin. *Stewardess with the Moustache!* Miami: Parameter, 1980.

Taylor, Steve, and Melissa Tyler. "Emotional Labour and Sexual Difference in the Airline Industry." *Work, Employment and Society* 14, no. 1 (2000): 77–95.

Tyler, Melissa. "Women's Work as the Labour of Sexual Difference: Female Employment in the Airline Industry." Ph.D. diss., University of Derby, 1997.

Tyler, Melissa, and Pamela Abbott. "Chocs Away: Weight Watching in the Contemporary Airline Industry." *Sociology* 32, no. 3 (1998): 433–50.

Tyler, Melissa, and Steve Taylor. "The Exchange of Aesthetics: Women's Work and 'The Gift.'" *Gender, Work and Organization* 5, no. 3 (1998): 165–71.

U.S. Civil Aeronautics Administration. CAA *Statistical Handbook of Civil Aviation, 1956.* Washington: U.S. Government Printing Office, 1956.

U.S. Department of Labor, Bureau of Labor Statistics. *Handbook of Labor Statistics 1969.* Washington: U.S. Government Printing Office, 1969.

U.S. Department of Labor, Women's Bureau. *1969 Handbook on Women Workers.* Bulletin 294. Washington: U.S. Department of Labor, 1969.

——. *1975 Handbook on Women Workers.* Bulletin 297. Washington: U.S. Department of Labor, 1975.

U.S. Department of Transportation, Federal Aviation Administration. FAA *Statistical Handbook of Aviation 1972.* Washington: U.S. Department of Transportation, 1972.

van der Linden, F. Robert. *Airlines and Air Mail: The Post Office and the Birth of the Commercial Aviation Industry.* Lexington: University Press of Kentucky, 2002.

Vecsey, George, and George C. Dade. *Getting off the Ground: The Pioneers of Aviation Speak for Themselves.* New York: E. P. Dutton, 1979.

Vosko, Leah F., and David Scott Witwer. "'Not a Man's Union': Women Teamsters in the United States during the 1940s and 1950s." *Journal of Women's History* 13, no. 3 (autumn 2001): 169–88.

Walkowitz, Daniel J. *Working with Class: Social Workers and the Politics of Middle-Class Identity.* Chapel Hill: University of North Carolina Press, 1999.

Walsh, David J. "Accounting for the Proliferation of Two-Tier Wage Settlements in the U.S. Airline Industry, 1983–1986." *Industrial and Labor Relations Review* 42, no. 1 (1988): 50–62.

——. *On Different Planes: An Organizational Analysis of Cooperation and Conflict Among Airline Unions.* Ithaca: ILR, 1994.

Wandersee, Winifred D. *On the Move: American Women in the 1970s.* Boston: Twayne, 1988.

——. *Women's Work and Family Values, 1920–1940.* Cambridge: Harvard University Press, 1980.

Ware, Susan. *Still Missing: Amelia Earhart and the Search for Modern Feminism.* New York: W. W. Norton, 1993.

Watson, Elwood, and Darcy Martin, eds. *"There She Is, Miss America": The Politics of Sex, Beauty, and Race in America's Most Famous Pageant.* New York: Palgrave Macmillan, 2004.

Weinlein, Craig. "Flight Attendant Weight Requirements and Title VII of the Civil Rights Act." *Journal of Air Law and Commerce* 45 (1980): 483–507.

Wells, Helen. *Silver Wings for Vicki.* New York: Grosset and Dunlap, 1947.

Wenzel, Bill, and Cornelius Wohl. *How to Make a Good Airline Stewardess.* Greenwich, Conn.: Fawcett, 1972.

West, Candace, and Don H. Zimmerman. "Doing Gender." *Gender and Society* 1, no. 2 (1987): 125–51.

Wheeler, Ruthe S. *Jane, Stewardess of the Air Lines.* Chicago: Goldsmith, 1934.

Whitelegg, Drew. "Cabin Pressure: The Dialectics of Emotional Labour in the Airline Industry." *Journal of Transport History* 23, no. 1 (2002): 73–86.

——. "From Smiles to Miles: Delta Air Lines Flight Attendants and Southern Hospitality." *Southern Cultures* 11, no. 4 (winter 2005): 7–27.

——. "Touching Down: Labour, Globalisation and the Airline Industry." *Antipode* 35, no. 2 (2003): 244–63.

Whitesides, Pamela. "Flight Attendant Weight Policies: A Title VII Wrong without a Remedy." *Southern California Law Review* 64 (1990): 175–233.

Willett, Julie. *Permanent Waves: The Making of the American Beauty Shop.* New York: New York University Press, 2000.

Williams, Christine L. *Gender Differences at Work: Women and Men in Nontraditional Occupations.* Berkeley: University of California Press, 1989.

Williams, Claire. *Blue, White and Pink Collar Workers in Australia: Technicians, Bank Employees and Flight Attendants.* Boston: Allen and Unwin, 1988.

——. "Sky Service: The Demands of Emotional Labour in the Airline Industry." *Gender, Work and Organization* 10, no. 5 (November 2003): 513–50.

Willis, P. P. *Your Future Is in the Air: The Story of How American Airlines Made People Air-Travel Conscious.* New York: Prentice-Hall, 1940.

Willson, Dixie. *Hostess of the Skyways, and of Train, Ship, and Hotel.* New York: Dodd, Mead, 1941.

Winchell, Meghan K. "'To Make the Boys Feel at Home': USO Senior Hostesses and Gendered Citizenship." *Frontiers* 25, no. 1 (2004): 190–211.

Witwer, David. *Corruption and Reform in the Teamsters Union*. Urbana: University of Illinois Press, 2003.

Wolf, Naomi. *The Beauty Myth: How Images of Beauty Are Used against Women*. New York: Vintage, 1990.

Young, Joanna L., and Erica Hayes James. "Token Majority: The Work Attitudes of Male Flight Attendants." *Sex Roles* 45, nos. 5–6 (2001): 299–319.

Zieger, Robert H. *American Workers, American Unions, 1920–1985*. Baltimore: Johns Hopkins University Press, 1986.

INDEX

Domesticity; Flight attendants:
popular image of; Glamour
Feminist movement, 1–5, 126–31, 136,
140, 153, 173–76, 186–207, 222, 266 n.
61. *See also* Flight attendants: activism of; Flight attendants: women's
movement and; Stewardesses for
Women's Rights
Fields, Jill, 5–6
Fifth Circuit, U.S. Court of Appeals,
163, 165, 168–69
Fletcher, Joanne, 118
Flight attendants: activism of, 1–5, 9–
10, 207–9, 212; African American,
114–21, 172, 191, 211, 217; antifeminism among, 137, 204; class identity
among, 22, 26, 65–68, 87–90, 209;
demographic changes among, 37,
111, 114–15, 117–20, 169, 172–73, 217–
18; deregulation's effects on, 212–14;
discrimination opposed by, 113, 121–
26, 130–65, 169–72, 188, 205–6, 218;
duties of, 3–4, 27, 45–49, 78–79, 166;
earliest, 11–12, 15–23; feminist movement and, 153–54, 175–76, 186–97,
204–7; feminist protests against
image of, 139–40, 189–90, 192–96;
feminization of, 19–23, 166, 217; gay
and lesbian, 56–57, 191, 217–18, 263
n. 33; growth among, 21, 111, 197; invisibility of, 4, 37–39, 42, 45, 48–49,
53, 58–59, 78, 137–39, 208–9; labor
movement and, 2, 7, 208–9, 221;
male, 1, 15–18, 21, 42, 53–58, 112, 115,
156–57, 159, 161, 166, 170, 188–89,
217–18; as "new face of labor," 59–62,
65–68, 215; nursing and, 18–19, 23–
24, 32–35, 37, 51, 75; occupation
viewed by, 2–3, 6, 28–29, 33–34, 36–
37, 58, 96–97, 104–11, 137, 174–75,
185–86, 188–90, 204, 205, 207, 214,
221; other pink-collar workers vs.,
7–9, 27–29, 33, 65–67, 175–76, 206–
9, 217; pilots and, 19, 27, 28, 29, 31,

56–57, 70–72, 79–80, 91, 197; popular image of, 1–3, 9–11, 19, 28, 30–31,
33–38, 50–53, 58, 61–62, 102, 110,
130–32, 135–37, 143, 145–46, 200, 211,
214–17, 221–22; racial discrimination and, 115, 118, 120, 153–54, 209,
248 n. 36, 249 n. 37; safety duties of,
78–79; sex discrimination and, 145,
156–59, 161, 169–70, 188, 199, 204;
sexualized image of, 174–86; Title
VII lawsuits concerning, 157, 162–
70, 218, 260 n. 9; training of, 46–47;
turnover among, 3, 26, 65, 111–12,
126, 172, 207; uniforms of, 1, 47–48,
51, 173, 179–84, 189, 193, 206; wages
of, 29, 36, 63, 65, 68, 229 n. 36
Flight Attendant Safety Professionals'
Day (1990), 214
Flight attendant unions, 60–95, 212–
17; autonomy drives of, 72–73, 80–
93, 124, 197–205, 209, 221, 237 n. 23,
239 n. 38, 265–66 n. 53; difficulties in
organizing, 64–68; founding of, 63–
64, 69–70, 72, 87, 198, 200–203; international, 215–16; men active in,
60, 70, 73, 83–85, 91, 189, 199–200,
204, 241 n. 43, 243 n. 56, 262 n. 27; sex
discrimination opposed by, 122–26,
131–53, 157–59, 188, 205, 218, 221;
racial discrimination opposed by, 117,
120, 153, 250 n. 46; safety activism by,
73–80, 137–40, 109–10, 175, 193, 203–
4, 214, 220; strikes by, 2, 60, 104, 175,
213. *See also individual unions*
Flight engineers, 70, 76
Flightlog, 213, 218, 221
Fly Girls, The (Glemser), 185, 261 n. 19
Flynn, Alice, 202–3
Freidin, Jesse, 157
Friedan, Betty, 129–30, 153, 192, 222
Frontier Airlines, 148
Fuentes, Sonia Pressman, 152–53, 156,
159
Fulsom, Jan, 190

Women's Strike for Equality (1970), 188
Women's movement. *See* Feminist
  movement
Women's work, 3, 8, 207–9, 228 n. 26,
  247 n. 28; Depression and, 11, 25, 111;
  protective legislation and, 162, 251 n.
  8, 252 n. 10; during and after Second
  World War, 61. *See also* Pink-collar
  workers
Working conditions, 3–5, 29–30, 125;
  deregulation's effects on, 211–14; as
  feminist issue, 174–75, 188–89, 193–
  96, 204–7, 214; glamour image's
  effects on, 37, 45–49, 58, 186, 208; jet
  aircraft's effects on, 82, 96–97, 103–
  11, 211; male vs. female, 53–57, 70–

72, 166, 170, 188; occupational
  health and safety, 74, 82, 104, 175,
  190, 193–95, 204, 214, 263 n. 37; routinization, 105–6, 246 n. 17; September 11, 2001, terrorist attacks' effects
  on, 211–12, 220–21. *See also* Age ceilings; Appearance regulations;
  Employment restrictions; Flight
  attendants: duties of; Flight attendants: uniforms of; Maternity
  restrictions; No-marriage rules;
  Weight rules
World Wings International, 211
Wyman, Jane, 51

Young, Phyllis, 96

KATHLEEN M. BARRY

was a Mellon Research Fellow in the Faculty of History

at Cambridge University and has taught American history

at New York University and Cambridge.

Library of Congress-Cataloging-in-Publication Data
Barry, Kathleen M. (Kathleen Morgan)
Femininity in flight : a history of flight attendants
/ Kathleen M. Barry.
p. cm. — (Radical perspectives)
Includes bibliographical references and index.
ISBN-13: 978-0-8223-3934-2 (cloth : alk. paper)
ISBN-13: 978-0-8223-3946-5 (pbk. : alk. paper)
1. Flight attendants—United States—History.
2. Flight attendants—Labor unions—United States.
3. Feminism—United States. I. Title.
HD6073.A432U62 2007
331.4'813877420973—dc22   2006031837